DATE DUE		
Jul 8 '81		
Feb 20 '84		

Orthography,
Reading,
and
Dyslexia

Orthography, Reading, and Dyslexia

edited by

James F. Kavanagh, Ph.D.
Associate Director
Center for Research for Mothers
and Children
National Institute of Child Health
and Human Development
National Institutes of Health

and

Richard L. Venezky, Ph.D.
Unidel Professor of Educational Studies
University of Delaware

University Park Press
Baltimore

UNIVERSITY PARK PRESS
International Publishers in Science, Medicine, and Education
233 East Redwood Street
Baltimore, Maryland 21202

Copyright © 1980 by University Park Press

Composed by University Park Press, Typesetting Division
Manufactured in the United States of America by
The Maple Press Company

Library of Congress Cataloging in Publication Data
Main entry under title:

Orthography, reading, and dyslexia.

"Proceedings of a conference...in a series entitled
'Communicating by language,' sponsored by the National
Institute of Child Health and Human Development [et al.]"
Proceedings of the 7th series of meetings; proceedings
of the 6th are entered under the title: Speech and
language in the laboratory, school, and clinic.
Bibliography: p.
Includes index.
1. Language and languages—Orthography and spelling
—Congresses. 2. Reading—Congresses. 3. Reading
disability—Congresses. I. Kavanagh, James F.
II. Venezky, Richard L. III. United States. National
Institute of Child Health and Human Development.
P240.2.O77   411   79-26451
ISBN 0-8391-1559-8

Contents

Overview
FROM SUMER TO LEIPZIG TO BETHESDA
Richard L. Venezky
1

Section I
ORTHOGRAPHY AND READING
A Cross-National View

Section V
DYSLEXIA AND RELATED LINGUISTIC DISORDERS

Contributors

Jonathan Baron, Ph.D.
Department of Psychology
University of Pennsylvania
Philadelphia, Pennsylvania 19174

Linnea Ehri, Ph.D.
Department of Education
University of California
Davis, California 94616

Dina Feitelson, Ph.D.
School of Education
University of Haifa
Mt. Carmel
Haifa 31 999 Israel

Christopher Frith, Ph.D.
CRMC Division of Psychiatry
Harrow, England

Professor Uta Frith
MRC Developmental Psychology Unit
Drayton House, Gordon Street
London, England WC1H OAN

Raymond G. Gordon, Jr.
Department of Modern Languages
  and Linguistics
Cornell University
Ithaca, New York 14850

Joseph E. Grimes, Ph.D.
Department of Modern Languages
  and Linguistics
Department of Anthropology
Cornell University
Ithaca, New York 14850

Hans U. Grudin, Ph.D.
Department of Educational Research
University of Linköping
581 83 Linköping
Sweden

Wayne Holm, Ph.D.
Rock Point Community School
(via) Chinle, Arizona 86503

Daisy Hung
Department of Psychology
University of California
Riverside, California 92502

James F. Kavanagh, Ph.D.
Center for Research for Mothers
  and Children
National Institute of Child Health
  and Human Development
National Institutes of Health
Bethesda, Maryland 20205

O. K. Kyöstiö, Ph.D.
University of Oulu
Faculty of Education
12240 Hikia 4
Oulu, Finland

Alvin M. Liberman, Ph.D.
Department of Psychology
University of Connecticut
Storrs, Connecticut 06710
and
Haskins Laboratories
270 Crown Street
New Haven, Connecticut 06510

Anatoly Liberman, Ph.D.
Department of German
University of Minnesota
Minneapolis, Minnesota 55812

Isabelle Liberman, Ph.D.
Department of Educational Psychology
University of Connecticut
Storrs, Connecticut 06710

Georgije Lukatela, Ph.D.
Faculty of Electrical Engineering
University of Belgrade
P.O. Box 816
11001 Belgrade, Yugoslavia

Eve Malmquist, Ph.D.
Department of Educational Research
University of Linköping
581 03 Linköping
Sweden

Dominic Massaro, Ph.D.
Department of Psychology
University of Wisconsin
Madison, Wisconsin 53706

Ignatius Mattingly, Ph.D.
Department of Linguistics
University of Connecticut
Storrs, Connecticut 06710

John W. Ryan
Division of Literacy, Adult Education
and Rural Development
United Nations Educational, Scientific
and Cultural Organization
7, Place de Fontenoy
75700 Paris, France

Takahiko Sakamoto, Ph.D.
Noma Institute of Educational
Research
Kodansha, Otawa 2-12-21
Kunkyo-Ku, Tokyo, Japan

Donald Shankweiler, Ph.D.
Department of Psychology
University of Connecticut
Storrs, Connecticut 06710

Rebecca Treiman
Department of Psychology
University of Pennsylvania
Philadelphia, Pennsylvania 19174

Ovid Tzeng, Ph.D.
Department of Psychology
University of California
Riverside, California 92502

Michael T. Turvey, Ph.D.
Department of Psychology
University of Connecticut
Storrs, Connecticut 06710
and Haskins Laboratories
270 Crown Street
New Haven, Connecticut 06510

Renate Valtin, Ph.D.
Pädagogische Hochschule
Berlin, West Germany

Vincent J. van Heuven, Ph.D.
Rijksuniversiteit Leiden
Afdeling Fonetiek
Schuttersveld 9 (6.06)
Leiden
The Netherlands

Frank Vellutino, Ph.D.
Child Research and Study Center
Albany Medical College
Albany, New York

Richard L. Venezky, Ph.D.
Department of Educational Studies
University of Delaware
Newark, Delaware 19711

Preface

This volume is the edited proceedings of a cross-language conference on Orthography, Reading, and Dyslexia held at the National Institutes of Health in Bethesda, Maryland, on September 18–20, 1978, under the joint sponsorship of the National Institute of Child Health and Human Development (NICHD), the National Institute of Mental Health, the National Institute of Education, the National Institute of Neurological and Communicative Disorders and Stroke, the Office of Maternal and Child Health (Health Services Administration), and the John E. Fogarty International Center. Dr. James F. Kavanagh, Associate Director of the Center for Research for Mothers and Children, NICHD, and Professor Richard L. Venezky, Unidel Professor of Educational Studies at the University of Delaware, were co-chairpersons. Central to the conference interests was the relationship of different writing systems to the languages they represent and their influence on success or failure in learning to read. Participants, who came from 12 countries, including the United States, were asked to address the special nature of the written symbol system used to represent a particular language, especially in regard to the following questions:

1. What is the beginning reader's task?
2. What must a child learn to become a successful reader?
3. What is the rationale for the instructional (including remedial and therapeutic) procedures for teaching reading in that language?
4. What research should be conducted to illuminate the reading process and the relationships between orthography and reading?

As in the previous seven conferences in the NICHD's "Communicating by Language" series, the meeting was structured primarily for participant interaction, rather than for addressing an audience. Papers were circulated before the meeting so that conference time could be spent in discussion.

Following the meeting, the conferees had an opportunity to revise their papers and to incorporate any new ideas that were generated by the conference discussions. This volume contains these revised papers, edited and arranged in an order more appropriate for the book than the original conference agenda.

The conference was organized around five areas: 1) orthography and reading in different languages (reports on Chinese, Japanese (hiragana),

Hebrew, Navajo, Finnish, Dutch, Serbo-Croatian, and Russian); 2) processing of orthography in learning to read; 3) information processing in experienced readers; 4) reading failure; and 5) the design of literacy programs and the methodology of cross-national research.

One issue raised in the meeting was how to define an optimal writing system. Dr. O. K. Kyöstiö (University of Oulu, Finland) reported that reading problems occur in Finland even though Finnish has the most uniform letter-sound relationship of any widely used alphabetic system. Dr. Takahiko Sakamoto (Noma Institute of Educational Research, Japan) indicated that although the hiragana syllabic alphabet is well suited to Japanese phonology and is easily acquired by young children, reading problems occur, revived from the logographic characters (kanji) representing the content words in written Japanese. Speaking about the design of new orthographies, Dr. Joseph Grimes (Cornell University) reported that a one phoneme-one symbol system is still preferred, even though evidence remains against the efficiency and learnability of such representations. Dr. Wayne Holm (Rock Point Community School, Chinle, Arizona) reported that in the Navajo language, for example, the full marking of Navajo vowel contrasts, including quantity, tone, cavity, and nasalization, is confusing to adult readers. The possibility was raised that what is an optimal system for a beginning reader might not be optimal for an experienced reader.

A second issue discussed was the appropriateness of particular writing systems for representing different languages. Several participants pointed out that the selection of an orthography often is based upon political, cultural, and social considerations rather than linguistic ones. Dr. William Wang (University of California-Berkeley), using Chinese as an example, described how, in the areas adjacent to China, many of the languages most similar in structure to Chinese have adopted alphabetic writing systems (e.g., Tibetan, Burmese), while many quite distinct from Chinese (e.g., Korean, Japanese) have borrowed Chinese logographs. Both Dr. Grimes and Dr. John Ryan (formerly at the International Institute for Adult Literacy Methods, Tehran, Iran) stressed the need, when designing an orthography, to consider the language of wider communication that speakers of a minority language will eventually need to learn.

A third issue discussed concerned the notion of linguistic awareness and what role it plays in learning to read. Although the subject appeared and reappeared in presentations and discussions, little agreement was reached on the nature of linguistic awareness or its role in reading acquisition. Some participants (e.g., Dr. Isabelle Liberman, University of Connecticut, and Dr. Alvin Liberman, Haskins Laboratories, New Haven, Connecticut,) held that linguistic awareness is required to read an orthography that taps more than the surface level of a language. Others, including Dr. Jonathan Baron (University of Pennsylvania) and Dr. Anatoly Liberman (University of Minnesota), suggested caution in assuming that such so-phistication is a prerequisite for reading, rather than a result of experience in reading.

Closely related to this concern was the notion of rule learning, particu-larly the role played by rules as compared with analogy in reading. Dr. Lee Brooks (McMaster University, Hamilton, Ontario) presented examples of training tasks in which adults failed to acquire letter-sound patterns in an artificial orthography, yet continued to abstract some features to facilitate transfer beyond the training items. Drs. Georgije Lukatela (University of Belgrade, Yugoslavia) and Michael Turvey (University of Connecticut) dis-cussed a variety of experiments with Serbo-Croatian readers, in which the researchers tried to assess the degree of interference created by the two scripts (Cyrillic and Roman) used in Yugoslavia. They found, in general, that the patterns derived from the script learned first dominate reading habits into adulthood even though the second script is usually learned within a year of the first.

Information processing in competent reading, a topic that links linguis-tic awareness and rule learning, was discussed in several presentations. Dr. Dominic Massaro (University of Wisconsin) presented new empirical sup-port for the view that orthographic structure serves primarily to aid letter identification when visual information is incomplete, but does not facilitate recognition of the features of the letters themselves. Dr. Ovid Tzeng (Uni-versity of California-Riverside) reported from his own studies with Chinese characters that phonological mediation is not necessary for lexical access, but is used to facilitate retention in short-term memory. These results are similar to reports on processing of alphabetic script. The Serbo-Croatian studies, however, tend to support the opposite view. Nevertheless, the three sets of studies reported here demonstrate that information processing para-digms are directly applicable to cross-language comparisons of reading pro-cesses.

Another set of papers discussed the nature of spelling ability and its re-lationship to reading ability. Both Dr. Uta Frith (MRC Developmental Psy-chology Unit, London) and Dr. Linnea Ehri (University of California-Davis) reported studies on spelling indicating that the visual component in spelling may be more prominent than a rule-derived phonological compo-nent. Dr. Dina Feitelson (University of Haifa, Israel) pointed out that in Israel, where many citizens are not native speakers of Hebrew, a fully marked Hebrew script helps teach proper pronunciation. For Navajo, Dr. Holm speculated that a common spelling system would serve as an "arbiter between idiolectal variations."

Another issue commanding attention was the nature of reading failure, particularly the problem of dyslexia. The arbitrariness of current definitions of dyslexia was addressed by Dr. Renate Valtin (Pädagogische Hochschule,

Berlin, West Germany), who reported on her own and other German studies of this topic. Controlled studies have shown no predominance of letter or word reversals in dyslexic readers. Dr. Frank Vellutino (Albany Medical College, Albany, New York) reviewed the evidence for eliminating visual deficits as a major cause of extreme reading problems. Instead, he claimed, reading problems lead to visual inefficiencies that result from a failure to use verbal regularities to process textual material. This view relates to the issue of linguistic awareness discussed earlier.

Adapting instruction to the peculiarities of a language and its script was discussed but not examined closely. Dr. Feitelson reported on studies of instructional methodology used to teach Hebrew script. In particular, it was found that for maximal learning, letters with the same sound should be presented together, but letters with similar shapes or similar sounds should be presented farther apart in an instructional sequence. Dr. Vincent van Heuven (University in Leiden, The Netherlands) reported on a study in Holland that attempted to discover the degree of difficulty for oral blending created by different monosyllabic syllable structures. Questions of methodology in investigating instruction were also discussed. Dr. Eve Malmquist (University of Linköping, Sweden) presented a proposal for a large-scale comparison of reading across cultures.

Many participants maintained, however, that problems, such as scaling the complexity (or regularity) of orthographies, need to be resolved before comparative studies on initial reading can profitably be done. Similarly, between-subjects designs in comparing an established orthography with variations upon it were thought to be inadvisable, although no acceptable alternatives to such comparisons materialized.

More work is needed on defining the theoretical relationships between different writing systems and the languages they represent and then in exploring the degree to which these relationships represent demonstrable habits of competent readers. Whether or not use of analogy can be distinguished from use of rules in translating from spelling to sound also needs study, as do the possible alternatives to hard-core rules that readers might use. For exploring instructional methodology, new investigative procedures may be required to achieve ecological validity. The typical laboratory approaches, particularly those using training-transfer techniques in relatively brief sessions, have not mirrored the sustained learning of an ongoing class.

Finally, comparisons across languages of stage-by-stage processing during reading need to be pursued with a variety of different writing systems. Many of the equivocal results emerging from studies done in the United States in the last 10 years on word recognition might be explained through the use of information processing paradigms with different types of writing systems. These approaches to the analysis of reading processes also might be applied to the diagnosis of severely retarded readers in an attempt to identify those processing deficits that are peculiar to specific writing systems and those that are not.

Acknowledgments

Vincent J. van Heuven is supported by a grant from the Dutch Organization for the Advancement of Pure Research (Z.W.O.).

John W. Ryan indicates that the opinions and assertions expressed in his paper are the responsibility of the author and do not necessarily represent the views of his employer, the International Institute for Adult Literacy Methods.

Isabelle Liberman, Alvin M. Liberman, Ignatius Mattingly, and Donald Shankweiler acknowledge that the preparation of their paper, as well as the research on which it is based, was supported by grant HD 01994 from the National Institute of Child Health and Human Development.

The research of Jonathan Baron and Rebecca Treiman was supported by NIMH grant MH-29453. They thank Nora Coffey and Maita Schneiderman who ran their subjects. The Powel School (Thomas Young, Principal; Wanda Will, Reading Teacher) provided a model of how schools can help researchers, it is hoped to the benefit of both.

Ovid Tzeng and Daisy Hung are grateful to Isabelle Liberman and Lila Gleitman for suggesting the experiment reported in their paper.

Georgije Lukatela and Michael T. Turvey acknowledge that their research was supported in part by NICHD grant HD 08495 to the University of Belgrade, and in part by NICHD grant HD 01994 to the Haskins Laboratories.

Frank R. Vellutino indicates that much of the research that he conducted and reported in his paper, was supported by grant HD 09658 awarded by the National Institute of Child Health and Human Development, DHEW; and grant G007604369, awarded by the Bureau of Education for the Handicapped, U.S. Office of Education, DHEW.

The editors would like to thank the many people who helped them develop the conference and this publication. They thank the staff of the Conference and Seminar Program Branch of the Fogarty International Center, NIH, Dr. Earl C. Chamberlayne, Mrs. Toby Levin, Mrs. Michiko Cooper, and Miss Janice Kamp, for their expert assistance in preparing for and conducting the conference. Richard L. Venezky also is grateful to his secretary, Mrs. Cathi Hollenbeck, for her sustained help during the planning of the meeting and the preparation of the conference proceedings.

James F. Kavanagh expresses his sincere appreciation to his secretary, Miss Janet Thomson, for invaluable help during the planning and conduct of the conference, the revision of parts of the manuscripts, and their assemblage into this book.

Finally, the editors thank the conferees without whose enthusiastic participation and complete cooperation, this publication would not have been possible.

Orthography,
Reading,
and
Dyslexia

Overview
FROM SUMER TO
LEIPZIG TO BETHESDA

Richard L. Venezky

The Cross-National Conference on Orthography, Reading and Dyslexia, upon which the chapters of this volume are based, was the first to bring together a world-wide range of scholars from many disciplines to discuss the role of orthography in reading and in reading failure. Other conferences on orthography have been held, such as the International Convention for the Amendment of English Orthography, which convened in Philadelphia in 1876 as part of this country's centennial celebration. But that gathering, like so many others of similar title, began with the assumption that English orthography was a menace to health, public safety, and early acquisition of literacy, and spent its time seeking a marketable replacement. The Bethesda conference, while not rejecting the possibility of merit in this position, sought instead to inspect what evidence might be adduced for discovering the role that orthography plays in reading and in reading failure, and what steps might be taken to overcome dyslexia in the United States. To achieve these ends an exceedingly wide range of topics and investigatory approaches were included, from how various national orthographies relate to language and reading, to the initial teaching of reading, to reading failure, to how adults and children process orthographic information, to the design and reform of orthographies, and finally to the problems of conducting cross-national research on reading.

The conferees shared a view that is common to those who have bothered to study carefully the evidence on reading achievement. Namely, that even with languages in which translation from writing to speech is highly predictable (e.g., Finnish), problems in reading instruction are found (see especially the chapter in this volume by Kyöstiö, chapter 3). There was a recurring theme, however, in some of the cross-national papers presented, and that was the partial independence of initial reading, which is heavily involved with symbol-sound translation, from comprehension, which is more closely tied to intellectual functioning. Within the area of initial reading, particular interest was expressed in defining specific research issues, particularly those that might reveal what facets of an orthography are relevant to the design of rational instruction (Grimes & Gordon, chapter 7, this volume; Holm, chapter 6, this volume).

Orthographies might relate to language on a variety of levels, and the processing of printed symbols into a form of language from which the reader can acquire meaning might proceed by a variety of means, yet ultimately our speculations in these areas, which we value for their contribution to fundamental knowledge, must be related to diagnostic or instructional procedures. In other words, we require not only that hypotheses be subject to empirical validation, but also that they pass a strong test of relevance to the issues at hand. At the same time we must guard against assumptions about reading that might limit our ability to discover particular solutions. Orthographies involve language, which leads us naturally to an examination of the specific relationships between writing and language for a particular system. Yet as several chapters in this volume indicate, we should not automatically assign a psychological reality to the full range of linguistic entities that are proposed. For complex orthographies like English, as an example, we have yet to determine which orthographic relationships competent readers acquire.

Similarly, we should try to avoid the simplistic dogmatism of the English spelling reform advocates, on one hand, who attribute without empirical justification all reading problems to spelling-sound irregularity, and on the other hand, the anti-orthography school that equally, without justification, would exorcise all attention to orthography from reading instruction.

The aim of this volume, viz., to assess what we know and what we might reasonably expect to learn about the role of orthography in learning to read and in reading failure, may appear quite unimpressive to those who traffic in the harder sciences. After all, in most of the physical and biological sciences only a single cutting edge exists, with strong agreement throughout the disciplines on which lands should be explored next and by what means. But no such consensus can be found in the social sciences and particularly not in those that contribute to the science of education. For example, the speller reformers, who have counted among their ranks such notables as Charles Darwin, William James, and Leonard Bloomfield, assume that the deleterious effects of orthographic irregularities on learning to read are obvious and without need of demonstration. For others, this point is far from well established. For some who are responsible for the design of new orthographies, an inviolable one-phoneme, one-symbol rule holds (see, in particular, Pike, 1947); but others (e.g., DeFrancis, 1950; Hockett, 1951) hold that such factors as the functional load that a contrast carries should also be considered before a feature is overtly marked in the orthography. And in the analysis of reading processes, disagreement can be found on many of the most basic matters. We seem to stand like Tantalus does in Hades; each time we reach for the fruits that seem so near, they recede from our reach. As we seem to approach consensus on one component of reading, the stage shifts, the understanding we sought vanishes and a new set of problems moves into sight. Ambrose Bierce, in his *Devil's Dictionary,* defined *education* as "that which discloses to the wise and disguises from the foolish their lack of understanding." By this definition, the task presented here is to seek education as the wise.

But before tackling the immediate concerns of the twentieth century, it may be informative to review some of the trends, anomalies, and curiosities that emerge from an examination of the last 6,000 years of orthography and reading, particularly those that seem to bear most directly on our understanding (or lack thereof) of reading processes. History may be, as Edward Gibbon wrote, "...little more than the register of the crimes, follies, and misfortunes of mankind," but without examining past practices much of the richness and complexity of our current interests may be lost. First, two anomalies are presented which might merit discussion; but yet again, like anomalies in general, may be no more relevant to reality than lightning is to a lightning bug.

THE CONSONANT-VOWEL DICHOTOMY

The first anomaly concerns the contrast between consonants and vowels, a topic that crops up here and there in current reading related research, but that also figures in controversies over the origin of alphabetic writing. In the earliest alphabetic writing system we know of, the Semitic system, which is first evidenced in the Sinai Inscriptions that date from approximately 3,500 years ago, consonants, but not vowels, are overtly marked. One might claim that since the 22 original symbols in the Semitic alphabet were derived from Egyptian syllabic symbols, that in fact vowels were represented in the Semitic orthography.

Gelb (1963) claims that West Semitic writing, of which Old Hebrew is an example, was syllabic and not alphabetic. The evidence for this conclusion is based primarily upon spelling similarities to cuneiform, which is obviously syllabic, and the introduction, under later Greek influence, of (among others) a special diacritic, *schwa,* for marking a consonant that had no following vowel. According to Gelb's analysis, a transition to alphabetic writing began in West Semitic writing with the *scriptio plena* system, an imperfectly used device for indicating vowel quality with weak consonant symbols. Greek became the first true alphabet system when the *plena* system evolved into the consistent use of symbols specifically for vowels. Diringer (1948) objects to this view on the grounds that ancient Semitic, like modern Hebrew, was adequately served by consonant representations alone. The basis of his claim is that since vowel pronunciations varied considerably more than consonant pronunciations across the various Semitic dialects and languages, a consonant marking system, like Chinese logographs, allowed communication across dialects and languages. On the Semitic script in particular, Diringer (1948, p. 217) exclaims, "It was not perfect. But perfection has not yet been reached by any alphabet."

Although Gelb's views have gained considerable popularity, they suffer from one major flaw, namely, that a writing system that has only a single symbol for each consonant hardly qualifies as a syllabary, especially in a language that had at least four and possibly eight vowel contrasts. A full syllabary for old Hebrew, for example, would need at least four symbols for each consonant, each representing a pairing with a different vowel, as is done in modern Japanese katakana or in the Cherokee syllabary. There seems to be no path around the obvious conclusion that Semitic languages chose to represent consonants but not vowels, even though both classes of sounds served to separate meaningful elements in the languages involved. Although the differences between Gelb and Diringer may be strictly semantic, hinging on the precise definition of *syllabic,* the existence of writing systems that mark consonants but not vowels, especially when found in full use today (e.g., modern Hebrew), indicates differences between the two sound classes that may be intrinsic to the manner in which each is perceived.

For Semitic languages, consonant writing probably did not pose as many problems as it did for the various Indo-European languages that the Semitic alphabet was borrowed from, mainly because Semitic language roots are characterized by their consonant schemes, the vowels serving primarily as grammatical markers. Thus, while ambiguities existed in writing from a phonological standpoint, native speakers could generally use word order to select a semantically significant alternative. Nevertheless, the analysis of the speech stream into consonants and vowels, with the assignment of consonants, but not vowels, to written representation is evident.

If we move forward in time about 1,400 years from the earliest Sinai Inscription, and across the Mediterranean to the Italic peninsula, we find the second component of the vowel-consonant dichotomy. Latin orthography, from which Modern English writing is most directly descended, is based in part upon the orthography of two sister Italic languages, Oscan and Umbrian (although Latin and at least Oscan derive their letter forms and letter names from Etruscan). Ancient Latin had phonemic contrasts for length or quantity in both consonants and vowels, as apparently did Oscan and Umbrian, which used geminated symbols to mark the long form of each, just as Finnish does today (Buck, 1929). But curiously, Latin scribes adopted consonant gemination but failed to establish any mechanism for distinguishing vowel quantity. Old English, which also had phonemic contrasts between long and short vowels and long and short consonants, continued the Latin writing practices, thereby neglecting to mark vowel quantity.

Old English spelling changed dramatically over the Old English period, particularly in marking spirant contrasts that were absent from Latin. Runic letters were borrowed (*wynn* and *thorn*) and in one case, a new letter created *(eth)*. Consonant quantity, as it lost its phonemic status, was no longer marked consistently. But nowhere other than in a few feeble attempts at gemination in some early glossaries, does a scheme for marking vowel quantity appear in Old English. When late Middle and early Modern English digraph vowel letters became widely used, the quantity contrast became one of quality through what is called in English philology The Great Vowel Shift.

Science fiction may not be needed to justify speculating on the psychological differences that might exist between consonants and vowels, especially as to their importance in a writing system. Some work on dichotic listening has been interpreted in terms of different hemispheric localizations for consonants and vowels in speech perception. I'm not altogether sure what to make of this in relation to orthography and reading, but I began by labeling this an anomaly and I think I'll leave it under that cover and move to a second such beast.

SILENT READING

The existence of writing implies quite strongly the existence of reading. Therefore, homo sapiens or some subset thereof has been reading for nigh 6,500 years. But does this mean that the processes by which Hammurabi or Alexander the Great or Horace or Charlemagne read are the same as those that adults today use in reading? We have one thin thread of evidence that implies a negative answer to this question. I won't delineate the full details of this evidence, because it is amply presented elsewhere (Hendrickson, 1929–1930), but mainly through historical anecdote it is clear that even among the most scholarly and literate, silent reading was exceedingly rare up to perhaps as late as the time of Chaucer. Even in complete privacy one read to himself with the full participation of tongue, glottis, and the other elements of the articulatory system and therefore considerably more slowly than the better adults in silent reading today. This leaves open the possibility that human reading processes, particularly for alphabetic languages, may have evolved dramatically over the last 600 years or so. While I doubt that the neocortex or any other component of the central nervous system has undergone changes during this period to facilitate silent reading, there may be processes that silent reading requires that profoundly influence other cognitive functions.

Oral reading, because of both its slower pace and its attention to complete articulation of each word, is probably not as demanding of higher cognitive processes as rapid, silent reading. In rapid, silent reading, visual processing, which tends to be relatively slow, is traded off for greater syntactic/semantic processing, which appears to be relatively fast. Furthermore, the reader learns to rely on the various levels of redundancy in a text, such as orthographic structure, to reduce his need to receive a fully composed visual image. But this implies that the reader is pushing himself to attend to and digest the text at a reasonably deep level in silent reading—processes that may not be required in oral reading. The net result might be that through silent reading, comprehension is more thoroughly practiced than through oral reading, and furthermore, the textual structures, that is, the textual redundancies, are more thoroughly acquired. These conclusions may have implications for the study of literacy in human history.

WRITING AS MYSTERY

Beyond these anomalies, several trends in the history of reading instruction and reading research bear on the concerns of this volume. The first trend, which carries us from Sumer in the southern portion of Mesopotamia to the Germanic tribes, which Tacitus described in the second century of the common era, to Medieval England, and then to post-revolutionary United States, traces the mystery and power of orthography.

Writing, at least according to some archaeologists (Pritchard, 1958; but cf. Sarton, 1952), occurred first among the Sumerians perhaps as much as 6,500 years ago. To the Sumerians also goes the prize for the first schoolhouse, which dates from Hammurabi's time. But in ancient times writing was, in addition to its various direct functions, an object of both power and mystery. In the continual contests for power in ancient times between the kings and the priest class, control over both reading instruction and the archives of written works was highly prized. Thus, while the earliest schools and the earliest collections of Sumerian tablets were found in the temples, with a shift of political power away from church control, libraries began to be associated with the King's palace, as evidenced most convincingly by the great library of Ashurbanipal, which was excavated at Ninevah.

The same was true in Egypt at the end of the 18th Dynasty, when Amenhotep attempted to deprive the priests of their power by adopting a monotheistic religion and by moving the capital, including its literary archives, to a new site. These same Egyptians, according to Plato, attributed the invention of writing to one of their gods. But Plato claims further that when writing was first offered to the reigning Egyptian King, he refused the gift on the grounds that "the alphabet would create forgetfulness in the learners' souls because they will not use their memories." (For a more light-hearted view of the origin of the alphabet, see Rudyard Kipling's "How the alphabet was made" [Kipling, 1902].)

The Germanic tribes who conquered England perhaps 1,500 years ago brought with them a writing system that was used almost exclusively for religious functions. The term for the letters of this alphabet, *rune,* means mysterious. In the United States, orthography has demonstrated an unexpected power since the inception of the country. Noah Webster, an ultra-patriot of the post-revolutionary period and the father of American lexicography, contributed to the intellectual independence of the newly formed nation by establishing a distinctively American spelling system. The results, as evidenced by such purely U.S. spellings as *meter, honor, traveled,* and *criticize,* are a testament to Webster's tenacity and marketing ability. In this century, one of America's most powerful presidents, Theodore Roosevelt, totally underestimated the reverence that the masses have for a spelling system to which they are accustomed. By attempting to encourage the reform proposals of the Simplified Spelling Board in 1906, Roosevelt triggered an outcry from both the press and Congress. The man who led the Rough Riders up San Juan Hill, broke up the Northern Securities Trust, and settled the Japanese-Russian War was quickly forced into a hasty retreat from spelling reform.

Today, orthography is no longer mysterious, nor is it any part of the struggle between Church and State; yet we cannot ignore the practical reality of spelling reform in some cultures. Russia, for example, has managed several orthographic reforms in this century, as have other countries (see A. Liberman, chapter 4, this volume). But for English, even if we should find that spelling irregularity seriously impedes learning to read, change in orthography may not be a practicable alternative. Writing systems have a sociopolitical reality as well as a linguistic one, and often what might appear desirable from a philological or pedagogical standpoint may not be acceptable to a society that has become accustomed to a prevailing standard or that derives its models for writing from systems with different features. Similarly, while it is commonly assumed that since the Enlightment most technologically developed countries have promoted widespread literacy, there are some political writers who have detected the opposite trends, particularly in nineteenth century England (Aspinall, 1949; West, 1970).

THE STATUS OF READING INSTRUCTORS IN SOCIETY

The second trend of interest concerns the public and their attitude toward the academic requirements for reading instruction. Since the classical period in Greece, educated citizens have expressed the belief, either directly or indirectly, that learning to read is quite simple. This attitude has expressed itself in three distinct ways up to this day. First, persons from the lowest political and social status have often been recruited for teaching reading, a practice that occurs from ancient Greece until modern times. At first slaves and others of limited rights and means were recruited. Then it was the impecunious country pastor, the newly arrived immigrant, and others of limited upward mobility. Elementary school teachers today are no longer drawn from the lowest strata of society, yet in many so-called enlightened countries, the amount of required training in reading pedagogy for classroom teachers is minimal at best.

Second, popular literature often perpetuates the image that persons with adequate intelligence can teach themselves to read. Thus, the Russian poet Mayakovsky (1960) wrote that

> The human fledgling—
> barely out of the egg—
> grasps at a book,
> and quires of exercise paper.
> But I learned my alphabet from signboards,
> leafing through pages of iron and tin.

And Tarzan, the creation of Edgar Rice Burroughs, taught himself to read English even before he ever heard it spoken. This feat, wrote Burroughs, was possible because of the "active intelligence of a healthy mind endowed by inheritance with more than ordinary reasoning powers."

Third, and most important for this volume, even the educated, including academics, treat reading processes and reading instruction as matters where common sense is sufficient for full understanding. For example, the late C. C. Fries, a linguist of considerable stature, dismissed the entire empirical literature on eye movements and most of what else has been done on reading research as being nothing but chasing after the wind. "In spite of the great number of studies dealing with eye movements..., very little of a positive nature has been contributed from these studies to our understanding of reading ability..." (Fries, 1963, p. 30). Fries was his own authority on the psychology and pedagogy of reading, as was Bloomfield before him. And both had an impact on reading practice, although the reading programs they separately produced have had limited acceptance.

But more surprising is the history of the design of orthographies for preliterate societies. In the middle of the nineteenth century when a group of missionary societies wanted assistance in bringing literacy to African and South American tribes, they sought the services of a prominent philologist who specialized in Egyptology, C. R. Lepsius. Lepsius developed an awkward scheme for designing new orthographies (Lepsius, 1863), replete with superscripts and subscripts, a scheme that took no account of the pedagogical concerns of literacy instruction. One can only assume that to Lepsius and to his employers, teaching to read was too trivial to require specialized assistance.

The first change in this attitude toward pedagogy and psychology did not come until 1930 when the International African Institute adopted a new set of principles for orthographic design (International African Institute, 1930). Deviations from pure phonemic representation were countenanced and psychological and pedagogical principles were invoked, based primarily on Huey's work (Huey, 1908). Similar concerns began to appear in the United States in the 1950s (e.g., Hockett, 1951; Jones, 1950; Nida, 1954). But what is most curious is that when Lepsius was hired in the 1840s, the educational reforms of Pestolazzi, particularly in the teaching of reading and spelling, were taking hold in Europe and in North America. But information on the learning process and on pedagogy was apparently not considered necessary for teaching reading. We might consider ourselves beyond this folly, yet it is not altogether clear that we are.

THE ROLE OF PSYCHOLOGISTS IN STUDYING READING

The third and last orthographic trend concerns the relatively late entry of psychologists into the study of orthography in reading. Experimental psychology traces its modern origins to Leipzig where Wilhelm Wundt established the first psychological laboratory in the 1870s (Boring, 1950). In Wundt's laboratory, as in others that sprang up shortly afterwards in Europe and then in North America, reading processes were a central focus in the attempt to measure the speed of mental events. In this era Cattel, Erdmann and Dodge, Quantz, and a variety of others investigated a wide range of reading processes, including word recognition, subvocalization during reading, the eye-voice span, and eye movements (Venezky, 1977). Yet in all of the empirical work and in all of the theorizing, not once is orthography— whether English, German, French, or Amharic—mentioned as a matter important to reading or as a subject for scientific investigation. Almost every major effect in the area of reading now being investigated was studied sometime between the foundation of Wundt's laboratory in Leipzig and Edmund Huey's seminal text in 1908, *The psychology and pedagogy of reading*. Yet the current focus of word recognition studies, orthographic structure, is curiously absent from this early work. And what makes this neglect even more curious is that various societies in both England and the United States were actively campaigning during this period for the simplification of English spelling, under the claim that irregular spellings seriously retarded the acquisition of literacy.

Following the International Convention for the Amendment of English Orthography (1876), the Spelling Reform Association was formed in the United States and a companion organization was organized in England. The English group, which was associated with the Philological Society of England, counted among its Vice-Presidents Charles Darwin, Alfred Tennyson, Sir Issac Pitman, and James Murray, editor of the *Oxford English Dictionary*. The American group had a list of no less impressive luminaries

(Venezky, 1980). Yet experimental psychologists ignored the spelling reform claims then, as they continued to do until the late 1950s when a group of psychologists and linguists at Cornell University began to study, among other reading topics, English letter-sound correspondences and their acquisition (Levin, 1966).

Prior to the Cornell studies, the only major investigation that attended to orthography and reading was a cross-language study of eye movements during reading, done by William S. Gray as part of his UNESCO survey, *The Teaching of Reading and Writing* (Gray, 1956). The absence of psychological interest until recently in orthography is difficult to explain. In part it may have resulted from the absence of an adequate linguistic base for describing different orthographic systems and in part it may have been derived from the psychologists' concern not with reading per se, but with the speed of mental events and other more general processing variables. Whatever the cause for past neglect, now it appears that experimental psychologists have a serious concern for the reading process, as a number of chapters in this volume demonstrate. If, however, the mistakes of the past are not to be repeated, it is important that psychologists strive for a fundamental understanding of reading and how it relates to other perceptual and cognitive functioning. The cross-national study of reading processes is one avenue through which hypotheses generated in this country about reading might be tested and a more basic understanding of underlying processes uncovered (see Lukatela & Turvey, chapter 15, this volume; Tzeng & Hung, chapter 14, this volume). It is interesting to note that modern linguistics dates approximately from the time when linguists began, after nearly a century of neglect, to test their philological theories on non-Indo-European languages. From early twentieth century work on American Indian languages (e.g., Boas, 1911) and Tagalog (Bloomfield, 1917), in particular, arose a totally new perspective on linguistic structure, as reflected in Bloomfield's seminal text, *Language* (Bloomfield, 1933). Similarly for American and British researchers, new ideas (or new conformations of old ideas) might arise from the systematic study of reading processes in widely divergent languages and orthographies.

But if psychological studies are to lead to new, fundamental understandings about reading and reading failure, then it is important that they be subjected to the criticism, encouragement, and scholarly competition of reading related disciplines, such as are represented in this volume. Although the normal association of experimental psychologists is with other experimental psychologists, the value of their reading related work may depend strongly upon the degree to which they can interact with clinical psychologists, linguists, educators, and others who are involved in investigating reading instruction and reading failure.

Thus, this volume is intended to serve a dual function. On one hand it presents a knowledge base viewed from highly diverse disciplines, but organized around a concern for the role that orthography serves in the acquisition of literacy. And on the other hand it attempts to foster communication across disparate methodologies, orientations, and technical dialects.

Section I
ORTHOGRAPHY AND READING
A Cross-National View

Chapter 1
READING OF HIRAGANA

Takahiko Sakamoto

SOUND-SYMBOL REGULARITY IN HIRAGANA

Although the Japanese orthography consists of kanji, hiragana, and kata-kana (Sakamoto, 1976), this chapter is limited to the reading of hiragana, which is a set of phonetic symbols.

RELATIONSHIP BETWEEN HIRAGANA AND HAKU

In the Japanese spoken language, the *Haku* is the smallest unit of sound. Although the term *Onsetsu* has traditionally been used in this context, the author prefers to use the term *Haku* to avoid confusion. Haku are short sounds spoken one after another for approximately equal lengths of time. For instance, *Sakamoto,* the author's name, has four Haku and the length of each Haku, *sa, ka, mo,* and *to* is about the same when the name is spoken in normal speech. Haku may be translated into English as *mora,* meaning the unit of time equivalent to the ordinary or normal short sound or syllable. Basically, a Haku is: 1) one of the five vowels in Japanese *(a, i, u, e, o)*, or 2) one of these five vowels preceded by a consonant, or 3) a special usage of the *n* consonant. Some examples of the first and second uses are shown in Table 1.

There is no Haku for a closed syllable in which a word ends with a consonant, such as *top* or *cat.* In Japanese, all consonants are followed by a vowel, with only one exception, the case of *n.* An *n* is usually followed by a vowel to make the Haku *na, ni, nu, ne,* and *no.* But an *n* can also exist with-

Table 1. Examples of haku

Word	Number of Haku	Hiragana	Meaning
AI	2	あい	love
KAI	2	かい	shell fish
AKAI	3	あかい	red
TAKAI	3	たかい	high
ATATAKAI	5	あたたかい	warm

Table 2.   The *n* haku

Words	Number of Haku	Number of Syllables	Hiragana	Meaning
KI<u>N</u>	2	1	きん	gold
HO<u>N</u>	2	1	ほん	book
SHI<u>M</u>BU<u>N</u>	4	2	しんぶん	newspaper
NI<u>N</u>GE<u>N</u>	4	2	にんげん	human being

out being followed by a vowel, except when it appears at the very beginning of a word; that is, *n* without a vowel can appear only in the middle of or at the end of a word. This *n* is regarded as an independent Haku. When it appears in the middle of a word and is followed by one of the consonants *m, o,* or *p,* its phonetic value changes from [n] to [m], but it is still regarded as the same Haku as *n.* Examples of this special *n* (or *m*) Haku are shown in Table 2.

First, there are 46 Haku which are called *Seion,* voiceless sound. These are actually the Haku that do not include voiced consonants. The 46 Haku consist of 5 vowels, 40 consonant-vowel combinations, and the *n* Haku. Each of the 46 Seion is written with a single hiragana letter and the 46 Seion might be called the basic hiragana.

Second, there are 20 additional Haku called *Dakuon,* voiced sounds. A Dakuon is one of the five vowels preceded by a certain voiced consonant such as *g, z, d,* or *b.* In order to write a Dakuon, two tick marks are placed at the right upper side of the particular hiragana of a corresponding Seion. For instance, if two ticks are put next to the hiragana for *ka,* the phonetic value changes from [ka] to [ga]. In the same way, the two ticks change *sa* to *za, ta* to *da,* and *he* to *be* (see Table 3).

Third, there are five more Haku called *Han-dakuon,* half-voiced sounds. A Han-dakuon is simply one of the five vowels preceded by the *p* consonant. When a small circle is put next to the hiragana for *ha, hi, fu, he,* and *ho,* the reading of the hiragana becomes *pa, pi, pu, pe,* and *po.* Examples of Han-dakuon are shown in Table 4.

Thus, although there are no special hiragana for Dakuon and Handakuon, they can be written by putting two ticks or a circle next to one of

Table 3.   Examples of Seion and Dakuon

か	が	さ	ざ	た	だ	へ	べ
ka	ga	sa	za	ta	da	he	be

Table 4. Examples of Seion and Han-Dakuon

は	ぱ	ひ	ぴ	へ	ぺ	ほ	ぽ
ha	pa	hi	pi	he	pe	ho	po

the Seion hiragana. When it is said that there are 46 symbols in hiragana, one is referring to the 46 hiragana for Seion, and when it is said there are 71 hiragana, one is talking about the three usages of hiragana mentioned above.

Each of the 71 Haku is written with a hiragana (with any necessary additional marks) and the relationship between a Haku and a hiragana is always perfect.

In addition to the 71 Haku, there are 34 special Haku that need extra arrangements of some of the 71 hiragana when they are written. Among the 34 special Haku, there is one called *Sokuon,* assimilated sound. This actually is a short pause as long as a normal Haku within a word. The Sokuon is also regarded as an independent Haku and is written with the hiragana for *tsu* smaller than the regular-sized hiragana (see Table 5).

The other 33 special Haku are called *Yō-on,* contracted sound. Yō-on are those Haku with a [j], or *y* sound between a consonant and a vowel, for instance, *kya, kyu,* or *kyo.* A Yō-on is written with a hiragana that has a consonant and an *i* vowel plus a smaller than usual hiragana for *ya* or *yu* or *yo.* For example, a hiragana for *ki* plus a small *ya* makes the Yō-on *kya.* Some examples of Yō-on are shown in Table 6.

Thus, hiragana for *tsu, ya, yu,* and *yo* are written smaller in size when the special Haku are indicated. Those smaller hiragana should be written to the right of the line in vertical writing, or below the center of the line in horizontal writing. The smaller hiragana are examples of the exceptions to the rule that a symbol perfectly corresponds to a sound, and Yō-on is the only exception to the rule that one Haku is written with one hiragana.

Table 5. Examples of Sokuon

	Sokuon	Number of Haku	Meaning
さ き sa ki	No	2	ahead
さ つ き sa tsu ki	No	3	azalea
さ っ き sa <u>k</u> ki	Yes	3	some time ago

Table 6.   Examples of Yō-on

	Yō-on	Number of Haku	Meaning
き　や　く ki　ya　ku	No	3	rule
きゃ　く kya　ku	Yes	2	guest
ひ　や　く hi　ya　ku	No	3	leap
ひゃ　く hya　ku	Yes	2	hundred

There are two more exceptional cases in which a hiragana should be read differently from its original sound, *Chō-on,* a prolonged sound, and *Joshi,* a particle. When a Haku with an *o* vowel is prolonged for about twice as long as the length of a regular Haku, the hiragana for *u* is sometimes added, rather than the hiragana for *o*, after the prolonged hiragana, although this *u* hiragana should be read *o*. Similarly the *i* hiragana is sometimes read *e*. See Table 7 for some examples of Chō-on.

When a hiragana for *ha* or *he* is used as a Joshi, or particle, it is read *wa* or *e*. Some examples of Joshi are shown in Table 8.

LEARNING TO READ HIRAGANA

Japanese children enter elementary school at age 6, at which time the Ministry of Education requires that they start to learn the hiragana letters. However, many children begin to learn hiragana before they reach school age without receiving any formal instruction by naturally absorbing Hiragana in their daily life through books, magazines, toys, TV programs, and other means with the help of their family (Sakamoto, 1975).

The National Language Research Institute (1972) published the results of a nationwide research survey on preschool children's reading abilities.

Table 7.   Examples of Chō-on

う　ん　ど　う u　n　do　o	movement
い　い　せ　ん　せ　い i　i　se　n　se　e	good teacher

Table 8.   Examples of Joshi

は	は	は	へ	や	へ	も	ど	る	(My) mother returns
ha	ha	<u>wa</u>	he	ya	<u>e</u>	mo	do	ru	to the room.

The subjects were 1,399 5-year-old children and 818 4-year-old children. This test was given in November when the 4-year-olds were 17 months away from entering elementary school and the 5-year-olds were due to enter school in 5 months.

It is clear that 14% of the 4-year-olds and 36% of the 5-year-olds could read all 71 hiragana (Figure 1). This figure also indicates that learning to read hiragana is completed in a rather short period of time once the child starts to learn. This is supported by Ishikawa (1970) who traced the learning of hiragana of 18 children. Murata (1974) shows the learning of hiragana by 11 children for whom the Ishikawa test data are complete (Figure 2). Apparently, the number of hiragana learned does not increase gradually, but rather shoots upward rapidly.

The National Language Research Institute (1972) also investigated its sample's reading of the special Haku: Yō-on, Chō-on, Soku-on, and Joshi.

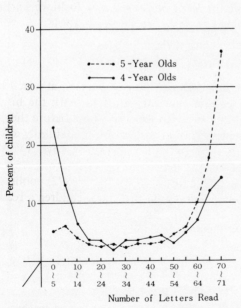

Figure 1.   Hiragana reading of 4- and 5-year olds. (Reprinted by permission, The National Language Research Institute, 1972.)

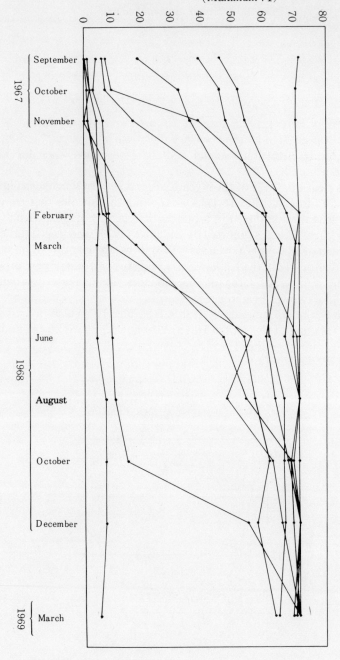

Figure 2. Development of hiragana reading of 11 children.

Table 9.   Developmental stages of hiragana reading

| Stage | Hiragana mastered | | Features |
	Number of hiragana (total 71)	Kinds of special Haku[a] (5 kinds)	
A	0	0	Totally unable to read
B	1–5	0	Begin to read the hiragana in own name
C	6–20	0	Become ready to read; can read either first name or family name
D	21–59	0	Period of rapid learning
E	60–71	0	Can read all Seion plus a good amount of Dakuon and Han-dakuon
F	60–71	1–2	Completes learning of 71 hiragana; begins to learn special Haku
G	60–71	3–4	Learning period of special Haku
H	60–71	5	All learning completed

[a]including Yō-chō-on
Reprinted by permission, The National Language Research Institute, 1972

The institute also added *Yō-chō-on,* which is a combination of Yō-on and Cho-on, to the test of special Haku. From the results, the institute set forth the developmental stages of hiragana reading (Table 9). A breakdown of the institute's subjects by the developmental stages indicated in Table 9 is shown in Figure 3. According to this figure, children who could not read at

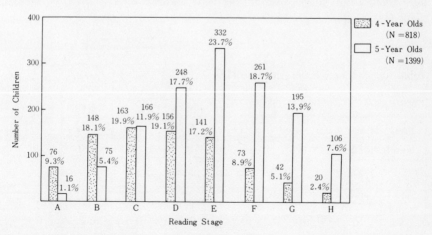

Figure 3.   Developmental stages of 4- and 5-year olds' hiragana reading. (Reprinted by permission, The National Language Research Institute, 1972.)

all are only 9% of the 4-year-olds and 1% of the 5-year-olds. On the other hand, children who completed the learning of all hiragana, including the reading of special Haku, are only 2% of the 4-year-olds and 8% of the 5-year-olds. Considering that the children in the E, F, G, and H stages can read almost all the 71 hiragana, there seems to be a great difficulty for children to learn the special Haku.

The report also stated that hiragana is easiest to learn in the order of Seion, Dakuon, Han-dakuon, Joshi, Sokuon, Chō-on, Yō-on, and Yō-chō-on.

A Japanese child is considered ready to begin to read when he/she can divide the spoken language into its constituent Haku. Amano (1970) investigated preschool children's abilities to divide a word into its constituent parts. Although he used the term *Onsetsu* in his report, his research can also be discussed in terms of Haku. The subjects were 3-, 4-, and 5-year-old children at a day care center in Tokyo. Table 10 shows the details of the subjects including how many hiragana they could read out of the 46 Seion.

In his experiment, children were instructed to divide a word into its constituent Haku. During the instruction session, the experimenter showed a picture to the subject and turned on a lamp as each Haku was spoken, while pronouncing the word depicted. The subject was instructed to imitate the actions of the experimenter. During the experimental session, the subject was to perform the task by himself. Among the items tested were five pictures of objects familiar to children, but which contained only Seion and Dakuon. The number of Haku in any picture ranged from 2 to 5.

The percentages of children's correct responses to the words with only Seion and Dakuon are shown in Figure 4. This figure shows that all children over 4-and-a-half years old could perfectly divide the words into the constituent Haku.

Table 10. Subjects in the Amano study

Group		3A	3B	4A	4B	5A	5B
Range of ages		3:2 ~ 3:6	3:7 ~ 3:11	4:0 ~ 4:4	4:6 ~ 4:11	5:1 ~ 5:6	5:6 ~ 5:11
Number of Ss		10	10	10	10	10	10
Number of Ss who could read	Hiragana						
	41–46				1	1	6
	11–40					2	1
	1–10			1	5	5	2
	0	10	10	9	4	2	1

Reprinted by permission, Amano, 1970.

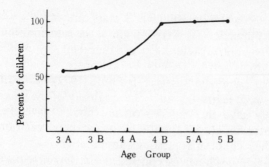

Figure 4.   Children able to divide words into Haku. (Reprinted by permission, Amano, 1970.)

All the data quoted here support the proposition that Japanese children are ready to read hiragana at age 4. This early reading is mainly attributed to the fact that hiragana is a good writing system that fits Japanese spoken language very well (Sakamoto & Makita, 1973).

THE MOTHER'S ROLE IN TEACHING HIRAGANA

Japanese children begin to read hiragana at age 4 and are generally at an advanced level of hiragana recognition before they enter elementary school. In addition to the sound-symbol regularity of hiragana, the mother's role in teaching is also a key factor behind this high achievement. Sugiyama and Saito (1973) reported that 36% of the surveyed preschool children's parents in Niigata prefecture, usually the mothers, began to read books to their children when the children were 1 year old, 31% of them began when the children were 2 years old, and 23% of them began when the children were 3 years old. Those parents who had not read to their children until they were 4 years of age comprised only 7% of all the parents. Sugiyama and Saito also concluded that the earlier the parents began to read to their children, the better the children could read by themselves when they were 5 years of age. To the extent that the mother's concern for the reading of her child is insufficient, the child's reading development is delayed.

Izumoji, Takenoya, and Mitsui (1975) reported that 92% of the preschool children they surveyed were read picture books at home. Mothers were the persons most often cited as the person who read picture books to their children, followed by both parents together and then older siblings. Fathers alone rarely read to them. Mothers answered that they gave picture books to their children because they wanted to let children know the joy of reading and to foster their children's interest in reading. Twenty percent of the mothers gave their children their first picture book when the child was less than 1 year old, 50% when the child was 1 year old, 21% when the child was 2 years old, 6% when the child was 3 years old, and 2% when the child was 4 years old. Picture books were bought at the rate of about one or two titles a month. The books were selected by mothers, by children, by both parents and children, and by fathers, in that order.

The National Language Research Institute (1972) asked 2,094 parents: "How did your child learn to read?" The majority of the parents reported that they usually gave the children picture books, gave them hiragana blocks (which were bought by about 70% of parents), read books to them, and answered their children's questions about letters.

From these findings it can be concluded that Japanese parents, usually the mothers, help their children develop abilities of hiragana reading although they do not actually teach their children to read.

Chapter 2
RELATING INSTRUCTIONAL STRATEGIES TO LANGUAGE IDIOSYNCRACIES IN HEBREW

Dina Feitelson

BACKGROUND

Hebrew was a so-called dead language from 200 C.E. to the beginning of the present century. Its successful revival has been called "a unique event in sociolinguistic history" (Fellman, 1979). One side-effect of this revival was that during the greater part of the 80-year history of the Hebrew school system in Israel, children were learning to read in a language that was not the language spoken in their homes or at least not the language in which their own parents had received their education. Despite this, learning to read was not considered a problem until the advent of mass immigration from Arab countries in the early 1950s.

Approaches to beginning reading instruction in the 1920s, 1930s, and 1940s were strongly imbued with progressive educational ideals, especially those practiced in English-speaking countries. The child and his own interests were to be the mainspring of all educational activity. Consequently, especially in the early grades, any rigid division according to subject matter was dropped in favor of a center-of-interest approach. Levy, one of the leading theoreticians of the language arts of the day, held that the child's own motivation, rather than any innate structure of subject matter, is of paramount importance in reading instruction. According to him there is no "easy or hard," no "before and after." Levy acknowledged only one distinction: "words which *interest* the child and those that do not" (Levy, 1952). The basic teaching approach was "look-and-say," with the unit of instruction being a whole sentence or phrase in preference to single words. A further aspect of this teaching approach was that it rested entirely on the personal efforts of each individual classroom teacher, unaided by any commercial teaching materials. Reading activities were based on teacher-prepared charts or on blackboard texts developed in the classroom through the cooperative efforts of teachers and children.

School entry was at 6 years of age, and by April or May of their first year in school, children used to receive their first reader at a special ceremony attended by their proud parents. In the book-centered culture of the early settlers, this ceremony was in fact invested with some of the significance of a rite de passage. Henceforth, the child was considered a "reader," and, in the second grade, moved on to the study of Bible, a subject that would remain one of the core subjects throughout the rest of his school career (Feitelson, 1973).

Until the 1950s, this way of teaching reading was widely used and, in general, considered eminently successful. The advent of mass immigration was accompanied by a dramatic reverse in this happy state of affairs. During the first 3 years of the existence of the State of Israel, the population doubled, and it doubled once again within the next 15 years. The educational system has been considered to have grown sevenfold within the first 27 years of Statehood (Central Bureau of Statistics, 1977). However, the problems inherent in the tremendous growth of population have been compounded beyond imagination by dramatic changes in demographic characteristics. As a result of the waves of refugees who arrived from Arab countries, a predominantly European-American society with a comparatively high educational standard changed in less than 20 years to a society in which the families of more than 60% of first grade entrants originated from Middle Eastern or North African countries, and had only scant traditions of formal schooling, especially for the women (Ormian, 1973). Within a very few years there were alarming reports of widespread failures in school, especially failures in learning to read (Adar, 1956; Dror, 1963; Enoch, 1950; Simon, 1958). A failure rate of 50% at the end of first grade became acceptable to many teachers and headmasters who tended to attribute it to the extremely deprived living conditions of immigrant children at the time and to a lack of interest and motivation on the part of their parents—many of whom had received very little education themselves, or even none at all.

In 1958 the Ministry of Education initiated concentrated efforts aimed at ameliorating the situation (Adiel, 1970). The impetus to these efforts was a study that had been published a few years earlier and that had drawn considerable attention. The study was designed to gain a better understanding of the factors affecting a child's success or failure during the first year of school.

Nine matched first grade classes, from schools in which failure was rampant, were studied intensively throughout one year and compared to control classes in schools in middle class established neighborhoods. Children were tested at the beginning, in the course of, and at the end of the year, and were also observed in class. Homes were visited and rated on several criteria. Teaching practices were observed and recorded, and teachers were interviewed at great length.

Within this framework only the results pertaining to reading are discussed. Contrary to expectations, rates of success and failure at the end of the year were not evenly dispersed among the nine matched classes. The pattern was one of the *whole class* doing exceptionally well, fair, or poorly. When these results were related to classroom observations, it turned out that the pupils of teachers who had not adhered to the accepted method, but who had in fact devoted considerable time to reading activities per se, including syllable drill, achieved better results than the pupils of teachers who had all along been considered to be the more resourceful and inspiring teachers. Also, the correlation between the teacher's way of instruction and the individual's success or failure in reading at the end of the year turned out to be significantly higher ($r = 0.71$; $p < 0.01$) than correlations with any home-related factor. On the other hand, in the control classes, the rate of success was very high despite the fact that reading had been taught informally and sometimes even casually (Feitelson, 1953).

The fact that the method of instruction rather than the sociocultural attributes of pupils' homes had been implicated as the crucial variable, in addition to an untenable situation created by continued high incidence of reading failure in a school system in which accomplished reading by the second grade was a must (due to the central role of Bible studies), led to an intensive search for alternative teaching approaches. The Ministry of Education set up six independent exploratory teams charged with developing comprehensive educational programs for the first year of school for children in immigrant areas. Each team was granted free access to a small number of schools. Within 2 years this overambitious master plan was translated by attrition and empirical reality into four sets of structured materials for teaching beginning reading (Bloom, 1966; Adiel, 1970). Three of these sets had many common elements, and the fourth has adopted more and more of those same elements in recent years. Commercial publishers followed suit, and, in time, a first grade teacher could choose from a wide range of available programs, most of which shared several underlying principles.

The new materials spread very rapidly, so much so that within only 4 years from the completion of the project one or the other of the initial four new programs was already in use in more than one-half of all first grade classrooms throughout the country (Feitelson, 1967). A survey conducted by the Ministry of Education in 1966 showed that great improvements had indeed occurred in the wake of the new teaching strategies. Not only had reading disability at the end of the first grade, as described by researchers in the fifties, virtually disappeared, but by 1966 achievements in technical reading in immigrant areas were better than scores on the same test batteries in the well-established areas in 1949 (Adiel, 1968).

Also, more recent reviews of the impact of numerous approaches to compensatory education, tried out over the years, singled out this initial project for special mention, noting that difficulties in beginning reading had indeed been satisfactorily overcome, and in one instance even calling the case of beginning reading, "the spectacular success story of compensatory educational efforts" (Adler & Peleg, 1976).

HEBREW ORTHOGRAPHY

In the team of which the author was a member, work on developing alternative teaching approaches was preceded by an analysis of phonological and visual characteristics of Hebrew orthography (Feitelson, 1961; 1966), as well as of supposed special needs of students who were typically unsuccessful in mastering decoding during their first year in school (Feitelson, 1968). One of the assumptions of the team was that once elements that are liable to cause difficulty are pinpointed in advance, it should be possible for the educator to structure instruction in such a way as to minimize potential difficulties. Within the present framework, mainly the first set of factors, language related variables, are of concern. However, in order not to lose sight of the fact that in every case decisions were based on a fusion of considerations from both sets of factors, two brief examples of population-related decisions might be helpful:

1. Children whose home environments differ markedly from the norms of the culture (or the teacher) are often considered to have a poor self-image and to lack necessary confidence in attacking learning tasks. The team judged that such children might feel threatened by being presented with the usual primers in which unlearned portions are constant evidence of hurdles still to be overcome. Instead, individual readers were designed as binders in which pages were collected one by one according to learning rate. Thus, primers became tangible evidence of knowledge already acquired, rather than a reminder of the size of the task still to be overcome.
2. When children's parents have had only scant education themselves, or are even illiterate, or when whatever education they had was in a language different from the one used in school, planned instructional sequences will have to cover all possible eventualities because at no point can the classroom teacher fall back on auxiliary teaching going on in the home. It was indeed sophisticated parental help that in the past

made instructional techniques, which were in fact particularly ill-suited to the special characteristics of the writing system, appear eminently successful (Feitelson, 1973).

Let us now return to language-related variables. The view that processes involved in initial reading acquisition are affected by various aspects of the specific writing system that is being learned has become more widely accepted. However, so far, interest in this field has been restricted mainly to two key areas; to the extent that a writing system is alphabetic and to the quality of symbol-sound relationships.

It is on purpose that the term *symbol-sound relationship,* rather than sound-symbol, is used consistently here. The reason is that it seems that, in reading, sound has to be deduced from symbol and not vice versa. Furthermore, the two sets of relationships are by no means symmetrical. For instance, in Hebrew, symbol-sound correspondences are highly consistent, while sound-symbol ones are much less so. Clearly, implications for mastering spelling will differ from those concerning decoding (see Frith and Frith, chapter 18, this volume). A redundancy of symbols over sounds is thus but one of the numerous idiosyncracies of Hebrew orthography with which a beginning reader will have to come to terms. This and many others are an outcome of the fact that the existence of a sanctified codex in a language generally impedes processes of orthographical adaptation to speech.

Hebrew is read and written from right to left. Except for instructional materials in the early grades, children's books, prayer books, and the Bible, vowels are omitted in all printed matter. Hebrew is highly inflected so that prefixes and suffixes serve in place of auxiliary words in English. Overall, Hebrew is considered to have less redundancy of information on a printed page than English, and translations of English materials into Hebrew are about one-third shorter. There are 22 basic consonant symbols and 9 vowel symbols. However, five consonants change form at the end of a word, and three (including two of the former) change sound depending on the presence or absence of a mid-line dot. The sound of another consonant depends on the location of a dot above it. Altogether a single dot signals seven different vocal meanings in Hebrew, serving in the capacity of a vowel in two of them. One of these two vowel sounds is also indicated by an additional symbol. One consonant can turn into two different vowels. Each of these vowel sounds is also represented by an additional symbol. Except for vowels indicated by this consonant, all vowels are much smaller than consonants and are placed most often below and in one case above consonants, but never beside them. In reading, consonants usually precede the vowels below them, except in one case, when a *patach* below a *chet* in final position is read first. However, the same combination in all other positions is read the regular way—consonant first.

This list by no means exhausts all idiosyncracies of Hebrew writing. Its aim is mainly to show that symbol-sound irregularities are far from being the only obstacles a beginning reader can encounter. Also, a writing system with highly consistent symbol-sound correspondences can be beset by a great number of potential difficulties for a beginning reader. It is the contention of the author that fully indexing potential difficulties of a given writing system is an essential step preceding efforts to devise strategies aimed at minimizing these difficulties.

RELATING INSTRUCTIONAL STRATEGIES TO LANGUAGE IDIOSYNCRACIES

In line with the work reported in several other chapters of this volume, our work is based on the assumption that the novice reader should acquire correct strategies. Thus, intermediary stages in which confusion about the real nature of reading could develop will hopefully be prevented. Contrary to laboratory-based experimentation in which subjects have to grapple on their own with tasks set them by an experimenter, a student in a real-life educational situation has a highly trained professional at his side. In fact, the image just evoked is misleading in a sense because even a so-called "real-life educational situation" is not an entity existing on its own, but has in most cases been contrived by an educator with a specific aim in mind. Thus, in most teaching approaches, including traditional "look-and-say," the educator mediates in one way or another between the learner and the full complexities of a naturalistic reading situation by way of providing simplified reading experiences, and carefully sequencing and spacing the introduction of additional elements. In traditional "look-and-say," for instance, the principle underlying both simplification and sequencing is most often mere vocabulary control.

On the other hand, a detailed preliminary analysis of specific characteristics including potential difficulties of a given writing system enables the educator to intervene much more fundamentally. He could, for instance, structure instructional sequences so that regularities will be highlighted and problematic issues will be interspersed only at carefully spaced intervals. Also, by using a synthetic approach, he could aim at achieving crucial insights with only a minimal information load.

It should be remembered that the oft-implied incompatibility between sequencing reading instruction according to considerations of decoding processes and attention to meaning is unfounded, and that it is possible to satisfy simultaneously both sets of criteria. That is, one can have totally meaningful material that, at the same time, has fully controlled grapheme content. Sequencing decisions would thus be based both on considerations of learning stage as well as on practical considerations, such as which particular grapheme will be handy in order to construct needed words. A few examples follow of ways in which language characteristics can influence choice of instructional strategies.

Word Shapes

Early theoriticians of "look-and-say" in English-speaking countries stressed the importance of distinctive word shapes and unchanging words (Gagg & Gagg, 1955; Schonell, 1946). Words in which there were no capitals and no ascenders and descenders were considered to lack distinctive shape, which was assumed to be helpful in word identification, and were therefore not to be introduced in early stages of learning. Nor were slightly changed forms of words which had already been introduced permissible. Neither of these conditions can be fulfilled in Hebrew where, due to the absence of ascenders, descenders, and capital letters, the great majority of all words would in fact consist of such "shapeless" words. Moreover, in Hebrew, both noun and verb forms are derived from basic sets of common consonants so that common clusters of numerous words are in fact slightly changed forms of each other.

The fact that in Hebrew writing extremely minor differences between graphic symbols (quite often no more than location of a single dot) are of significance would be an additional factor that would question the wisdom of using a basic teaching approach that directs a learner's attention only to overall word shape instead of training him right from the start to pay attention to the most minute detail. Under these conditions, "look-and-say," which had been developed within the context of writing systems with very different premises, did not seem very suitable for Hebrew. Indeed, at this stage the question became not what had caused failure in the 1950s, but rather how "look-and-say" could possibly have been successful for nearly 30 years. As already mentioned, it turned out that highly motivated and knowledgeable parents had been able to provide additional home instruction that successfully overcame the disadvantages of "look-and-say" in Hebrew. But once the majority of students came from homes in which such help was unavailable, failure in learning to decode became a widely spread phenomenon (Feitelson, 1973).

Word Sounds and Symbols

The fact that Hebrew orthography has a redundancy of symbols over sounds has already been mentioned. Consequently, there are pairs of letters that are sounded identically, as *f* and *ph* or hard *c* and *k* are in English. On the other hand, there are also pairs and triads of letters that closely resemble each other in either shape or sound. Once these three contingencies are identified, it becomes possible to formulate clearly differentiated hypotheses:

1. Sets of symbols with identical sounds (which resemble each other in both shape and sound) are acquired most easily when they are introduced concurrently.
2. Sets of symbols with identical sounds (which resemble each other in both shape and sound) are acquired most easily when they are introduced sequentially following upon each other.
3. Sets of symbols with identical sounds (which resemble each other in both shape and sound) are acquired most easily when they are introduced sequentially with a string of neutral symbols intervening between them.

Classroom experimentation showed that in the first instance—sets of symbols with identical sounds—the first alternative, concurrent introduction, yielded best results. Sequential introduction, on the other hand, resulted in negative transfer—one symbol of the pair being retained and the other consistently forgotten.

Conversely, in the case of similarities, either of shape or of sound, a strategy of dispersed introduction, with a string of neutral symbols intervening between the pair that was liable to cause confusion, yielded the best results. This finding is in direct contradiction to Smith's (1971) contention that letters that are liable to cause confusion, for instance lower case b and d in English, should be taught concurrently. It has to be remembered that at this stage of our work identification of difficulties has already proceeded from a stage of experience gained in the field to verification by controlled experimentation (Cohen, Stilitz, & Feitelson, in preparation). In the area of instructional strategies, our results are based at present only on extensive field experimentation, and have not yet been replicated in fully controlled situations. Williams' (1968) experiment, which relates to part of the issue raised here, confirms our experience, although her subjects had already had a few years in school, while we were dealing exclusively with beginners.

One further example should suffice to clarify the many ways in which instructional strategies can be modified as a result of a detailed mapping of orthographical contingencies.

Omission of Vowels

As detailed previously, Hebrew vowels are usually much smaller than consonants in addition to being somewhat tucked away below them. Also, vowels are omitted altogether in a great portion of the printed material that a child is exposed to in daily life—books, periodicals, newspapers, and television. A typical pattern of reading failure in Hebrew is that a child recognizes many consonants, but is largely unaware of the modifying effect of vowels. In a reading aloud task at the end of first grade, vowel errors were more frequent than any other kind, and made up 38% of all errors. At the end of second grade the vowel errors were down to only 22% and the overall picture had changed to that familiar from Goodman's writings with content-consistent miscues more numerous than decoding related ones (Goodman, 1970).

The strategy that proved effective in this case was focusing substantial learning sequences on one particular vowel sound. Thus, learning stages were segmented into the /a/ stage and the /i/ stage, and so on, instead of the previously predominant practice in which single consonants were the focus. Each was studied with all possible combinations, e.g., *ba, bi, be.*

The report of the Storrs group found more vowel errors than consonant errors despite the fact that, in English, written vowels are not graphically different from consonants (Shankweiler & Liberman, 1972). This raises an interesting question: over all alphabets, are vowels more difficult than consonants, or do vowels in English cause special difficulty quite unrelated to the causes of vowel difficulties in Hebrew (cf. Lukatela & Turvey, chapter 16, this volume). According to Shankweiler and Liberman (1972), this may well be so.

In recent meetings of the Israeli Ministry of Education Reading Steering Committee, there was general consensus that specific instructional techniques in the initial stages seem to be especially closely related to vowel problems. For instance, the recent wide adoption of teaching materials in which syllables (or more specifically consonant + *a* combinations) are introduced as entities, was held responsible for difficulties of transfer to combinations with other vowels (Israeli Ministry of Education, 1977–1978). This view would be in line with the findings of Bishop (1964) and of Jeffrey and Samuels (1967).

Agreement on underlying didactic principles does not imply uniformity of materials used in class. In fact, for a population of only 3 million, there are at present well over 20 different programs on the Israeli market for teaching beginning reading in Hebrew.

CONCLUSION

A fluent adult reader has a myriad of interrelated skills at his command. Decoding strategies are but one aspect of these skills. However, early and complete mastery of decoding strategies is an essential prerequisite for all further development of reading ability.

In this chapter, achieving decoding strategies was envisaged as a time-limited, adult-directed, tightly sequenced, and structured process. According to this approach, all sequencing decisions would be based on a detailed analysis of language contingencies, with painstaking experimentation used to find possible ways of simplifying potentially difficult issues. It has to be remembered that there is much similarity across languages, so that quite often specific contingencies will tend to reappear in several orthographies. In such cases it should be theoretically possible to apply insights gained in relation to one language to other writing systems. That such an approach is more than a mere possibility is being proved at present by a group of Arab students at the University of Haifa. This group is preparing sets of instructional material for teaching decoding in Arabic—the medium of instruction in schools for the Arab minority in Israel. The materials, which are already in their second year of field testing, are being developed in the wake of a thorough analysis of Arab orthography, and rely, wherever it seems warranted, on adaptations of strategies that proved effective in Hebrew (Feitelson, 1978a). It is hoped that it is to this area of relationships between language contingencies and learning strategies that both basic and applied cross-language research of the future will address itself.

Chapter 3

IS LEARNING TO READ EASY IN A LANGUAGE IN WHICH THE GRAPHEME-PHONEME CORRESPONDENCES ARE REGULAR?

O. K. Kyöstiö

SOME CHARACTERISTICS OF THE FINNISH LANGUAGE

Finnish belongs to the Finno-Ugric language group that is not related to other European languages. The ancestors of the speakers of this language lived about 4,000 years ago in the central parts of present-day Russia. Many Finno-Ugric tribes spread out in different directions from this area. For example, to mention only the biggest tribes, the Hungarians wandered to Hungary, the Finns and the Estonians moved to the coast of the Baltic Sea, and the Mordvinians and the Cheremiss remained in approximately the original place. The linguistic relationship of these tribes to Finnish depends on the time at which the peoples separated from each other: Hungarian represents the most remote relationship, and Estonian the closest. Present-day Finnish is derived from Proto-Finnic, which was spoken among tribes (Finns, Estonians, and some smaller ones) living east of the Baltic Sea in the first centuries B.C. In this sense Estonian could be called a Finnish dialect in the same way that Swedish, Norwegian and Danish are closely related to one another. Finns moved from this area to present-day Finland during the first centuries A.D. as three tribes speaking their own dialects. Linguists are of the opinion that the Finnish language in the proper sense took on its characteristic structure between the eleventh and fifteenth centuries, a time referred to linguistically as the period of Early Finnish. At that time the development of the language took place without any noteworthy written expression. The few manuscripts written in the late Middle Ages had no great linguistic influence.

The cultivation of writing began properly in the sixteenth century when the earliest Finnish books were printed. Written Finnish was of course a great deal different from that of the present time, as were the then prevailing spoken dialects. A glance at the first version of the Bible (Agricola's in 1548) and at the present version illustrates the differences in written expression and suggests that the then spoken language may also have been diverging (Kyöstiö, 1973). Irregularities were very numerous in written forms at that time, e.g., the sound /k/ was written in eight different ways *(c, ch, ck, g, k, ki, q, x)*, instead of only one as at present. The greatest weaknesses in old literary Finnish were due to the formulation of diphthongs and the gemination of consonants and long vowels. Some sounds (e.g., /δ/ and /θ/— comparable to the English phonemes in the words "mother" and "nothing") which later disappeared were still common in southwestern dialects.

It is difficult to say how many Finnish words are derivatives, compound words, or stem words. According to a small investigation, about one-half may belong to the last category, especially where an everyday text is concerned (Hakulinen, 1961). With regard to the origin of words, Finnish may be one of the purest western languages, only about 20% of its vocabulary is clearly loan words; the indirect foreign influence of spoken and written expression is, of course, greater. The whole Finnish vocabulary has been estimated to be about 320,000 words.

The following features characterize the present-day Finnish language and affect learning to read and to write.

1.   Standard Finnish has only 13 consonants *(d, g, h, j, k, l, m, n, p, r, s, t, v)* and 8 vowels *(a, e, i, o, u, y, ä, ö)*. The foreign letters *b, c, f, q, x,* and *z* are used only in some loan words. All letters have a sounding role and are not used only as markers as in English orthography (Weir & Venezky, 1973, p. 199). So, for instance, the phoneme /a/ is always indicated by the same letter, *a*, and vice versa.

2.   The relative frequency of the use of vowels compared to consonants is greater in Finnish than in other languages. (The ratio of vowels to consonants is 100:96, the nearest being Italian, 108:100, French, 141:100, and German, 177:100, are far from Finnish.) The most common vowel is *i* (12%) and the most common consonant is *t* (11.5%). All Finnish vowels, as well as consonants, are sounded (always in the same way) irrespective of their place in a word. The grapheme-phoneme correspondence is nearly perfect. (The one exception is /ŋ/.) The correspondence between sounds and letters also means that one sound is not indicated by two letters, nor is one letter used to indicate a combination of sounds. The preference for vowels is also reflected in the prevalence of diphthongs, of which there are 16, more than in other European languages. (Compare English diphthongs and glides or diphthongized vowels, Betts, 1973.) The relationship of the general occurrence between long vowels, and diphthongs and short vowels is 1 to 3.3.

The ratio between dental, labial, and palatal consonants is 4:1:1 compared with a ratio of 6:1:1 in most other European languages.

3.   A dominant principle in the formation of words from sounds is the avoidance of all phonemes that are difficult to articulate, although there are small phonetic differences, or allophones, as there are in English (Lefevre, 1964). There are several applications of this principle: the phenomenon of vowel harmony (back and front vowels do not occur together in the same noncompound word, *e* and *i* are exceptions), a syllable (and, of course, likewise a word) never begins with a cluster of consonants, a limited number (two) of consonant clusters appear at the end of a syllable, and final consonants other than dentals *(l, n, r, s, t)* are to be avoided in all words. No Finnish word ends with two or more consonants (e.g., a loan word like "bank" is, in the Finnish form, *pankki*).

4.   From a phonetic point of view Finnish is a slack language. Therefore, for example /k/, /p/, /t/ sound softly (their oppositions /b/, /d/, /g/ did not originally belong to the Finnish phonological system) and no variation between /s/ and /š/ exists. There is only one /s/ sibilant in the written form.

5.   The duration of (long) vowels and (geminated) consonants is of greater importance in the Finnish orthography than in other European languages as the following examples show: *tule, tulee, tulle,* and *tullee* (all forms of the verb "come") and *tuule, tuulee, tuulle,* and *tullee* (all forms of the verb "blow"), each word having a different meaning. The differences in the duration of short and long vowels (and respectively single and geminated consonants) is at least twice, or even three times, as long. The opposition of front vowels /y/, /ä/, /ö/ to back vowels /a/, /o/, and /u/ is very clear. Both these phonological characteristics require greater accuracy in speaking (and writing) than is needed in most European languages. They compensate a little for the poverty of the morphemic resources of Finnish (lack of consonants and avoidance of consonant clusters).

6.   The main stress is always on the first syllable, which facilitates the correct pronunciation; but, in an open stressed syllable (e.g., *sataa*) vowels can be short, and in an unstressed one they can be long (as in Latin, Czech, and Serbian). This is a controversial feature that can cause difficulties to foreigners. Long vowels in any syllable other than in the first are, however, developmentally secondary.

7.   Finnish words generally consist of a relatively large number of syllables (the synthetic character of Finnish) and the number of monosyllabic words is very limited (about 50). This latter characteristic stems from the fact that no word begins with two or more consonants and that only one-third of the potential combinations of consonants, and diphthongs or long vowels have been used. Therefore, to write an English paragraph in Finnish usually requires one-quarter more space. In Finnish the syllables are often

short, e.g., *a-ja-u-tu-a*. An average Finnish word contains more semantic information than an average English word, and thus a word is semantically and perhaps perceptually (reading!) a more important unit than in English. This can be illustrated by the fact that Finnish infinite verbs have seven position classes (Karlsson, 1977) as the following example word *(syöte-ttäviämmehän)* shows:

Root + Derivative + Passive + Functor + Number + Case + Possessive + Clitic
syö   *te*   *ttä*   *v*   *i*   *ä*   *mme*   *hän*

8. Word order in Finnish sentences is comparatively free without changes in meaning of the thought, but an attribute usually precedes the main word.

LEARNING TO READ AND WRITE ACCORDING TO THE CHARACTERISTICS OF THE FINNISH LANGUAGE

General Characteristics

Compulsory education begins in Finland in the autumn of the year in which a child becomes 7 years old. Some of them may then be 7 years, 8 months old, and others may be a year younger because the intake happens only once a year. This great difference in age should, of course, be borne in mind by the teacher, but in practice it has not been regarded methodologically in Finnish schools. (Organizationally, in reading, however, the class is divided at the beginning stages into two groups.) The fundamental factor in learning to read is the understanding of the symbolic role of written or printed signs. Its basis is a complex psycholinguistic process. According to many investigations (e.g, Downing, 1973a), children normally reach this stage of development by the age of 6, although a large variation exists. Some experiments show possibilities of beginning reading instruction very early, even at the age of 2 years when children learn to speak (Doman, 1964). We can, however, pass over these hasty proposals because their public realization is impossible, at least at present.

In Finland test results of initial reading among school beginners show that about 15% of the early intakes are able to read well enough (according to the norms for reading) to have gone straight into the second grade of the primary school. These children have not had any regular instruction because kindergartens, which some children have attended, do not teach reading. However, the majority of children have had many kinds of incentives in literacy skills at home or elsewhere before entering school. No doubt they have reached such a stage of operational reading readiness that even unsystematic hints have helped them to pick up basic reading skills. What role the regularity of Finnish spelling plays in this process it is difficult to say. What is well known, however, is that when parents guide small children in reading they usually teach them the letter names first. The same method, in principle, is used at school, too. In Finnish the letter names of vowels are absolutely identical to the respective phonemes and help children to understand easily the corresponding graphemes. The proportional richness of vowels and diphthongs mentioned earlier facilitates learning at the beginning stage. In the names of consonants, a vowel is always involved and this causes a little confusion to children, especially if the vowel sound comes after the consonant, as is the case in stop sounds. But, by using short words and sometimes phonetic pronunciation, it is usually easy for the teacher to get children to understand the correspondence between graphemes and phonemes. The method is almost universal. It is a synthetic beginning with the smallest elements, phonemes (letters), and then syllables, words, and sentences.

Instructional Methods

The basic technique of initial reading in Finnish passes through the following stages:

1. Producing phoneme-grapheme correspondences
2. Identifying the syllabic division
3. Forming a syllable out of phoneme-grapheme correspondences
4. Assembling a word out of syllables
5. Reading words and sentences aloud

This technique seems to correspond best to the structure of the English language in another sense too. (Inflective character has already been mentioned.) The initial writing runs parallel with reading and follows the sequence below:

1. Repeating the word
2. Identifying syllables
3. Identifying phonemes
4. Converting phonemes into graphemes
5. Writing words and sentences

A typical feature of Finnish preprimers is that they are printed in capital letters and the words are divided into syllables with a hyphen. Discriminating syllables is the most difficult phase in the writing process. Its basis is the acoustic intonation of the word.

Some examples from a Finnish preprimer may illustrate the method of the teaching of initial reading and the simplicity and regularity of Finnish orthography at the same time. The letters are at present learned approximately in the order of their frequency, so that *i* usually comes first, then *a, t, e, s, n* and so on. The order varies a little in preprimers from different publishers. In some books *i* and *e* are learned first. There are many pictures in the books and children must find the missing letter and write it in the blank space below the picture. For example, when children are learning the letter *t*, many words can be found using the already learned letters *i* and *e* plus the *t*. There are many examples in the book, and the children find and draw more independently. Some other letters, not learned yet, may be within the words. This gives the pupils who know more an opportunity to use their knowledge, e.g., ☐S-T☐ "obstacle", P ☐ ☐ -R☐ "circle", MA-☐O "worm", ☐UO-LI "chair", and KEN-GA☐ "shoes". At the same time, the important concepts of the phoneme, the letter, the syllable, and the word become understood. In Finnish, reading and writing can be learned simultaneously.

The procedure described does not then mean rote learning of the letter names, which is a rather useless activity (Downing, 1973a). How far a knowledge of the alphabet predicts later reading skills is also dubious.

In this period, children learn instinctively to use long vowels (e.g., *uu-si, sa-taa*), geminated consonants (e.g., *pal-lo, mum-mo*), and consonantal gradation in inflective forms (change of consonants *k, p,* and *t* in closed and open syllables). The following examples illustrate the gradation: *lakki* (normal)–*lakin* (general), *kaappi–kaapin, hattu–hatun, jalka–jalan, sota–sodan, kipu–kivun,* and *henki–hengen.* Of course many children make mistakes in length in writing and it is only in the fourth grade that they learn these matters from the grammatical point of view. In particular, *d–t* and *nk–ng* cause many difficulties because they are artificial products of the written language.

The orthographic system of Finnish, its high regularity between the grapheme and the phoneme, and the synthetic structure of the Finnish language gives a good opportunity to apply the synthetic method, that is, to begin the teaching of reading by using the smallest units of language, phonemes, and their correspondent signs, letters. In this way children are able to form syllables and combine them into words. Syllables in speech and in print are the same in Finnish. When Lefevre (1964, p. 177) says that "division of words into syllables is primarily a printer's device rather than a problem of reading or writing" this does not hold true for the Finnish language. Venezky's (1973a) study among Finnish pupils (first, second, and third graders) confirms their high skill in reading even artificial words. It is true that single words are thus overemphasized and we cannot always be sure whether children have understood the meaning of a large unit. But this part of reading grows stronger in the course of time when the child no longer needs to give his main attention to the mechanical skill. Experience shows that children use syllabification spontaneously even later when a word is long and quite strange. Teachers are also of the opinion that the synthetic method is the best guarantee of good spelling. Kyöstiö and Vaherva (1969) also support the use of the synthetic method among preschool children.

Reading and Writing

The advantages of a regular orthographic system are perhaps still greater concerning writing skill rather than reading skill. The relationship between reading and writing skills is rather high in Finnish, a correspondence that does not hold true for English (Lefevre, 1964). The errors children make in dictation tests concentrate on alien and geminated consonants and missing letters in general. The reason may be the slack tone of Finnish pronunciation and the influence of colloquial language in which many words are shortened. Other characteristics of writing, e.g., punctuation, vocabulary, sentence structure, and style, in general depend more on individual abilities and the standard varies in all languages. Vähäpassi (1977) shows that most Finnish pupils in the third and sixth grades have reached an acceptable standard in mechanical reading (and writing), but that the comprehension is not at so high a level. The question here, however, is rather one of individual capacity in which variation is and will always be large. Intelligence is the basic factor, but school can do much to raise the standard of weak students (Kyöstiö, 1977).

LEARNING DIFFICULTIES IN LITERACY SKILLS

Chall (1967), says in her review in *Learning to Read* that "in almost every class, there are some children who do not learn to read along with their classmates. These are reading failures." According to Lefevre (1964) about one-third of American elementary school pupils have difficulties in reading. Downing's *Comparative Reading* (1973a) points to high percentages in many other countries, too. How common is this phenomenon among Finnish children who have the advantages of a regular orthography?

In Finland there is only one university department particularly devoted to special education and the training of teachers for different kinds of learning disabilities. Teachers in this department have estimated that about 15% of Finnish children in the second grade have difficulties in reading and writing (Ahvenainen, Karppi, & Aström, 1977). Disability cases have then been checked operationally using Ruoppila-Västi's test (1971) in which pupils below 1.4 standard deviations of norm value (IQ > 85) belong to this group. According to Ruoppila and Västi (1971), reading and writing errors are specific, which means that it is not possible to predict on the basis of reading errors what kind of writing errors a child will make and vice versa, although achievements in these skills correlate at the 0.5 level. On the basis of factorial studies it has been revealed that the most common writing errors among disabled children are: 1) missing letters, especially ones of the long vowel or geminated consonant, features that can be considered typical of the structure of the Finnish language (a missing letter at the end of a word syllable has again been proved to be a common writing error in all languages); 2) confusing letters (*m-n, nk-ng, d-t*; reversals; and rotation); and 3) other errors (wrong or additional letter, wrong dots, and word wrecks).

From another point of view, writing errors have been grouped into such categories as auditory, visual, speech, grammatical rule, and others. Reading errors from the same point of view are guessing (wrong word or wrong end of word), repeating, wrong discrimination of syllable, and late syllabification. (The list is, in principle, different from that presented by Hansen and Rodgers, 1968, p. 83.)

In spite of a regular orthographic system, Finnish children have difficulties in initial reading as well as in writing. They do not discriminate long vowels and geminated consonants clearly enough, or, from the point of view of the child, the question may be one of memory. That long vowels and geminated consonants must be written with two similar signs is a matter of grammatical rule that requires more practice than the writing of single sounds.

Both assumptions are supported by some investigations. Alahuhta (1976) has shown that children who are handicapped in the field of linguistic expression also suffer from great disturbances in auditory, visual, tactual, and olfactory discrimination. Children who received low marks in reading and writing were especially weak in rhythmic manipulation. These children needed speech therapy. Kuusinen (1972), who has standardized the American Illinois Test of Psycholinguistic Abilities (ITPA) test for Finnish circumstances, has shown that children with reading and writing difficulties differed significantly from the control group, especially in those subtests in which the communication channel of hearing and speech is common (cf. Myklebust, 1968, p. 13). Disabled children in reading and writing differ from normal children in those psychological abilities and aptitudes in which auditory discrimination and integration, short-term memory, and understanding of meaning are essential. Kuusinen emphasizes particularly the importance of short-term memory. In the case of dysgraphia, the deficit probably concerns a lack in memory of motor patterns (McGrady, 1968). The investigations of Alahuhta (1976), Kuusinen (1972), Lyytinen (1977), Ruoppila and Västi (1971), and Tuunainen (1977) have shown that the so-called risk group can be revealed in advance, for, as Delacato (1967, p. 29) says, "children have reading problems long before they enter school, the school only points them out." (This quotation does not imply any approval of Delacato's theory.) Such is the situation among Finnish pupils, too, at the beginning stage, although probably in a smaller proportion than in languages in which the orthography is irregular or at least very complicated, as in English. The extent to which different dialects cause difficulties in reading and writing has not been investigated thoroughly in Finland.

RECENT RESEARCH EVIDENCE FOR THE IMPROVEMENT OF READING

Specific Difficulties

Kyöstiö (1973) has described the situation and problems of reading in Finland. Some previous investigations are also mentioned among the references. Since that time (at the end of the 1960s) more attention has been given to reading problems and new investigations have been published.

The school medical service has initiated some medical doctors into speech and reading problems. Thus, Arajärvi, Louhivuori, Hagman, Syvälahti, and Hietanen (1965) analyzed specific reading and writing difficulties (N = 33) in childrens' hospitals and arranged a treatment period. Two-thirds of the children had some neurological abnormalities and one-third had speech defects. In the reading and writing tests children with an auditory disturbance displayed most often mixed or wrong letters and wrong durations of sound or missing letters (in a long vowel or geminated consonant). If the visual disturbance was stronger, more cross-dominance of eyedness and handedness occurred than in the other group. During the training it was observed that auditory progress was more rapid and more clearly noticeable than visual.

Siirala's study (1969) concerned delayed speech development, which usually hinders normal learning of reading and writing. Her sample consisted of 335 children (between 1 and 14 years of age) from the whole country. It proved possible to determine the causes and nature of speech disorders (according to Arnold's classification). Children with speech defects were usually found to show poor concentration, incoherence, intellectual immaturity, mental deficiency, minor brain injuries, EEG changes, and weaknesses of both visual and auditory perception. The individually organized treatment consisted of handicrafts, play therapy, painting, drawing, speech therapy, articulation exercises, widening of vocabulary, improvement of sentence building, correction of errors in grammar, reading and writing practice, speech reading, auditory training, exercises, and correction in the use of the voice. The best results were reached with the following groups: 1) central disorders of language development, 2) pathology of the speech organs, and 3) stutterers; altogether the speech of 63% of the children was found to have improved. Siirala (1969) stated, however, that there still remained a great number of articulatory disturbances and disorders of reading and writing for which continued rehabilitation was needed. This study clearly emphasized the great importance of speech for effective learn-

Table 1. Finnish communicative intonation system

	Communication proper		Communication with an appeal to the listener
Schematized form	⌐‾‾‾⌐__	⌐‾‾‾‾‾	⌐‾‾‾⌐__
Descriptive label	Normal-breath group	Open-breath group	High-breath group
Use	Complete statement	Incomplete statement	General questions Particular question Imperatives

ing of reading and writing. The following investigations concentrate on the same matter but more from the point of view of linguistics, psychology, and education.

English-Finnish Contrastive Studies

Some contrastive studies made in the University of Turku (Hirvonen, 1970; Wiik, 1965) examine problems that are important in teaching English to Finnish students. In Wiik's investigation, a group of Finnish pupils who did not know the English language wrote English words using only their Finnish orthographic knowledge. In this way it was possible to clarify how Finns transcribe English phonemes in their phonetic structure and orthography. Wiik showed typical errors made by Finns and gave valuable guidance to avoid them. Of special interest to those learning Finnish was the classification of pronunciation difficulties because many of the illustrations involved a speaker of English struggling with Finnish phonology (Rowe, 1969). Hirvonen (1970) analysed English and Finnish communicative intonation models (Table 1).

Hirvonen concludes that intonation has a more specific distinctive function in English than in Finnish. Lehtonen, Sajavaara, and May (1977) also describe contrastive problems between English and Finnish (Contrastive Studies Project, University of Jyväskylä). The contrastive analysis is probably a linguistic answer to the problems of language teaching of which reading is a part.

Linguistic Development

Kuusinen (1972) had suggested that Finnish children have not reached such a level of linguistic maturity to begin school attendance at age 5 as English children do. This is a result of the difficulties of Finnish morphology. Lyytinen (1977) followed the morphological development of children between 2–5 years of age and arranged several experiments in kindergartens. A comparison of the learning results between the experimental and control groups revealed that the nontrained groups also improved their performance from one measurement to another, but that the changes were minor compared to those caused by systematic training. The starting point for the examination of children's linguistic errors was the thought that erroneous utterances at the early stage of development are not random, but that they appear as the result of the reasoning and thinking processes typical to each age level. The analysis of the errors was also motivated by the knowledge that Finnish, with its special characteristics, makes possible a more versatile and wider description of the children's errors than do the Indo-European languages. The results of the error analyses indicated that the correct inflections are achieved stage by stage. The clearest changes were found in 3-year-olds. At the age of 5 years, the cognitive performance of children exceeds the level necessary for mastering the basic forms of Finnish morphology. In interpreting linguistic errors, the age and the children's cognitive level of development must always be taken into account, as the same error means different things at different age levels. Among environmental variables, those stronger than others were 1) the mother's daily use of time with her child, 2) explaining behavior to the child in everyday problematic situations, and 3) the quality of the child's play material. Thus, in spite of the many morphological difficulties of the Finnish language, Kuusinen considers that children normally reach a satisfactory level of language skill, but that without help the variation is rather great.

Alahuhta (1976) has stated that linguistically handicapped children also suffer from defects of perception, reasoning, and spatial orientation abilities. She administered a modified version of the Borel-Maisonny test to 8 subgroups of different handicapped children (50 subjects each), and to a control group of 50 children. The results show that disturbed groups were weaker in all ability areas than the normal group. Differences between disturbed groups in background factors were quantitative in general. Main difficulties for the RE-WR group also existed in all speech disabled groups. Factor analysis gave as a result three factors: 1) reasoning ability, 2) perception and orientation, and 3) rhythmic manipulation on which marks in reading and writing were loaded. The RE-WR group differed clearly in the weakness of rhythmic manipulation. Boys were overrepresented (54%–80%) in all disturbed groups as well as in left-handedness, except among stutterers. The result concerning poor laterality (one-sidedness) (experiment group, 28%, control group, 6%) supports Delacato's (1967) findings of the importance of laterality for reading. The key point of all speech, reading, and writing disturbances is common according to Alahuhta: erroneous auditory-verbal memory traces.

The studies of Kuusinen (1972) and Blåfield and Kuusinen (1974) concern the earlier analyzed Finnish version of the ITPA. The latter indicates the psychometric characteristics of the test. Absolutely identical factor structures were not found in any age group (3–9 years); but, nonetheless, the Finnish and American versions correspond well to each other. There were large differences among the Finnish individual subtests in stability. Interesting from the point of view of literacy skills is the fact that the auditory tests had a higher stability than the visual subtests. The intercorrelation of 0.54 and 0.68 between the Finnish ITPA (total score) and achievement in reading, writing, and mathematics at the first and second grade of primary school shows a rather good predictive validity for the test. In general, auditory subtests were related more to reading and writing and visual subtests than to achievement in mathematics. The results reached by the ITPA test support the idea of the great importance of the auditory-vocal abilities for reading and writing (cf. McGrady, 1968).

Comparisons of Good and Poor Readers

Reading results at different stages of primary school have been analyzed. Ylinentalo (1970) found the differences in traits between good and poor readers matched for general intelligence, age, sex, and achievement in mathematics. There were 154 subjects; 86 were good readers and 29 were poor readers. (It was not possible to find enough poor readers fulfilling the sampling conditions in the all age schools used.) Good and poor readers differed significantly in tests of verbal ability and silent and oral reading. (The especially strong differences in oral reading show that teachers evaluate particularly on the basis of reading aloud.) Verbal ability accounted best for the traits of silent reading, whereas those traits of oral reading formed a highly independent vector cluster. The analysis of reading interests indicated that a good reading ability is one of the prerequisites for interesting pupils in reading; home is another essential stimulating factor. The investigation also showed a very large variation in pupils' reading ability, even among good and poor readers. The examination raised the question of how to decrease the differences in reading performance in a way that would be useful, particularly for pupils suffering from reading difficulties. School should provide more individual guidance in learning and the home should give richer stimuli for reading activity.

Viitaniemi (1971) concentrated on a comparison of oral and silent reading in grades 3–5. The total number of pupils who took part in the beginning and final tests was 1,845, with drop-out rates varying from 7% to 20%. After the initial tests, the teachers used in their teaching either oral, silent, or mixed methods, according to instructions sent to them. The following results were obtained after a 1-year experiment when pairs of method differences were investigated using t tests.

According to Viitaniemi, the results support the use of oral reading in the third grade, but in the fourth grade they slightly favor the silent reading method (see Table 2). The results were not clear in the fifth grade. This

Table 2. Comparisons of reading methods taught in grades 3–5

Grade	Comparison of teaching method	Variable measured	Level of significance
3	Oral reading > silent reading	Oral reading speed	0.001
	Oral reading > mixed method	Oral reading speed	0.01
	Mixed method > silent reading	Skimming	0.05
	Mixed method > oral reading	Skimming	0.05
	Mixed method > silent reading	Synonyms	0.05
	Oral reading > silent reading	Comprehension	0.05
4	Silent reading > oral reading	Skimming	0.05
	Silent reading > oral reading	Synonyms	0.05
	Silent reading > oral reading	Comprehension	0.05
5	Oral reading > silent reading	Oral reading speed	0.001
	Silent reading > oral reading	Skimming	0.01
5 (after 2 school years)	Oral reading > silent reading	Oral reading speed	0.001
	Silent reading > oral reading	Skimming	0.001

result was unreliable because the whole of the age class did not participate in the experiment in this grade. In their answers, both teachers and pupils were in favor of the mixed method. Viitaniemi argues further that weak pupils should progress as far as possible at the same level as others in the group, and that, therefore, remedial instruction should be given to these pupils.

Environmental Factors

Kyöstiö (1977) followed the same pupils through the whole elementary school period (grades 1 to 6) to study the effect of different environmental factors on children's cognitive, social, and physical development. From six communities an age cohort entering school in 1970 was measured periodically. At the start of the study, there were 767 children in the group; at the end of the 6-year period 597 remained. The main results show that the children in remote rural areas in the north represent a significantly lower stage of development in all measured aspects at the starting point. Pupil development in intelligence, reading, and mathematics shows, however, that children in those areas catch up with their coevals in other areas. When average test scores are corrected using regression coefficients, the children gained most in these skills during the 6-year period. Equality in schooling has thus been achieved by the basic school reform, but how far it satisfies varied individual abilities in literacy skills is still an open question.

Materials

Vähäpassi (1977) examined the level of reading ability in relation to the goals and materials in reading in 60 third grade classes of the new comprehensive school (931 subjects). Reading skill was studied from the viewpoint of the following variables: reading comprehension, speed of silent and oral reading, fluency, expressiveness, and correctness of reading. The results showed that the variation of performance was generally great, particularly in the reading speed test. For this reason pupils continuously need some graded reading material. In general, pupils were most successful in the areas of correctness of reading and the speed of oral reading. On the other hand, results indicate that reading comprehension, especially the practicing of deductive and evaluative reading, should be emphasized more in teaching. On the basis of her study, Vähäpassi drew the conclusion that about 20% of Finnish third graders have not achieved the reading skill level required to enter the fourth grade of the comprehensive school and that about 25% of the pupils had reached a good and versatile reading skill. In addition, Vähäpassi proposed that the level and content of textbooks and other learning materials of different subjects in the third grade should be studied and specified so that the great differences in reading skill would not be an impediment to pupils' interest in school learning. In a later study among sixth graders, Vähäpassi concluded that only about 50% of these pupils had attained the level of reading and writing needed at the upper stage of the comprehensive school.

CONCLUSIONS ABOUT LEARNING TO READ

On the basis of the investigations presented in this chapter, the answer to the question of easiness in reading the Finnish language is affirmative as far as mechanical reading is concerned. But if by reading we mean a higher level skill, the answer might be the same as in other languages: children have difficulties in comprehension and other more developed literacy skills. However, the frequent use (10 visits/100 persons/year) of libraries and the subscription rates for newspapers (60 of every 100 persons) show that adults in Finland have a continuing interest in reading. How this is evident of the excellence of Finnish orthography is difficult to say because it has not been comparatively studied. The IEA study, for example, did not examine the so-called developmental functional literacy, which is the goal of all reading instruction.

Chapter 4
ORTHOGRAPHY AND PHONEMICS IN PRESENT-DAY RUSSIAN

Anatoly Liberman

Russian spelling is a major item in the education of Russian-speaking children. The subject called *Russian* in the curriculum disregards all problems of oral delivery, let alone elocution, and concentrates entirely on the written form of the language. The study of written Russian takes 7 years, and almost all of that time is devoted to spelling and punctuation. The results are as poor as those in this country, and high school graduates are, on the whole, sadly illiterate. Even though Russian spelling is somewhat more rational than English and French, it is difficult enough to offer stubborn resistance to its students.

The concept of spelling covers both graphemics and orthography. Graphemics covers all the means that a language has for rendering a complex of sounds (phonemes) in writing. Thus, *nite, nyte, knite, knyte, night, knight, neit, nuite, kneit, knuite,* are all graphemically correct ways of expressing [nait]. Orthography is a set of rules stating which of the graphemically admissible variants is correct in each individual case. It is quite clear that at the initial stage of education, graphemics is a very important problem, but as time goes on, students learn all the existing possibilities and have to grapple only with orthography. However, a serious analysis of spelling presupposes separate treatments of graphemics and orthography.

PROBLEMS OF GRAPHEMICS

Differentiating Allophones of One Phoneme by Letters or Diacritics

It is not quite clear why people sometimes designate allophones of one phoneme by different letters. It happens very seldom and all the examples are from dead languages, so they remain largely a matter of reconstruction. In Russian, as could be expected, there are no instances when phonetically conditioned allophones would need special designation. However, the point of designation is often wrong. Thus, although the words ряд [r'at] 'row', рёв [r'of] 'howling', and жарю [žár'u] 'I fry' are distinguished from рад [rat] 'glad', ров [rof] 'trench', and жару [žáru] 'heat' (m., dat., sg.) in that they have a palatalized (soft) /r/ (in transcription /r'/), as opposed to a nonpalatalized (hard) /r/ in the latter three, in spelling it is the vowels that are different. Besides, one and the same distinctive feature can be designated in different ways: palatalization can be rendered by a special letter (the so-called sign of softness), as in Обь [op'] 'Ob' (the river), соль [sol'] 'salt', семь [s'em'] 'seven', корь [kor'] 'measles', etc., but it is left without any marker before ц , for consonants are always soft before it. Consider the datives of the first, second, and fourth words: Оби, соли, and кори . Finally, when the letters е, ё ,ю, and я follow a consonant, they perform two functions: they are signals of palatalization and they denote the phonemes /e/, /o/, /u/, /a/. The confusion is greatly enhanced by the fact that palatalization is an assimilating feature, and in clusters, if the last consonant is soft, the preceding one(s) often will be soft too. (Progressive assimilation is only dialectal.) Only in extremely rare exceptions is their palatalization left undesignated. A word like вскользь[fskol's'] 'in passing,' with the sign of softness after *l* and after *z* looks unusual. One of the most common mistakes that Russian children make is the insertion of an extra sign of softness after C_1 in C_1C_2'. And I constantly observe that my 6-year-old son (who has been bilingual all his life) refuses to understand that the letters е, ё ,ю, and я designate palatalization by their very presence and he tries to use the sign of softness after every palatalized consonant.

Using One Letter to Designate Different Phonemes Or Different Letters to Designate One Phoneme

One and the same letter can designate a nonpalatalized (hard) and a palatalized (soft) consonant. Thus, the letter *c* renders /s/ in вес [ves] 'weight', but /s'/ in весть [ves't'] 'information'. Different people use regressive palatalization in clusters to a varying degree; besides, phonetically, C_1 in C_1C_2 may be half-palatalized. (The same confusing notion occurs in the history of Russian.) However, there are numerous clear-cut examples where palatalization in Russian clusters is left undesignated. The fact that the palatalization in question is phonetically conditioned in C_1C_2 is immaterial, for the opposition hard:soft is relevant for the system. Very much in the same way the choice between final /t/ or /d/ in the English forms *asked* and *begged* is determined by the preceding phoneme, but that will not preclude a semiliterate person from spelling them *askt* and *begd*.

Another similar situation concerns voiced and voiceless consonants. In modern Russian, voiced obstruents do not occur when word-final or before other voiceless consonants. For this reason, the letters б , д , г , в , з , ж will designate /b/, /d/, /g/, /v/, /z/, /ž/ in годы[gódy] 'foreheads', лбы [lby] 'years', рога [rʌgá] 'horns', рвы [rvy] 'trenches', возы [vʌzý] 'cart-loads', and ножи [nʌzí] 'knives' (plural), but in the respective singulars: лоб [lop], год [got], рог [rok], ров [rof], воз [vos], and нож [noš] the same letters stand for voiceless sounds.

Those are the most important and the most systematic cases, but there are other situations where one and the same letter can designate different phonemes. Thus г is usually [g] or [k], but it denotes a homorganic fricative; i.e., [x] before [k] as in мягкии [m'áxkij] 'soft', and лёгкии [l'óxkij] 'light, not heavy', and [v] in genitive endings of adjectives and some pronouns: того [tʌvó] 'of that', etc. The letter ч, normally a sign of [č], sometimes stands for [š], as in что [što] 'what', конечно [kənéšne] 'of course', and подсвечник [pətsvéšnik] 'candlestick' (more often in the Moscow variant than in the Leningrad). Other instances are less regular and are not discussed.

The Russian language often uses different letters to designate the same phoneme. Thus, there are the words рог 'horn' and рок 'fate' (or the name of the fabulous bird *roc*). They are homonyms but are spelled differently for morphological considerations. There is a debate whether English has the same phoneme (or archiphoneme) in such words. Naturally, those who, like the representatives of the Moscow phonological school or generativists, deny the phonological identity of homonyms, will not consider the рог/рок example. (Generativists will probably disagree with the whole frame of reference chosen here, for they do not work with 'autonomous' phonemes and they find the spelling of English and Russian natural and intuitively justified.)

Since one and the same letter can designate different phonemes in Russian, it is to be expected that in some cases different letters designate one phoneme. Some of the examples given above can be easily used here. Thus, the phoneme /v/ is usually rendered by the letter в, but in того, and the like, it is rendered by г. In similar fashion, /š/ is almost always designated by ш, but in что there is ч, not ш.

A final example in this rubric concerns the phoneme /j/. After vowels, if it stands before a consonant or before a pause, it is designated by a special letter, called short *i*, й. But in other cases the letters ё, ю, and я perform the function of й.

Designating Groups of Phonemes by Single Letters and Single Phonemes by Groups of Letters

Both situations are possible in Russian. Of special interest here are the letters е, ё, ю, and я. After consonants they show that the consonant is palatalized and designate the vowel phonemes /e/, /o/, /u/, and /a/. Initially, the same letters designate /je/, /jo/, /ju/, /ja/, although /j/ and palatalization are different things in Russian, where we come across contrasts of the /kól'a/:/kól'ja/ type (Коля 'Nick', and колья 'poles' plural). The status of the letters щ and ц is also ambiguous. They are graphic symbols of [š:], which is always soft, and [c], monophonemic, respectively, but they may indicate /š/ + /č/ and /t/ + /s/, although many examples here are controversial. Modern Russian makes very wide use of double letters, but geminates as phonological units are of marginal importance in it. The words классный [klásnyj] 'pertaining to class' (adjective) and гласный [glásnyj] 'vowel' are a perfect rhyme, but in the first word /s/ is designated by cc and in the second by c.

Returning to the problem of palatalization, when the softness of a consonant is designated by a special sign, as in Обь (see the examples on page 52), there is a case of a phoneme rendered by two letters. As a matter of fact, the sign of softness has no other function apart from denoting palatalization.

PRINCIPLES OF ORTHOGRAPHY

It is convenient to distinguish four principles of orthography: 1) morphological, when words are spelled alike to preserve the identity of the morpheme (*wrapped* and *robbed,* although *-ed* in them stands for different pronunciations); 2) phonematic, when words are spelled as they are pronounced, i.e., according to their phonemic make-up (*spelt* and *burnt* rather than *spelled* and *burned*); 3) traditional, when nothing but tradition justifies the spelling, as in *gnaw* or *knight*; and 4) hieroglyphic, when words are spelled differently, even though they are homonyms: *right, Wright, rite, write.*

Modern Russian spelling makes use of all four principles. It is phonemic up to a point (more so than English, perhaps), very morphological, and largely traditional. The hieroglyphic principle is of little importance, although some instances are worth mentioning. Thus, capital letters serve to distinguish *sandwich* and *Sandwich,* exactly as in English. Also, some grammatical forms are really hieroglyphs: злиться 'to get angry' and злится '(he) is getting angry' are homonyms [zlíc:a], but are spelled differently. Hieroglyphic spellings of the [zlíc:a] kind or of the *write/right* type (of which few Russian examples are usually cited: cf. компания 'company' versus кампания 'campaign' [kəmpanija], туш 'flourish of trumpets' versus тушь 'Indian ink' [tuš], ожог 'burn' (s.) versus ожёг 'burned' (pret.) [ʌžók]) can be subsumed under ''Problems of Graphemics'' or ''Principles of Orthography.''

SPELLING REFORMS

The first attempts to unify, normalize, or regularize Russian spelling (which includes both graphemics and orthography) go back to the middle of the eighteenth century. The main dilemma has always been phonetics (later the term *phonematics* was used) versus morphology. Proposals turned around paradigmatic problems (what letter to write) as well as syntagmatic ones (whether two words should be spelled together, separately, or with a hyphen). The history of punctuation ran parallel to the main discussion, but seldom aroused too much interest. The polemics concerned the following main paradigmatic aspects: 1) treatment of functionless or mute letters, 2) treatment of ё, ю, я , 3) vowels after ж, ш, ч, ц, and 4) spelling of unstressed vowels. Russian spelling was rather dramatically reformed in 1917 and 1918, and somewhat regularized in 1956; the latest outburst of reformatory activities took place in the mid-1960s.

LITERATURE

There are hundreds of works devoted to Russian spelling. The most interesting single book is *Obzor predlož enij po usoveršenstvovaniju russkoj orfografii* [*An Overview of Proposals Concerning the Improvement of Russian Orthography*] (1965). All of the 500 pages of this book read like a thriller. It also contains a superb bibliography for works spanning two centuries. Another good book is *Russkoe pravopisanie* [*Russian Spelling*], (Šapiro, 1961). A more popular exposition of the same problems can be found in *Orfografija i russkij jazyk* [*Orthography and the Russian Language*] (1966). A curious overview of popular ideas on Russian spelling, i.e., opinions of nonlinguists, is contained in *Pis'ma ob orfografii* [*Letters on Orthography*], (Bukčina, Kalakuckaja, & Čel'cova, 1969). Other books of interest are *Nerešennye voprosy russkogo pravopisanija* [*Unsolved Problems of Russian Spelling*] (1974) and *Sovremennyj russkij jazyk. Punktuacija* [*Present-day Russian Punctuation*], (Šapiro, 1974). A strict differentiation between graphemics and orthography goes back to Baudouin de Courtenay. See, for example, *Obščaja fonetika* [*General Phonetics*] (Zinder, 1960, pp. 306–316) or *Sovremennyj russkij literaturnyj jazyk* [*Present-Day Literary Russian*] (Gvozdev, 1973, pp. 84–206).

Chapter 5
ASPECTS OF DUTCH ORTHOGRAPHY AND READING

Vincent J. van Heuven

LETTER TO PHONEME CONVERSION

When trying to place orthographies along a scale, ranging from e.g., Finnish, as an illustration of a near-optimally regular set of letter-phoneme correspondence rules, to English, which has traditionally been considered as highly irregular, Dutch would presumably be located toward the regular end of this scale.

Complete regularity is usually taken in the sense of perfect one-to-one letter-phoneme correspondences. However regular these correspondences in Dutch may be, there is no single one-to-one letter-phoneme correspondence in Dutch orthography, contrary to what has been suggested in the literature (for an opposing view see Damsteegt, 1976).

Relevant Letter Symbols in Dutch Orthography

Dutch spelling has been changed by governmental decree a number of times this century, and, in fact, public clamor for additional changes is still heard today. The changes involved are all intended to alleviate the problems that confront the (would be) writer of Dutch. One important category of spelling problems is constituted by the spelling of nonnative words, notably words of Latin and French origin. I would like to dispense with this class of words in this survey for a number of reasons:

The spelling of Latinate words will in practice be mainly a matter of rote learning

Latinate words are nearly always polysyllabic and of low frequency, and are therefore not dealt with in the initial reading stages

There is a tendency to use alternative, native spellings, which although not always officially approved by the government, are socially acceptable.

A consequence of leaving out Latinate words is that 23 letters are used in Dutch orthography, the usual set of 26 minus *q, x,* and *y*. However, *c* remains only as part of the digraph *ch*.

Phoneme Inventory of Dutch

Phonemic analyses of Dutch vary to some extent as to the number of relevant contrasts. There are some major issues in Dutch phonology that may affect the outcome of a phoneme count.

The Analysis of Trigraph Vowels (Sometimes Referred to as Long Diphthongs)   The issue at stake is whether such complex vowels as [aːi] or [eːu] in *vlaai* [vlaːi] 'pastry' or *geeuw* [χeːu] 'yawn' are to be thought of as single phonemes or as sequences of two phonemes. Most analyses today take the position that these complexes should be regarded as a long vowel followed by a separate consonant /j/ or /w/ (for a survey and references in English see Brink, 1970), which is the practice followed in this chapter.

Loan Words from the French   Supposedly due to French occupation of the Netherlands in the early nineteenth century, a large number of French loan words have been incorporated in the Dutch lexicon, retaining more or less their original pronunciation. Although there is considerable overlap of Dutch and French near-equivalents in the respective phoneme inventories, a number of foreign sounds had to be added to the Dutch phonemic system. Moreover, these loan words have also retained much of their original French spelling, although partial adaptation to the standard conventions of Dutch orthography has been allowed, or even advocated, in the course of the last two decades. In spite of this, the Dutch spelling of French loan words is often considered uneducated, especially in the eyes of the older and middle generations.

Since there is still no official uniform settlement on the spelling of French loan words, part of the French letter-phoneme correspondence rules are duplicated in the Dutch system. This, of course, causes serious problems to anyone who wants to read and write Dutch.

Even though many of these loan words are frequently used in Dutch, and may have no native equivalent, e.g., the words *douche* [duːʃ] 'shower', or *serre* [sɛːrə] 'glass house', I omit these words, too, from further consideration, mainly on the strength of the argument that their spelling is, understandably, not dealt with in the initial spelling and reading stages in Dutch primary schools.

The Phonological Status of the Neutral Vowel Schwa [ə]   There is still some dispute on the correct interpretation of a central vowel in Dutch which can only occur in unaccented syllables: [ə]. It has a variety of representations in spelling: *e, ij, i* (for details cf p. 64). In terms of vowel quality it does not differ from another central vowel [œ], spelled *u,* with which it is allegedly in opposition. Error analyses of spontaneous spellings of preschool children (van Rijnsoever, 1977) indicate that the distinction is highly obscure to untrained speakers of the language. Certain radical spelling reform proposals, which have not (yet) been accepted, advocate reduction to one phoneme, and consequently to one symbol.

Table 1.   Conversion from single vowel symbols to phonemes

Symbol	Phonemic value	
	Initial/medial position	Final position
a	/ɑ/ *al* 'already', *pak* 'grab'	/a:/ *pa* 'dad'
e	/ɛ/ *er* 'there', *weg* 'road'	/ə/ *de* 'the'
i	/ɪ/ *in* 'in', *kin* 'chin'	
o	/ɔ/ *os* 'ox', *bos* 'wood'	/o:/ *vlo* 'flee'
u	/œ/ *uk* 'tod', *buk* 'stoop'	/y:/ *nu* 'now'

Velar Fricatives   Perceptually there is no difference between voiced and voiceless velar fricatives (van Heuven & van den Broecke, 1977), although the most recent textbooks on Dutch phonetics (Nooteboom & Cohen, 1976) maintain that the distinction exists. From a transformational point of view there are compelling arguments to accept the difference as an underlying distinction, which is captured in the spelling in a rigorous fashion. Analysis of spelling errors of first graders, however, shows that the distinction is lost: usually only the symbol for the voiced variant, *g,* is written, although it is the voiceless sound that is pronounced throughout. The reason for this spelling behavior is probably that the symbol for the voiceless fricative, *ch,* a digraph, is taught at a later stage than the voiced symbol.

Incidentally, the voiced/voiceless distinction, which has always been neutralized in final position in all Germanic languages except English, and which has hardly any functional load in Dutch, seems to be disappearing in all fricatives in initial positions, and even medial positions as well. In fact, in certain urban dialects the distinction is lost completely, which leads to additional spelling difficulties for such dialect speakers.

Letter-Phoneme Correspondences in Dutch

In view of the facts that have been given in the preceding sections, it seems reasonable to limit the discussion of Dutch letter-phoneme correspondences to monosyllabic, native words, which, as a matter of fact, also constitute the subject matter for the first grade reading and writing skills at primary schools. An extension to polysyllabic words follows in the next section.

Under the restrictions made here, pronunciation of Dutch words is fully predictable from spelling, although the converse does not hold. Using 23 letters to cover 33 phonemes (34 including /ə/), among which are 15 (16) vowels that have to be represented by only 5 vowel symbols: *a, e, i, o* and *u,* some conventions had to be used in order to have combinations of vowels represent the various vowel phonemes.

Strictly speaking, the 18 consonant letters could quite adequately serve to represent the 18 consonant phonemes, but this turns out not to be the case.

Table 1 shows how to relate single vowel symbols to phonemes, in syllable initial and medial position on the one hand, and in final position on the other.

Table 2. Conversion from digraph vowel symbols to phonemes

| Symbol | Phoneme | Position | | |
		Initial	Medial	Final
aa	/a:/	aal 'eel'	zaak 'case'	
au	/ɑu/	au 'ouch'	paus 'pope'	au 'ouch'
ee	/e:/	eed 'oath'	leed 'sorrow'	zee 'sea'
ei	/ɛi/	eik 'oak'	reis 'voyage'	kei 'boulder'
eu	/ɸ:/		reus 'giant'	reu 'dog'
ie	/i:/	iep 'elm'	biet 'beet'	wie 'who'
ij	/ɛ:/	ijs 'ice'	pijn 'pain'	rij 'row'
oe	/u:/	oer 'prehistoric'	boer 'farmer'	koe 'cow'
oo	/o:/	oog 'eye'	boog 'bow'	
ou	/ɑu/	oud 'old'	goud 'gold'	kou 'cold'
ui	/ʌy/	uil 'owl'	kuil 'pit'	bui 'shower'
uu	/y:/	uur 'hour'	buur 'neighbour'	

The reason why a single *a, e, o, u* (and in foreign words, *i*) could be used to represent long vowels in final position, is that no short vowels are permitted in that position by phonotactic constraint. Notice further that long /e:/ is not expressed by *e* in final position, as this represents the neutral vowel /ə/. As a final remark on Table 1 it should be noted that *u* in nonfinal position represents long /y:/ if followed by *w*. All other vowel representations are digraphs (see Table 2).

Curiously enough, *au* in final position only occurs in onomatopeic *au* [ɑu] 'outch'; in all other words it is followed by *w*. The digraph *ou,* which represents the same phoneme, may or may not be followed by *w* in final positions, leading to homophones: *jou/jouw* [jɑu], 'you/your' and *kou/ kouw* [kɑu], 'cold/chew'.

The letter-phoneme conversion for consonants is relatively simple. Unless stated otherwise, any consonant symbol has the value given to it in the International Phonetic Alphabet (IPA). There are, however, some exceptions:

ch is pronounced as [χ], *ng* (only occurring in final position) is pronounced as [ŋ], and *n* before *k* is pronounced as [ŋ].

A final consonant symbol representing a voiced obstruent is pronounced as as a voiceless sound: *word* [wɔrt] 'become' and *heb* [hɛp] 'have'.

The symbol traditionally representing a voiced velar stop, *g,* is pronounced as a voiceless velar fricative, irrespective of its position in the word: *graag* [χra:χ] 'voluntarily'.

The final combination *dt,* which occurs in verb forms only, is pronounced as [t]: *wordt* [wɔrt] 'becomes'.

i and *u* as the last element of a trigraph vowel (cf. p. 58) represent the consonants [j] and [w] respectively. However, *u* is not used to designate a semivowel after another symbol *u*. This graphotactic constraint was apparently introduced to avoid such illegal letter sequences as *ruu¹ [ry:w], which is correctly spelled ruw 'rough'. ¹Notice that the symbol u is not geminated here, as should be expected, since it is no longer in syllable final position.

In a comprehensive treatment of the letter-phoneme correspondences in the Dutch monosyllable, there is at least one further complication that should be dealt with. There are quite a few words in Dutch that are spelled with only one vocalic center, but are regularly pronounced as two syllables. This phenomenon arises when a liquid or nasal is followed by a nonhomorganic consonant in the postvocalic position. In such cases an epenthetic unstressed neutral vowel [ə] is inserted between the two consonants. This rule explains, for example, why the name of the bulb flower tulp ['tœləp] was understood as 'tulip' by English speakers. Thus melk 'milk' is pronounced ['mɛlək], and berg 'mountain' as [bɛrəχ], but lamp 'lamp' remains [lɑmp]. There is a small group of historically motivated exceptions to the epenthesis rule that need not concern us here; for a survey of some relevant data and extensive references see Brink (1970, pp. 145-146).

In conclusion to this section, one allophonic variation, viz., the influence of /r/ on preceding [+tense] vowels must be mentioned. For high vowels the effect is mainly a matter of lengthening. For mid vowels, which are clearly diphthongized in all other environments, the change in quality disappears. After /a:/ the change is usually towards [ɛ] ('t Hart, 1969). Young children, who tend to listen to sounds very analytically, are often found to spell *vir for veer 'feather' or *bur for beur 'lift', which contain the vowel symbols that normally represent the short vowels with the same quality.

Underlying Principles of Dutch Orthography

The Phonemic Principle Unless another rule takes precedence, all contrastive sounds are uniquely represented by letters or letter combinations. Thus, audibly quite different sounds such as long vowels followed by final /r/ have the same spelling as when occurring in other environments, because they are allophonic variants. The sounds /ʌy/ and /au/, which speakers of English find very difficult to distinguish, are spelled differently because they function contrastively in Dutch.

The Congruence Principle Stem morphemes are not spelled differently when they undergo predictable phonetic changes in morphological alternants. The final devoicing rule for obstruents is ignored in the spelling using this principle; similarly, a number of low level phonetic assimilation processes are not reflected in the spelling.

---

¹An asterisk (*) denotes a nonoccurring form.

The Analogy Principle   Some deep level suffixes are consistently represented in the orthography, even if they are absent in pronunciation, for example, the practice of spelling *dt* at the end of verbs. The inaudible addition of *t* signals, for example, the grammatical function of third person singular indicative present, on the analogy of the audible addition of /t/ to other verb stems such as *zwemt* [zwemt] '(he) swims'. As a consequence of this principle, the first and third persons of verbs with stems on *d* are homophonous: (ik) bid [bɪt] '(I) pray' versus *(hij) bidt* [bɪt] '(he) prays'. Notice, however, that no inaudible addition of *t* is allowed to stems ending in *t* themselves: *(hij) schiet* [sχ:t] '(he) shoots', but not **schiett*.

The Etymological Principle   Different letter codings with identical sound values may be employed to capture distinctions that existed in older stages in the development of the language. The spelling alternatives for /εi/ *(ei, ij)* and /ɑu/ *(au, ou)* are examples of this principle. Contrary to English orthography, where a similar principle may be used (cf. Chomsky & Halle, 1968), these distinctions seem to have no significance in a synchronic description of Dutch (morpho-) phonology. This renders the etymological principle an unnecessary source of error in the eyes of many specialists on Dutch orthography, and reduction to single representations of these phonemes has often been proposed.

On the basis of the particulars given so far it turns out that automatic letter-phoneme conversion for native Dutch monosyllabic words is a relatively simple task, and will always have error-free results. In order to determine the phonemic value of a particular letter, a moving context window should span three adjacent letters. This would at least partly explain why Dutch is more regular than English. In English many letter-phoneme correspondences are idiosyncratic: *great* (/εi/) versus *beat* (/'ː/), or even worse, *read* with either /'ː/ or /e/, in which case a decision cannot be made without recourse to higher order morpho-syntactic information. The phonemic value of Finnish letters, however, can probably be derived by taking only two adjacent letters into account, as would also be the case in Spanish orthography.

Polysyllabic Words

The first important complication of letter-phoneme conversion in polysyllables is the following convention, pertaining to the spelling of certain vowels and all single letter consonants. As we have seen in the discussion of monosyllables, a vowel which is normally spelled with reduplication *(aa, ee, oo, uu)* is simplified (reduced to one letter) in syllable final position, or, as it is traditionally called, in an 'open' syllable. One of the few clear principles of Dutch syllabification is that, unless a word boundary intervenes, a single intervocalic consonant is the first element of the next syllable. This implies that when, for example, *beek* 'brook' is pluralized (by adding *en* [ən]), the syllable division is *bee-ken,* leaving *ee* in final position. Consequently the stem vowel is now spelled with single *e: beken.* To complicate matters further, vowel simplification does not take place when the next syllable begins with a digraph consonant: *goochel* [χoː-χəl] 'juggle'.

Conversely, a single letter consonant is reduplicated in the intervocalic position after a stressed short vowel. Thus the plural of *gek* 'fool' is spelled *gekken* and *sok* 'sock' as *sokken.* Understandably, this rule is a direct consequence of the vowel simplification rule. If the intervocalic consonant would not be reduplicated, the stem vowel would be assigned the value of a long vowel.

This consonant/vowel reduplication system is not dealt with until the second grade, and spontaneous spellings produced when the rules have not yet been taught, reveal no tendencies to use such conventions. The exact advantages of this system, if any, are neither known, nor have they ever been investigated. One advantage would be that average word length in Dutch is now slightly lower than when a Finnish kind of spelling would be used (always reduplicate letters representing long phonemes). In an average Dutch text, vowel simplification occurs about twice as often as consonant reduplication, with relevant cases in roughly every fifth word.

In spite of this, the system clearly goes against the grain of the morphophonemic basis of the Dutch writing system: it obscures a direct one-to-one letter-phoneme correspondence and it interferes with uniform spellings of both free and bound morphemes. There is, however, no clear indication that these conventions constitute significant spelling or reading problems, once the rules are dealt with.

This practice of geminating vowel and consonant symbols, ultimately, warrants my earlier claim that there is no single one-to-one letter-phoneme correspondence in Dutch.

Unsoluble Cases

Correct letter-phoneme conversion in Dutch polysyllables presupposes two extra sources of information:

Where are the syllable boundaries?
Which syllables are unstressed?

Unfortunately, proper syllabification and stress assignment is not always possible on the basis of formal criteria. Phonological syllabification is dependent on internal word boundaries. A difference in position of an internal boundary alone may create a homographic pair:

boordraad	*boor-draad*	[boːrdraːt]	'spiral thread of a drill'
	boord-raad	[boːrtraːt]	'council on board a ship'
haardrek	*haar-drek*	[haːrdrɛk]	'filthy mess of hairs'
	haard-rek	[haːrtrɛk]	'fire guard'

Because the *d* in these pairs is alternatively in syllable final or in initial position, the final devoicing rule may or may not apply, creating phonemic differences. Obviously, the correct placement of internal word boundaries in these compounds can only be done on the basis of the semantic context in which these words occur.

As another example of unavoidable error, consider the following compound: *darmonderzoek* 'intestinal examination'. Assuming that the typical Dutch syllable is a CVC sequence, the straightforward syllabification of this word would be *dar-mon-der-zoek,* which would be pronounced [dɑrmɔn-dərzu:k]. However, the word is a compound of *darm* 'bowel' and *onder-zoek* 'examination', so that an internal word boundary occurs between *m* and *o*. Since *rm* is now a final cluster, the epenthesis rule becomes applicable, giving the pronunciation [dɑrəmɔndərzu:k]. In cases like these each attempt at syllabification should be preceded by some lexical decision process in order to ensure correct division.

Brandt Corstius (1970) has evaluated his syllabification program, which is currently used by Dutch newspapers for automatic typesetting, on the basis of the error rate obtained in the automatic syllabification of a 43,712 word token (4114 types) corpus of newspaper texts (van Berkel, Brandt Corstius, Mokken, & van Wijngaarden, 1965). He found that 64 of the 4,114 types (1.6%) were hyphenated incorrectly. It seems to me that these results are somewhat misleading, as a large part of the words in the corpus were monosyllabic. Brandt Corstius mentions a percentage of 54, which (probably) refers to word tokens.

A second source of ambiguity is the decision whether certain syllables in a word are part of the stem or separate morphemes. If they are separate morphemes, they will be unstressed. Normally, stress differences have no phonemic consequences, but there are some exceptions:

ij, which is normally pronounced as [ɛi], must be pronounced as [ə] in the suffix *lijk* [lək], which has a variety of uses. Unfortunately, there is also a stem form *lijk* [lɛik] 'corps', so that a correct analysis of a word like *kinderlijken* depends on semantics: when *ij* is unstressed, [kɪndər-ləkən], the meaning is "childlike persons'; when stressed, [kɪndər-lɛikən], it means 'children's corpses'.

e stands for [ə] when unstressed, but represents [e:] in stressed, open, non-word final syllables:

geren	'geren	[χe:rən]	'taper(ing) out'
	ge'ren	[χərɛn]	'repeated act of running'
bedelen	'bedelen	[be:dələn]	'beg'
	be'delen	[bəde:lən]	'hand out'

i, which regularly represents [ɪ], is pronounced as [ə] in the suffix *ig,* as in *prachtig* [prɑχtəχ] 'beautiful'.

Kok (1972a, 1972b) describes a program for automatic letter-phoneme conversion for Dutch texts, and mentions an error rate of 6%, on the basis of word types in a 44,299 word token corpus (9,380 types). Nine percent of the errors were due to incorrect syllabification, 16% to the foreign status of certain words, 24% to the absence of diacritics that are normally written in Dutch, and 51% to incorrect stress assignment. These figures illustrate once more that Dutch orthography is problematic as soon as one goes beyond the scope of the monosyllable.

PROBLEMS IN THE INITIAL READING STAGES

There are two sources of literature that may contain information on the aspects of Dutch orthography that constitute learning problems in the initial reading stage: 1) experimental studies on initial reading, carried out by educational psychologists and 2) textbooks for prospective primary school teachers.

In this discussion of possible reading problems the survey is limited to technical or mechanical reading, the process of correctly pronouncing sequences of letters (words), no matter whether or not the reader understands what their meaning is.

The experimental studies referred to, however, limit their scope even further to sound pure words (Kooreman, 1974, 1975), words selected from an artificially constrained lexicon in which only one-to-one phoneme grapheme correspondences hold. Although a number of interesting learning problems can be tackled in this way, the procedure eliminates any possibility to investigate reading problems specifically due to the peculiarities of Dutch orthography. In other words, studies on the basis of such a constrained orthography might as well have been conducted in another language with a writing system with a one-to-one grapheme-phoneme relationship. These studies are therefore not taken into further consideration.

Research specifically directed toward investigating whether certain types of letter-phoneme conversions are intrinsically more difficult to learn than others has never been carried out in the field of Dutch orthography. In order to get some idea as to what might be the outcome of such an investigation, one could perhaps analyze initial readers' performances on a number of mechanical reading skill tests. It should be pointed out, however, that none of the tests was constructed with this goal in mind. One might, as a matter of fact, wonder whether the authors of such tests were at all aware that quite a few items in their tests contained deviations from one-to-one letter-phoneme correspondences, and potentially constituted additional difficulties, over and above those inherent to the mechanical reading skill as such.

Unfortunately I have not been able to perform any such post hoc analyses, partly because no score distributions of the tests are readily available in the literature and partly for reasons of time.

For the second source of information we may turn to the more or less intuitive claims as to what causes reading problems in Dutch, that can sometimes be found in textbooks for prospective teachers. Although most textbooks (and teacher's handbooks that come with reading primers) contain some thoughts on this matter, the most comprehensive listing of reading difficulties is given by Caesar (1971, p. 36):

Reading vowels followed by -r, which leads to a change in quality
Reading digraph consonant symbols: *ch* and *ng*
Reading words in which a final voiced symbol is pronounced as a voiceless sound: *bed, heb*
Reading words with nongeminate digraph vowels (but not with geminate digraphs)
Reading the final sound in trigraph vowels (*aai, eeu,* etc)
Reading [ə] for *e* in final position
Reading words in which a single letter vowel represents a long vowel phoneme in word final position and open syllables in general
Pronouncing [ə] for *e* or *ij* in unstressed syllables
Reading words with syllable final nonhomorganic [+sonorant] [+consonant] clusters (epenthesis rule)
Reading final *nk* as in *bank* 'bank, bench', which a beginning reader would be tempted to pronounce as [bɑnək] by erroneous application of the epenthesis rule, and consequently fail to recognize
Reading polysyllabic words
Reading words deviating from the simple CVC structure, where CVCC is claimed to be easier than CCVC

Although this is a rather elaborate list, one might wonder if it is exhaustive. It is the result of an a priori crude analysis of letter-sound discrepancies and the impression of classroom errors that were informally observed. A more rigorous analysis of letter-sound discrepancies will undoubtedly reveal additional potential difficulties; in fact, a number of omissions will be detected if one compares the listing here with the discussion of letter-phoneme correspondences given earlier.

All but a few of the listed problems are traced to complications in letter-phoneme correspondence. One problem has to do with difficulties that come up when longer and more complex words are read, and two more problems originate in markedness of syllable structure. I should like to enlarge on this last issue, and discuss an experiment in which deviations in syllable structure were methodically investigated as a source of problems.

Rispens (1974), who investigated the relationship between children's abilities to synthesize words from isolated sounds, and reading perfor-

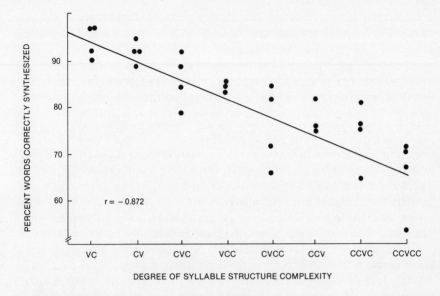

Figure 1.   Percentage of correctly synthesized (blended) words as a function of syllable structure complexity. Each dot represents the results for one test word, based on the responses of 91 subjects (adapted from Rispens, 1974).

mance, hypothesized the following order of difficulty in monosyllabic words: 1) VC, 2) CV, 3) CVC, 4) VCC, 5) CVCC, 6) CCV, 7) CCVC, and 8) CCVCC. His crucial test measured difficulty of synthesis (blending individual sounds to a word) as a function of syllable structure complexity. A group of 91 initial readers responded to 32 test words presented as sequences of isolated sounds, 4 different test words per syllable structure type. The results are as indicated in Figure 1, in which the percentage of correctly synthesized words is plotted along the vertical axis, and syllable structure complexity increases along the horizontal axis.

It appears from the graph that there is a fairly strong relationship between the two variables ($r = 0.875$). However, Rispens' data are confounded by word frequency. Correlation of percent correctly synthesized words with log transformed word frequency, as established in a recent 600,000 word count of Dutch texts (uit den Boogaart, 1975), turns out to be 0.524. If my claim that high frequency words are easier to synthesize than low frequency words (and, in fact, correlation of syllable complexity and log word frequency was -0.559) is accepted, then Rispens' findings, suggestive though they may be, should be regarded with caution. A rerun of his experiment with adequate control for word frequency seems to be in order.

Insufficient experimental data are available to warrant any definite conclusions as to what constitutes a reading difficulty in Dutch. Nevertheless, the author feels that initial reading instruction would greatly benefit from clearer insights both in the consequences of discrepancies of letter-phoneme correspondences and in the effects of syllable complexity.

EXPERIMENTS ON THE EFFECTS OF SOME CHARACTERISTICS OF DUTCH SPELLING ON SENTENCE PROCESSING IN ADULT READING

Dutch orthography is basically a morphophonemic writing system, in which uniform spelling of stems and affixes is preserved, even if this leads to complications in letter-phoneme correspondence. As a result, there are a large number of morphologically complex homophones whose spelling differences are caused by differences in underlying morphological structure. Correct spelling of such words is only possible if the writer realizes that alternative morphological analyses may correspond to a particular sound sequence, selects the right alternative, and reflects this in his spelling.

An example of this is the inaudible spelling difference between first and third persons of verbs in the present tense with stems ending in d (cf. pages 57–65). It turns out that the correct spelling of verb forms, which is taught from third grade onward, presents tremendous problems, which situation has once been called "the tragedy of the verb forms" (Van der Velde, 1956). All spelling reform proposals that are currently entertained suggest simplifications on these points.

In a discussion of spelling reforms two distinct groups of users should be kept in mind: those who have to learn to read and write, and those who have mastered the system. It is at least conceivable that certain characteristics of an orthography that are difficult to learn, may greatly facilitate the processing of text in a later stage (see Frith & Frith, chapter 18, this volume; Lukatela & Turvey, chapter 15, this volume).

In 1974–1977 I worked on a project that aimed to investigate if reflection of underlying morphological structure in homophonous verb forms might be beneficial to adult readers. Because the correct morphological analysis of the verb forms (and consequently their spelling) depends on the syntactic structure of the sentence in which they occur, it was hypothesized that the resulting redundancy of verb inflection and syntactic structure might guide the reader when processing a sentence.

From a theoretical point of view, Dutch orthography is an interesting system to conduct this kind of experiment in, because it provides the means to compare different ways in which underlying morphological distinctions may be reflected in spelling and pronunciation:

type I: An underlying distinction is maintained in the spelling and in pronunciation: *(ik) speel* [spe:l] '(I) play' / *(hij) speelt* [spe:lt] '(he) plays'.

type II: An underlying distinction is neutralized in pronunciation but maintained in the spelling, thus creating a homophone: *(ik) bid* [bɪt] '(I) pray' / *(hij) bidt* [bɪt] '(he) prays'.

type III: An underlying opposition is lost both in spelling and in pronunciation: *(ik) schiet* [sχi:t] '(I) shoot'/ *(hij) schiet* [sχi:t] '(hij) shoots'.

The experiment to be discussed presently is one of series, carried within the framework of the project referred to. It has been described in more detail together with a number of related experiments (van Heuven, 1978). Preliminary reports of a more informal nature have appeared in the Progress Reports of the Institute of Phonetics of Utrecht University (van Heuven, 1976, 1977a, 1977b).

Cue Value of Tense Marking Suffixes in Plural Finites in Silent Reading

In Dutch plural finites, grammatical person is not expressed, but there is a formal difference between present and past tense, which may be reflected in pronunciation and spelling in each of the three ways mentioned. Weak verbs add *ten* or *den* to the verb stem in the past if the stem ends in an underlying voiceless or voiced segment respectively. The present tense plural is formed by suffixing *en* to the stem. Thus the three opposition types are as follows:

type I: *werken* [wɛrkən] 'work'/ *werkten* [wɛrktən] 'worked'
           zwaaien [zwa:jən] 'wave'/ *zwaaiden* [zwa:jdən] 'waved'
type II: *feesten* [fe:stən] 'have a party'/ *feestten* [fe:stən] 'had a party'
           branden [brandən] 'burn'/ *brandden* [brandən] 'burned'
type III: *dutten* [dœtən] 'nap'/ ditto 'napped'
           wedden [wɛdən] 'wager'/ ditto 'wagered'

Note that the gemination of *t* and *d* in the past tense of type II is caused by the analogy principle (the past tense morpheme is spelled uniformly in type I and type II). In type III, however, gemination is caused by the general spelling convention stating that stressed short vowels must be followed by two consonant symbols (cf. pp. 57–65).

The actual stimulus material consisted of 40 sentences constructed by systematic variation of opposition type (see above) and three other variables, to be discussed presently.

Sentences were complex, beginning with a temporal clause followed by the main clause. The subclause started with a conjunction that can be used with both present and past tense. Both clauses contained a finite. On account of concord the tense of the second clause is predictable from the tense of the first. The temporal clause contained the crucial verb, the second clause contained a strong verb, in which the difference between the tenses was visible only in one short letter in the middle of the word. Assuming that the perception of such strong verbs takes the same amount of time in the present and in the past (e.g., *trekken/trokken* 'draw/drew'), the speed and accuracy with which readers may decide that the tense of the second clause is compatible with that of the first, will depend on the relative salience of the tense cue contained in the crucial verb form.

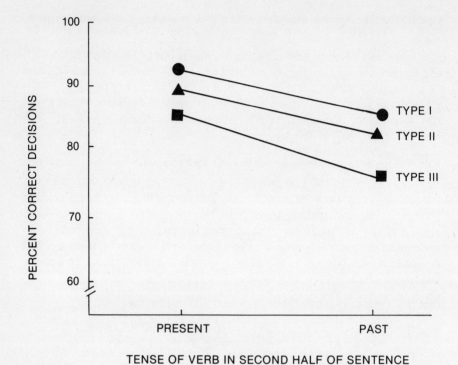

Figure 2.   Percentage of correct decisions as a function of opposition type (type I: audible and visual difference; type II: only visual difference; type III: no difference) and tense of verb in second half of the stimulus sentence. Each mark is based on 624 responses (312 for type III).

Four different sentence frames were used, two of which contained verbs with *t*-stems (underlying voiceless stem final segment) and two more with *d*-stems (with voiced stem final segment). With the exception of the type III crucial verbs, whose tense cannot be varied, both first and second verbs could be either present or past, leading to violation of tense concord in half of the type I and type II sentences.

The sentences were presented twice, in different quasi-random orders, to a group of 39 readers (male and female staff and students at Utrecht University, right-handed and with normal vision, paid volunteers, and all native speakers of Dutch) with the aid of a line stepper (Bouma & De Voogd, 1974). The subclause was presented for 1 sec, and then replaced by the main clause, which remained visible until the subject responded by pressing one of two buttons marked "right" or "wrong." The subjects were instructed to decide for each pair of clauses, as fast and as accurately as possible, whether or not the combination was a correct sentence. One-half of the subjects pressed right for "right" and left for "wrong"; positions were reversed for the other half.

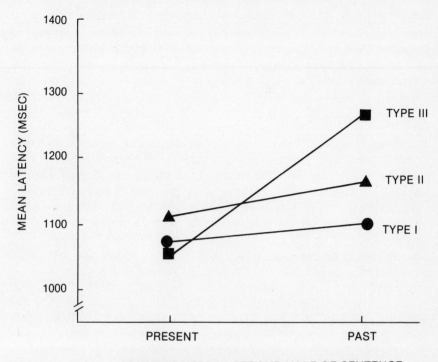

Figure 3.   Decision latency (msec) for correct responses only, as a function of opposition type and tense of verb in second half of stimulus sentence.

Response latency (time interval between moment of presentation of the second part of a stimulus and moment of response) was measured, and the correctness of the response was established. Since type III crucial verbs are compatible with both present and past tense continuations, a "wrong" response here was regarded as an error. The results are given in Figure 2 for mean percentage correct decisions and in Figure 3 for mean latency obtained with correct decisions only.

The general level of accuracy is 87% correct. Type I verbs are responded to more accurately (90% correct) than type II (87% correct), which in turn is superior to type III (82% correct). There is a small effect due to the four different sentence frames used, but differences disappear completely when the sentence frames are lumped together two by two on the basis of *t*- and *d*-stems. Present tense continuations are responded to with 90% accuracy, past tense continuations with only 84%.

The particular sentence frame has no influence at all on latency, nor is there an effect when the sentences are combined on *t*- and *d*-stem characteristics. Shortest latencies are obtained with type I oppositions (1086 msec), longest for type III (1165 msec), and intermediate latencies are found for type II (1121 msec). Present tense continuations lead to faster correct responses than past tense (1080 msec versus 1157 msec). However, the advantage of the present tense continuation is much stronger for type III contrasts than for the other types.

DISCUSSION OF RESULTS

In general it appears that the percentage of correct decisions and their response latencies supply more or less parallel information, which is what one expects to be the case. The results of this experiment clearly supported our earlier findings that the grammatical cue provided by a potentially audible contrast (i.e., type I) is more effective than when the difference exists only in the spelling (type II). However, the results forced us to qualify an earlier claim that type II cues would not be any different from the control type containing no cue at all (type III). Rather it should be said that the inaudibility of a spelled difference reduces its cue value to some extent.

This finding seems to be in line with later weak versions of the speech recoding hypothesis as formulated by, for example, Kleiman (1975) and Baddeley (1976, 1979). In their view speech recoding is not strictly necessary for reading, but it may provide a means to perform tasks in which memory plays a role. There is a striking resemblance between one of Kleiman's experiments, from which it appeared that subjects had great problems in judging the semantic acceptability of strings of consecutively presented words while recoding to speech was precluded by imposing a concurrent shadowing task, and our experiment. In our experiment the tense information derivable from the verb in the first clause had to be remembered for some length of time to be able to arrive at a decision after viewing the second part of the sentence.

Past tense forms in type II oppositions *(feestten, brandden)* were responded to more accurately and faster than type III forms *(wedden, dutten)*. This means that the gemination of the medial consonant letter is perceived in most cases, and that it is used as a cue to determine the grammatical tense of the clause. However, when forms such as *dutten* and *wedden* were presented, i.e., without informative suffixes and hence compatible with both present and past tense, correct decisions that a present tense continuation of the sentence is grammatical, are taken faster than with a past tense continuation.

In view of these facts one must assume that the perception of the word final letter strings *tten* or *dden* is not automatically associated with past tense. Rather it appears as if the subject performs a more sophisticated analysis of the verb forms: only if *tt* or *dd* is preceded by another consonant symbol, does he know that gemination is due to the past tense suffix. If the letter preceding the *tt* or *dd* is a single vowel symbol, he realizes that gemination is the direct consequence of a general spelling rule, and that no information relevant to performing his task is given.

Section II
DESIGN AND IMPROVEMENT OF LITERACY PROGRAMS

Chapter 6
LEARNING TO READ AND WRITE IN NAVAJO

Wayne Holm

THE NAVAJO LANGUAGE

The Navajo are an Apachean group of Native Americans living in the southwestern United States. Numbering about 150,000, they are by far the largest tribal group in the United States; one out of every five or six Indians in the United States is a Navajo. Living on or near a reservation comparable in area to the whole state of West Virginia, the Navajo are one of the most economically disadvantaged groups in the United States.

There is a relatively high degree of language retention among the Navajo. Language census data have shown that despite marked differences between communities (having to do, as one might have suspected, with the degree of accessability to English-speaking population centers), an overwhelming number of Navajo children on and near the reservation are entering school dominant, or monolingual, in Navajo. There is an increasing number of children who are, to some extent, bilingual in Navajo and English. Because of the high birthrate and the high rate of retention of Navajo as the language of the home, the absolute number of speakers of Navajo is still increasing (for language census data on Navajo 6-year-olds, see Spolsky, 1969, 1970). Navajo is not at this time a dying language!

Given the continuing high incidence of Navajo monolingual children entering school and the relatively high degree of language insulation on much of the reservation, one would think that initial literacy in Navajo would be the logical basis of elementary education on and near the reservation. Such is not the case.

THE DEVELOPMENT OF WRITTEN NAVAJO

In 1812, Pedro Bautista y Piño, the deputy from New Mexico to the legitimist parliament of Spain, published what seems to be the first attempts at written Navajo: a list of 10 Navajos words and phrases glossed in Spanish

---

Although the form *Navaho* occurs in much of the anthropological literature, the Navajo Tribal Council has sanctioned the older Spanish form, *Navajo*. The latter form will be used throughout except in citing titles in which the h-form is used.

(Bautista y Piño, 1812)[1]. There were a number of Navajo wordlists taken by army officers and others in the decades after 1850. Some of the transcriptions are surprisingly good, given the orthographic "resources" of most of these amateur philologists (see Saville-Troike, 1973).

The first attempts to write connected text in Navajo seem to have been those of Washington Matthews. Matthews, an Army physician, was the first serious student of Navajo mythology and ceremonialism. He began publishing some sections of Navajo text in the 1880s or 1890s[2].

The Franciscan Fathers began writing Navajo around the turn of the century. Their *Ethnologic Dictionary* (1910) is still an important reference work. Various Protestant groups began writing Navajo sometime after the turn of the century.

The noted American linguist Sapir (1922) noted that Sarcee (an Athapaskan language of northern Canada) "has a well-developed system of pitch accent." "So fundamental is tone to Sarcee," he wrote, "that it should be entirely absent in any other Athabaskan dialect." Such indeed was the case, Sapir found. The orthography he developed in *Navaho Texts,* an apparent grafting of his analysis of Navajo vowels onto Fr. Berard's analysis of Navajo consonants, was used throughout the 1930s and, by some, in the 1940s.

The first *practical* orthography, as contrasted with a *technical* orthography, was that of Robert Young and William Morgan, Sr. (1943). While consciously reducing the inventory of graphemes to those that could be typed (and printed), the orthography also captured some significant relationships not captured by earlier orthographies (while giving up some surface contrasts losing ground in the language).[3] Their orthography, which is contained in *The Navaho Language* (Young & Morgan, 1943), with one relatively minor change has been used for most serious work on Navajo and the Navajo people after the mid 1950s.[4]

Navajo lacks, then, not a practical orthography, but readers. Navajo has been used extensively by both Catholic and some Protestant missionaries. There are Navajo language bibles, hymnals, catechisms, and tract lit-

---

[1]A translation of an 1849 edition of Bautista y Pino's work was published (in a limited edition) by the Quivira Society in 1943. Somewhat surprisingly, there are minor differences in the Navajo forms from those in the 1812 original. See n. 10 in Holm, 1972.

[2]Matthews must have been writing Navajo as early as 1883, according to a comment in the *5th Annual Report* of the then-new Bureau of American Ethonology (Powell, 1887) (XXX). But the earliest published running Navajo text known to the author is a text with interlinear translation, "Beginning of Origin Legend" (Matthews, 1897).

[3]A detailed comparison of Young and Morgan's practical orthography and Hoijer's technical orthography is found in chapter IV of Holm, 1972.

[4]The Navajo Orthography Conference in 1969 adopted the existing Young and Morgan orthography, eliminating (predictable) word-initial ' (glottal stop.) Although several recommendations for changes in functional units were received at the Second Conference, no such changes were approved.

erature. Written Navajo may have been taught at some mission schools before 1920, although the information available is sketchy at best (see Holm, 1972, p. 13). Although the U.S. Indian Service (now called the Bureau of Indian Affairs, BIA) published two sets of beginning readers (and a number of other books) in Navajo, there is no indication that these were ever used as *initial* reading materials at any school. World War II seems to have gotten in the way.[5] A Navajo language monthly newspaper, '*Ádaahooníłígíí,* was discontinued in 1957. Politics and the lack of an adequate adult literacy effort seem to have led to the untimely demise of the paper. With increasing emphasis on assimilation, relocation, and termination in the 1950s, literacy in Navajo came to seem an anachronism. It was not until 1967 that there were serious efforts to implement initial literacy in Navajo programs at Rough Rock and Rock Point.

LEARNING TO READ NAVAJO

Rock Point is a relatively poor (even by reservation standards) Navajo community of approximately 1,400 people on the middle reaches of Chinle Wash in far northeastern Arizona. The school initiated intensive EFL (English as a Foreign Language) activities in 1963–1964. In 1967, the school undertook modest initial literacy Navajo activities. These activities have since become part of one of the more comprehensive bilingual education programs on the reservation.

> The current Navajo orthography represents four surface vowels that are written as $<i>$, $<e>$, $<a>$, and $<o>$.[6] Vowels may be short or long in duration; this distinction is marked by doubling the vowel graph: $<v>$ versus $<vv>$. Vowels may be oral or nasal in cavity; this distinction is usually marked by a cedilla or nasal hook: $<v>$ versus $<ɣ>$. Vowels may be low, high, rising, or falling in tone. The high tone is marked by an acute accent: $<v>$ versus $<v́>$. Since rising or falling tone occurs only with long (in duration) vowels, these can be marked as sequences of low + high tone $<vv́>$ and high + low tone $<v́v>$ respectively.

---

[5]Two sets of Navajo language preprimers, primers, and readers became available in the 1940s and 1950s. These were bilingual texts written in English with Navajo translations on the same page. The intent of these materials was "to speed up the acquisition of English", to assist Navajo students "learning to read a language other than their native tongue...with comprehension..." (Holm, 1972, p. 27). Bauer (1970) to the contrary, finds no indication that *initial* literacy was ever taught in Navajo in any Bureau school in the 1940s or 1950s.

[6]Throughout this chapter, broken brackets, $< >$, are used to mark functional units in the writing system; slashes will be used to mark phonemes in the sound system. A v is used to represent any vowel. *Functional unit* is used throughout this paper to indicate a unigraph, digraph, or trigraph that represents a given phoneme. From this, we will sometimes refer to "vowel units" or "consonant units". The term "functional unit" is, as far as I know, Venezky's.

English vowel names are used to name the vowel units. Back translations are used to designate diacritics:

déigo 'up' for v́ high tone
ninééz 'long' for vv long duration
bichį́įhdę́ę́ 'from the nose' for ɣ nasal cavity

Navajo consonant units occur as unigraphs, digraphs, and trigraphs. Navajo consonant names are used to name the consonant units. The < ɫ >, representing an voiceless lateral, is called *el;* < ' >, representing the glottal stop either as an independent phoneme or as a component of a glottalized phoneme, is simply called *stop.* Thus the triad:

< dl > "dee-el"
< tɫ > "tee-eɫ"
< tɫ '> "tee-eɫ-stop"

The first-generation initial literacy materials at Rock Point were, of necessity, put together at night and on weekends. Navajo language teachers, most of whom were from the community, were trained on-site. Given these circumstances, one should not be too surprised to find the first generation materials rather mechanical; they had to be.

Navajo verbs are not simple. There is only one one-syllable verb in the language; despite word boundary conventions intended to shorten verb forms, what are written as five- or six-syllable verbs are not at all uncommon in the speech of school children. The makeup of the Navajo verb is such that mode and person tend to be marked just before the prefix-stem boundary, i.e., in the middle of the verb. Attempts to teach Rock Point students to read Navajo by a *sight* approach in the mid-1960s confirmed observations that the initial and final letters (or syllables) tend to be most salient. Navajo seems to cry out for a *word attack* or *analytical* approach to reading instruction.

Attempts were made to teach students to read syllables. It was assumed that if a student could sound out syllables, could remember a given string of syllables, and if these syllable strings were a word the student knew, he would be able to read the word.

The first-generation materials consisted of two separate strands: a sound-to-letter strand and a letter-to-sound strand. Although students were led to relate given written units to given spoken sounds, the notions of "sound" and "letter" were kept separate in all presentations.

The sound-to-letter materials made use of an insight of a Russian educational psychologist, Zhurova (1963); but contrary to received opinion in the United States, kindergarten-age children *can* isolate sounds.[7] Going through lessons in order of consonant unit frequency, children repeated words after the teacher, isolated the first (or last) sound, watched the teacher write the word, supplied words of their own to exemplify the sound, repeated each other's words, isolated the first (or last) sound, watched the teacher write the word, and, hopefully, generalized: same-sound same-unit, or vice-versa. Students were taught to deal with vowel attributes orally before they encountered the diacritics. Two-syllable words were used that involved a contrast of the marked and unmarked forms. The index finger is pointed down to mark low tone, up for high tone. Thus *jiní* was marked left-low right-high; *díítįį́ł* was marked left-high right-low. The distance between the thumb and index finger marks short and long duration. Thus *shédléézh* would be marked left-short right-long; *náádá* or *naa'na'* would be marked left-long right-short. Oral cavity was marked with thumb and fingers in a circle; nasal cavity with a closed fist. Thus *hólǫ* was marked left-open right-closed; *tsintah*[8] would be marked left-closed right-open.

The letter-to-sound strand made use of, among other things, a set of 55 blending cards. These consist of three cards, side-by-side, on rings. A change in any of the three cards produced a new CV(C) syllable involving the contrast being taught (or a summary of the contrasts taught to date). Completing the 55th set successfully, a student should be able to sound out any possible Navajo syllable.

The problem with the first generation materials was that, except for language experience stories, students practiced syllables for a long time before they ever read connected text. The second generation materials embody a helical presentation of material: vocabulary made available by a new contrast is used almost immediately in reading. These materials are now presented in a programmed format and have been published as commercial quality texts by the Native American Materials Center in Albuquerque.

Rock Point initiated a modest bilingual program in 1967. In 1971, the program was funded by Title VII (Bilingual Education). In 1972, the community contracted with the school. That is, the local Navajo community-elected Board contracted for the operation of what had, up until then, a school operated by the Bureau of Indian Affairs. This arrangement was formalized by the signing of PL 93-638 in 1975; there are now more than 30

---

[7]The linguist's argument that children cannot/should not isolate sounds always makes use of words with stopped consonants to prove their point: one does not say /k-æ-t/ but /kᵊ'ae tᵊ/. But Navajo students have little trouble with /n - ow -z/. Note, however, that only 6 of the 24 English consonants are stops. Starting with Navajo continuants, students seem to have little difficulty with Navajo stops.

[8]The /i/ of /tsin/ is automatically nasalized by the syllable-final /n/; an unwritten spelling convention has determined that one does not overtly mark such vowels as nasal. I.e., tsintah contains the sequence of vowels /...i...a.../.

such schools in the country. By 1975, it became possible to see some of the effects of the bilingual program. Studies of standardized achievement test results in reading and arithmetic in 1975–1977 showed that the Rock Point students, compared to students who had received English-only instruction in comparable BIA schools, were

a month or less behind at the second grade
a month or two ahead at the third grade
two to four months ahead at the fourth grade
1.0 to 1.5 years ahead at the fifth grade
1.5 to 2.5 years ahead at the sixth grade

on standardized achievement tests (Rosier & Farella, 1976; Rosier & Holm, in preparation; Vorih & Rosier, 1978).

SYLLABICATION

Navajo verbs might be thought of as (semi-) sentences of one-syllable morphemes compressed by complex morphophonemic processes. Verbs tend to be long; only one one-syllable verb exists. Despite spelling conventions that tend to detach a number of elements from the verb complex, verbs of five or six syllables are not uncommon even in the language of 6-year-olds of which "experience stories" might be made. For example, the word *nináhisooka-hígíí* 'those of you who are returning' shows up on bulletin boards each fall. Half-spaces between syllables have been used in an attempt to help students induce the relatively simple syllabication rules of Navajo. Thus:

ni ná hi soo ka hí gíí
ni ná hi soo ka hí gíí

This may cause as well as solve problems. It seems to make it easier for initial readers to sound out long words. But the resulting sound-based syllables are not always congruent with meaning-based morphemes. Thus, in the example given above, the verb stem/*kah*/ is followed by one of the few vowel-initial elements in Navajo /*ígíí*/. Morphemically, the word ends /...*kah-ígíí*/; phonologically, the word ends /...*ka hí gíí*/. While this scheme aids the student in sounding out material, it may sometimes make it a bit more difficult to comprehend. Teachers feel that there comes a time when syllabification actually seems to get in the way and slows students down. We would like to be able to be sure syllabication *does* help students and, if so, when (as we suspect) it ceases to be helpful. (Examples of syllabication in Navajo are found in Figure 1.)

ERROR ANALYSIS

In the course of evaluating the Navajo language activities, a considerable amount of written material was obtained from students and an analysis of

(MAXIMAL SYLLABICATION)

Shíʼ si láo nish łį. Shíʼ éíʼ
chi díʼ daal gaiʼ gíʼ ni dzi tʼi.
A bíʼ níʼ go tsee bíʼi di go hi dish níʼsh.
Łaʼ yée go bił daʼ íʼl taa łíʼ gíʼ éíʼ
ne hesh tłááad. Łah da éíʼ a dláa nii
ii hish níʼł. ...

(MINIMAL SYLLABICATION)

Shíʼ si láo nish łį. Shíʼ éíʼ
chi díʼ daal gaiʼ gíʼ ni dzi tʼi.
A bíʼ níʼ go tsee bíʼi di go hi dish níʼsh.
Łaʼ yée go bił daʼ íʼl taa łíʼ gíʼ éíʼ
ne hesh tłááad. Łah da éíʼ a dláa nii
ii hish níʼł. ...

(NORMAL---NOT SYLLABICATED)

Shíʼ siláo nishłį. Shíʼ éíʼ
chidíʼ daalgaiʼgíʼ nidzitʼi.
Abíʼníʼgo tseebíʼidigo hidishníʼsh
Łaʼ yéego bił daʼíʼltaałíʼgíʼ éíʼ
neheshtłááad. Łahda éíʼ adláanii
iihishníʼł. ...

Figure 1. Examples of syllabication in Navajo.

student errors was begun. There weren't many. Elementary students today transcribe more accurately than many of the college students tested 9 years ago. And the distribution of errors seems to be somewhat different.

Having learned to read (and write) Navajo first, the children make none of the English orthography influenced errors that the poorer adult transcribers made 9 years ago. Most of the children's functional unit errors had to do with the choice of one of three syllable- or (more often) word-final consonants: $<'>$ (glottal stop), $<\emptyset>$ (zero), or $<h>$. Syllable- or word-final $<\emptyset>$ versus $<h>$ is the one essential morphophonemic contrast in a strongly phonemic orthography. All words that do not end with one of the 10 syllable-final consonants may be said to end with a phonetic [h]. In this sense, there are no vowel-final words. Both /da/ and /dah/ are pronounced [da^h]. The decision of whether or not to write $<h>$ is determined by whether or not the /h/ is retained when one adds certain enclitics.

$$[da^h + go] \rightarrow /dago/ \therefore <da>; [da^h + go] \rightarrow /dahgo/ \therefore <dah>$$

The principle that, unless you have learned to spell a given word through familiarity, you must test it seems to be one that is learned slowly. The problems with syllable- or word-final $<\emptyset>$ versus $<'>$ are harder to understand.

Like the better adult transcribers of 9 years ago, most of the children's errors involved diacritic errors. But the children seldom wrote a diacritic that should not have been there; most of the children's errors involved omission of a diacritic. Impressionistically, the children's diacritic errors (even more than the adults') seemed to come not from confusion but from haste, which seems to suggest that older children may come to sense diacritics as being unnecessary. Considerably more analysis will have to be done to confirm this and to determine the developmental patterns.

DIACRITICS

A computer-assisted analysis of a large corpus of 6-year-old children's Navajo yielded the following information:

1. One-third of the vowels are marked for (long) duration.
2. One-half of the vowels are marked for (high) tone.
3. One-tenth of the vowels are marked for (nasal) cavity. There is a somewhat higher incidence of nasal vowel sounds in oral Navajo. One of the spelling conventions of Navajo is that nasal vowels are not so marked in /n/–initial or –final syllables, the contrast having been neutralized.

Roughly one-half of all vowels are marked for duration, tone, cavity, or some combination thereof.

Although all unmarked forms are more common than their marked counterparts, diacritics are extremely pervasive in written Navajo.

On tests of Navajo transcription (Holm, 1972), three groups of Navajo adults at the University of New Mexico (all of whom had learned to read and write Navajo relatively recently and *only* long after having learned to read in English) averaged between 79% and 91% in functional unit accuracy. In making a distinction between unit errors and diacritic errors, the distribution of errors was roughly half and half for the poorest group of transcribers. But for the two better groups of transcribers, two-thirds of the errors were diacritic errors. The distribution of diacritic errors was surprisingly uniform among the three groups:

tone errors	45%
length errors	40%
nasality errors	15%

In summary, the proper use of diacritics is a major problem for Navajo adults in transcribing Navajo (Holm, 1972).

On tests that had an equal number of the marked and unmarked vowels, Holm (1972) found that:

1. There were more errors with tone (81% correct) and fewer with duration and cavity (both 92% correct).
2. Within each dichotomy, there were more errors in leaving what should have been a marked form unmarked than vice-versa. Unmarked duration and cavity, it may be remembered, occur much more frequently than marked.
3. The most errors came from leaving what should have been high tone low (unmarked): 69% correct compared to 92% correct for the reverse error. The relative frequency of high and low tone is approximately half-and-half. More diacritic errors, then, seem to involve failure to mark (73% correct) rather than over-marking (94% correct).

A word reading test, making use of the same words used in the test just described, was given some months later to some of the more experienced transcribers. The results are summarized:

1. People did better on the reading task (97% correct) than on the transcription task (91% correct).
2. Approximately two-thirds of the reading errors involved diacritics.
3. Of the diacritic errors, one-half of the errors were tone errors, two-fifths were duration errors, and one-tenth were cavity errors. These are roughly the same percentages of diacritic errors that were found in transcription (Holm, 1972).

Between the diacritics, the frequency of errors seems to be related to the amount of information involved. Within a given diacritic distinction, the frequency of errors seems to be related in part to haste or forgetfulness.

DIACRITIC REDUCTION/ELIMINATION

There are relatively few Navajo adults who read Navajo. No one knows how many. Perhaps there are as many as one thousand school children, most of these in the community controlled "contract" schools; a hundred or more adults, teachers, and aides in such programs; and an unknown number, perhaps as many as a thousand, of adult members of Navajo congregations making use of Navajo language Bibles and hymnals.

Among Navajo adults, there are only a few who may be said to be monoliterate in Navajo. Most adults who have learned to read Navajo have learned to do so only after having learned to read English. Their orthographic expectations are those of English. What seems to deter many adult Navajos from learning to read Navajo are the diacritics: all those funny little marks, which are contrary to their (English-induced) orthographic expectations.

This situation had led us to look at the possibility of eliminating, or at least reducing, diacritics, which mark the attributes of vowels.

As discussed earlier, the four simple vowel graphs in Navajo are supplemented by gemination and diacritics to mark duration, cavity, and tone. This leads to 12 theoretically possible forms of each:

v	low, short, oral
v́	high, short, oral
vv	low, long, oral
v́v́	high, long, oral
y	low, short, nasal
ý	high, short, oral
yy	low, long, nasal
ý́y	high, long, nasal
vv́	rising, long, oral
yý	rising, long, nasal
v́v	falling, long, oral
ýy	rising, long, nasal

There are, therefore, (theoretically) 48 simple vowels in Navajo and an as yet undetermined number of diphthongs. Relatively simple sorting activities carried out at Rock Point in 1969 suggest that 6-year-old Navajo children not yet exposed to reading readiness activities do, in fact, tend to perceive Navajo as having four (not 48) surface vowels (Judy Martin, personal communication).

Tone, duration, and cavity are phonemic; any one of the three can cause confusion between two words similar, or quite dissimilar, in meaning.

nílį	he/she is
nílį	you are

| binii' | his/her face |
| biníí' | his/her waist |

| yilghał | he/she eats |
| yiilghał | we (2) eat |

| bitsi' | his daughter |
| bitsii' | his/her hair |

| bitsi' | his daughter |
| bitsį' | his/her meat/flesh |

Diacritics are needed, then, for nonnative speakers when citing words in isolation. The question is: does one need to mark all diacritics in connected text for native speakers? One finds that there are a number of reasons for thinking that it would be possible to write a less marked Navajo.

There are any number of languages in which certain contrasts that occur in the language are not fully marked in the orthography without seeming to cause undue problems for readers (cf. Grimes & Gordon, chapter 7, this volume).

Perhaps of most interest is the Cree-type syllabaries that are used with a number of Canadian Athapaskan languages (Walker, 1969). Cree-type syllabaries are based upon the rotation of what might be thought of as consonantal units to indicate vowel quality.

The fact that other Athapaskan languages like Carrier, Dogrib, and Sarcee, which, like Navajo, have phonemic tone, duration, and cavity contrasts, have been written in orthographies that fail to mark these distinctions suggests that Navajo too could be written in such an orthography.

One's concern about reducing diacritics has to do with what DeFrancis (1943) called *homography:* the number of *homographs* (different meanings, different sounds, same marks) created above and beyond the existing *homophones* (different meanings, same sounds, same marks).

An analysis involving every tenth verb paradigm in *The Navajo Language* (Young & Morgan, 1943) showed that, within the paradigm, taking the incidence of homophones as 1.0:

Neutralizing duration increased homography to 1.52
Neutralizing duration and tone increased homography to 2.23
Neutralizing duration, tone, and cavity increased homography to 4.88

The elimination of diacritics, then, might cause a fivefold increase in homography. But the fivefold increase is of an insignificant base. There were 2,070 verb forms cited (69 paradigms × 5 modes × 6 cited forms). The number of possible homographs within paradigms would be 69• ½ •(30•29) or 30,015; the number of homographs within and between paradigms would be ½ (1,870•1,869) or 17,747,515. The actual numbers of homographs are relatively small.

	n	between
homonyms	66	.0000037
homonyms + duration-neutralized heteronyms	99	.0000056
homonyms + tone-neutralized heteronyms	145	.0000081
homonyms + duration-neutralized heteronyms + tone-neutralized heteronyms	233	.0000131

Thus, for a relatively limited sample of all verbs, the elimination of diacritics marking duration and tone would cause homography of about 1/1000th of one percent![9] An unacceptable level of homography is not known; it's hard to believe this even remotely approaches it.

READING UNMARKED/LESS-MARKED TEXT

The most effective measure of the effectiveness of the reduction/elimination of diacritics would be how well people read unmarked/less-marked text. In 1969–1971, there were few children who could be considered intermediate or advanced readers. Studies of five competent adult readers of Navajo showed that, despite a lack of previous experience with less-marked text, they read less-marked Navajo text more rapidly than they did fully-marked text (Holm, 1972). Stating the average time in which the fully-marked text was read as 1.0, the other length-adjusted average times were:

type of text	average speed
cavity-neutralized text	1.02
tone-neutralized text	0.70
duration-neutralized text	0.92
unmarked text	0.94

The same studies showed surprisingly little difference in the number of errors made on fully marked and on an unmarked text:

type of text	average number of errors
tone-neutralized text	1.2
fully-marked text	3.5
duration-neutralized text	3.8
unmarked text	3.8
cavity-neutralized text	4.1

---

[9]The data presented here is analyzed differently than in Holm, 1972.

One must be careful of making generalizations from studies of five readers; still, it does seem that less-marked Navajo text might be read more easily by intermediate or advanced readers than the fully-marked text.

Since 1971, Rock Point has published a student newspaper on a more-or-less monthly basis. The paper makes parallel use of fully-marked text (for younger students) and less-marked text (for older students. (See Figure 2 for examples of marked texts.) Students 'rehearse' the newspaper in class in the hopes that children will be able to read to their families at home.

(NORMAL TEXT)   (UNMARKED TEXT)

izhidi'nóoltsąął   izhdinoltsał

At first, all diacritics were omitted. But we have since retained duration while omitting tone and cavity. We cannot give any principaled reason for doing so.

(NORMAL TEXT)   (LESS-MARKED TEXT)

izhdi'nóoltsąął   izhidi'nooltsaał

The retention of the duration contrast would seem at first blush, letter-centric Anglo thinking. It is of interest to me that Paul Platero (personal communication), one of the first of the formally-trained Navajo linguists, seems to have come to the same conclusion quite independently.

MORPHEMIC/MORPHOPHOMEMIC SPELLING

Alphabetic orthographies have been characterized (Vachek, 1945–1949) as symbol systems that attempt to represent both sound and meaning. No alphabetic orthography can represent both optimally and simultaneously. Any given alphabetic orthography, then, is an elaborate set of (sometimes inconsistent) compromises between these two principles: same-sound same-symbol(s) and same-(underlying)-meaning same-(underlying)-spelling.

Depending upon the compromises made, orthographies might be ranged along a continuum from more phonemic to more morphophonemic. Navajo, like most "new" orthographies, tends to be highly phonemic. Navajo may write the same verb stem –lí as:

–lį in	Ch'ííłį	Chinle (a place)
–lįį in	Ch'ínlį́įgóó	toward Chinle
–lįį in	Ch'ínlįįdi	at Chinle

Most Navajo readers are not at all upset at this sort of apparent inconsistency.

Navajo verbs may be thought of, as noted earlier, (semi-) sentences of one-syllable CV morphemes compressed by complex morphophonemic processes. Young and Morgan (1943) attempt to detach those elements that are

(NORMAL TEXT)

Shɽ siláo nishɬ[.   Shɽ éɽ
chidɽ daalgaiɽgɽɽ nidzit'i.
Abɽnɽgo tseebɽidigo hidishniish.
ɬa' yéego biɬ da'ɽltaaɬgɽɽ éɽ
neheshtɬááad.   ɬahda éɽ adláanii
iihishnɽɽɬ.   ...

(UN-MARKED TEXT)

Shi silao nishɬi.   Shi ei
chidi dalgaigi nidzit'i.
Abinigo tsebidigo hidishnish.
ɬa' yego biɬ da'iltaɬigi ei
neheshtɬad.   ɬahda ei adlani
ihishniɬ.   ...

(LESS MARKED TEXT)

Shi silao nishɬi.   Shi ei
chidi daalgaaigii nidzit'i.
Abinigo tseebiidigo hidishniish.
ɬa' yeego biɬ da'iltaɬigii ei
neheshtɬaad.   ɬahda ei adlaanii
iihishniiɬ.   ...

Figure 2.   Examples of marked texts in Navajo.

fairly regular and fairly far from the prefix-stem boundary (where morphophonemic change or reduction is most intense).

For example, the practice is to detach, wherever possible, postpositions from the rest of the verb complex, for example, *shaa ní'*aah 'to me/you give (bulky) object'. But one must make a choice between *shaa yíní'ą* and *sheííní'ą* 'to me/you gave (bulky) object when one says the former only in slow and overly careful speech.

And if one opts for the morphophonemic spelling, where does one stop? Given the apparent high degree of reduction or elimination underlying representation in surface Navajo, an orthography based on underlying lexical representation would involve a high degree of overwriting, e.g., the two-syllable verb *déyá* 'I'll go' might be represented as a four-syllable *disishighá (di-si-shi-ghá)*.

CONCLUSION

Most of the work now needing to be done on Navajo orthography cannot be done by non-Navajos and may not be done by linguists, Navajo or non-Navajo. The standardization of written Navajo will depend ultimately upon Navajo-language writers and, perhaps even more important, Navajo-language editors. But whether or not these writers and editors emerge depends on how successful reservation schoolteachers are in convincing Navajo parents and educators that initial literacy in Navajo is worthwhile. After 10 years and some local successes, bilingual education is still a precariously new and untried program on the Navajo reservation.

Chapter 7
DESIGN OF NEW ORTHOGRAPHIES

Joseph E. Grimes and Raymond G. Gordon, Jr.

Two out of three of the world's languages have no writing system of their own. One out of five has acquired a system only in the last few decades. In 1978 a couple of dozen writing systems were put into use for the first time.[1] This chapter reviews the more constant characteristics of the writing systems being developed today and sketches some research in graphemics that could help make new systems adequate for the people who need them.

CHARACTERISTICS

New orthographies, those developed for vernacular languages during the last 40 years, have a lot in common with each other and differ from traditional orthographies in noticeable ways.

Phonemic Orientation

First, the newer orthographies are strongly phonemic. That is, they maximize consistent correspondence between symbols and individual segments of sound. Mixed strategies and other strategies are possible, for example, strategies that maximize the consistency with which each meaningful element is symbolized regardless of environment; but the current practice has been phoneme-oriented.

There are two consequences of a phonemic orientation. One is the degree of inconsistency, greater in some languages than in others, among the different representations of a single word or morpheme. For example, if English were written phonemically, the plural, which is written as *–s*, would be written that way in words like *hats,* as *–z* in words like *dogs,* and as *–vz* (leaving aside for the moment the question of how the vowel would be written) in words like *houses.*

The other consequence of a phonemic orientation in writing is the proliferation of homographs: words that are lexically different, but are pronounced and written the same.

---

[1]This information is based on B. Grimes, 1978, the most recent publication from the computerized Cornell-SIL Language Archive.

One reason why phonemic consistency figures so strongly in current orthography design is that linguists know how to do a good job in a short time on sound segments for most languages. This know-how provides a verifiable basis for stating that certain distinctions in sound have to be captured in a feasible writing system, or else serious misunderstanding can result.

We have all heard stories about how missing a contrast produces awkward social situations. From Huichol of Mexico it is noted that the difference between a flap and a trill at the beginning of a word, which is not symbolized in that position in the Spanish spelling that influences Huichol orthography, makes the difference between the word for "pencil" and the word for the term of a body part which Huichols consider inappropriate to use in public (McIntosh & Grimes, 1954). A simplistic adaptation of Spanish writing practice, therefore, would lead to predictable trouble. Since examples of this kind crop up in language after language, making sure that all the phonemic distinctions get encoded in the orthography is at least safe.

In the area of suprasegmental distinctions, linguists are divided into two groups, those who feel confident around tone languages and those who do not. If a linguist insists that the segmental distinctions provide enough redundancy to make tone marking unnecessary, without proving his point linguistically, it may be that he finds it hard to tell whether the pitch goes up or down, and hopes that if he keeps quiet about tone it will be lost in the next round of historical development. If, on the other hand, he insists that all stress, pitch, and length distinctions have to be symbolized, without again a batch of charts to show why, he may be a tone freak who won't let an opportunity to symbolize tone go by unnoticed. One feels safer with the latter breed, because if the information is there, then it can at least be ignored by users of the writing system when the orthographer's back is turned; but if he has kept out symbols that are really needed, writers in the language are unlikely ever to remedy the problem by inventing their own tone marks (Gudschinsky, 1973, especially chapter 12).

There is no known writing system that has been in use for long that symbolizes all the phonemic distinctions all the time. There seems to be a conventional wisdom that recognizes some differences as functionally less critical than others in certain contexts.

In other words, one distrusts blanket statements about what should and should not be represented in a writing system. It takes a detailed linguistic analysis to know what might not be needed for a particular language. One could do worse than to derive a writing system from a straight phonological analysis up to the level of the word, and possibly the phrase or pause group. Some of the distinctions turned up by that analysis might, however, get dropped out of the symbolization as time went on, at least in certain positions.

The dropping of distinctions is most likely to occur in contexts where they do not differentiate lexical items: this is a hypothesis that could be investigated by comparing earlier and later stages of popular orthographic usage.

For example, linguists have done a fairly thorough job of documenting how the stress of an English word relates to its grammatical function, and secondarily to its internal complexities. There are words whose stress does not fit the normal patterns; but they are adequately identified by their consonants and vowels, and so there is no pressure to distinguish them from the better behaved words by writing stress marks on them. Nevertheless, demonstrating that English works this way has taken an impressive amount of research, without which we might haggle meaninglessly over accents (Chomsky & Halle, 1968; Vanderslice & Ladefoged, 1977).

Typewriter Orientation

The second characteristic of the newer orthographies is their orientation toward the typewriter. Most orthographies are basically a Roman alphabet, togged out with overstrikes, accents, or other diacritics and combinations of two and three characters like "sh" or "kkw" to represent single segments where needed. Some variations on the Roman alphabet that match one segment to each symbol, such as the International Phonetic Alphabet, do not fit a typewriter keyboard. They have had limited popularity in the former British colonies of Africa; but even there, ways are being found now to circumvent having to type Greek *e*s and broken *o*s. (Current policy in Cameroon seems to run counter to this trend, but the approved orthographies are certain to be impossible to type and probably impossible to print.)

The other main orthographic traditions, other than Cyrillic, have their own problems with the typewriter keyboard. The Indic or Devanagari family of scripts, in use from the Middle East to Java with considerable local diversity, often require character sets of 250 symbols and up. They can be simplified, and have been for office practice, but the simplified form carries with it an air of inelegance or crude utilitarianism. The same is true of Arabic and its derivative scripts, such as Urdu, and also of the Ethiopic writing used for Amharic and other languages of that area.

Here again there is the tendency of writing systems that have been in use for awhile to depart from merely reproducing the sounds of speech on paper. Such systems reach out in the direction of providing a constant representation for each lexical item—what the Dutch call the principle of congruence. In English, for example, all the regular plurals are written as -*(e)s* whether they represent an *s* sound, a *z* sound, or a vowel + *z* combination. At the same time older orthographies tend to distinguish lexical items even when they sound the same: homophones do not necessarily imply homographs.

Writing systems in the Chinese sphere of influence seem to rely on matching ideographs with phonetic values for syllables or segments, rather than on the lexically oriented match between a character and a particular word in standard Chinese usage. There is experimentation going on both in Chinese and in minority languages, with official interest in both phonetic character writing and in romanization. There is no typewriter tradition, but these writing systems do fit within the capabilities of ordinary printers' fonts.

Influence of Another Language

The third characteristic of currently developed writing systems is that nearly all writing systems show the influence of a particular prestige language, not just of typewriter technology as such. Nobody has suggested a hiragana notation for any language of South America, or an Arabic-like script for Canadian Indians. There are practical reasons for this other than the difficulty of finding Arabic typewriters in the Yukon: speakers of nearly all minority languages need to communicate with speakers of the official or trade language of their area. Compatibility between writing systems seems to facilitate this, although we have no proofs of this. The idea that one can learn to read fairly easily in a language he already knows, then turn that knowledge into a stepping stone to get into another language he doesn't know so well, is a powerful one, widely recognized by speakers of vernacular languages, and increasingly recognized by educators.

The writing conventions of a prestige language, however, restrict how the minority language can look on paper. For example, in Otomi of the Mezquital Valley in central Mexico the tones of verb proclitics have to be distinguished in writing or chaos results. The first syllable of verb stems and of most noun stems also has to have tone symbolized, but it takes a three-way set of distinctions rather than the two-way split that operates with the proclitics (Wallis, 1968). Early phonological analyses of Otomi turned up these facts, together with the observation that nasalized and nonnasalized vowels are phonemically distinct. Writing systems based on these analyses incorporated all these distinctions, and ran into a snag.

Even illiterate Otomi speakers had seen Spanish billboards and road signs around their valley. They knew that Spanish used the acute accent, and so they had no quarrel with acute accent to represent Otomi high tone. A wedge, or hachek, accent for a rising tone, however, and a cedilla under a vowel for nasalization, were condemned by literate and illiterate persons alike as "little horns" that had no place in a civilized alphabet.

A compromise was finally worked out. It required a closer understanding of the linguistic system than the first work had given. The rising tone, it turned out, was always phonetically long, and could be taken as a double vowel with high tone (or stress in some analyses) on the second member.

This high tone, written with an acute accent, permitted the Spanish-like symbol to be retained in place of the unfamiliar wedge, yet kept the three-way split between high tone (one vowel, one accent), rising tone (two vowels, accent on the second), and low tone (one vowel, no accent).

The other linguistic evidence that turned up was that except for a̲, the presence of nasalized vowels could nearly always be predicted. The a̲ was written with a line under it when nasalized, and without the line otherwise. Nasalization could be ignored for the other vowels. Underlines were part of the readers' image of what a real language could look like, and so the nasalization contrast was preserved at the point where it really mattered.

The attitudes held by speakers of a prestige language toward their own writing system extend to others in their spheres of influence, and thus exert sociopolitical pressure on the way those other writing systems fit the languages they are intended for. For example, English uses no tone marks; but most of the languages of Ghana really need some means of indicating tonal differences. We have heard of instances, not independently verified, where a West African orthography deprived of tone marks by the pressure of English, forces readers to go over each sentence twice, once to guess at the meaning from the inadequate transcription, and a second time to try to fill in the tones. The underdifferentiation of vowel symbols in English catches readers out much less frequently, since the interplay with syllable structure, vowel combinations, and silent letters usually permits an unfamiliar word to be sounded out even if it is not recognized directly.

A prestige language can force a writing system to overdifferentiate as well as underdifferentiate. In Southeastern Tepehuan of Mexico, for example, Thomas Willett (in press) reports that syllable final voiced stops are written as -'m, -'n, and -'ñ rather than as the -b, -d, and -dy suggested by the phonological analysis because bilinguals who learned their alphabet in Spanish schools equate the sequence of a glottal stop (') plus a nasal that manifests the voiced stops at the end of a syllable with a Spanish spelling rather than with its Tepehuan function.

This influence of an outside writing system is vivid in the writing of the Yao people of northern Thailand, reported Herbert Purnell (personal communication). There is a rich literature of songs in Yao, written in Chinese characters. These characters take Cantonese readings, although the result is unintelligible in Cantonese. Due to a general similarity of syllable structure and stock of phonemes, it comes out as a good approximation of Yao, including the tones. Yao readers learn the Chinese symbols, mixed with a few of their own, in order to read Yao.

Recent attempts to introduce a Roman writing system for Yao on the one hand, and a Thai-based system on the other, have not met with success even though the time required to learn either alphabetic system is less than what the Chinese characters require, and the Thai script provides a way to learn the national language as well. The Chinese character system is adequate for the sounds of Yao and has a valued tradition among them, so people are willing to put in the work it takes to master it.

The amount of work required to learn to write in one's own language brings up the teaching strategies that go with the writing system. Here again the effect of majority languages is felt. From the standpoint of speakers of a minority language, the role of pedagogical traditions appears to go something like this: schools are institutions that the national government has and we don't. Schools open the door for our young people to make their way in the national life, in both its good and bad aspects. Schools are coming to us from people with a lot of experience in running them. Therefore the way they run a school is the way people ought to learn things. Whatever the pedagogy of the schools is, that is what we should follow if we want to learn.

The trouble with the widespread tendency of minority groups to follow the educational models that are offered to them, is that those models may not be useful to begin with. Bad pedagogy is more likely to be exported into vernacular cultures than good pedagogy, since there is so much more of the former around.

In teaching Huichol Indians to read, for example, Grimes has noticed that men and women follow characteristically different patterns. When asked "Who taught you to read?", most Huichol men who do read reply, "I taught myself." They mean that someone helped them get the hang of what reading was about, whereupon they learned enough key phrases to back them up when they got stuck, then figured out the rest on their own. Women, on the other hand, appear to follow a school model. As far as they have been able to observe, it consists of having the teacher go over and over a book until the pupil has it by heart. Women answer "Who taught you?" by naming the individual they learned from, and may go on to point out "Now I can read this book" with a demonstration that suggests that they memorized it rather than learned to understand its message.

This is in the beginning stages of reading. There are enough fluent readers of Huichol of both sexes that one might be hard put to show that either strategy is inferior in the long run. If there is any principle to be drawn here, it is probably that a successful writing system tolerates various teaching strategies, so that as long as it is adequate to represent the language, almost anything goes.

ENCODING ADEQUACY

Writing systems can be learned even if they are taught badly. This does not imply that good pedagogy doesn't count, or that any old orthography that people like meets their needs, but it has been observed that there is more latitude in orthographic systems than we used to think possible.

One question for research that new orthographies pose is along that line: What factors limit adequacy in an orthography? Can we predict adequacy from a linguistic analysis, together with a study of prestige language orthographies in an area? Can we recognize and repair a bad orthography?

Gordon gives his attention to completing orthographic proposals. His research is a study of alternative writing systems, directed toward such questions as "Can one orthography be learned more easily than another?", and "Are there general principles in orthography design that maximize learnability?" Progress in answering these questions should arise from an understanding of the limits of encoding adequacy.

Gordon is currently testing hypotheses about the limits of adequacy in orthographies. The first hypothesis is that, as features are eliminated from an orthography, there will be a point beyond which even the most skilled readers have serious difficulty. At the other extreme there could be a point beyond which an increase in the richness of features encoded would not improve even the poorest reading behavior. It is not clear, however, how this point could be identified if it exists. An orthography that lies between these extremes is adequately encoded.

English is the current target of study; several Native American languages are in view for later research. The primary measures of reading behavior are oral reading rate and oral error rate. They are evaluated for alternative orthographies against the standard orthography, or where there is none, against the orthography that the subject already reads best. His performance is examined over time as he is introduced to alternative orthographies. Because English deals with one thoroughly learned writing system as opposed to test systems the subject has never seen before, the subject's reading and error rates on standard English are used as an indication of where his learning curve has leveled out. From test data we try to estimate where the learning curve for each alternative orthography appears to level out. This estimate, in comparison with the subject's performance on standard English, leads to one of three experimental outcomes.

The first outcome, when the long-term learning curve on the test orthography approaches substantially the same asymptote as that of the subject's best orthography, indicates that there is no difference in efficacy of one orthography over the other. The second outcome is indicated when the learning curve crosses the line of the subject's performance with his original orthography. If the difference is significant, this indicates that the test orthography is really better: it enables the subject to read faster or with fewer errors, and thus puts fewer stumbling blocks in his way. The third outcome, where the learning curve stays worse than what the subject can do in the existing system with practice, indicates that the test orthography is not as adequate for written communication as is the existing one.

The learning curve approach looks at the level of proficiency that the learner approaches rather than at its initial slope. In the first place, there is no way of knowing the rate at which the subject originally learned his more familiar orthography, so that a high rate of learning in the test is as likely to be due to a motivated teacher or the experimental situation as it is to the orthography itself. Later on, one may find a measure of ease of learning when controlled experiments can be carried out.

Looking at the asymptote also corrects for temporary interference in the subject's capability to handle his normal orthography, which is caused by his learning a new one. Linguists who have lived through major orthography changes in various parts of the world report that the trauma one might expect such changes to impose on readers appears mainly when the orthography change is made a political issue. Otherwise readers take change in stride despite the apprehensions of outsiders, most of whom are not comfortable in either the old or the new way of writing. Test subjects are expected to react with similar aplomb, and indeed this has been the case in preliminary tests.

This research differs from the kind of orthography study in which word boundaries are replaced by dummy characters or are omitted, the size or the case of the letters is switched, or the text is transformed geometrically by inversion, reflection, rotation, or letter reversal. All these tests change the graphic shape, but not the symbolic representation; whatever was represented in the original writing comes to be represented by a different shape, but keeps the same relation to the linguistic elements.

There are, however, many ways to manipulate the symbolic aspects by which an orthography relates to linguistic elements, and that is what this research does. Some testable manipulations include:

1. Symbol deletion in all environments or in specified environments. This reduces encoding relationships.
2. Symbol addition. This is possible where linguistic features have been left uncoded, and enriches encoding relationships.
3. Symbol reduction. By neutralizing the representation of contrasts such as voicing, encoding relationships are reduced in a way similar to the reduction brought about by symbol deletion; yet the number of characters per phonological unit or segment is unchanged.
4. Symbolic shift. Shift refers to the change of level of encoding: from the phonetic to the phonemic, or from the phonemic to the morphophonemic.

These manipulations are similar in their effect to the mutilations studied by Miller and Friedman (1957), but are introduced systematically. This research concentrates on symbol reduction.

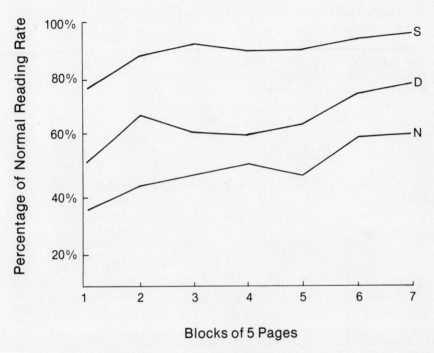

Figure 1.   Mean reading rate in words per minute expressed as percentages of normal reading rate.

The results of a pretest on three test modes are shown in Figure 1. A narrative text was altered in three ways.

1. In the *substitution mode* (S), symbol substitutions were made without altering the sound-symbol relations *(trail–trale, smelled–smelt).* In some cases the alteration resulted in a shape that formed another lexical item in English *(some–sum, days–daze).*

2. In the *neutralized mode* (N), symbols were collapsed in a regular way by eliminating the voicing distinction across the following stops and fricatives: *p* and *b* were collapsed to *b; t* and *d* to *d; k* and *g* to *g; s* and *z* to *z;* and *f* and *v* to *v.*

3. In the *deletion mode* (D), vowels were preserved according to the following rules: retain the vowels in the 100 most frequently used words in English, retain the vowels in words with only one consonant, and retain initial vowels or vowel sequences. All other vowels were deleted.

These alterations resulted in a character change level of about one character out of every six for each mode.

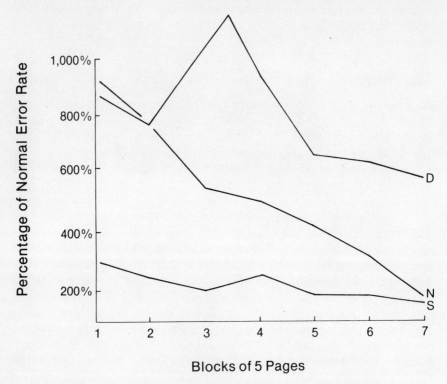

Figure 2.   Number of gross errors expressed as percentages of normal error rate.

In the pretest two adult subjects were assigned to each mode and were asked to record orally 35 pages of double-spaced, typewritten narrative text. Immediately following this, they read six pages written in normal English orthography. The mean improvement in performance over time in terms of reading rate in words per minute for the seven blocks of 5 pages each is shown in Figure 1. Figure 2 shows the number of gross errors in each block of five pages. The data in both figures are expressed as mean percentages of the corresponding baseline rates taken from the unaltered text. The baseline is represented as 100% in both figures.

Although no demonstrable conclusions can be drawn from such a limited sample, the data do anticipate the general direction of a long-term study now under way. Another pretest with sixth graders gave comparable results.

The present long-term study will monitor the reading rate and the error rate for leveling out to an asymptote. The asymptotes will be studied for both stabilized improvement and for degree of variation. A further hypothesis to be tested is that as a performance peak is approached, the variability in both reading rate and error rate will be reduced. Another aspect of these results that needs further looking into is the interaction of reading rate and error rate.

DISCUSSION

Recognizing symbolic shift opens up the possibility of examining what time-tested orthographies do. Whereas the newer orthographies emphasize phonological regularities, the older ones maximize consistency of morpheme shape, and distinguish one meaningful form from another, even when they are pronounced the same. We have little experience with this as a deliberate strategy for orthography design, yet it seems potentially powerful.

Some approaches to orthography design, including the investigations of Chomsky and Halle (1968) on English, suggest that orthographies ought to approach some optimum. However, an orthography could be considered optimal in terms of one kind of linguistic encoding, without necessarily being optimal in terms of another, or from the standpoint of learnability. It is possible, for example, that a phonemic orthography may be easy for a pupil to get the hang of, but may slow him down for lifetime reading because it leaves too many homophones undifferentiated. Correspondingly, an orthography that maximizes the constancy with which each form is represented in all environments, and that distinguishes different forms even though they may sound alike, might be harder to begin with because the pupil does not have pronunciation so readily accessible to fall back on (this is called "sounding out" words); yet over the years it may make him a better reader. The research the authors have undertaken should help sort out these issues.

Chapter 8
LINGUISTIC FACTORS IN ADULT LITERACY

John W. Ryan

The problem of adult illiteracy in the world is massive and complex. On the basis of quite uncertain statistics, the number of adult illiterates is estimated to be 800 million (Bataille, 1976). If, however, literacy were to be defined as linguists have suggested it be (cf. Gudschinsky, 1977, p. 39), that is, to mean the ability to read and write with comprehension and fluency rather than by the nominal standards applied by census takers, the estimate of 800 million would probably be found to underestimate rather than to exaggerate the magnitude of the problem. Expressed as a ratio rather than in absolute terms, this statistic means that one person in three, 15 years of age and older, is unable to read and write.

It is an obvious fact, but an important one, that illiteracy is not distributed randomly across the continents, but is concentrated geographically and socially. A map of illiteracy would cover much the same terrain as a map of poverty, disease, high infant mortality, malnutrition and other causes and symptoms of underdevelopment and inequality. Illiteracy is related to sex, with women having a higher illiteracy rate; to rural residence; and to membership in social, cultural, and ethnic minorities. It is this set of pernicious interrelationships that gives urgency to the problem of illiteracy and makes its solution complex. Foster (1977) has noted that literacy may be a prerequisite for economic development, but that it cannot be inferred that it is a sufficient condition. Fishman, on the other hand, asserts that the implementation of writing systems, and by extension the diffusion of literacy, are "revolutionary rather than narrowly technical acts. They succeed or fail on the basis of the success of larger revolutions with which they are associated: revolutions in the production and consumption of economic goods and revolutions in the distribution of power and influence" (quoted in Gorman, 1977, p. 277-278). These are complementary rather than contradictory assertions and serve to emphasize that the quest for a more literate world is complexly related to fundamental social, economic, and political issues.

This is true because, in the final analysis, efforts to promote literacy depend upon the learner's motivation to learn and this inclination is strongly conditioned by his social, political, and economic circumstances, perceptions, and aspirations. The landless peasant of Asia cannot be made literate until the basic conditions of his life are transformed. The same is true of the Arab housewife, the African tribesman, and the dwellers in a Latin American favella or an American ghetto. Literacy has meaning and is actively sought only when it leads to fuller participation in culture and society and to a more equal sharing of social, economic, and political rights and privileges.

Learning to read is an arduous task. Research can contribute to an understanding of the processes involved and suggest ways in which teaching and learning can be made more efficient and effective. This is an important contribution. But the learner's will to read remains an essential determinant of success. Where that will exists, the limited opportunities for learning provided, for example, in the schools of the American frontier during the last century, will suffice to produce literate communities. Where it does not exist, clever pedagogy, elaborate equipment, and fancy buildings are likely to prove of no avail.

Improvements in orthographies and better educational techniques and technology can be of crucial importance once the social, economic, and political conditions conducive to literacy are present. There is ample evidence that adult literacy programs falter and fail because orthographic systems and other linguistic factors make the burden of learning heavier than it need be. The most successful literacy campaign of this century, that in the USSR, owes a great deal to the systematic language planning that accompanied and guided it. Yet, this reform would not have been possible or sufficient without the social, economic, and political revolution of which it was a part.

LINGUISTIC FACTORS IN ADULT LITERACY

"People can be taught to read any alphabet provided ample time is given and provided they desire to read strongly enough" (Pike, 1947). This assertion may be correct, but in the context of adult literacy the two conditions established severely limit its applicability. The challenge of adult literacy is to teach reading in a limited period of time under difficult conditions and in ways that sustain and develop the learners' motivation for literacy.

The difficulty of this undertaking is considerable. The increasingly detailed descriptions and analyses of the mental process of the skilled reader demonstrate convincingly that reading is a complex and demanding cognitive transaction. The reader is required to exercise skills of association and discrimination, to apply a system of logical conventions, to draw upon memory for background information, and to use the contextual and grammatical clues in the opening words or phrases of a passage to anticipate its conclusion. Reading, in brief, involves an active and skillful quest for meaning. Writing requires the learner to be able to apply the logic of language in encoding meaning. Thus, the challenges of teaching and learning literacy should not be underestimated. Historically, the school came into being as a response to the need for systematic instruction to achieve literacy. Literacy cannot be "picked-up" by observation or through social interaction, but has to be purposefully taught and systematically learned.

The adult literacy class seeks to teach reading and writing, but does so under different and generally more difficult conditions than the primary school. An adult learner, assuming he is becoming literate in his mother tongue, possesses one major learning advantage over a child: his knowledge and control of the spoken language. His disadvantages are several: limitation of time, duties and obligations that conflict with regular class attendance, and a level of motivation that may not be sufficient or long enough sustained to achieve an enduring level of literacy. The child's motivation is not necessarily higher, but it is compensated for by the coercive powers of the school, whereas the adult learner is usually freely participating in a literacy course and can abandon it at any time he chooses. Moreover, in many rural societies, the social definition of *adult* does not include and is not easily compatible with the role of student or learner, even when this role is disguised by euphemisms such as "participant" or "group member." Adults, almost invariably, desire literacy for their children. They are often less certain about their own need for literacy. Their intuitions on this point may or may not be correct, but their sentiments are realities with which adult literacy work must contend.

The time factor is particularly crucial in adult literacy programs. Even in the rural areas of developing nations where schooling tends to be intermittent and where drop-out rates are high, a child who is enrolled for three or four years (the period usually considered a minimum for achieving lasting literacy) is likely to have 2,000 or more hours of school experience devoted primarily to the acquisition of literacy and numeracy skills. By contrast, many adult courses provide 200 or fewer hours of instruction (International Institute for Adult Literacy Methods, IIALM, 1971). Moreover, as punctuality and regular attendance are not enforced as in the school system, the actual number of hours of class participation per adult learner is likely to be considerably less than would be inferred from the class schedule. In one program where systematic observations were made of three classes, it was found that participants, on average, were in attendance for only 40 minutes in a 90-minute class period (Bazany, 1972, pp. 147–148). In addition to reducing the number of hours of attendance, tardiness and absenteeism interrupt the continuity of instruction. This poses a serious difficulty in literacy courses where a system of knowledge rather than a set of loosely related learning tasks must be mastered. Moreover, whereas the emphasis in the primary school, particularly in developing nations, is on the three R's, the trend in adult programs is toward functional literacy. This term has been variously defined, but implies that the teaching of literacy must be related to and, if possible, combined with vocational or other training considered to be of practical value to the learner and his community. Although the value of this approach, and in particular its ability to sustain motivation, is widely recognized, it does further reduce the already limited time available for literacy and numeracy instruction. Finally, the instructional methods used in the adult class are (or should be) dialogical rather than didactic. The class is frequently organized as a discussion group and explanations are interwoven with discussion. As a consequence of these factors, the time available for mastering and practicing the complex and demanding skills of reading and writing is extremely limited.

The success experience of adult literacy efforts is, at best, mixed. Many programs have been conspicuous failures and others only lukewarm successes. As noted in the preceding paragraph, the learning opportunities offered in literacy courses are limited by time and organizational factors. Many adults require more time to achieve literacy than the classes provide. On the other hand, increasing the duration of courses by dividing them into stages has usually had the effect of increasing drop-outs. Moreover, the degree to which literacy skills are retained and developed is problematic. There is strong evidence that when opportunities and incentives for reading do not exist skills rapidly atrophy (Roy & Kapoor, 1975).

Earlier in this chapter, mention is made of the social, economic, and political preconditions of literacy. In the subsections that follow, important linguistic factors that condition the success of literacy programs are discussed. This discussion should be seen in the light of the special and particularly challenging instructional situation of the adult literacy class. The issue is not whether adults can be made literate, that has been answered in the affirmative, but rather the probability that they will achieve literacy in adult classes as they are presently organized and conducted.

The answer to this query, it is contended, is closely related to five issues: 1) literacy readiness, 2) language knowledge, 3) the correspondence between the spoken language and the written language to be mastered, 4) the adequacy and complexity of the orthography employed and the skill and thoroughness with which it is taught, and 5) the provision of opportunities and the incentives for reading. More detailed attention will be paid to orthography, including the teaching of punctuation and format, than to other matters, as this bears most directly upon the theme of the present volume. In the context of adult literacy, however, this issue is closely related to questions of language use and language learning, and can, it is believed, be most usefully examined in this broader context.

LITERACY READINESS

In teaching children to read, a great deal of attention is given to readiness. It is usually tacitly assumed that adults, because of their maturity, are ready to begin literacy instruction immediately. But it has to be remembered that the term *illiterate* does not denote a precise state but rather a continuum including, at one end, those who have never encountered a written language and at the other, the semiliterate. The latter, who in most developing countries will be primary school drop-outs, may indeed be ready to proceed immediately to literacy instruction. Their months or years in school may not have made them literate, but they will have acquainted themselves with the "secrets" of the written code. The "naive" illiterate, on the other hand, will have to develop powers of recognition, association, and discrimination before literacy instruction can be usefully begun. Indeed, it has been observed that the life experiences of adults may complicate rather than facilitate the learning task to be mastered. A hoe, for example, is still a hoe regardless of what direction its blade is turned or its handle pointed. A letter form, by contrast, may have several different values, which are entirely dependent upon its positioning: for example, *b* or *d,* and *p* or *q.* Knowledge of such conventions cannot be assumed, but must be systematically and carefully taught. The danger in classes of mixed ability, which is the usual situation in adult literacy courses, is that the teacher may assume that because basic principles are understood by some, they are understood by all. When this occurs, the unschooled illiterate is lost at the outset.

Word recognition is another area where essential skills have to be developed before literacy instruction can begin. A principle of pedagogy is to begin where the learner is. In the teaching of literacy, the obvious entry point is with the spoken language, assuming the learner commands it adequately. The success of such a teaching strategy, however, depends not only upon the degree of correspondence between the written and the spoken media, but equally upon the ability of the learner to recognize such similarities. The concept of a graphic system isomorphic to a sound system is a demanding abstraction that usually becomes apparent to the learner only by degrees and through careful instruction.

This is suggested by the finding that illiterates are frequently unable to recognize words in isolation. Gudschinsky (1977) notes that illiterates differ widely in their ability to recognize content words but that very few are able to recognize functors, which indicate grammatical relationships rather than physical realities. For the naive speaker, orthographic words do not necessarily possess psychological reality, i.e., they are not perceived as the intuitive units from which language is constructed. Speech is perceived as a stream of meaning rather than as a delicate mosaic of words. Thus, it is often necessary to begin literacy instruction with explanations and drills intended to develop word recognition skills.

The principal social determinant of literacy readiness is probably the extent to which literacy is used in a society. A literate individual is conscious of letters and words as basic language units and conveys his awareness to those around him. In preliterate or illiterate societies, there may be a sophisticated language consciousness, but it is not necessarily focused on those aspects of the spoken language upon which the learning of the written language will depend. An awareness of these features will, therefore, have to be developed. Unfortunately, this is often neglected. It is a personal observation, confirmed by the pattern of dropout statistics, that the first lessons of a literacy course are the most critical. Once the fundamental ideas of the written language are understood and the requisite auditory and psychomotor skills developed, literacy instruction can proceed with surprising speed and success in supportive environments.

LANGUAGE KNOWLEDGE

On the basis of what is known of the reading process, particularly the finding that fluent reading appears to depend upon an ability to anticipate the meaning of passages, it would be expected that one of the important factors in achieving literacy in a language would be the learner's mastery of its spoken form. Empirical evidence confirms this expectation (see Gorman, 1977). Recognizing this relationship, international meetings have recommended that initial literacy should, wherever possible, be achieved in the learner's mother tongue.[1] Yet, even a cursory examination of the language situation in developing nations suggests how difficult it will be to apply this recommendation. To seek to do so is to confront two obstacles: 1) the vast multiplicity of languages spoken in many developing countries and 2) the meagerness of available resources, both financial and manpower, for rendering the spoken language into effective media for literacy instruction.

Gorman in his review, "Literacy in the Mother Tongue: a Reappraisal" draws a striking comparison between the language situation in the Soviet Union and Europe and that in Africa.

> There are more languages spoken in Tanzania than in the USSR and more languages spoken in the Cameroon than in the Soviet Union and Eastern and Western Europe combined. Yet there are almost three times as many languages spoken in Nigeria as in Cameroon (Gorman, 1977, p. 281).

The situation in many developing states outside Africa is similar. There are, for example, over 800 languages spoken in Indonesia and over 600 in Papua, New Guinea, a country of fewer than three million inhabitants. Moreover, the vast majority of the languages in developing countries are unwritten, unstandardized languages spoken by communities of a few hundred or a few thousand persons.

Confronted with these facts, it becomes apparent that a rational policy for literacy promotion imposes a harsh necessity to choose the languages in

---

[1] A review and commentary on the recommendations of international meetings in respect to the use of mother tongue in literacy is presented in Gorman, 1977, pp. 271–281.

which literacy instruction is to be offered and literacy to be attained. A corollary to this conclusion is that in many countries a majority of participants in adult literacy courses will be seeking to attain literacy in a language other than their mother tongue. The alternative is to wait decades, or more probably centuries, for orthographies to be made and for languages to be standardized and developed into media capable of conveying information and ideas that a modernizing society will require. Moreover, the pedagogical advantages of teaching in the mother tongue are sometimes offset by resistance from learners. Halvorson (1970), for example, notes the difficulty of persuading Tanzanians that they should first attain literacy in their mother tongue before proceeding to the study of Swahili, the national language. A recurrent complaint expressed by learners was: "Why are we wasting our time on our own language; we already know that. We are being delayed in learning Swahili."

The planners of literacy programs are thus faced with a dilemma. For pedagogical reasons, it may be best to begin with the mother tongue, or more accurately with a language that the learner commands fluently, be it his mother tongue or a language learned later in life, but this best choice will often prove a practical impossibility or if possible, may lead to a dead end if there are not opportunities and incentives to read and write regularly in the mother tongue.

The practical implication of this situation for the adult literacy class is that many learners will be seeking to achieve literacy in languages that they do not command fluently. Thus, the literacy class is going to be engaged in two distinct forms of instruction: second language learning and literacy training. Baucom (1978) cautions that these are fundamentally different operations and should not be confused with one another, as they too often are. Gorman (1977), endorsing Pike's proposal, suggests that in such situations greater use might be made of "diglot" materials; i.e., materials using two languages, one better known to the participants that serves as a bridge to the language in which literacy is ultimately to be attained. He notes, however, that such materials, although often recommended, have seldom been used because of the practical difficulties that their preparation presents.

One aspect of the issue of language choice relates directly to the development of orthographies. Recognizing that learners in multilingual societies will frequently be required to achieve literacy in more than one language, it has been recommended that related or adjacent languages make use of the same or similar orthographies. In this way, the task of achieving literacy in a second language is facilitated. A related advantage is that the same typesetting and printing equipment can be used for several languages. The outstanding example in this respect is the experience of the USSR, which has combined a policy of language preservation and development with measures directed toward an increasing standardization of national orthographies based on the Cyrillic alphabet (Lewis, 1977). In West Africa, an agreement has been reached among neighboring states to develop a unified orthographic system for six language groups: Hausa, Kanuri, the Mande group, Fulani, Songhai-Zerma, and Tamashek. This latter development represents a considerable departure from the colonial period where two or more orthographies were sometimes developed and put into use for the same transnational language by different colonial authorities. The general point to be made is that the development of orthographies must be seen as one aspect of national or regional language policies and not as a technical exercise to be performed in isolation. The promotion of literacy, in many countries, will not be able to progress far until coherent language policies are formulated and instructional approaches developed that take into account the realities of the learning situation these policies impose.

CORRESPONDENCE BETWEEN THE
WRITTEN AND SPOKEN LANGUAGE FORMS

Teaching someone to be literate is usually based upon the assumption that a high degree of correspondence exists between the spoken and written forms of a language. If this is not the case and the two forms are sharply divergent, a learner seeking to become literate in his own language is confronted with a difficulty analogous to that of attaining literacy in a second language. He is required to learn a new language medium in addition to mastering the system for its graphic representation.

In most, if not all languages, the written and spoken forms differ considerably. Writing may closely resemble formal speech, but it differs substantially from everyday conversation. Writing tends to be more formal, more concise and precise and tends to employ words and forms that rarely occur in speech. Thus, becoming literate usually requires achieving mastery of new language forms. There are, however, two special and extreme cases: 1) the problem of unstandardized languages and 2) the special situation of diglossia.

In the developing regions of the world, where revolutions in communication and transportation have only recently brought communities into regular contact with one another, languages often have many dialects that differ considerably from one another. One dialect may be recognized as the standard form of the language and may be in general use in the urban areas, but the unstandardized dialects continue to prevail in the countryside. Or, as is frequently the case in Africa, there is no recognized standard form of the language. In either case, speakers of different dialects of the same language may encounter communication difficulties of varying degrees of severity.

Dighe (1977) relates the difficulties encountered in the use of standardized Andra in a rural maternal-child health care program, which included a literacy component. In pretesting instructional materials, it was discovered that the word *chulalu,* meaning pregnant in the standardized language, was not readily understood by speakers of the village dialect who used the term *nindumanisi* instead. Because this was one of the key words in the program, failure to make this discovery could have led to confusion.

The problem in teaching someone to be literate is obviously complicated in situations where it is necessary to first teach the lexicon of an unknown standardized form of the language. To fail to do so, however, is to provide the new literates with mastery of a language form of very restricted usefulness because most written materials are published in the standardized language.

Diglossia refers to situations where in addition to dialectical and standardized forms of a language, there exists a divergent and highly codified form used for most writing and in formal speech. This situation is relatively common in parts of Asia and the Middle East where ancient and highly revered literacy traditions exist. Maamoori (1977) describes the situation in Tunisia as a state of diglossia aggravated by French-Arabic bilingualism. He notes that two related languages, Modern Standardized Arabic (MSA) and Tunisian Arabic (TA) are used "side by side, but with clearly defined role differentiation" (p. 212). MSA, the official language, is used for writing and for formal speeches, particularly of a religious or cultural nature. It, however, is not spoken natively by Tunisians and sounds stilted and unnatural when used informally.

In Tunisian adult literacy classes, all discussions and explanations are in TA, but writing is done exclusively in MSA. This situation considerably complicates the teaching and learning of literacy skills. The instructional strategy adopted seeks to use the commonalities in their lexicons as a bridge from TA to MSA. Nonetheless, a complex language form has to be mastered before the learner can express himself in MSA. Maamoori (1977, p. 212) quotes Foster's comparison (after noting that it contains a degree of exaggeration) that to become literate the Tunisian child must learn classical Arabic "which is rather like modern British and American children having to learn Anglo-Saxon before they can attempt to write or read personal letters."

In situations of diglossia, the usefulness of teaching literacy by strategies based on sound-symbol correspondence will be severely limited. The orthography of the MSA, for example, does not reflect how words are pronounced today in Tunisia, but rather is based upon the pronounciation that prevailed in Arabia thirteen centuries ago. On the other hand, basing the orthography on contemporary TA pronunciation would cut Tunisia off linguistically and culturally from its neighbors in the Arab region as well as from Arabic literature, science, and the sacred writings of Islam.

ORTHOGRAPHIES AND LITERACY PROMOTION

The orthography best suited to the needs of adult literacy programs would be one that can be efficiently learned, easily read and written, and economically reproduced. The first point is the most critical. Complex and difficult orthographies may be easily handled by skilled readers, but they are laborious to teach and learn, more especially so under the challenging conditions that commonly prevail in adult literacy programs. As has been noted, instructional time is limited in literacy classes. It is also important to remember that for many participants the literacy class is one additional activity in a full and demanding day. The learner's energy and attention are often in short supply. Finally, there is ample evidence that slow learning frequently leads adults to discouragement and dropping out.

The second criterion, ease of reading, is of particular importance to the new literate or the semiliterate. Ambiguities present more serious difficulties for the inexperienced and uncertain reader than they do for the skilled and experienced one. The former can be easily confused and discouraged, whereas the latter is able to draw upon his experience and upon contextual clues to decipher the meaning of a puzzling passage. If, for example, an experienced reader so misreads an introductory passage that he finds it contextually or grammatically inconsistent with the conclusion, he will in all likelihood reread the passage and discover his error. The beginning reader, however, may lack the confidence or experience to do so. Thus, orthographic decisions that introduce ambiguity, whether unintentionally or to gain simplicity or other advantage, may seriously complicate the reading task for the new literate or semiliterate, a category that represents a large percentage of the potential reading public in many developing countries.

As a result of her experience in developing orthographies for literacy programs, Gudschinsky was acutely aware that inexperienced readers were more likely to encounter difficulties than a "green" expert might suppose:

It may be expected that if a beginning reader misreads an ambiguous word he will immediately think of the other word he should have read. This is not the case. For example, suppose vowels were omitted from some English words. If a pupil found *b...t* sitting in the middle of a sentence, would he immediately think of all the possible words it might represent? Would he think of *boot, bet, bought,* etc., to see if they fit? Probably not. A better example is found in the Mazatec language. There are these minimal tone pairs: *ti* (with low falling tone) 'boy', *ti* (low rising tone) 'water jug', *ti* (high level tone) 'particle on a verb'. When the semi-literate Mazatec reads *ti* as 'boy' and finds it is wrong, he does have on the tip of his tongue a whole set of tone pairs to draw from—that is, pairs of words identical in letter sounds but different in tone. He does not know what choice to make next. It is even more difficult for him to think in tone pairs than for English speakers to think in vowel pairs. It cannot be assumed that if an element such as a tone symbol is omitted from an orthography the reader can resolve ambiguities automatically (Gudschinsky, 1973, pp. 121-122).

Unfortunately, the ease with which an orthography can be read is often diametrically opposed to the ease with which it can be written. Diacritics, accents, and tone markings, while increasing the clarity of text to the reader, complicate its reproduction for the writer. These complexities also have the indirect consequence of encouraging the development of speed scripts that omit those features of the orthographies that literates do not require in corresponding with one another. These omissions, however, can be profoundly puzzling to a new literate who has been trained in the official or formal script, but has not been introduced to its informal derivatives. An overly elaborate orthography can also cause difficulties in reading and, more particularly, in writing. For example, if the linguist is able to identify and represent more vowels than the speech community generally recognizes, the learners may find difficulty in choosing between symbols that represent different values to the linguist but have the same value to their ears. In the development of orthographies, an awareness of the distinctions that have psychological reality to the speech community is usually a better criterion than technical accuracy.

The last consideration, the simplicity and economy of reproducing the orthography, is of obvious concern. The development of orthographies is of little practical importance unless it leads to the implementation of writing systems and the development of mass media. Complex orthographies that require special typesetting and printing equipment or that are otherwise uneconomical are less likely to be implemented and widely used than are simpler systems for which trained labor and equipment are already available.

LEARNING PROBLEMS RELATED
TO ORTHOGRAPHIES: SOME EXAMPLES

To discuss in more concrete terms the problems that orthographies can pose to literacy learning, the Persian language and the modified Arabic script in which it is written have been chosen as an example. Reference is also made to research on related problems encountered in the use of Arabic in Egypt.

Since the seventh century A.D., the Persian language has been written in a modified Arabic script. It thus shares the virtues and problems of the Arabic script and, because it is from a different language family with a different phonetic structure, adds a unique difficulty of its own.

In the Arabic script a small number of basic letter forms are used to represent the letters of the alphabet: 28 in Arabic and 32 in Persian. These are differentiated from one another primarily by the use of dots in different numbers and positions. Two examples illustrate this point (adapted from Nickjoo, undated):

Basic Form	Letters	Arabic and Persian	Persian only
ٮ	ٮ Bi	ٮ Ti ٮٮ Si	ٮ Pi
ر	ر Ri	ز Zi	ژ Zhi

The basic form is used for four different letters and the second form for three. Students encounter the same difficulties in differentiating these forms from one another as do English speaking children in distinguishing between *b*s and *d*s and *p*s and *q*s.

A second difficulty is that the same letter may have many variant forms depending upon the script in which it is written, where it appears in the word, and which letters precede and follow it. For many letters, there is an initial form (when used as the first letter in a word), a medial form (when the letter occurs between two other letters), a final form (when connected only to the preceding letter), and an independent form (when the letter stands alone). Thus the 32 letters of the Persian alphabet are represented by over 100 forms in common use. In the first grade school textbook, a reduced set of 61 forms is used. If all the variant letter forms used in different scripts are included, the total would be 400 or more.

The Arabic Language Academy in Cairo has examined the learning and reading problems posed by this multitude of letter forms (Arab Regional Literacy Organization, 1977). It has proposed the use of an orthography employing 80 characters: 66 basic letter forms and certain common combinations. This alphabet is now in use in some newspapers in Egypt and is widely employed in adult instructional materials. The keyboards of Arabic typewriters use a similar orthography of approximately 80 characters. In most printing houses, 119 letter forms are now in use. Formerly, the basic matrix of Arabic letters consisted of the 470 forms still in use in religious publications.

The relationship between the number of letter forms and the speed and success with which literacy can be attained is a natural research issue. The Arab Regional Literacy and Adult Education Organization, ARLO, which operates under the Arab League, undertook a study of this matter in 1975. Three experimental orthographies consisting respectively of 32, 80, and 119 letter forms were compared in an experiment. Nine adult classes took part in the experiment: three classes were assigned texts in each of the orthographies being tested. The rates of learning success were then compared. Although full details of the experiment are not available to the author, the conclusion reached was that literacy success is inversely correlated with the number of letter forms taught. All students in the classes using only 32 letter forms were reported to have passed the criterion examination. The classes using the 80 character orthography had a higher success rate than those using 119 characters, although the difference was not statistically significant. This research would appear to confirm the common sense assumption that a reduced set of letter forms would be more easily mastered than the numerous forms previously taught.

A third and perhaps the most difficult problem in reading the Arabic script, is the absence of diacritics indicating the short vowel sounds. Nickjoo (undated) notes, for example, that the combination 'KRM' may be read in Persian in five different ways depending upon the vowel assignment the reader makes: *kirm* 'a worm', *kurum* 'chrome', *karam* 'generosity', *kirim* 'cream', and *karam* 'I am deaf'.

To convey to English readers the skill required for reading the Arabic script, Maamoori (1977, p. 219) suggests that the reader attempt to quickly peruse the following text from which the vowels have been omitted:

Tm, wh ws wrkng (a) lng wy frm hm, wntd t snd (a) lttr t hs wf, bt h cld nthr rd nr wrt, nd h hd t wrk ll dy, s h cld nly lk fr smbd t wrt hs lttr lt t nght. T lst h fnd th hs f (a) lttr-wrtr whs nm ws Bll. Bll ws lrdy n bd. "T s lt," h sd. "Wht d y wnt?" "(I) wnt y t wrt (a) lttr t m wf," sd Tm. Bll ws nt plsd. H thght fr (a) fw scnds nd thn sd, "Hs th lttr gt t g fr?"
"Wht ds tht mttr?" nswrd Tm.
"Wll, m wrtng s s strng tht nly (I) cn rd t, nd f (I) hv t trvl (a) lng wy to rd yr lttr t yr wf, t wll cst y (a) lt f mny."
Tm wnt wy qckly.

The reader's skill would probably improve rapidly with practice on such texts, but some sentences such as the following from Nickjoo (n.d.) would remain problematic.

Bll rdrd thr blls fr hs sthrn bll's sstr nd pd th bll rght thr."[2]

In Iranian first year classes and literacy courses diacritics are used to assist the new reader in sounding out words. These aides, however, are not in common use. Therefore, the reader has to graduate from instructional materials that include diacritics to general reading materials that do not. Transitional materials are provided to assist the learner in this passage.

A problem encountered in Persian, but not in Arabic, is the representation of a single phoneme by more than one grapheme. This overrepresentation of the orthography is historically rooted. Persian adopted all of the Arabic letters, but not the phonetic values they represent in Arabic. Thus, the letters *ti*, ت , and *tain,* ط , which represent different phonemes in Arabic, represent the same phoneme in Persian. Similarly, the sound si is represented by three different graphemes. Literacy students encounter relatively little difficulty in reading the various letter forms, but serious difficulty in deciding which one to use in writing.

The choice of one grapheme as opposed to another usually indicates the origin of a word. Arabic loan words, for example, are commonly written in Persian with the same graphemes used in Arabic, although pronounced in the Persian manner. In some instances, the different graphemes are also used to distinguish words containing the same consonantal pho-

---

[2]Maamoori (1977, p. 224) provides this rendering: "Bill ordered three balls for his southern belle's sister and paid the bill right there."

nemes from one another. There has been a tendency in recent years to use the more common grapheme in place of the less common. Tehran, for example, is now usually written with *ti* rather than *tain*. Both graphemes, however, continue in use and continue to complicate the task of becoming literate in Persian.

It would be a mistake to exaggerate the importance of the orthographic problems discussed above. An individual well schooled in Arabic or Persian reads his language with fluency and accuracy. The learner, however, does face difficulties. This is particularly true of the adult learner who has neither the time nor the motivation to spend several hours daily in class or doing homework. To diffuse literacy widely, it becomes necessary to simplify the learning task as far as possible. Learning efficiency, of course, has to be weighed against traditional and cultural values that mediate against tampering with orthography. Although one encounters occasional proposals for the kind of drastic orthographic revolution Ata Turk imposed in Turkey in 1928, this is probably neither politically feasible nor educationally necessary. More moderate reforms such as the reduction of the number of letter forms in use and the provision of abundant easy-to-read materials are likely to prove more effective means for the promotion of literacy.

TEACHING ORTHOGRAPHIC CONVENTIONS

Orthography includes not only letters, but also diacritics, tone marks, punctuation, and features of format. An understanding of all of these features is important for fluent reading. Rarely, however, are these latter aspects of orthography systematically taught in literacy classes. The instructor usually introduces words or short sentences by writing them on the blackboard. Attention will be given to word space and periods, but other format features and punctuation are often ignored. As a consequence, the learner is puzzled when confronted with a printed page. The function of paragraphing, the purposes of capitalization, the use of italics, and the choice of punctuation is not clear to the untrained reader. One encounters reports of readers who treat each line of print as a sentence and consequently find a text unintelligible (see, for example, Gudschinsky, 1977). These are extreme cases. The more common result of neglecting to teach the meaning of orthographic conventions is that the reader's progress is slowed and his uncertainty increased. As a result, reading becomes more laborious and less rewarding. Reading skills are, thus, less likely to be regularly practiced and further developed.

This difficulty can ony be resolved through more thorough and systematic training of literacy instructors. It has to be remembered, however, that literacy teachers are usually engaged only part-time in teaching adults, are generally poorly compensated for this work, and often have had little schooling and only a few days of preservice training in preparation for their assignments. In parts of Africa, one encounters primary school dropouts, barely literate themselves, who are endeavoring to conduct a literacy class (cf. IIALM, 1978).

PRODUCTION OF LITERACY MATERIALS

If the provision of literacy is to serve a useful purpose, it has to be accompanied by the provision of opportunities and incentives for reading. This is a complex matter involving fundamental economic, social, and cultural issues. Incentives for reading are created and the habit of reading developed when a need for more and new forms of information arises through social change and economic development. The role of the linguist is not decisive in promoting this development.

The linguist can, however, play a crucial and creative role in the production of literacy materials and follow-up literature. Although such materials have been produced in abundance for several decades, their instructional efficiency and interest-holding ability has generally not been high. The conundrum confronting the author of a primer, and to a somewhat lesser extent the writer of a follow-up publication, is to exercise a careful control over the rate at which graphemes and words are introduced and repeated and, at the same time, avoid Primerese and "Dick and Jane" lingo (Longacre, 1977). It is also desirable that the discourse genres used approximate as closely as possible the oral language the learner already controls. The need is, therefore, for carefully controlled creativity.

As proof that this is possible, Gudschinsky (1977, p. 42) mentions a Mozambique primer that begins with a well-known song. The song is not only attention catching, but it permits the learner to compare an oral text known by heart with its written representation. Another example cited is that of an Indian primer, which while observing the need to keep the language used in reach of the beginning learner, manages, nonetheless, to consist of a lurid melodrama from beginning to end. A form that is appropriate in one language or culture, may not, of course, be appropriate in another. Primers have to be language and culture specific. The same themes or problems may be used in different primers, but the treatment must be appropriate and natural to the language communities concerned. Longacre (1977) suggests ways in which discourse analysis can be used to assure that literacy materials are appropriate for and intelligible and pleasing to learners.

The purpose of careful linguistic analysis in the preparation of primers is to assure that they are educationally efficient and capable of holding the attention of adult learners. As noted in the section entitled "Linguistic Factors in Adult Literacy,'' the challenge of adult literacy is to enable the learner to achieve literacy in a limited period of time, often under distracting circumstances, and in ways that sustain and develop his motivation to read. The need for better literacy materials, including follow-up literature, to achieve this end is widely recognized. The success of literacy programs depends very largely on two factors: 1) the ability of such programs to teach literacy in ways that are interesting and effective, and 2) developments in society that render literacy a useful and rewarding skill to possess. There is much yet to be achieved in both of these areas.

CONCLUSION

Illiteracy has been called a political problem, a socioeconomic problem and a linguistic problem (see Bataille, 1976; Maamoori, 1977). It is all of these, as are all global problems. This chapter has examined selected language and learning issues that condition the success of literacy programs. These include the language readiness of the learner, the choice of the language in which literacy is to be attained, and the quality and interest holding capacity of the learning materials used. Special attention has been given, and examples provided, of the problems that ambiguities and complexities in orthography can create for the beginning reader. For reasons of space, many matters that might have been discussed in this chapter have been excluded. The special linguistic problems presented by the need to introduce technical vocabulary at an early stage in functional literacy courses and the reorganization of language sequences in experimental programs to adapt them to the fact of irregular adult attendance are, for example, issues that might have deserved, but did not receive, consideration.[3]

---

[3]The concept and application of functional literacy is discussed in the Experimental World Literacy Programme (1976). A discussion of new trends in adult literacy programs is presented in Harman (1977).

Chapter 9

CROSS-NATIONAL STUDIES ON PRIMARY READING
A Suggested Program

Eve Malmquist and Hans U. Grundin

BEGINNING READING INSTRUCTION OF CRITICAL IMPORTANCE

The development of reading ability must not be looked upon as an isolated technical teaching problem. Rather it is a phase in the child's total growth process, closely related to his all-around personality development. There is a dynamic interaction between progress in general maturity (physical, intellectual, emotional, and social) and the development of reading ability. Since reading is vital to an individual's ability to adapt to the environment, success or failure in attaining elementary reading proficiency may affect a child's entire behavior and general attitude toward the world. The ability to read is so essential to life, both in and out of school, that a failure in the early stages of learning to read may adversely affect a child's entire personality development. In other words, beginning reading instruction is of critical importance. Good habits are crucial in the acquisition of any new skill. Repetition is good only if what is being repeated is appropriate and desirable; otherwise, it can be very harmful. Inappropriate attitudes, as well as inappropriate techniques, can be extremely difficult to unlearn. Therefore, the first stages of learning are extremely important for the whole learning process. They constitute the basis for all subsequent work.

It is not surprising to note, therefore, that concerned efforts have been made in most countries to ensure success in learning to read during the initial stages, and that the majority of the scientific studies carried out within the field of reading are directed to problems concerning primary reading. In reviewing this area of research, two other interesting observations have been made: 1) the number of items of research are extremely unevenly distributed among different geographical regions of the world, and 2) very few cross-national studies have been accomplished.

SOME PROBLEMS OF INTERNATIONAL
INTEREST IN RELATION TO PRIMARY READING

Age of School Entrance

During the past few years additional strength has been given to the viewpoint that experiences during the early years of life have a profound influence on an individual's development in accordance with his potential resources. The age at which the majority of children are introduced to the teaching of reading varies from country to country. For example, in Great Britain, Australia, and New Zealand, formal reading instruction begins at the age of 5. In countries such as Western Germany, Hungary, France, Japan, and the U.S.A., the general practice is to start teaching reading at the age of 6. Schools in the Scandinavian countries (Denmark, Finland, Norway, and Sweden) and also those in the Soviet Union do not introduce reading instruction until the age of 7, and sometimes even later, depending upon the maturational level of the individual child. Very little is known about the considerations behind the choice of different ages of school entrance in different countries. In most cases these decisions were made a long time ago. At present there has been a tendency in many countries to reconsider the regulations of their school systems as to beginning age. In this process of reconsideration the results of comparative cross-national studies of a kind such as the one proposed in this chapter should be of value.

Language Differences and Their Implication for Reading Instruction

It is, of course, trivial to observe that languages differ greatly in a number of respects. The world's approximately 3,000 languages (there seems to be some lack of agreement as to the exact number) represent an enormous range of variation along different countries. A project trying to cope with the whole of this variation would meet with insurmountable difficulties. However, in the study proposed in this chapter, this range is very much restricted, since only a handful of languages are included.

Because of the lack of cross-language studies in this field, it is not well known what linguistic differences are of importance for the reading process or the reading instruction. There are, nevertheless, some factors that can safely be assumed to be important in these respects. Differences in the writing system is one such factor. According to a common classification, three main types of writing systems are used today (Gray, 1956, p. 11):

1. Systems using ideograph or word-concept characters (e.g., Chinese)
2. Systems using syllable-sound characters (e.g., Japanese)
3. Systems using alphabetic or letter-sound characters (e.g., English)

Problems of reading and reading instruction are to some extent different for different types of writing systems. Because this study proposes to include only languages using alphabetic writing systems, this question will not be further discussed.

Within the group of languages using alphabetic writing, there are still great differences. This seems only natural in view of the fact that this group includes languages from all continents. One important dimension of difference between alphabetic languages is their degree of letter-sound correspondence, or, to use the terms of the linguists, the degree to which their orthography is phonematic. Some languages have almost perfect correspondence in this respect, e.g., Finnish. At the other end of the continuum there are languages such as English whose orthography is notoriously unphonematic. Between those extremes, among numerous other languages, are German and the Scandinavian languages. Hungarian, being a Finno-Ugrian language, is quite close to the Finnish end of the continuum. These differences in letter-sound correspondence have been quite thoroughly studied by linguists in various countries and detailed descriptions of them are readily available for a number of languages. It is much less well known, however, to what extent the reading process or the process of learning to read is affected by the lack of letter-sound correspondence in the writing system. (However, see Gibson, 1971.) On the basis of studies of alphabetic as well as non-alphabetic languages, Gray (1956, p. 50) concludes that "the basic processes of silent reading are essentially the same" for languages as different as English, Spanish, and Chinese (to mention only a few examples). Gray bases his conclusions on, among other things, analyses of eye movement records that are strikingly similar irrespective of the language read.

Still, even if one accepts that the basic reading process as it is manifested by the mature reader is similar for most languages, this does not exclude the possibility of an interaction between language characteristics and the effects of different methods of initial reading instruction. It is also conceivable that although the final product of reading instruction may be the same behavior irrespective of the language read, some languages are more difficult to learn to read than others, e.g., in the sense that it takes more training time to reach mastery. The languages that are of interest in this context differ in other respects than that of letter-sound correspondence. They differ greatly in their degree of morpheme-word correspondence, i.e., the extent to which they tend to let morphemes form separate words. Here too, the extremes are represented by English, where a great number of morphemes form separate, short words in writing, and by the Finno-Ugrian languages, where morphemes corresponding to possessive pronouns, prepositions, etc. usually do not form separate words. As an example, take the English prepositional phrase *to my father*. It contains three morphemes, each forming one word, but its Finnish equivalent, *isalleni* is written in one word, although it also contains three morphemes: *isa* 'father' + *lle* (dat.) + *ni* (possessive pronoun). The German and Swedish languages are more similar to the English than to the Finno-Ugrian languages in this respect. In German, the prepositional phrase is *zu meinem Vater* (3 words and 4 morphemes), and in Swedish, it is *at min far* (3 words and 3 morphemes). In view of the differences discussed it is obvious that the concept word must be very carefully defined, if it is to be used in cross-language studies. Alternatively, this concept will have to be replaced by a more suitable concept, based for instance on the identification of morphemes, or other morphological units of language.

This discussion may be summarized by the conclusion that a study such as the one proposed in this chapter must include a thorough analysis of language differences and of their implications for the organization of elementary reading instruction and for the choice of instructional methods. In this task the advice and help of linguists knowledgeable in the languages concerned must, of course, be solicited. It is, for instance, desirable that the degree of letter-sound correspondence of each language involved in the study be objectively measured.

Aspects of the Instructional Process

For many years controversial points of view have been offered regarding methods of teaching reading. A great number of studies comparing different methods of instruction have been carried out in various countries.

Gray (1956) categorized the methods, labeled in many different ways, under the following headings: methods that place initial emphasis on elements of words and their sounds (alphabetic, phonic, and syllabic methods); methods that emphasize meaning from the beginning (word, phrase, sentence, and story methods); and the "learner-centered" trend (author-prepared reading matter, learner-teacher prepared reading matter, and materials integrating reading with other communication skills). Gray also pointed out that methods that emphasize word elements may neglect the development of comprehension, and methods that emphasize meaning may fail to develop enough skill in word identification.

Feitelson (1967b) has elaborated that instructional methods should be chosen to fit the nature of the language, its written representation, and the characteristics of the learner (See also Feitelson, chapter 2, this volume). Chall (1967) reviewed the research on this issue and came to the conclusion that some advantage lay with the code-first methods, but that there was no basis for asserting the superiority of one code-first approach over another. Chall also observed that methods professing to be different are often similar in some respects and vice versa. (See also, Chall, 1977; Feitelson, 1978b; Kozma, 1972).

After having compared the results of those children in English schools taught at the beginning by a method stressing phonics with those children initially taught by an analytic or whole-word approach, Morris (1966) concluded that the nature of the community, the brightness of the children, and the quality of the teachers and the school principal were more important influences on later reading than the method used in beginning reading instruction. Similar conclusions were reported from 27 cooperative first grade reading studies in the United States (Bond & Dykstra, 1976). However, a cross-national comparative study of different methods of instruction in beginning reading (involving countries having beginning ages ranging from 5 to 7), may give valuable information about the order in which the children acquire component reading skills under different conditions. It has commonly been asked which method of beginning reading is best, or which method produces more good or more bad readers. It would be easy to pose a similar kind of question in comparative research and ask which method is best for which language.

NEED AND FEASIBILITY OF INTERNATIONAL COMPARISONS IN THE FIELD OF PRIMARY READING

More and more countries are aware of the advantages of international cooperation within the field of education. The value of an exchange of practical experiences and results of scientific studies within nations with regard to educational organization, teaching procedures, etc. is mostly clearly recognized. The awareness of the fact that cross-national research studies in many instances would be even more profitable for participating countries is also growing, although slowly.

As Husén (1969) has pointed out:

> both cognitive and non-cognitive outcomes of schooling can be related to the different patterns of "input" factors, such as per pupil expenditure, teacher competence, number of hours of instruction, grouping practices, and so forth. Within countries, particularly in those with national policymaking and centralized administration in education, many practices are very uniform, whereas the cross-national variations in practice may cover a much longer range. One can therefore take advantage of the cross-national variability of the socioeconomic structure and educational practices to relate them to measures of outcomes. For instance, the long-range effect of sex differences on science achievement cannot be studied with any prospect of success within a system in which input variables cover a narrow or no range, whereas they can be studied cross-nationally with reasonable expectation of success.

Further language differences and their implications for effective reading instruction could be studied. The age of school entry and its implications for achievement are not readily studied within countries. The cross-national differences regarding the beginning age of learning to read allow for valuable comparisons, provided that other variables can be controlled in an acceptable way. Much useful information could be gathered about the ways in which the sequential changes of reading behavior are different for children who begin to learn at different ages and use different languages.

OBJECTIVES OF A CROSS-NATIONAL STUDY

A cross-national study at the initial stages of learning to read would focus on the effectiveness of different methods of teaching related to the characteristics of languages and to the different ages at entering school. The kinds of questions that might be posed are:

1. Is it easier for beginners to learn to read a language that has a more regular letter-sound correspondence?
2. Will disadvantaged groups profit by an earlier age of entry to school?
3. In what ways will the efficiency of a particular method or combination of methods in learning to read vary with language structure, background of the child, and age of school entry?

The main objective of the proposed study is to make a cross-national comparative evaluation of the process and product of elementary reading instruction in relation to a number of different types of variables such as:

1. Characteristics of the pupil, notably chronological age and reading readiness at the school start
2. Characteristics of the school system and its personnel
3. Methods and materials of elementary reading instruction, especially those of the initial reading instruction
4. Nature of the target language for the elementary reading instruction, especially regarding grapho-phonic aspects
5. Characteristics of the child's cultural, social, and economic environment

These relationships can best be studied by examining the course of development in reading ability from age of entry to school until 9 years of age, taking into consideration the variables encompassed in variables 1 to 5 above. The data should be gathered in such a way that the relationships between the variables and the extent of reading difficulties can be studied.

SOME IMPLICATIONS OF EXPECTED PROJECT OUTCOMES

The outcomes of the proposed project may be expected to have implications of theoretical, as well as of practical, importance. In the theoretical field, the study may contribute to a more thorough understanding of the processes of reading and of learning to read, mainly because it makes possible interlanguage contrasts that add a dimension to the study of reading that is usually not found in research at the national level. An outcome of the study that will be of both theoretical and practical interest will be the result of the test construction phase. The efforts to construct equivalent test versions in different languages for the purposes of this study are likely to give experiences of great value to the whole field of cross-national research, as well as to the field of test construction in general. The resulting set of parallel tests in different languages will also be an important achievement in itself, and it is expected that these tests can be useful for other cross-national projects too.

As to the project's possible implications for educational practice, it is expected that it will contribute to a better basis for decision making regarding some vital issues of primary reading. The age of school entrance, for instance, and its implications for achievement are not readily studied within countries, so the cross-national comparison will lead to a better assessment of this factor. It is not only a question of which entrance age produces the highest reading attainment at the age of 9 years, but it is also a question of possible differences in the learning sequence among groups of children who start learning to read at different ages. Considerations of a varied set of linguistic differences could lead to clearer insights regarding how best to simplify materials for beginning readers. The understanding of the interactions of linguistic variables and the impact of primary reading instructions on beginners of different ages should provide valuable information to countries considering lowering or raising the age of school entrance. Should the child be kept longer in preschool and should the start of reading instruction consequently be delayed? Or should the child leave his preschool environment earlier and enter school earlier? Once in school, should he be taught to read immediately? These and similar questions are no doubt asked in many countries and the availability of cross-national data concerning these problems may well make it possible to obtain better answers.

HYPOTHESES

The exact formulation of testable hypotheses for the proposed project must be postponed until after a great deal of the preparatory work has been accomplished. The question of whether a hypothesis concerning some international (or interlanguage) difference is testable or not cannot be answered before it is known exactly which countries will participate in the study. Whether or not a hypothesis is testable may also depend upon whether test versions of acceptable equivalence can be constructed in the different languages included in the study. The planning of the project must be guided by a set of working hypotheses concerning the relationships between variables that may be included in the analysis. A list of such working hypotheses is given below. This is only a preliminary list of hypotheses intended to guide our work until more definite hypotheses can be formulated.

1. Children introduced to formal instruction in reading at different age levels will have reached at the age of 9 years approximately the same level of reading achievement
2. Beginning readers will make faster progress in learning to read when the degree of letter-sound correspondence is high
3. Those children within an age group who are least well prepared for formal instruction in reading (e.g., due to their home background) will profit the most from being given a greater number of years in schooling before the age of nine
4. Potential reading "failures" can be identified before the beginning of formal reading instruction by means of a combination of reading tests and teacher observations
5. There will be an interaction between the methods used in initial reading instruction and the nature of the language the children are learning to read
6. Reading achievement at the age of 9 years will be correlated with such school system variables as number of hours of reading instruction, pupil-teacher ratio in reading groups, teacher competence, proportion of male teachers in the infant school, attitudes of teachers as to reading readiness, and similar concepts
7. Girls will learn to read faster than boys and maintain their superiority at the age of 9 years

It should be noted that some of the hypotheses can very well be tested within a single country. Cross-national research is therefore not the only way of studying those problems, but it is likely that the increased variation that the cross-national project entails makes possible much safer generalizations and, thus, more definite answers to the questions posed.

RESEARCH DESIGN

In a study like the one proposed in this chapter, different research designs are, of course, possible. Given three groups of countries with school entrance age of 5, 6, and 7 years respectively, and given the desire to test the reading development until the age of 9 years, there are three main types of design to choose among, viz., simple cross-sectional, modified cross-sectional, and longitudinal.

The simple cross-sectional design yields simultaneous measures of reading ability at different age levels. Certain inferences regarding the development of different reading skills can be drawn on the basis of these data, but no true measures of change will be obtained. The only advantage of this design is that the period of data collection is very short. The design yields results quickly but they are of limited value.

The modified cross-sectional design yields the same kind of data as the simple cross-sectional design, but it also yields measures of change over a 1-year period for each of the age levels concerned. Since one of the major objectives of the proposed study is to study the development of reading ability, this is a very important design feature. A study with this design will take 1 year more to complete than would a simple cross-sectional study.

The longitudinal design yields, as do the two other designs, data regarding the status of reading skills at different age levels. But the longitudinal design also yields true measures of change over the whole age range that is of interest in the proposed study. When it comes to describing the development of reading skills this design must, therefore, be considered superior to the others. However, data collection will have to be extended over a 5-year period. Comparing the longitudinal design (LG) and the modified cross-sectional design (MCS), one may conclude that:

1. The LG design can be expected to yield data that are more adequate in view of the objectives of the study
2. The costs of the LG design will not exceed those of the alternative design
3. The LG design will lead to a delay in obtaining final results of less than 2 years

In view of the above conclusions the longitudinal design is recommended for the study proposed.

THE SELECTION OF COUNTRIES
FOR PARTICIPATION IN THE PROJECT

In the selection of countries for participation in the cross-national project, two partly conflicting objectives must be realized. On the one hand, it is desirable that the variation between countries should be increased as much as possible (in order to get the maximum out of the cross-national approach). On the other hand, the full range of international differences is so enormous that it is hardly possible to cope with it in a single project. Therefore, the selection of countries will have to be restricted in certain respects. The cross-national variation in the proposed study should be restricted in terms of the character of the countries' national languages and their levels of literacy.

To avoid the extreme difficulties involved in comparing reading instruction in languages with different types of writing systems, the study should be restricted to languages using an alphabetic system. Regarding the level of literacy, the problems of developing nations with high illiteracy rates require separate study; therefore this study should be restricted to countries with a high level of literacy and well-established traditions of elementary schooling for all children. It is particularly important that participating countries represent different categories such as age of children at school entrance and degree of letter-sound correspondence in their language. It is also desirable that a wide range of differences regarding methods of primary reading instruction be included in the study.

SAMPLING OF CHILDREN WITHIN COUNTRIES

The number of children involved in the study will depend upon whether the longitudinal or the modified cross-sectional design is chosen. For a longitudinal study one sample of children entering school is needed for each participating country. For a modified cross-national design several samples are needed for each country: four samples if the school entrance age is 5 years, three if it is 6 years, and two if it is 7 years. Each of those samples, however, should be of the same size and the same principles of sampling should be followed in both designs. The following observations are therefore valid regardless of which of the two designs is chosen. First, it has to be decided whether samples should be nationally representative, i.e., represent each country as a whole, or whether the *representative-regions approach* should be preferred; i.e., sampling should be restricted to a geographically compact and reasonable representative region within each country. In view of the difficulties of sampling and testing on a national level, especially in large countries, the representative regions approach is recommended.

There is also the problem of whether entire school classes or individual children should be sampled. Both procedures have their advantages and disadvantages. Administratively, class sampling is much simpler than individual sampling. Since children are usually instructed in school class units, it may also be argued that this is the natural unit of sampling corresponding to one degree of freedom in the statistical analysis of differences between subpopulations, e.g., countries. Individual sampling has the chief advantage of permitting strict random sampling from a given population of children, regardless of how these children are distributed in different schools, classes, etc.

The size of national samples of children can, of course, be determined only after consultations with representatives of the participating countries. As in all research based on the study of samples there must, however, exist some minimum size of samples that must be attained in order to keep the error variance at an acceptable level. The minimum sample size within a country participating in the study should include not less than 30 classes. This minimum sample size can be considered acceptable if the variations within a country (or its sampling region) regarding the methods of primary reading instruction are small or moderate. If a national sample has to cover a greater variation of instructional methods, it may be necessary to include a considerably larger number of classes, since it is desirable that each method be represented by several classes.

EQUIVALENT TESTS IN DIFFERENT LANGUAGES

Besides all the problems one encounters in any effort to evaluate the product of elementary reading instruction, one is here confronted with the problems of linguistic differences between the samples of children studied, or, to be more exact, with the problems of a complex set of linguistic and cultural differences between samples. The objectives of the proposed study call for the construction of sets of tests that are in different languages but still equivalent to the various gradients of difficulty, such as content, concepts, number of high frequency words, word or morpheme length, sentence or clause length, spelling regularity, and syntax (cf. Bormuth, 1970; Henry & Grisay, 1972). Equivalent versions in different languages may be obtained by means of a translation of a set of tests from one language to the other, or such versions may be obtained through parallel construction of tests for each language. It has been suggested that the parallel construction approach is more likely to yield tests of acceptable equivalence. It is also possible that a combination of approaches may prove feasible, or that different approaches may be used for different types of tests. If translation is used, it is vital that the character of texts for reading tests is not unduly influenced by one of the languages included in the study or by the cultural sphere connected with a certain language. A means of circumventing this difficulty might be to choose basic texts written in a language that is not included in the study. In that way all texts used in tests would be translations from a foreign language.

TYPES OF TESTS AND TESTING PROCEDURES

The choice of test types and testing procedures may to some extent depend on the overall design and organization of the study, and, of course, on the economic resources available. If entire classes (or corresponding groups of children) are sampled, it will be most economical to use group tests as much as possible, and test individually only such skills as oral reading that cannot be tested in groups of children. If samples of children are large, it may prove too expensive to test all of them individually. In that case it would seem advisable to administer group tests to all children and to select random subsamples within each class and test those subsamples individually in oral reading, etc. To obtain fairly accurate measures of the level and distribution of skills in each class, such subsamples should include at least 25% of the children.

Exactly what types of tests will be included in the study cannot be determined at this stage, but the main areas of testing within the project may be listed tentatively. They are:

1. School and reading readiness (e.g., such factors as language development, visual and auditory perception, and visual-motor coordination)
2. Fundamental reading skills connected with decoding (e.g., word attack skills, letter-sound correspondences, letter identification, etc.)
3. Oral reading skills (e.g., such factors as accuracy, speed, types of errors)
4. Reading comprehension skills (e.g., ability to extract information from texts, to summarize texts, and to follow written instructions)
5. Spoken language abilities (e.g., listening comprehension)

DATA COLLECTION THROUGH QUESTIONNAIRES

Several types of data needed for the purposes of the proposed study are to be collected by means of questionnaires. In the construction of these questionnaires one will meet with problems of equivalence between countries and language areas similar to those encountered in the field of test construction. Naturally the translation approach will have to be used rather than the parallel construction approach, but even so a number of problems remain. Chief among these is probably the lack of an internationally accepted terminology of education. In some cases the problem is even greater, since this lack reflects a lack of nationally accepted terminologies. The construction of questionnaires may therefore have to be preceded by a comparative study of the terminology related to primary reading in the countries concerned.

It is not possible to state at this stage exactly what kind of questionnaires will be needed, but it can be foreseen that the following ones will be required:

1. Questionnaire to national, regional, or local school authorities regarding the organization and resources of primary reading instruction, provisions for remedial instruction, etc.
2. Questionnaire to teachers of the classes sampled regarding methods and materials of instruction actually employed and the teachers' attitudes toward selected issues of reading and reading instruction
3. Questionnaire to parents of children sampled regarding the child's home environment, his educational experiences before entering school, etc.

COLLECTION OF PRINTED MATERIALS

Closely related to the collection of data by means of questionnaires is the collection of printed materials relevant to the proposed project. Problems of equivalence between countries do not arise in this collection process, since the objective is to collect such relevant materials that exist within each country. There may, of course, be problems of terminological differences involved in the interpretation of the materials collected. Different types of materials will have to be collected. The main types are:

1. Official documents containing regulations, statements, etc. concerning primary reading
2. Instructional materials and tests used in the classes sampled

Official documents are an important complement to the responses to questionnaires addressed to school authorities. It should in many cases be possible to obtain information regarding the objectives and methods of instruction through the analysis of such documents. The analysis of such documents can also be a reliable means of determining whether or not national differences exist. The question of school entrance age is an example of this. In many countries compulsory schooling starts at the age of 6 years. Still, it is possible that these countries differ as to the mean age of the beginners. They may also have quite different policies regarding the treatment of children whose school readiness is not considered normal. And the possibilities of letting a child start school before the stipulated age could vary. In other words, only a careful analysis of the regulations pertaining to the school start can reveal all the existing differences between countries.

The collection of instructional materials is mainly intended as a complement to the teachers' questionnaire responses regarding their use of methods and materials of elementary reading instruction. In view of the somewhat confused terminology in this field and the lack of clear definitions of the methods used, it is possible that teacher responses of this kind may be misleading, in spite of the efforts that are made to remove ambiguities of terms and concepts. In such cases a direct analysis of the reading materials and the teacher manuals can provide a valuable check on the questionnaire responses.

Reading tests used in the participating countries will, of course, be collected during the pilot phase of the project, but it will be useful to obtain data regarding tests actually used in the classes sampled for evaluation purposes. Analyses of tests used in the classes can give information about the objectives of reading instruction and the priorities attached to different objectives (assuming that the choice of test items reflects the objectives rather than the availability of this or that type of test).

Section III
READING PROCESSES
Initial Stages

Chapter 10

ORTHOGRAPHY AND THE BEGINNING READER

Isabelle Liberman, Alvin M. Liberman,
Ignatius Mattingly, and *Donald Shankweiler*

Most of our research has been concerned with the processes and problems that occur in the beginning reader. It divides quite naturally into two parts. One deals with the importance to the reader of having some degree of sophistication about the linguistic structures that the orthography represents, and with the difficulty that attends the development of such sophistication in many beginners. While the importance of that sophistication is fixed, the difficulty of achieving it ought to vary greatly with the nature of the orthography and also, although perhaps less obviously, with the relation of the orthography to certain characteristics of the language. The other part of our research has to do with the importance to the reader of recovering a phonological representation of the language that he reads, especially for the purpose of meeting the short-term memory requirements that language imposes on those who would store the words long enough to understand the sentence. Since all languages impose that requirement—the meaning of a sentence is always distributed among the several words it comprises—we should expect that the results we have obtained with English would apply universally, but it remains to be determined whether, in fact, they do.

LINGUISTIC SOPHISTICATION:
PROBLEMS OF THE BEGINNING READER
THAT MAY VARY ACROSS LANGUAGES AND ORTHOGRAPHIES

The point of departure for our earliest research on the tribulations of the beginning reader was the assumption that we were, after all, asking him to do something quite unnatural. That assumption appeared obvious to us, if only because reading and writing seem rather far removed from their biological roots in the universals of language. We know that reading and writing appear late in the history of humankind, just as they do in the development of the individual; and also that there is considerable variation among orthographies in the nature and size of the linguistic units (phonemes, morphophonemes, syllables, moras, morphemes) they represent. We therefore supposed that the (less natural) processes of reading and writing would need to be more deliberate than the (more natural) processes of listening and speaking. In particular, we put our attention on the possibility that, in contrast to the listener and speaker, the reader and writer must be a kind of linguist. The largely tacit command of language that serves the nonlinguist, when, in speaking and listening, utterances roll trippingly off his tongue or pass readily into his comprehension, is not sufficient for the reader and writer; like the linguist, he requires a greater degree of sophistication about linguistic structures, including, in particular, those that are represented by the orthography he reads or writes (I. Y. Liberman, 1971, 1973; I. Y. Liberman, Shankweiler, A. M. Liberman, Fowler, & Fischer, 1977; Mattingly, 1972).

The sophistication that is required has two aspects, corresponding approximately to two aspects of the way an orthography represents speech. The first, *phonological maturity,* has to do with the often abstract but nonetheless regular nature of the link between the orthography and the phonetic (or phonemic) structures it conveys. In English, for example, the spellings of words such as *telegraph, telegraphy,* and *telegraphic* are irregular except as the reader comprehends the (morpho-)phonological rules that rationalize them. Phonological maturity is, as in the case just cited, of some importance to the beginning reader, although it is not crucial. More important by far is an explicit understanding by the reader of the relation in segmentation between the orthography and speech. It is patent that an alphabet can be used properly only if the reader (and especially the beginner) is quite aware that speech is divisible into those phonological segments that the letters represent. This aspect of sophistication about language is referred to as *linguistic awareness* (I. Y. Liberman, 1971, 1973; Mattingly, 1972).

The Role of Phonological Maturity in Learning to Read

A reader is able to recognize a written word because he can equate it with some representation of that word stored in long-term memory. This stored representation is linguistic, and an orthography appeals to the reader's appreciation of the grammatical structure of utterances. Specifically, Chomsky's (1970a) argument states that the orthographic transcription of a word corresponds approximately to the way generative phonologists assume the word is represented in the ideal speaker-hearer's mental lexicon. This representation is often morphophonological: the word is conveyed as a sequence of systematic phonemes divided into its constituent morphemes. For example, the words *heal, health, healthful,* have the morphophonological representations[1], /hēl/, /hēl + θ/, /hēl + θ + ful/, respectively.

---

[1]Chomsky refers to this form as the *lexical representation.* But since we wish to consider later whether this or some other representation is the actual basis of lexical lookup, and so deserves to be called *the* lexical representation, we use the neutral and descriptive term *morphophonological representation* instead.

The morphophonological representation of a word is quite distinct from its phonetic representation, that is, from what the speaker-hearer thinks he pronounces and perceives. In the phonetic representation, *heal* and *health* are realized, approximately, as [hīyl] and [helθ]. Notice that in the phonetic representation, the underlying morphophonological forms are to a considerable extent disguised, and explicit morpheme boundaries are absent. Moreover, the same morpheme has various phonetic representations depending upon the phonological context (Chomsky & Halle, 1968).

Clearly, the transcriptions of *heal* and *health* in English orthography approximate the morphophonological representations rather than the phonetic. The orthographic forms differ from the morphophonological representations only in the omission of morpheme boundaries and in the conventional substitutions of *ea* for /e/ and *th* for /θ/.

Chomsky's argument about the morphophonological nature of orthographies applies, of course, to logographic and syllabary scripts as well as to alphabetic scripts. Since English is written alphabetically, a distinct symbol is used for each of the distinct systematic phonemes: /h/, /ē/, /l/, and so on. If English were written logographically, a distinct symbol would be used for each of the morphemes /hēl/, /θ/, /ful/; and, if it were written in a syllabary, a distinct symbol would be used for each of the syllables /hēl/, /hēl + θ/, /ful/. But in all cases, the morphophonological representations would be transcribed.

An orthography makes the assumption that readers know, tacitly, the phonology of the language, so the representation of words in their personal lexicon matches the transcriptions of the orthography. In the example, English speakers have the morphophonological representations /hēl/ and /hēl + θ/ in their lexicons, and not [hīyl] and [helθ]. In the course of acquiring English, they have mastered the morphophonological rules, and have inferred that [hīyl] and [helθ] can both be derived from /hēl/, /θ/ being a separate morpheme.

Thus, to the extent that English is written morphophonologically, and then to that extent it assumes an ideal reader, who commands the grammatical rules in terms of which spelling makes sense. That is, it assumes a reader who has achieved phonological maturity. To a reader who lacks that maturity, the linguistic regularities that justify the orthography are simply opaque, and the spellings can only appear exceptional.

Research by various psycholinguists indicates that young children are, in fact, quite immature phonologically, hence they are not well equipped to take maximum advantage of the morphophonological aspects of English orthography. Rather, they appear, as speaker-hearers, to learn enough to permit pragmatic communication and only later, if at all, to approach the phonological competence of the ideal speaker-hearer (Berko, 1958; Moskowitz, 1973; Read, 1975). Moreover, there is evidence that, given free rein to spell as they will, such children tend to be better as phoneticians than they are as phonologists (Read, 1975; Zifcak, 1977). If so, and if, indeed, a morpho-phonological orthography is, as some claim, the best one for adults, then English puts the child at odds with the adult.

It is fortunate, therefore, that, while phonological maturity may be of some importance in reading, it is, in no sense, critical. That is, it appears that children who are more at home with a phonetic structure than with a morphophonological one can, nevertheless, learn to read. At all events, their problem could certainly be minimized by controlling the vocabulary used in early reading instruction. Moreover, informal observation and some experimental evidence suggest that the experience of reading itself serves to stimulate phonological development. Thus, Moskowitz (1973) has shown that a by-product of learning to read is that the child is led to acquire the Vowel Shift rule.

Children who profit from the linguistic stimulation of reading, internalizing the phonological rules they induce from orthographic transcription, and accordingly revising the representations of words in their lexicon to make them more nearly morphophonological, are the sort who continue the process of language acquisition far beyond the pragmatic level. Obviously, they cannot do this except as they read analytically, that is, with attention to the relation between the internal structure of the printed word and the phonology of the spoken word. But, given that strategy, they are likely to become more competent users of their language and also superior readers.

The Role of Linguistic Awareness in Learning to Read

So much, then, for the difference between a morphophonological representation and a phonetic one, and for the phonological maturity that enables a sophisticated reader to bridge the gap. We turn now from that gap to one that yawns equally wide and presents a much greater hazard for the beginning reader. For if orthographies are morphophonological rather than phonetic; they are *a fortiori,* not acoustic or auditory. Although closer to the speech signal, the phonetic representation is far from isomorphic with it. To bridge the gap between the phonetic level and sound, the reader must have linguistic awareness. To see just what that is, and why it might be hard to achieve, we should consider first one of the peculiar complications that characterizes the relation between phonetic structures and their acoustic vehicles.

Given the way speakers articulate and coarticulate, the segments of the phonetic structure do not correspond in any direct way to the segments of the sound. Thus, a word like *dog* that has three phonological (and ortho-graphic) segments has only one isolable segment of sound (A. M. Liberman, Cooper, Shankweiler, & Studdert-Kennedy, 1967). The information for the three phonological segments is there, but so thoroughly overlapped (encoded) in the sound that there is no way to divide the sound into segments so that each acoustic segment carries information about only one phonetic segment. Nor is the opposite possible. That is, one cannot begin with prerecorded sounds for each of the three segments that are written as *d, o,* and *g* and in any way put them together to form the word /dɔg/. An obvious consequence is that many of the segments—in particular, many consonants—cannot be produced in isolation, as syllables and words can; hence these segments might be expected to have little salience and to escape the conscious awareness of the ordinary user of the language.

This characteristic of speech offers no obstacle to the listener, because all speaker-hearers of a language, even very young children, are presumably provided with a neurophysiology that functions quite automatically, that is, below the level of awareness, to extract phonetic structure from the continuous acoustic signal in which it is so peculiarly encoded (A. M. Liberman et al., 1967). To understand a spoken utterance, therefore, the child need not be explicitly aware of its phonetic structure any more than he need be aware of its syntax. But that explicit awareness of phonetic structure is precisely what is required if the beginning reader is to take full advantage of an alphabetic system of writing.

Returning to our example of the word *dog,* consider the child who, knowing the word, sees it in its printed form for the first time. In mapping the three letters onto the word he already knows, it will avail him little to be able to recognize the three letters and to sound them out. He must also be consciously aware that the word he knows has three phonetic segments. Without that awareness, and given the impossibility of producing the phonetic segments in isolation, the best the child can do is to say something like [də] [ɔ] [gə], thus producing a nonsense trisyllable that bears no certain relationship to the word /dɔg/.

Indeed, neither the child nor any other reader can recover speech from print on a letter-by-letter basis. Rather, he must group the letters so as to have put together just those strings of phonetic segments that are, in the normal processes of speech production, collapsed into a single coding unit. (A syllable is sometimes thought to be such a unit.) But there is no simple rule by which a reader can do this. The properly speakable unit may comprise almost any number of letters from one to nine or, at the level of prosody, even more. We suspect that acquiring the ability to do this, that is, knowing how to combine the letters into units appropriate for speech, is an aspect of reading skill that, as much as any other, separates the fluent reader from the beginner who has only just succeeded in discovering what an alphabetic orthography is all about (I. Y. Liberman et al., 1977).

Considerations of the kind we have just reviewed led us to suppose that linguistic awareness—awareness of the phoneme in the case of an alphabet—might be difficult for young children, but also important if they are to become readers.

Development of Linguistic Awareness: Some Experiments

Given the way most consonant phones are encoded in the sound, it is not possible to produce them in isolation.[2] But syllables can be so produced. (Vowels can, of course, be treated as if they were syllables.) We should suppose, then, that it might be easier for the child to become aware of syllables than of phonemes.[3] Indeed, more generally, this difference may account for a fact about the history of writing systems, to wit, that syllabaries appear early and as a result of several quite independent developments, in contrast to an alphabet, which appears later and only once. Looked at this way, the alphabet can be seen as a triumph of applied linguistics, a cognitive achievement by the race. Is it so for the child, too? Experimental studies designed to compare the development in the child of awareness about syllables and phonemes have been carried out.

The object of the first experiment (I. Y. Liberman, Shankweiler, Fischer, & Carter, 1974) was to compare the ability of children in nursery school, kindergarten, and first grade (4-, 5-, and 6-year-olds) to count the phonemes in spoken utterances with the ability of matched groups of children to count syllables. The procedure was in the form of a game that required the child to repeat a word spoken by the experimenter and then to indicate, by tapping a wooden dowel on the table, the number of segments in the word. In order to teach the child what was expected of him, the test list was preceded by a series of demonstration trials. The test proper consisted of randomly assorted items of one, two, or three segments, presented without prior demonstration and corrected, as needed, immediately after the child's response. Testing continued until the child reached a criterion of tapping six consecutive items correctly, or until the end of the list.

It was immediately apparent from this experiment that syllables were more readily counted than phonemes. The number of children who reached

---

[2]This circumstance presents a hazard for anyone who has to teach beginners to read an alphabetic orthography. Given the impossibility of producing many consonants in isolation, how does the teacher help the child to identify the linguistic units that the orthography represents? If the teacher sounds out the consonants by coarticulating them with the neutral vowel [ə], a very common strategy, he runs the risk of confusing the child, for surely the syllable that results is inappropriate for almost all of the contexts in which the consonant will be represented in printed text. Possible ways around this difficulty have been discussed in detail elsewhere (I. Y. Liberman & Shankweiler, in press; I. Y. Liberman, Shankweiler, Camp, Heifetz, & Werfelman, 1977).

[3]We should note that other investigators besides ourselves have remarked on the difficulty of becoming aware of the phonemic segment, and also on the possibility that this might be a problem in learning to read. Among these are Calfee, Chapman, & Venezky, 1972; Downing, 1973a; Elkonin, 1973; Gibson & Levin, 1975; Gleitman & Rozin, 1977; Rosner & Simon, 1971; Rozin & Gleitman, 1977; Savin, 1972; Vellutino, 1977.

criterion was markedly greater in the syllable group, whatever the grade level. None of the nursery school children and only 17% of the kindergarteners could count phonemes, while 46% of the nursery school children and 48% of the kindergarteners could count syllables. The first graders performed much better on both tasks, but only 70% could count phonemes while 90% were successful with syllables. Similar results have been found with different subject populations in two other investigations by our research group (Treiman, 1976; Zifcak, 1977). At this point, suffice it to say that in all these studies it was found that explicit analysis of spoken utterances into phonemes is significantly more difficult for the young child than analysis into syllables, and it develops later.

Although awareness of syllables was found to be greater for young children than awareness of phonemes, it was also true that both increased over age, with the steepest increase occurring in the 6-year-olds. As it happens, that is the age at which the children in our schools begin to receive instruction in reading and writing. The question immediately arises whether these measured increases represent maturational changes or the effects of experience in learning to read. Whatever the effects of instruction, our findings strongly suggest that a higher level of linguistic awareness is necessary to achieve the ability to analyze words into phonemes than into syllables (see also Baron & Treiman, chapter 12, this volume).

Linguistic Awareness and Success in Learning to Read

The argument that linguistic awareness is an important condition for reading has been based thus far on an appeal to sweet reason: that a reader must have explicit knowledge of (at least) the linguistic units that the orthography represents, else he cannot read properly. We should now consider two such other bases of support, both empirical in nature, that the argument may have. One has to do with the actual correlation between awareness of segments and success in reading, and also with the possibility that this correlation reflects a causal connection of some kind. The other deals with tests of the correspondence between the errors that beginning readers make, and those we should expect them to make, given the assumption that they are caused in significant measure by the lack of linguistic awareness as revealed by the studies reported in the previous section.

Correlational Studies   Recall, now, the gross correlation between the spurt in awareness of phonemic segmentation and the onset of reading instruction. One interpretation of that correlation is, of course, that both are related to age but not to each other. In this connection, we do indeed suspect that age is important for linguistic awareness *and* reading because, being cognitive achievements of sorts, both must require the attainment of some level of intellectual maturity. But, as has been so often implied, it is also suspected that the relation between the two is causal, although in a reciprocal way: the awareness is important for the acquisition of reading; at the same time, being taught to read helps to develop the awareness.

Consider, first, the possibility that linguistic awareness is necessary for reading. Obviously, we should like to be able to report the results of experiments which show, other things equal, the effects on reading achievement of various kinds of training in awareness of segmentation. Unfortunately, no carefully controlled studies of that kind have been completed, or, at least, none that we know of. Such data are only correlational, but they are, nevertheless, encouraging.

We were motivated to initiate the correlational studies by a rough check of the reading achievement of the group of first graders who had taken part in our experiment on phoneme counting. Testing them at the beginning of their second school year, we found that there had been no failures in phoneme counting among the children who now scored in the top third of the class in reading; in contrast, one-half of the children who tested in the lowest third of the class in reading achievement had failed in the phoneme counting task the previous year (I. Y. Liberman et al., 1977).

Three subsequent studies by our research group (Helfgott, 1976; Treiman, 1976; Zifcak, 1977) have now substantiated these results. The consistency of positive findings in all these correlational studies, despite widely diverse subject populations, school systems, and measurement devices, gives us confidence that there is, at least, a correlation between awareness of segmentation and success in learning to read.

What, then, of the possibility that instruction in reading is important in the development of linguistic awareness? Morais, Cary, Alegria, and Bertelson (1978) took advantage of a kind of experiment created by particular conditions of life in Portugal. There, they were able to compare awareness of phonemic segmentation in two groups of reasonably matched adults: one illiterate, the other literate. The finding was that the illiterates failed the awareness test and the literate subjects passed, from which the investigators concluded that awareness of phonemic segmentation does not develop independently of instruction in reading. Assuming the generality of that conclusion, we are encouraged to believe that the connection between awareness and reading is not accidental.

Analysis of Error Patterns   It has seemed reasonable to us that the errors a beginning reader makes might enlighten us about his problems, including those that pertain to linguistic awareness, so we have conducted studies designed to make the appropriate observations (Shankweiler & I. Y. Liberman, 1976; Fowler, I. Y. Liberman, & Shankweiler, 1977; Fowler, Shankweiler, & I. Y. Liberman, in press). The study by Fowler et al. (1977) is more directly relevant to our assumption about the relation between linguistic awareness and reading.

In that study, second, third, and fourth graders were asked to read aloud from lists of monosyllabic words in which the position (within the word) of consonant and vowel letters was systematically varied. The children's errors were noted and examined, with particular attention to the effect of position on the likelihood that a particular segment would be misread. A clear pattern emerged. Consonants in the final position were consistently misread about twice as often as those in initial position. Although the frequency of all consonant errors dropped markedly from the second through the fourth grade, a 2:1 ratio of errors on final and initial consonants was maintained. Vowels yielded a very different result in that errors were independent of position, and that, too, was found in all three grades.

We can hardly claim that the pattern of errors just described falls inevitably out of our hypothesis about linguistic awareness, but we can see that the pattern and the hypothesis are, nevertheless, nicely consistent. Consider the fact that initial consonant errors are less frequent than final consonant errors, and assume a child who does not explicitly understand the segmentation of the words he speaks. Being able to recognize the letters, and knowing (presumably) that he should go from left to right, he begins with the initial consonant. But, lacking the ability to be sufficiently aware of the segmental structure of the word, and failing, therefore, to appreciate its relation to the structure of its orthographic representation, he cannot properly link the initial consonant to the segment represented by the letter that follows. What he often does then is to produce a word that has the same initial consonant but otherwise bears no particular resemblance to the word he is trying to read. Thus, given the word *dog,* he might say [dʌmp]. That procedure will give him a relatively high score on initial consonants, but a low score on succeeding ones.

Consider the opposite findings with vowels: errors were independent of position in the syllable. That, too, makes some sense in terms of our hypothesis. Recall that children find it relatively easy to count spoken syllables, presumably because the syllable (usually) has a vocalic nucleus and a corresponding peak of perceived loudness. Of course, a vowel is the essential part of the vocalic nucleus, and, for that reason, a vowel can be a syllable (as most consonants cannot); hence it can be produced in isolation. It should not be surprising, then, that such difficulty that the child might have with the vowels would not depend on their locations.

Two other results of the error studies are briefly described, although their relevance (if any) to linguistic awareness and its role in reading is uncertain. One of these, and the one that appears to be the less relevant, was that the consonant errors tended significantly to take the form of incorrect assignment of one segmental feature; that did not appear to be the case with the vowels. The other result was that the vowel errors were more numerous than the consonant errors by a considerable margin. That result lends itself to many possible interpretations, some of them interesting from our point of view and some not. Thus, we must consider that the most egregious irregularities of English spelling seem to be concentrated in the vowels, as in *precede* and *proceed*. But some of the regular phonological alternations lie there too, for example, *heal–health,* and beginning readers may lack knowledge, either explicit or tacit, of these. Finally, there is the possibility at least that vowels cause more trouble because, when produced (and perceived) in isolation, they are less nearly categorical than consonants (A. M. Liberman et al., 1967). To decide among these interpretations will require a great deal more research.

So much, then, for the relation between the pattern of errors in the beginning reader and our hypothesis about the importance, in reading, of a conscious awareness of at least some aspects of linguistic structure. The results of the error analysis emphatically support a hypothesis more general than, and basic to, the analysis about linguistic awareness, namely, that the problems of the beginning reader are primarily cognitive and linguistic, not visual or perceptual. Note the consistency with which the children's errors distinguish consonants and vowels: errors on consonants, but not on vowels, depend on position in the syllable; errors on consonants, but not on vowels, tend to be by segmental feature; and finally, errors on consonants are, by far, the less numerous. It is hard to see how such findings can be accounted for on the assumption that the child is having difficulty in the visual or, more broadly, perceptual sphere. Although we may have less than perfect confidence that our finger has pointed to the exact sources of the difficulty, we can be reasonably sure that, being oriented toward cognition and language, it is, at least, aimed in the right direction.

The Interaction of Phonological Maturity and
Linguistic Awareness with the Nature of the Language and the Orthography

Orthographies vary considerably in the demands they make on the beginning reader. This variation has two essentially independent aspects: first, the depth of the orthography, its relative remoteness from the phonetic representation; and second, the particular linguistic unit—morpheme, syllable, or phoneme—that is overtly represented. A deep orthography, like that of English, demands greater phonological development on the reader's part than a shallow orthography, like that of Vietnamese. Logographies (such as the Chinese writing system), syllabaries (such as Old Persian cuneiform), and alphabetic systems (such as English) demand successively increasing degrees of linguistic awareness. Neither sort of orthographic variation is to be attributed to historical accident alone: the structure of the language, and perhaps political and social factors, are typically involved. Moreover, advantages for the beginning reader with respect to the phonological maturity or linguistic awareness demanded are often offset by disadvantages of other kinds.

Orthographic depth depends upon two variables: the depth of the morphophonological representation itself and the degree to which the orthography approximates this representation. If the morphophonological representation is quite close to the phonetic representation, the orthography will, of course, be close as well. The reader needs to know little phonology because there is little phonology to be known. This seems to be the case not only with Vietnamese but also with Turkish and many other languages. In the case of Turkish, the orthography is even shallower than the morphophonological representation because the alternations determined by the Vowel Harmony rule (which is about all there is to Turkish phonology) are nevertheless transcribed in the orthography. It can be argued that this is not unreasonable because there are numerous borrowed words that are not subject to Vowel Harmony (A. Kardestuncer, personal communication). (By contrast, English orthography transcribes the underlying forms of vowel-shifted words, despite a great many borrowed words that are not subject to Vowel Shift). The orthographies of languages with limited phonologies ought, in general, to be easy for the beginner.

If the morphophonological representation of language is relatively deep, various compromises with the ideal may be observed in its orthography; in particular, phonologically predictable alternations may be explicitly indicated. Examples from English orthography have already been given. In Sanskrit, the alternations between aspirated and unaspirated stops (Grassman's law) are transcribed. In Spanish, infinitives are transcribed without the underlying, phonologically deleted, final /e/ of the morphophonological representation, e.g., /decire/, "to say," is written *decir* (Harris, 1969). In this respect, as in many others, French orthography, which has *dire,* is closer to the morphophonological representation. The orthography of Spanish, on the other hand, has a surface regularity that accounts in part for its reputation as an easy language among American secondary school students. If a language has an exceptionally deep phonology, it may well be the case that few native speakers actually control very much of it. It is reported that when a morphophonological orthography was devised for Mohawk, native speakers could not learn to use it, and a much shallower orthography had to be substituted (M. Mithune, personal communication).

To make clear that the depth of the orthography is independent of the unit of representation, it may be pointed out that the kana symbols of the hiragana syllabary used for Japanese represent morphophonological syllables, that is, moras. Thus, the kana for a syllable beginning with a voiceless stop is used even when the stop occurs in noninitial position, and so becomes voiced by phonological rule. Moreover, a two-mora sequence, e.g., *su ku,* will be transcribed with two kanas even though, in colloquial speech, it will often be realized phonetically as [sku]. Thus, the kana, which are usually learned by Japanese children by the time they enter school (Sakamoto, chapter 1, this volume) require at least a modest degree of phonological maturity. As for linguistic awareness, we should wonder whether moras or phonetic syllables are more readily available.

Languages with deep morphophonological representations appear to put the phonologically immature learner at odds with the more experienced and phonologically more mature reader. An orthography practical for the former may be cumbersome for the latter. But if we are correct in our emphasis on the contribution of reading to phonological maturity, a shallower orthography may reduce the reader's opportunities for learning more about his language.

We turn now to the advantages and disadvantages of transcribing linguistic units other than phonemes. In the case of Chinese writing, the use of a morphemic transcription has a number of advantages. The most obvious, from our point of view, is that it presumably makes minimal demands on linguistic awareness, for, to the extent that morphemes can be produced in isolation, they are salient and readily available to consciousness. In this connection, we should wonder if some difficulties nevertheless arise whenever the phonology makes more abstract the basis for recognizing morphemic identity across words. At all events, the availability of the units is not the only advantage. The various dialects of Chinese can use the same writing system, even though they have developed independently to such an extent that the systematic phonemic representation of a given morpheme will, in general, differ from dialect to dialect. Since the morphemes are, in general, monosyllabic, and since constraints on syllable structure permit only some 1,200 phonemically distinct syllables, a syllabary or an alphabetic system would entail substantial homography; this is avoided by the use of a logography. The price, obviously, is that the learner must devote several years to memorizing two or three thousand characters. Having acquired this basic stock, however, he can read a great many more words, since compounding is the basic method of word formation: Chinese content-words are ordinarily bimorphemic (Martin, 1972). In regularly written Japanese text, the kanji logograms are used for roots and the hiragana only for affixes. Thus the Japanese child, like the Chinese child, must devote years to the memorization of characters. The use of kanji, it is said, serves to avoid the homography that would result from a syllabic or phonemic transcription of an almost intolerably homonymic language. The kanji themselves, however, are typically homographic (Martin, 1972).

Syllabary systems are best suited for languages in which the number of possible syllables is small, as in the case of Old Persian, Hittite, and the classical Semitic languages (Gelb, 1963). Semitic had the further advantage that its root morphemes, which were relatively few in number, had the patterns C__C__ or C__C__C__, the intervening vowels carrying only inflectional and derivational information. In the Semitic syllabaries, each symbol stood for any one of the set of CV syllables beginning with a particular consonant. Thus an inventory of only 22 symbols was required, yet a word could be transcribed by only two or three symbols. This resulted in an extremely compact transcription that did not require the reader to be aware of phonemes. But, of course, he had to guess which of the many inflectional and derivational forms of each word was intended and this must have required both control of the complex morphology of Semitic and a keen awareness of it. Evidently this burden was not always endurable, since the practice of using supplementary symbols to disambiguate vowel quality arose early (Gelb, 1963).

From these examples, we might conclude that syllabaries and logographies are realistic possibilities only under rather special linguistic circumstances, and that, even then, the price may be high. For the modern Indo-European languages, which have fairly elaborate syllable structures, large and rather inefficiently exploited inventories of morphemes, and little homonymity, an alphabetic system is preferable, despite the requirement of a relatively greater degree of linguistic awareness.

PHONOLOGICAL RECODING: A PROBLEM OF THE BEGINNING READER THAT MAY BE MORE OR LESS INDEPENDENT OF LANGUAGE AND ORTHOGRAPHY

One of the advantages of the alphabetic writing system is that, in the ideal case, someone can read words he has never before seen. It is obvious, however, that one can do this only insofar as he is able to map the internal structure of the written word onto the segmental structure of the morphophonological representation of the spoken word he holds in his personal lexicon. This requires a degree of linguistic sophistication that many beginning readers do not have and find difficult to attain. If such beginners read at all, they must read holistically. If they do, there are two possibilities. They may be locating the lexical entry by recovering the morphophonological representation as if it were an arbitrary paired-associate of the orthographic transcription, just as the reader of a logographic system must do. Or they may be recovering some sort of semantic representation, attempting to go "directly to meaning." But if the latter is the case, then they stand to lose two advantages that the morphophonological representation affords the readers of all orthographies.

The first advantage relates to lexical lookup, the second to the interpretation of the sentence. It is important that the reader locate the lexical entry for the very word intended by the writer, so that the grammatical and semantic features peculiar to the word are available for subsequent sentence processing. Not everyone appears to concede this; there are some who seem to believe that readers do, or should, read the way aphasics are said to listen, relying heavily on a priori knowledge and common sense, and using the word in the text to narrow down the semantic possibilities a bit, or to suggest some semantically-related word. But if it is granted that the intended word is required, the morphophonological representation provides the most direct means of lexical lookup. Despite minor problems caused by homonymity, a search of the lexicon based on the morphophonological representation is rapid and self-terminating; either the word is there, properly specified, or it is not. This is obviously untrue of a search based on semantic information; how can the "semantic" reader know when he has found the most likely part of the conceptual forest or located the most plausible tree? It was exactly this difficulty that made picture-writing unsatisfactory. Is it also, perhaps, this difficulty that lies behind the tendency of some young readers, presumably those who do not recode phonologically, to land in the right semantic area but on the wrong word, as when, for example, on being shown the word *dog,* the child reads "cat."

Note also that, in listening, a normal nonaphasic person locates the lexical entry by what might seem rather a roundabout process: he recovers the phonetic representation by means of the mechanisms of speech perception, and then, either through analysis-by-synthesis, or, more likely, by using various shortcuts, determines what morphophonological representation would generate the phonetic representation consistent with the phonological rules he commands. Then he searches for the lexical entry that corresponds to this morphophonological representation. If Nature seems to find this cumbersome procedure preferable to "going directly to meaning" from the acoustic waveform, and has endowed us with the necessary special-purpose equipment to make the procedure workable in real time, it must be, in part, because of the virtues of the morphophonological representation as a means of locating a lexical entry.

In comparison with this account of the apparently complex processes that go on in understanding speech, the proposal that reading exploits morphophonological representations seems quite straightforward. And at any rate, since speech is prior to reading, the beginning reader has at his disposal a well-established and natural device for lexical lookup. Would it not be disadvantageous for him to set up an entirely new one, and unparsimonious for us to suppose that he must?

The second advantage of the morphophonological representation has to do with its relationship to the nature of the working memory that stores words long enough to permit the sentence they form to be interpreted. It is assumed that in the case of speech understanding, morphophonological representations are inferred in working memory from an input representation that is phonetic. It is an important and unsettled question, but one not relevant for our present purpose, whether, in reading, the working memory is essentially morphophonological, or whether a phonetic representation is generated as well even though it would appear to be redundant (Mattingly, 1972). What *is* relevant is whether, in reading as in speech, a working-memory representation, identical either with the morphophonological representation or with one of its phonetic derivatives, is used—a representation that is called, more for convenience than for precision, *phonological*.

In speculating about the working memory of a reader, we must consider that some nonphonological representation, visual or semantic, might be invoked. Surely, such a strategy is possible. Indeed, there is evidence that a visual representation is employed by some congenitally deaf readers, but, as with the matter of lexical lookup, we should suppose that its use is inadvisable.

There is evidence that, in the case of the normal adult, the nonphonological strategy is not very common. In some experiments (Baddeley, 1966, 1968, 1979; Conrad, 1964, 1972), where information was presented as printed letters, words, or syllables, it was consistently found that the confusions in recall were much greater when the items were phonologically similar than when the similarity was either visual or semantic. This suggests that the readers are storing the information phonologically, although it be disadvantageous to do so. Even when the information is presented in logographic form, strikingly parallel results are obtained. Here, some experiments used Japanese subjects reading the kanji (Erickson, Mattingly, & Turvey, 1973); others had to do with the reading of Chinese (Tzeng, Hung, & Wang, 1977). Finally, the strength of the tendency toward a phonological representation in working memory is underscored by the finding that even when the material presented is not linguistic at all, but pictorial, the information is nevertheless recoded into phonological form (Conrad, 1972). All these results support the idea that use of a phonological representation can be viewed as a generally appropriate strategy for holding linguistic information, however presented, in short-term store.

In view of the memory requirements of the reading task, and evidence for the normal involvement of a phonological representation in the service of that requirement, we were interested in learning whether those beginning readers who are progressing well and those who are doing poorly might be distinguished by the degree to which they rely on a phonological representation when working memory is stressed. We assumed that good beginning readers of an alphabetic orthography, having already related the printed word to the corresponding morphophonological representation, would have the word available for use in working memory in phonological form. Presumably, they would take advantage of that. As for the poor readers, we know that many have difficulty in going the analytic, phonological route and might tend, therefore, to forgo phonological strategies, relying more heavily, perhaps, on representations of a visual or semantic sort.

At all events, we thought it wise to determine whether, in fact, good and poor readers do differ in the degree to which they use a phonological representation in working memory. To that end, we carried out several experiments with children in the second year of elementary school. In the initial experiments (I. Y. Liberman et al., 1976) we borrowed a procedure devised by Conrad (1972) for adults in which the subject's performance is compared on recall of letters with phonologically confusable (rhyming) and nonconfusable (nonrhyming) names. Our expectation was that the rhyming items would generate confusions and thus penalize recall in subjects who use a phonological representation. Poor readers might then be expected to be less affected by the phonological similarity of the items than good readers, whether or not the groups differed in recall of the nonconfusable items.

The results showed that, although the superior readers were better at recall of the nonconfusable items, their advantage was virtually eliminated when the stimulus items were phonologically confusable. Phonological similarity always penalized the good readers more than the poor ones. A further experiment (Shankweiler & I. Y. Liberman, 1976) showed that it made practically no difference whether the items to be recalled were presented to the eye or to the ear. These results strongly suggest that the difference between good and poor readers in the recall of linguistic items will turn on their ability to use a phonological representation, whether derived from print or speech, and not merely on their ability to recode from print.

We might digress for a moment to ask whether the poor reader's problem may be a general deficit in short-term memory, or whether it is, indeed, a deficit specific to the processing of linguistic information. In a recent study directed to that question (I. Y. Liberman, Mark, & Shankweiler, 1978; I. Y. Liberman & Shankweiler, in press)[4] it was found that good and poor readers could not be distinguished on a recognition memory task employing photographed faces and abstract nonsense figures, but did differ significantly in their memory for nonsense syllables. This finding, and other existing evidence (see Vellutino, 1977, for a review), is consistent with the conclusion that the deficiencies of poor readers on memory tasks are limited to situations in which phonological representation can readily occur, either because the stimuli are linguistic items to begin with, or because they are objects to which verbal labels can readily be applied.

Returning, now, to the principal point, we should note that our original findings with letters apply to other linguistic materials and to other kinds of tasks closer to real reading situations. Two experiments speak to this matter. The first (Mark, Shankweiler, I. Y. Liberman, & Fowler, 1977)

---

[4]A full account of this study, which includes M. Werfelman as a co-author, is in preparation.

used rhyming and nonrhyming words instead of letters. It also had the advantage over the earlier study of a procedure that eliminated the possibility of differential rehearsal effects. Once again, the superior readers were much more strongly penalized by the confusable items than the poor readers.

In the second and more recent experiment, we have moved on to sentences. For this experiment we tested good and poor readers in recall of meaningful and semantically anomalous sentences, making a parallel comparison between conditions that did and did not offer the opportunity for phonological confusions to occur. A clear result of these new findings is that in recall of sentences, as with letters and words, good readers are much more affected than poor readers by phonological similarity.

There is, then, considerable support for the assertion that, for purposes of storing linguistic information in working memory, poor readers do not rely as much on a phonological strategy as good readers do. Given the effectiveness of the phonological strategy, and given that reading may put working memory under stress, especially in the beginner, we see that failure to use the phonology properly may be a cause, as well as a correlate, of poor reading.

The advantages of using phonological structures for short-term storage are independent of orthography and language. On that supposition, and given our results, we should anticipate that greater and lesser reliance on such structures might prove to be an important difference between good and poor readers everywhere.

Chapter 11
THE ROLE OF ORTHOGRAPHIC IMAGES IN LEARNING PRINTED WORDS

Linnea Ehri

One of the most important capabilities in learning to read is learning to recognize printed words. Research on beginning readers performed by Shankweiler and I. M. Liberman (1972) and by Firth (1972) reveals high correlations between the ability to identify printed words and skill in reading text. However, there is substantial disagreement about which skills and experiences contribute most to the word learning process. Some authorities stress letter-sound mapping skills (I. M. Liberman & Shankweiler, in press; Rozin & Gleitman, 1977). Others emphasize the importance of learning to recognize printed words rapidly and automatically (LaBerge & Samuels, 1974; Perfetti & Hogaboam, 1975; Perfetti & Lesgold, 1979). Still others proclaim the centrality of learning to recognize the meanings of printed words as they participate in larger sentence and story contexts (Goodman, 1972; Smith, 1973). We have attempted to integrate these components into a theory of printed word learning, referred to as word identity amalgamation theory (Ehri, 1978, in press). Rather than singling out one skill or experience, the theory makes room for the importance of several. The theory together with supportive evidence is reviewed in this chapter. The value of the theory is mainly heuristic at this point so it should not be construed as any fixed or final answer.

THEORY OF WORD IDENTITY AMALGAMATION

The most important capability to be acquired in learning to read is learning to recognize printed words accurately, rapidly, and also completely in the sense that all of a word's identities are apparent when the printed word is seen. Children already possess substantial linguistic competence with speech when they start learning to read. The major task facing them is to learn how to incorporate printed language into this existing knowledge. In English, the most perceptible and dependable units of printed language are *words,* not letters or sentences, so it is at a *lexical* level that beginners work at assimilating print to their existing linguistic knowledge.

The lexicon is conceptualized as a store of abstract word units having several different facets or identities. Every word has a *phonological* identity specifying the word's acoustic, articulatory, and phonemic structure. Every word has a *syntactic* identity indicating characteristic grammatical functions of the word in sentences (i.e., noun, verb, adjective, determiner, etc.). And most words have a *semantic* identity, which specifies the word's meaning in various contexts. These identities are acquired and known implicitly by children when they learn to speak. In the course of learning to read, another identity is added to the lexicon, the word's *orthographic* form, which gets established in memory as a visual image. The term *amalgamation* refers to processes by which this orthographic identity merges with the word's other identities to form a single unit in lexical memory.

Orthographic images are acquired not as rotely memorized visual figures but as sequences of letters bearing systematic relationships to acoustic or articulatory segments already stored in lexical memory. The word's orthographic form is secured to its phonological structure when at least some of the letters merge with and come to represent phonetic segments. In order for this process to occur, readers must already be familiar with those letters as *symbols* for the relevant phonological segments. When letters are built into memory in this way, an orthographic image is formed and becomes a visual symbol for the word.

The more systematic knowledge the reader has about how print maps speech, the easier it should be to form and retain orthographic images in memory. This general knowledge can be quite extensive and include not only information about single letter-sound relations but also information about more complex functional spelling patterns in which letters combine to determine sounds within words (Venezky, 1970), about syllabic print-sound structure, and about common spelling patterns shared by several words whose orthographic forms have already been stored.

In order for printed word storage processes to become operational, some preparation is essential to bring the learner to the point where the particular letters appearing in words are seen as belonging there and he can store them in memory. This preparation very likely includes some analytic capabilities: being familiar enough with the shapes, names, and sounds of letters so that the shapes can be imagined and remembered accurately and processed as symbols for letter names and sounds; being able to isolate relevant acoustic or articulatory segments in words and to detect systematic relationships between these phonetic segments and letters present in their spellings. Very likely, these analytic skills must be known well enough so that the reader can operate with the whole word and can coordinate and synthesize several visual-sound parts more or less automatically without giving separate attention to each segment.

When printed words are stored in lexical memory, their orthographic forms are amalgamated not just with phonological identities but also with syntactic and semantic identities. Amalgamation occurs as readers practice pronouncing and interpreting unfamiliar printed words while they are reading text for meaning. Contextual experiences are thought to be particularly important in learning the identities of printed words that perform grammatical functions and lack independent, distinctive meanings (i.e., *from, were, could*).

When all of a word's identities have been amalgamated to form a single unit in lexical memory, the process of recognizing that word changes qualitatively. Its printed form is processed as a single unit rather than a sequence of letters (Doggett & Richards, 1975; Terry, Samuels, & LaBerge, 1976), and its meaning can be accessed silently rather than through sound (Barron, 1978; Barron & Baron, 1977). Because a fairly exact copy of the word exists in memory, this visual image becomes a symbol for meaning as well as sound, and replaces sound as the address used for locating a word in memory from its printed form. When the word is seen, it is matched to the image stored in lexical memory, and the other identities become apparent simultaneously.

Some studies bearing on one or another hypothesis of amalgamation theory have been conducted. This chapter reviews evidence for the idea that orthographic images underlie the printed word learning process. (Fuller accounts can be found elsewhere in Ehri, in press, and Ehri & Wilce, 1979). Also, we have sought evidence regarding the semantic side of word learning. Ehri (1975, 1976, 1980) investigated lexical awareness in prereaders and found that they had difficulty recognizing the syntactic-semantic identities of printed words that were pronounced in isolation, particularly context-dependent words. This suggests that beginning readers may need to learn these words by reading them in meaningful text in order to ensure identity amalgamation. Ehri and Roberts (1978) showed that contextual reading experiences benefit semantic amalgamation. They taught two groups of beginners to read homonyms (i.e., words with the same pronunciation, but different spellings). Children who read the words in sentence contexts learned the meanings of these words better than children taught the words isolation on flash cards. However, isolation learners remembered spellings better than context learners. These findings support amalgamation theory's portrayal of printed word learning as a multifaceted process.

EXPLORATIONS OF THE ROLE OF ORTHOGRAPHY

Visual Representation of Sound in Memory

Our first experiments were intended to show that orthography can function as a mnemonic device, that it can be used by beginning readers to preserve sounds in memory when it provides an adequate printed symbol for those sounds. We observed in a previous study (Ehri, 1976) that young children had difficulty remembering sounds which were not perceived as meaningful. We devised a paired associate sound learning task to determine whether beginning readers might be able to improve their memory for meaningless sounds when shown relevant spellings. Four experiments were conducted to investigate this possibility (Ehri & Wilce, 1979).

In the first experiment, four paired associate (PA) learning tasks were given to first and second graders. In each task, the responses to be learned were four oral consonant-vowel-consonant (CVC) nonsense syllables. The tasks differed in terms of the printed test cues and most importantly the type of mnemonic aids provided during the feedback period. In three of the tasks, the test cues were single alphabet letters representing the first consonant in each nonsense response. In the fourth task, the test cues were meaningless but visually distinctive line drawings called squiggles. Mnemonic aids were provided in two of the letter cue conditions. In one case, correct spellings of the CVC sounds were shown (e.g., "Pab," "Des," "Nif," "Fug"). In the other case, misspellings which represented only the initial sound correctly were displayed (e.g., the foregoing sounds were spelled "Pes," "Dif," "Nuf," "Fab").

Children were tested individually. They were given 15 trials to learn each set of four sounds. The anticipation method of presentation was used. On each trial, the four test cues were shown one at a time, children tried to remember the CVC sound that had been paired with it, and then the experimenter pronounced the correct sound and showed them any spelling aids. It is important to note that, theoretically, the subjects did not have to be able to read in order to perform the task. All they had to do was remember the CVC sounds and match them up with the appropriate visual test cue. The CVC spellings were extra and were not present at the time of the test.

Based on the hypothesis that spellings provide a visual symbol for storing sounds in memory, children were expected to remember the four sounds best when they were shown correct spellings and to do worst with misspellings. Also, we expected memory to be better when the test cues were letters mapping initial sounds of CVC units than when test cues were unrelated squiggles. Results confirmed these predictions. Children took about 6 trials to learn the sounds with letter test cues and correct spelling aids, about 11 trials to learn sounds with initial letters but no spelling aids, 13 trials to learn sounds with initial letter cues and misspellings, and 13 trials with squiggle test cues. These differences were statistically significant. A second experiment replicated these findings. Analysis of recall errors revealed that most were response failures rather than pair mismatches, indicating that the effect of spellings was to facilitate response memory.

Two other experiments were performed to rule out some alternative explanations for the facilitative effects of spellings. It was reasoned that spellings may have caused subjects to repeat and rehearse the sounds one additional time. Or spellings may have clarified the separate segments in the nonsense sounds more than simple pronunciation. Or some nonvisual aspect of the letters may have helped.

In a third experiment, four variations of the PA task were devised and given to second graders. Rather than using squiggles or letters as stimuli, the numbers 1 through 4 were used to prompt recall of each of the four CVC nonsense responses. In all tasks, an initial study trial was followed by test trials with corrective feedback. The tasks differed in terms of the activity occurring during the feedback period. After the stimulus cue had been presented and the child had attempted to recall the response, either a visual spelling was shown, or the experimenter gave the spelling orally by naming the letters, or the experimenter articulated each phonetic segment separately, or the child repeated the nonsense sound one additional time.

It was reasoned that if spellings are helpful because they provide a visual image which subjects can use to remember sounds, then recall in the visual spelling condition should still be superior. Results confirmed predictions. Children recalled significantly more nonsense sounds when they were shown visual spellings than in the other three conditions. Performances in the letter tasks were almost identical.

These findings suggest that the visual properties of spellings are central in facilitating memory. The preferred interpretation attributes effects to the storage of orthographic images. However, in the above studies, children were simply shown spellings and no mention was made of images. A fourth experiment was performed to demonstrate the effect more directly. Recall under two conditions was compared: when children studied the sounds by imagining spellings, and when children studied the sounds by repeating each one twice.

In this experiment, the numbers 1 through 4 served as stimulus prompts for four oral CVC response sounds in each of two PA tasks given to second graders. In the orthograpic image task, the experimenter pronounced the trigram, had subjects repeat it, then the experimenter spelled it orally and had subjects close their eyes and create a visual image of the spelling. In the sound repetition task, the experimenter pronounced the word, subjects repeated it, the experimenter pronounced it again, and the subjects repeated it again. These events took place for each of the four CVC responses on the initial study trial and then following each recall attempt.

As expected, recall was significantly better with image instructions than with rehearsal instructions. These results further confirm the mnemonic function of orthographic images. They add to previous findings by suggesting that it is not necessary for printed forms to be seen outside the head in order to enter memory. Orthographic images can be constructed in the learner's mind.

One result which surprised us in these experiments was how difficult the sound learning task proved to be for first graders, particularly when no spellings were provided. Children who failed to learn the sounds with spelling aids never learned them in the other tasks. Many of the successful spelling-aided learners were unable to learn the sounds without spellings. If children were going to be successful in any task, it was the spelling-aided task. These results raise the possibility that children do not possess a very effective phonemic coding system for preserving meaningless sounds in memory, and consequently they have need for a representational system such as orthography which symbolizes these sounds.

Not only children but also adults have been found to benefit from orthography in a memory task. Sales, Haber, and Cole (1969) found that adults' short-term memory for six words displaying vowel variations (i.e., *hick, heck, hack, hook, hoak, hawk*) was better when the words were seen than when they were heard.

Importance of Orthographic Mnemonic Skill in Learning to Read

Two of the sound learning experiments were intended to determine when during beginning reading instruction orthography becomes effective as a symbol for sounds, and whether this capability is related to the acquisition of other reading skills, most importantly, the size of the beginning reader's lexicon of printed words.

Comparison of the performances of first and second graders indicated that this skill develops between the first and second year of reading instruction. Fewer first than second graders were able to benefit from spellings in remembering the sounds. Whereas 25% to 40% of the first graders failed to learn the sounds with spelling aids in 15 trials, only 8% of the second graders were unsuccessful.

To examine the relationship between performance in the sound learning tasks and beginning reading, various reading subskills were measured. It was reasoned that if the ability to form orthographic images contributes in learning to read, then performance with spelling aids in the sound learning task should be highly correlated with beginning reading skills, more so than performance in the other sound learning tasks without spellings. This was the general pattern observed. In Experiment 1, spelling-aided correlations ranged between -0.64 and -0.75 whereas the other sound learning correlations ranged between -0.29 and -0.56.

In Experiment 2, first graders were divided into two groups, those who were successful in learning the sounds to criterion with spelling aids ($N = 18$)

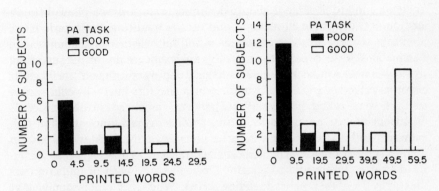

Figure 1.   Distributions of good and poor learners on the printed word identification tasks.

and those who were not ($N = 12$). The mean scores of these two groups on various reading skill measures were compared and found to be very different, all statistically significant ($p < 0.01$) favoring the successful learners.

If it is true that orthographic memory is important because it enables readers to store and remember printed word forms, then one would expect children who possess this skill to know many more printed words than those lacking it. In the first sound-learning experiment, children's familiarity with 27 high-frequency printed nouns was assessed. In the second experiment, 30 irregularly spelled context-dependent words (e.g., *when, every, could, might, once*) were added to this list to ensure that scores represented an estimate of the size of children's printed word repertoire rather than simply their ability to sound out unfamiliar words correctly. Clear evidence for a relationship emerged. To depict this relationship, histograms were constructed and are reproduced in Figure 1. First graders were divided into two groups: those who learned the sounds with spelling aids in fewer than 10 trials, represented in white, and those who took 10 or more trials, represented in black. To our surprise we discovered bimodal distributions. Our first graders were able to read either most of our printed words or very few. This was true in both experiments. Furthermore, in every case, subjects with sizeable print repertoires were successful in learning sounds with spellings while subjects knowing few words were unsuccessful sound learners. Although findings are correlational, precluding any causal inferences, they are at least consistent with the claim that when children learn to read, they acquire an orthographic mnemonic system and this capability enables them to begin building a repertoire of printed words in lexical memory.

Comparison of Silent and Pronounced Letters in Orthographic Images

In order to explore further the nature and operation of orthographic images, we undertook some studies to determine what sort of alphabetic information gets deposited in memory and can be used to access words (Ehri, 1980). In the first study, we wanted to find out whether beginning readers would be able to consult their orthographic images to answer questions about silent as well as pronounced letters, and whether these letters might serve as effective word retrieval cues in a memory task. Twenty second graders were tested individually. First they practiced reading 15 high-frequency adjectives and verbs, most of which proved familiar. After this, they spent 10–15 minutes at a filler task reading a list of 84 words and decoding some nonsense syllables. The central part of the experiment came next. Children were told to imagine the spellings of each of the adjectives and verbs they had practiced reading earlier. When they reported having an image, the experimenter presented a card displaying a lower-case letter, named the letter, and had subjects judge whether the word they were imagining contained that letter. Among the 15 words judged, five words contained a letter which mapped into sound (e.g., r–strong), five words contained a silent letter (e.g., l–talk), and five words did not contain the letter (e.g., m–hard). The contained letters came from noninitial positions in the word, and all 15 letters were different. Subjects judged the letters twice. Then they were surprised with a recall task. Each letter was shown, and they tried to remember the word imagined for that letter.

It was reasoned that if words are stored as orthographic images with all the letters represented, then subjects should be able to perform the letter judgment task easily, and they should be able to recall words containing the letter prompts much better than words lacking the letters. Furthermore, silent letters should be identified as easily as sounded letters and they should be as effective in prompting recall. An alternative possibility is that when children learn words, they translate letters into sounds and use sound to access word meanings. If this is true, then sounded letters should be easier to identify in words and they should serve as better retrieval cues than silent letters.

Results confirmed that children were able to form images and judge letters easily. Nobody complained about not understanding the instructions. Most letter judgments were immediate. In examining images, some children rolled their eyes upward and nodded their heads up and down. Negative responses were often adamant, "No way!" Sometimes "yes" responses were slightly delayed as children appeared to be locating the letter in the image before answering. For words requiring more time, children would close their eyes tightly or whisper spellings to themselves. They appeared to be engaged in constructing rather than simply retrieving a visual representation.

These observations make it hard to doubt that the children were indeed working with images.

On the letter judgment task, scores were close to perfect for all three letter types (i.e., means ranging from 4.3 to 4.9 correct out of 5). Although errors were few, the majority occurred with silent letters. These results reveal that memory for letters in familiar words is very accurate, with sounded letters having a slight edge over silent letters.

Remembering the words was somewhat more difficult than imagining spellings, the means ranging from 0.45 to 2.55 words correct out of 5. As predicted, word memory was much poorer with absent than with contained letters. Comparison of pronounced and silent letters disclosed a difference, but it was the opposite of any effect expected. To our surprise, silent letters prompted significantly better recall than pronounced letters (mean recall: 2.55 versus 1.70).

Why memory was superior with silent letters is puzzling. Several possibilities can be identified. It may be that the effect is real and reflects a characteristic of orthographic images. Frith (1978) reports a similar finding. She had 12-year-olds proofread a text containing misspellings and found that more omissions of silent letters (e.g., *sissors*) were detected than omissions of pronounced letters (e.g., *scarely*). It may be that silent letters are more salient because their presence in the image is not predicted by any phonetic segment and hence there is less redundancy for the letter slot. Also, learners may have devoted more attention to silent letters when they learned the orthographic forms originally, and so the letters may be more firmly planted.

Alternatively, the silent letter effect may be a consequence of the task we have chosen. Children may have spent more time or effort thinking about the silent letter words as they judged the letters. Error data indicated that silent letters were somewhat harder to detect. Or it may be that pronounced letters were verified by consulting word sounds whereas silent letters forced subjects to examine images. Since orthographic images are better mnemonics than sounds, word recall may have been boosted in the latter case. A third possibility is that silent letter words were easier to remember than pronounced letter words. This could have happened since a different set of words was used in each case.

To check on the latter possibility, another experiment similar to the one above was performed. This time, a set of 10 words thought to be familiar was selected, and these same words were presented for letter judgement and surprise recall to two groups of second and third graders, one given pronounced letters and the other given silent letters as recall prompts. These words and letter prompts are listed in Table 1. By using the same words, we eliminated any possible differences in recall due to the choice of words.

In the letter judgment task, children detected the presence of most of the letters (means of 9.8 correct for pronounced letters, 9.4 correct for silent

Table 1.   List of words and letter prompts employed and number of subjects recalling each word

Words	Silent letter	Subjects (Max = 19)	Pronounced letter	Subjects (Max = 19)	Difference
school	h	14	c	17	− 3
straw	w	10	t	5	5
wide	e	15	i	9	6
laugh	u	7	a	5	2
listen	t	14	s	4	10
friend	i	9	n	10	− 1
dead	a	12	e	10	2
young	o	13	u	9	4
comb	b	18	m	12	6
bright	g	14	r	13	1
Mean		12.6		9.4	

letters out of 10). In the recall task, the mean number of words prompted by silent letters was again significantly superior (6.6 words versus 4.9 words). When performance patterns for individual words were analyzed, the same pattern favoring silent letters was evident for 8 of the 10 words (see Table 1). These results show that the silent letter effect did not arise simply from the choice of words. Additional studies are needed to explore the other explanations.

To summarize, results of the word recall studies contribute support to the hypothesis that beginning readers have familiar printed words stored as orthographic images. Findings reveal that not just phonetically salient letters but all the letters participate in an orthographic image.

These results might be perceived as discrepant with one claim of orthographic amalgamation theory, that phonetic segments provide a base to which letters are secured as orthographic images of words are formed in memory. This might lead one to expect pronounced letters to have superior status. In support of this, performance in the letter judgment task was slightly better with pronounced letters, although scores were close to perfect in both cases. It may be that pronounced letters have an advantage over silent letters only during the learning period when orthographic images are being formed. Words used in the present study were not of this sort but had already been learned well by subjects.

Additional evidence regarding the salience of silent and pronounced letters was sought in another study involving younger beginners (37 first graders) who were required to identify and correct the misspellings of 18 words thought to be familiar (Ehri & Roberts, 1978). One-half of the words lacked one noninitial silent letter (e.g., wa*l*k; yo*u*r); half lacked a pronounced letter (e.g., he*l*p, aw*a*y). It was reasoned that if complete visual im-

Table 2.   List of nonsense names and misspellings

Original spellings	No. of errors	Misspellings[a]
1. Wheople	6	wheaple (3), wheeple, whopore, whepole
Weepel	4	weeple (2), weepl, wepol
2. Bistion	4	bistoin, bishtin, bshistun, bitson
Bischun	4	bischtun, bistchin, bischen, buchden
3. Crantz	4	cantz, cranttz, crants, crand
Crans	1	crane
4. Ghirp	4	ghrip (2), grirp, girp
Gurp	1	grup
5. Juild	2	juiled, jild
Jilled	0	
6. Proat	2	poat (2)
Prote	0	
7. Lutter	1	luter
Ludder	1	lutter
8. Knopped	1	knoped
Nopt	0	
Total	35	
(Max.)	(112)	

[a]Parentheses indicate that more than one child produced this misspelling.

ages of words are available in memory, then silent letter omissions should be as obvious and easily corrected as sounded letters. However, if letter importance is determined by whether they map sounds, and if word spellings are remembered in terms of sound-salient letters, then correction should favor pronounced letters. Results supported the former hypothesis. Mean scores were equivalent for the two letter types (6.0 for silent letters versus 6.1 for pronounced letters).

In the previous studies, real words whose printed forms had already been learned outside the laboratory were studied. In the next two experiments, we employed pseudowords. By teaching subjects the words during the experiment, we ensured that their orthographic representations came by way of reading the words and not by writing or memorizing word spellings. Knowledge of printed words was tested by having subjects spell the words following word training.

In the first study, we compared the extent to which phonetically regular and irregular orthographic patterns were preserved in beginning readers' attempts to recall spellings. Eight nonsense words were made up, and, for each, two distinctive spellings were created. In Table 2, the more deviant spellings are listed first for each word. Second graders ($N = 14$) practiced reading four regular and four irregular spellings until they could perform perfectly. The words were taught as names of pictured animals. Following a delay of 3-4 minutes, children wrote out names for each picture. It was reasoned that if, as children learn to read words, they spontaneously store orthographic images, then their spellings should resemble the original forms. If, however, they recode the print to speech and store the names phonetically, then their spellings should be strictly phonetic and original irregular versions should be forgotten.

Results revealed that children remembered original spellings quite well: 69% of their productions were perfect. Their errors are listed in Table 2. More of the phonetic spellings were recalled correctly than the deviant versions: 80% versus 59%. Analysis of the misspellings of irregular forms revealed that one-half were phonetic variants. Although this suggests weaker visual memory, inspection of the particular letters retained in these misspellings revealed that subjects did not completely abandon original forms. Rather they tended to retain salient letter patterns. This was clear from the fact that these patterns were produced only by subjects who had seen that original version of the spelling. Whereas every misspelling of *wheople* began with *wh,* every misspelling of *weepel* began with *we.* Every misspelling of *bistion* contained *st* whereas every misspelling if *bischun* had *ch.* Every misspelling of *ghirp* had an *i* and two included the *h* as well, whereas these letters never occurred with *gurp.*

These results suggest that both visual and phonetic factors participate in the storage and recall of word spellings, with neither dominating to the exclusion of the other. This is consistent with the concept of amalgamation suggesting that a coordination process between letters and sounds is involved in establishing orthographic images in memory.

The findings of a second pseudoword spelling study suggest how visual and phonetic properties of words might interact in setting up orthographic images. Some better first grade readers were taught to read 16 trisyllabic nonsense words, such as *petravamp, rostenlust, pimmican, termolent,* and *kempurgate,* pronounced with primary stress on the first syllable. The second syllable contained an unstressed schwa which theoretically can be spelled with any of the five vowels. In the spellings created for these words, the schwa sound was represented by each of the vowel letters. We were interested in how accurately children might remember these letters. It was reasoned that if sound determines which letters get stored, then accuracy should be poor. However, if visual properties of words are stored, then these letters might be remembered better than chance.

Children were given four study-test trials to learn the words. Then their memory for the schwa spellings was tested. Each word was printed on a card with a hole in place of the schwa letter. Behind the hole was a sliding row of vowels each of which could be positioned to fill the slot. The child was told to pick the letter that made the word look right.

Although children learned to read many of the words, most did not remember the schwa spellings very well. Out of 19 children, there were only 8 who performed above a chance level. No doubt visual memory for spellings was relatively weak in this experiment because the words were long and there were several to remember.

This study was designed to assess subjects' visual memory for letters that did not map into their characteristic sounds. However, observation of the children's learning strategies revealed that for some learners this was a false characterization of the task. Some children were observed to adopt a printed word learning strategy which *created* relevant sounds for the letters. In decoding the printed words, they pronounced each syllable separately with stress and, as a consequence, appropriate sound values were assigned to schwa letters. For example, when *salsify* was broken into syllables and pronounced slowly, /sə/ was pronounced /si/. This strategy illustrates the process of orthographic amalgamation, although in this case phonetic segments to be merged with letters were created rather than simply detected. Such a strategy might very well improve readers' memory for letters mapping into nondistinctive sounds and thereby ensure retention of a more complete orthographic image. Adoption of this strategy may explain how some of the children in the present study were able to remember spellings for schwa sounds.

To summarize, results of these studies offer evidence for the presence and operation of silent as well as pronounced letters in lexical memory. Pronounced letters may have an advantage as printed forms are being learned, whereas silent letters may have special status in fully formed orthographic images. To facilitate the storage of silent or nondistinctively pronounced letters, it may help if readers can create appropriate phonological segments for those letters, perhaps by modifying or embellishing the word's phonological representation. Blumberg and Block (1975) observed learners who appeared to be using this strategy to enhance their memory for word spellings (i.e., rehearsing *discipline* as *dis–ki–plin*). This may be linked to a more general process described by Kerek (1976) as the iconic principle. Kerek suggests that when people learn how spoken words are spelled, and when spellings are not iconic with sounds, there is pressure to change pronunciations to enhance the iconic relationship between letter and sound. Sounds symbolized by silent or nondistinctive letters may work their way into the actual pronunciations of words, particularly if strong oral traditions with the words are lacking (e.g., *victuals* previously pronounced *vittels*). In further studies of this process, very likely it will prove necessary to distinguish different types of silent letters, for instance whether or not they are perceived as markers altering the sound of other letters. Salience in memory or pressure to pronounce may be limited to only some types.

DISCUSSION

Although preliminary, results of our studies are encouraging and lead us to believe that we are on the right track in explaining how the printed forms of words are learned so that they can be recognized accurately, rapidly, and without being pronounced, and so that their spellings resemble conventional forms rather than phonetic variants. The interpretation given to our findings is that orthographic images underlie the printed word learning process. Images are acquired through visual experiences reading specific words, and they are formed in memory through amalgamation processes in which the various identities of words are merged so that the images come to symbolize these other identities. The presence of images serves to guide spelling as well as word recognition processes.

Support for the claim that orthographic representations are essentially visual can be drawn from other sources. Studies by Baron (1977), Brooks (1977), Hintzman and Summers (1973), Kirsner (1973), and McClelland (1977) indicate that there is a component of word memory that is purely visual rather than phonemic and that is specific to the original form of the word seen. For example, McClelland showed that altering the print case structure of pseudowords after adults had learned to read them created a delay in identifying them.

Given the claim that reading and spelling develop together, one may wonder how it is possible for good readers to be poor spellers. An explanation compatible with amalgamation theory is that poor spelling arises from less extensive knowledge of orthography as a speech mapping system. This inadequacy makes it harder to secure clear and complete orthographic images of words in memory via amalgamation processes and also harder to guess at spellings of unfamiliar words. The presence of adequate reading skill in poor spellers is possible because complete orthographic images are not necessary for readers to recognize words accurately, particularly in text where syntactic and semantic information contributes also.

Supportive evidence for this explanation is provided by Frith and Frith (chapter 18, this volume) who compared the capabilities of good and poor spellers (12-year-olds) who were good readers. She found that the two groups were equally accurate in processing the meanings of familiar printed words, although good spellers were faster in some cases. However, poor spellers displayed less adequate print-speech decoding skills, although their knowledge was not as deficient as that of poor spellers who were poor readers. Also, Frith found that poor spellers (good readers) knew less about how the printed forms of familiar words should look than good spellers. They were less accurate in identifying misspellings, although they detected over one-half of the errors successfully. Furthermore, their performance pattern in a proofreading task was different from that of good spellers. Whereas poor spellers detected about the same number of silent and pronounced letter omissions in word misspellings, good spellers were substantially better at detecting silent than pronounced letters. These findings can be interpreted to indicate that poor spellers possess orthographic images for words but that the images are less adequate or complete than those possessed by good spellers. The absence of a distinction between silent and pronounced letters may reflect the fact that poor spellers pay less attention to whether or not each letter symbolizes a separate, distinctive sound as they store orthographic images in memory. This may be one reason why their orthographic images are less accurate, because letters are not completely amalgamated with the phonological identities of words. This speculation awaits study.

Other evidence uncovered by Frith (personal communication) indicates that the occurrence of good reading without good spelling may be restricted to more proficient levels of reading. She was unable to locate poor spellers who were good readers among beginners (second graders). They were always poorer readers as well. It may be that the impact of inadequate orthographic images and decoding skills on reading abates as learners acquire enough reading experience to compensate.

Besides indicating how reading and spelling capabilities might develop together, amalgamation theory offers an explanation of how readers become able to access meaning from print directly without first pronouncing words. Baron's path model (see Baron & Treiman, chapter 12, this volume) does this also, so it is important to clarify how the views differ. According to Baron, there are two ways that beginners can learn to recognize word meanings: by establishing a direct path from print to meaning, or by establishing an indirect path via sound. However, according to Ehri (1980) there is only one way. All word learning is mediated through sound initially when letters are being amalgamated to the word's phonological structure. Once orthographic images are established as word symbols in lexical memory, this mediational function ceases, and images replace sound as the means of identifying a word from its printed form.

There appears to be little evidence that beginners can learn to read words effectively without some dependence upon print-sound regularities. Baron and Treiman (chapter 12, this volume) report that even for words whose spellings are phonetically irregular (i.e., exception words), the correlation between word recognition and nonsense decoding ability is substantial, $r = 0.49$, suggesting that letter-sound knowledge plays some role. As mentioned above, Frith was unable to locate good beginning readers who were not also good spellers. In preliminary studies, we have found that it is very difficult to teach printed words to kindergarteners who lack letter-sound skills. They retain very little from one day to the next.

One implication of amalgamation theory is that the process of learning to read printed language may affect children's competence with spoken language. The effect may be to enhance readers' metalinguistic awareness, that is, their conscious insight into structural aspects of their linguistic knowledge (Ehri, 1980). Or the effect may be more central and involve the acquisition of structural knowledge itself. Moskowitz (1973) proposes that children's ability to learn certain vowel shift patterns in a laboratory task stems from their knowledge of the spelling system of English. Ehri (in press) suggests that seeing Standard English in print complete with inflectional endings normally omitted in nonstandard dialects may enable dialect-speaking children to learn standard English word pronunciations. Valtin (chapter 17, this volume) discusses evidence suggesting that the difference between good and poor readers on auditory discrimination tasks may arise not from deficient auditory skills in poor readers, as is commonly believed; but rather from the greater use by good readers of a strategy of imagining written language symbols to improve their ability to discriminate sounds. This possibility is consistent with our findings that orthographic images can influence better readers' performance in auditory memory tasks and phonemic segmentation tasks (Ehri & Wilce, 1979). Specific effects of printed language acquisition on general linguistic competence merit further exploration.

Chapter 12
USE OF ORTHOGRAPHY IN READING AND LEARNING TO READ

Jonathan Baron and Rebecca Treiman

The advantages of different orthographic systems depend ultimately on the ability of readers and writers to make use of the principles embodied in each system. For example, the potential economy provided by spelling-to-sound rules is lost if the reader or writer cannot take advantage of these regularities. In this chapter, readers are asked how they learn and use the principles embodied in English orthography. The chapter focuses on the psychological processes involved in the learning and use of spelling-sound rules.

The chapter begins with an overview of the processes involved in the reading of single words. These processes can be understood in terms of the mental codes used in various reading tasks and the paths leading from one code to another. The evidence concerning adults' and children's use of these paths is discussed. We also focus on two particular aspects of learning to read: the learning of associations between whole printed words and whole spoken words, and the learning of spelling-to-sound rules. We are particularly concerned with the role of the child's awareness of speech segments as a possible prerequisite for the learning of spelling-sound rules. Finally, the results of a study of individual differences among children in the learning and use of the two paths of particular interest are reported.

CODES AND PATHS IN READING

Figure 1 (Baron, 1977) provides a framework for our discussion of the codes and paths used in the reading of individual words. The boxes represent the three major types of codes: print, sound, and meaning. The *print* codes are not the print on the page, but its psychological representations. These representations may include codes for letters, codes for letter patterns, and codes that represent the overall shapes of words. *Sound* codes are representations of speech. They may be acoustic or articulatory, and they may represent phones, phonemes, whole spoken words, or other units. *Meaning* codes represent the meanings of words (whatever those are). They are presumably used in understanding spoken words and in making other judgments of word meaning.

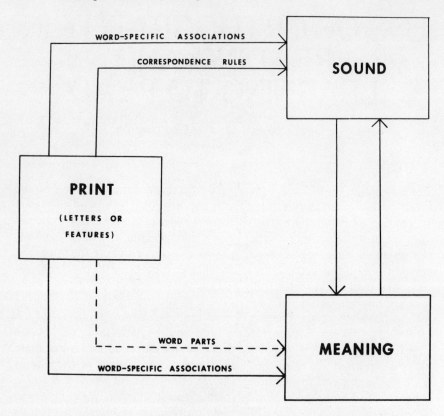

Figure 1.   Paths that might be used in extracting meaning and sound from print. Reprinted by permission, Baron, 1977.

The lines in the figure represent the paths that link one code to another. The paths between sound codes and meaning codes are presumably used in production and comprehension of speech as well as in reading. The paths from print to sound and print to meaning are acquired when one learns to read. Two kinds of paths from print to sound can be distinguished. One links whole printed words to whole spoken words. The other links parts of printed words (e.g., letters or groups of letters) to parts of spoken words (e.g., phonemes or groups of phonemes). The latter sort of path may exist when there are rule-governed correspondences between spellings and sounds, as in English. A parallel distinction can be made for the paths linking print to meaning. In certain cases (e.g., derived words), parts of the meaning of a word are represented by parts of its printed form. In these cases, a path from parts of printed words to parts of meaning may exist.

EVIDENCE FROM ADULTS

As yet, there is no conclusive evidence that the proposed codes and paths are actually used in fluent reading. The available evidence, most of which comes from speeded tasks that resemble reading to a greater or lesser degree, suggests that each path is used in at least one task. However, it cannot be said for sure which paths are used in fluent reading or how they interact.

Evidence that a direct print-to-meaning path is used by readers of English comes from studies of Baron (1973) and Meyer and Ruddy (1973). Baron found that subjects could classify phrases such as *tie the not* or *its knot so* as nonsense just as quickly as they could classify phrases such as *he is kill* or *ill him*. If subjects had been using speech codes, they would presumably have taken longer with the former phrases, which do make sense when read aloud. Meyer and Ruddy asked subjects to judge the truth of sentences such as *a pear is a fruit, a pair is a fruit,* or *a tail is a fruit.* The judgment was to be made either in terms of sound or spelling. When both sound and spelling led to the same response, decision time was less than when only one code could be relied upon. For example, when subjects judged according to sound, they accepted the first sentence more quickly than the second.[1]

The existence of a direct print-to-sound path is evident from our ability to read nonsense words quickly. Since there are no meaning codes for these words, the reader could not derive the sound from the meaning.

There is evidence that readers sometimes derive sound from print by means of spelling-sound rules. Baron and Strawson (1976) found that exception words, for which rules alone are not sufficient, are read aloud less quickly than regular words. This result suggests that the rule path is used for regular words and speeds their pronunciation. Furthermore, individuals differ in the magnitude of this effect: those who know the rules well show a larger effect than those who seem to rely on whole words in reading and spelling. Other evidence for use of spelling-sound rules comes from studies using artificial alphabets. Brooks (1977) and Baron (1977) taught subjects to read six words. In one condition, the words were written in an artificial alphabet with consistent letter-sound correspondences. In another condition, the printed and spoken words were re-paired so that the correspondences were no longer consistent. After 400 trials of practice, the words

---

[1] Experiments that use homophones have several potential problems. Words that sound alike when spoken aloud may not be represented identically in the speech code used in reading, for that code may involve a more abstract phonemic representation (Baron, 1977). When confusions between homophones do occur, the explanation might be not that the reader is using sound, but that he is confused about which spelling is correct, or (in Meyer and Ruddy, 1973) that he is confused because the words look similar.

with consistent correspondences were read aloud more quickly than the words with inconsistent correspondences.

Another approach to the question of whether spelling-sound rules are used is to compare reading in alphabets that use such rules with reading in alphabets that do not. Treiman, Baron, and Luk (1979) found that readers of English have more difficulty with homophonic sentences *(the beech has sand)* relative to control sentences *(the bench has sand)* than do readers of Chinese with comparable sentences in Chinese. This result suggests that the existence of spelling-sound correspondences in English encourages the use of the indirect path to meaning through sound, in some situations. (It must be noted that homophones look similar in English but not, generally, in Chinese. The English readers may have had greater difficulty learning which spelling was which.)

There is at present only suggestive evidence for use of a direct path from whole printed words to whole spoken words, a path not involving the use of meaning or of rules. Probably the best evidence is the existence of neurological patients who can read words aloud, even when the patients have apparently lost the ability to understand the words, and even when the words are exceptions to spelling-sound rules (M. Schwartz & E. Saffran, personal communication).

There is solid evidence that some path from print to sound uses the form of whole printed words. Brooks (1977) found that practice at reading a word in mixed type cases (such as *rEaDiNg*) did not transfer entirely to the task of reading the same word with different letters capitalized *(ReAdInG)*. Thus, some learning was specific to the form of the word and did not involve letter identities alone. Similarly, Baron (1977) showed that words usually printed with the first letter uppercase or lowercase (e.g., *Tom, top*) were read aloud more quickly in these familiar forms than in unfamiliar forms *(tom, Top)*. Finally, Rayner and Posnansky (1978) found that pictures could be named more quickly when the pictures contained a letter string similar in shape to the picture name (*baid* for *bird*) than when it contained a letter string that differed in shape *(bude)*. It is clear from these results that features of words other than the identities of individual letters are used in reading, but it is not known whether these features influence the path from print to sound, the path from print to meaning, or both.

There is evidence that an indirect path from print to sound through meaning is sometimes used. In particular, Meyer, Schvaneveldt, and Ruddy (1974a) found that a word is read aloud more quickly when the subject has just read a semantically related word. However, sounds of words may activate sounds of associated words because of prior contiguity, without use of meaning codes.

The possible use of an indirect path from print to sound to meaning has been the subject of extensive research. There is evidence that people "subvocalize" during reading, especially when the text is difficult to understand.

Such covert articulation is revealed by electrical activity in the muscles used in speaking (Edfeldt, 1960; Hardyck & Petrinovitch, 1970). When covert articulation is disrupted by making people speak or listen to irrelevant material while reading, their performance generally declines (Baron et al., 1980; Kleiman, 1975; Levy, 1975). However, covert articulation may be unnecessary for comprehension, even though it may occur so automatically that its suppression leads to disruption. Another line of evidence for the use of an indirect path to meaning involves the use of homophones (e.g., Baron & McKillop, 1975; Meyer & Ruddy, 1973; but see footnote 1). Some subjects do apparently have difficulty rejecting sentences such as *the beech has sand* as nonsense (Baron et al., 1980); these people may rely on the indirect path through sound.

In sum, any reasonable path that has been proposed seems to be used in at least some task involving reading. In any reading task, it seems, all paths that *could* be used *are* used. Although further research may discover a task in which this is not so, there is good theoretical reason to think that parallel use of multiple paths will be the rule rather than the exception in complex tasks such as reading (Baron, 1977). Two general working hypotheses about performance lead to this conclusion. One is the principle of automatization, first clearly stated by Bryan and Harter (1899), and rediscovered by Kahneman (1973), LaBerge and Samuels (1974), and Shiffrin and Schneider (1977). By this principle, practice at a task reduces the mental resources required to do the task (Norman & Bobrow, 1975). The principle of automatization also holds for subtasks, such as the use of each of the paths in Figure 1. With sufficient practice, a path becomes automatic and carries itself out with no effort or intention on the part of the user. The second principle is the "principle of continually available output," which states "that processes must continually provide outputs over a wide range of resource allocation, even when their analyses have not yet been completed" (Norman & Bobrow, 1975). This principle implies that a reasonably efficient path will have some influence on a task, even if its use is not yet completed at the time some other path has yielded sufficient information for the task to be done. Together, the two principles suggest that every possible path will have some influence on the performance of every task as long as the path is well practiced. Baron (1975) has argued that limits on the paths used may be present when a task takes its output from an early stage in a sequence of successive stages, for example, from the "Print" stage in Figure 1. However, the tasks discussed in this chapter all involve higher level codes such as sound and meaning.

EVIDENCE FROM CHILDREN

It is conceivable that the paths involved in reading are learned in different ways and at different times. In principle, any one of several paths could be adequate for initial reading. A child might begin to read by using only the whole-printed-word to whole-spoken-word path, for example. Through practice the child might develop "shortcut" direct associations between print and meaning (Brooks, 1977), or he might acquire spelling-sound rules by a process of implicit learning (Baron & Hodge, 1978). Studies of young competent readers could tell us what kinds of initial learning are sufficient for progress.

Early evidence (Edfeldt, 1960) suggested that children were more prone than adults to use an indirect path through sound to meaning. However, these results were based on electromyograph recording that may be differentially sensitive to subvocal speech as a function of age. Furthermore, since difficulty affects use of speech recoding in adults (Hardyck & Petrinovitch, 1970), it is reasonable to expect that children will show more evidence of subvocal speech if they find the material they are asked to read more difficult than the adults find the materials *they* are asked to read.

Barron and Baron (1977) examined the use of print-to-sound path and the print-to-meaning path as a function of school grade, from first to eighth. Children were asked to do two kinds of tasks. In the sound task, they were to say whether a printed word rhymed with the name of a picture presented next to the word (e.g., *tree–key*). In the meaning task, they were to say whether the word and the picture "went together" (e.g., *pants–shirt*). At each grade level, these two tasks took about the same amount of time, and led to about the same number of errors. Although overall performance improved with increasing grade level, there was no interaction between task and grade. Items that rhymed led to errors in the meaning task, items that went together led to errors in the sound task, and these two effects were equally strong at each age. Concurrent articulation (saying "double, double..." while doing the tasks) affected only the rhyme task at all ages. It thus seemed that in these children the two paths developed side by side.[2]

Another question about children's reading concerns their use of rules as opposed to other mechanisms, called word-specific paths, in reading words aloud. (The word-specific paths include the direct path from whole printed words to whole spoken words and the indirect path from print to meaning to sound.) Boder (1973) has noted that very poor readers often seem to be deficient mainly in one of these two paths. One type of poor reader can read a few words by memory, but cannot read nonsense words at all. Another type of poor reader treats almost every word as if it were a nonsense word, and thus mispronounces exception words such as *one* and *two*. (Marshall and Newcombe, 1973, have pointed out a parallel distinction in adults whose reading has been impaired by brain damage.)

---

[2]Other situations are possible. Children in Ethiopia often first learn to read a language they do not speak, apparently relying entirely on spelling-sound rules. They later use the same rules to read their own language with little difficulty (Ferguson, 1971).

Baron (in press) has shown that the individual differences described by Boder occur among children in regular schools as well. (Such differences have also been found in adults by Baron and Strawson, 1976, and Baron, Treiman, Wilf, and Kellman, 1980). Baron tested a diverse group of children ranging from first to fourth grade. The children were asked to read exception words, such as *are, both, put,* and *garage;* regular words, such as *bare, cloth, cut,* and *page;* and nonsense words, such as *lare, poth, lut* and *fage.* A child who relied on word-specific paths rather than on rules would be expected to read many of the exception words and few of the nonsense words. He should do moderately well on the regular words, but not as well as a child who could use rules to read words he did not remember by rote. A child who relied on rules should read many of the nonsense words, but few of the exception words. Such a child should tend to make sound-preserving errors on the exception words—errors in which the exception word is read according to the rules. We would also expect a child who relied on rules to be good at reading regular words. Rules could be used to sound out a regular word for the first time or to remind oneself of the identity of a word once known.

If children differ in reliance on rules, these differences should be reflected in the pattern of correlations between scores on the three tests. The correlation between N, the number of nonsense words correct, and E, the number of exception words correct, should be the lowest of the correlations, since these scores reflect different abilities. N reflects mainly the ability to use rules, and E the ability to use word-specific paths. The correlation between R (the number of regular words read) and N should be higher than that between E and N, since R and N might both reflect rule-using ability to some extent. Likewise, the correlation between E and R should be higher than that between E and N, since E and R might both be influenced by ability at word-specific paths. The results were in accord with these exceptions. The correlation between N and E was 0.49, the correlation between N and R was 0.88, and the correlation between E and R was 0.70. In addition, the tendency to make sound-preserving errors in response to exception words was more highly correlated with N than with R. Meaning-preserving errors (e.g., *twenty* for *twelve, paper* for *page*) tended to occur in children who were poor at using rules. This result suggests that these children were using an indirect path to sound through meaning, at least in part. Children were also asked to read lists of words in which adjacent words contained the same spelling pattern and were pronounced differently (e.g., *maid–said*). The magnitude of the confusion effect correlated more highly with N than with E, suggesting that children who use rules when reading difficult words also use them when reading familiar words.

Finally, children who relied heavily on rules tended to be better at reading regular words. Individual variation in rule use thus seems to be a more important determinant of reading ability than individual variation in use of word-specific associations (at least among these children). We are thus led to ask what determines the ability to use rules.

Many investigators (Baron et al., 1980; Calfee, Chapman, & Venezky, 1972; Dykstra, 1966; Firth, 1972; Gleitman & Rozin, 1977; I. M. Liberman, Shankweiler, A. M. Liberman, Fowler, & Fischer, 1976; Savin, 1972) have proposed that one of the major problems in the acquisition of spelling-sound rules is the fact that it is difficult to analyze speech into phonemic segments. Analysis into syllables is easier, and analysis into words easier still, so that orthographies that represent speech at these levels are simpler to learn than systems that represent phonemes. These claims have been supported by showing correlations between measures of segmental analysis ability and reading ability. Treiman and Baron (in press) have taken an initial step beyond this sort of evidence by showing that one test of segmental analysis ability correlates more highly with the use of rules than with the use of word-specific paths in reading words. The measure of tendency to use rules was the tendency to make sound-preserving errors when reading the list of words used by Baron (in press). The measure of segmental analysis was the ability to judge whether two syllables started, or ended, with the same segment.[3] Correlations between the segmental analysis measure and N and E were also computed, but while the correlation between the analysis measure and N was higher than that between it and E, the difference in correlations was not significant. One of the goals of the study reported here is to ask whether this difference in correlations can be found with a larger sample.

INTRODUCTION TO THE PRESENT STUDY

This study attempts to extend the previous studies of children's use of rule paths and word-specific paths from print to sound and to teach children to read new words with two methods of instruction, one emphasizing word-specific associations and the other emphasizing rules (but otherwise similar to the first method). We ask whether children can be distinguished by the method that is most effective for them and whether such differences can be predicted. The belief that emphasis on rules is more appropriate for some children than for others is a common one among teachers, but there is no

---

[3]Actually, three syllables were presented on each trial, the child was asked to say which two went together, and he was told he was correct if he picked the two with a common segment. In each triad of syllables, two shared a segment, and two other syllables were similar overall, as judged by adults, but had no segments in common. For example, if the three syllables were *bih, veh,* and *bo,* the first two would be considered more similar overall. The use of such triads was based on the work of Smith and Kemler, in press, who argued that there is a general developmental trend toward making judgments in terms of identical attributes rather than overall similarity.

evidence to support this belief, much less the claim that such differences can be predicted. In seeking these differences, we try to concentrate on the essential learning processes that might underlie the ability to benefit from each kind of instruction. We thus hold constant such other factors as the form of motivation and the use of word lists versus text. (However, we cannot claim that each of our methods is representative of all the methods of its type.)

Subjects were given measures of ability to read exception, regular, and nonsense words, a segmental analysis test, and the two types of instruction. They were also given a test of ability to learn associations between words printed in artificial letters and spoken words, with no spelling-sound rules available.[4] Some subjects were given a test of the ability to make inferences about the sound of a new, artificial letter by comparing words with and without the new letter. We thus ask whether ability to benefit from different kinds of instruction can be predicted from segmental analysis ability, from letter-inference ability, and from ability to learn new words by rote.

If segmental analysis ability facilitates learning of rules, we would expect it to predict learning from analytic instruction, which emphasizes rules, better than it predicts learning from whole-word instruction, which emphasizes word-specific paths. Ability to learn novel words by rote should show the opposite pattern of correlations.

Method

Subjects   Subjects were students at the Powel School in Philadelphia. Most were black and of working-class background. They ranged in age from 5.8 to 10.3 years. Reading instruction in the school emphasized phonics, but teachers were given freedom to pursue their own approaches. Students served as subjects if their teachers agreed, if their parents returned permission forms, and if their teachers indicated that their reading ability was not so great that they could read all the words on our lists. The subjects included 13 first graders, 30 second graders, 12 third graders, and 17 fourth graders. Testing began in the late fall of 1977. Subjects who read no words correctly (9 first graders, 10 second graders, 2 third graders, and 1 fourth grader) were considered nonreaders.

Measures   The tests are described in the order in which they were given to each child. Many children were unavailable for many tests, so the

---

[4]Rozin, Ponitsky, and Sotsky (1971) found that poor readers had little difficulty learning to name Chinese characters (in English), but others (e.g., Samuels & Anderson, 1973) have found deficits in visual-verbal paired-associate learning in poor readers. The present task measures ability to learn associations between multi-character strings and words. Firth (1972) found such learning ability to be correlated with IQ but not (otherwise) with reading ability, but Vellutino et al. (1975) did find a correlation with reading ability as such, although he used nonsense words.

analysis to be reported is based on the maximum number of subjects usable for each analysis. Several sessions with each subject were required.

The word reading tests were like those used by Baron (in press), except that exception words, regular words, and nonsense words (E, R, and N, respectively) were inter-mixed in a fixed random order, with more difficult words appearing later in the list. (See Appendix A.) The exception words were also "true" exceptions, as defined by Baron's inability to think of more than two other words with the same spelling patterns (e.g., vowel and final consonants) pronounced the same way. The nonsense words were counted as correct if they were read by analogy with either the regular word or an exception word, as done by Baron (in press). The three types of words were constructed in triples for number of letters and syllables (e.g., *put, cut, lut;* see Appendix A for all items). The words were printed in large letters on individual index cards. Each child was given the choice of an uppercase or a lowercase deck, and was asked to divide the cards into words he had seen before and words he had not. He was then given the deck again, in the original order, one card at a time, and asked to read as many words as possible. If the child was having great difficulty, he was simply handed the deck and asked to read any words he knew. Responses were transcribed phonetically. Many sessions were tape-recorded, and the reliability of recording responses was found to be nearly perfect.

Two types of instruction were given: whole-word instruction (W), which emphasized word-specific associations, and analytic instruction (A), which emphasized spelling-sound rules. For the whole-word instruction, words were selected from the original list that had not been read correctly. The child was retested on these words, and any word read correctly was replaced. Words were used in order of difficulty, that is, in the order in which they had been presented. Instruction began with six words, three regular words, and three exception words. The experimenter went through the six cards slowly and told the child what each word was. The child was tested on the six words repeatedly, in a different order each time. If the child erred or refused to answer, the experimenter again told the child what the word was. (In essence, this training method is paired-associate learning by the method of anticipation.) If the subject reached a criterion of two successive correct responses to all six words within 10 trials, six more words, selected as the original words, were added. (For some subjects, a sufficient number of words were not available, and these subjects could not be considered in some analyses. In fact, only the first 10 trials were analyzed.) Up to 18 words were taught in this way. (Before this limit was instituted, one child, an industrious but overactive second grader who originally read only 31 of the 153 items correctly, learned 42 more words in less than an hour by whole-word instruction! His data were not used.)

The analytic instruction was identical to the whole-word training except that nonsense words were used in place of exception words. Thus, instruction began with three nonsense words and three regular words. At the beginning of the session, and every time the subject was incorrect, the experimenter told the child not only the word itself, but also a number of parts of the word. These parts of the word retained their pronunciation when pronounced according to spelling-sound rules. The experimenter covered the irrelevant parts of the word with her fingers and read aloud the remaining parts. For example, for the word *maid,* the experimenter covered up the *m* and the *d* and read the sound of the *ai,* covered the *d* and read *mai,* and covered the *m* and read *aid.* Since some words (e.g., *counter*) could be divided into many parts in this way, a maximum of five parts was used, with an attempt made to choose large and small parts and parts from all positions in the word. The child was encouraged to try to read each word again after these parts had been presented, but only the initial response on each trial was actually counted.

The scores for learning ability were the number of correct responses made in the first ten trials; these are called W and A for the two tests, respectively. These scores could not be calculated if the experimenter ran out of usable words. However, even for such subjects, it could still be determined whether analytic or whole-word instruction was superior.

In the segmental analysis test (S), the child was presented with pairs of syllables spoken by the experimenter, in blocks of eight syllables. The child was first given three blocks in which he was asked to judge whether the two syllables ended with the same sound, followed by four blocks in which he compared first sounds. Corrective feedback was given after each response. (The experimenter repeated the syllables in giving the feedback, e.g., "No, *see* and *zay* end with different sounds.") The first block in each condition (last-sound and first-sound) was considered as training, and the data were not counted. In the training blocks, the first (last) sounds of the two syllables were the same, so the subject could simply judge whether the two syllables were the same or not. Each block was presented twice, unless a child got all eight items correct, in which case it was assumed that he would do so again on the second presentation. If a child got fewer than six correct on each of the two presentations, the next blocks of that condition were omitted. Since blocks were arranged in order of difficulty, it was assumed that children would perform at chance on subsequent blocks. (We tried in these ways to minimize the duration of this test, since children found it difficult.) Data from children who did not go beyond the training block on the first-sound or last-sound tests were not used. The score, S, ranged from 0 to 80 correct, with chance performance at 40.

In the next test, children learned responses to three-letter words printed in a novel alphabet. Since many of the letters were Greek letters, this task is called the Greek task (G). The procedure was the same as for the whole-word learning except that four words *(dog, cow, pen, fox)* were used instead of six, and four more *(run, his, sky, she)* were added if criterion was reached by the tenth trial. The score, G, was the number of correct responses in 10 trials. Note that letters or sounds were never repeated, so no spelling-sound rules were available to learn. This test proved to be the most enjoyable for the subjects.

The tests described so far were given to each subject within a span of a few days. The test of letter-inference ability was given to 26 of the poorer readers in the original sample (for reasons that are irrelevant here). In this test, children were first told the identity of two training words (to the left of the slash, in Appendix B) printed on index cards. They were then tested on these two words until they read them both correctly twice in succession. Then they were shown the two test words (to the right of the slash) and asked to figure out what they were. Some words contained artificial letters, so that ability to infer letter sounds could be tested with minimal specific transfer from prior instruction. In case a child did not learn the training words in five trials, the test words were not presented. The score (I) was the percent correct on the test words that contained an artificial letter.

Results

The major results consisted of correlation coefficients between various pairs of tests. In addition, ages were used in some correlations, as were scores on the California Achievement Test, which was given to the subjects in the early spring of the school year.

Use of Rule and Word-Specific Paths   The first hypotheses to be tested concern the use of these two paths, as measured by E, the number of exception words read correctly, and N, the number of nonsense words. For these analyses, we used only those 36 subjects whose total score (R + E + N) was between 15 and 138 (out of 153) to avoid floor and ceiling effects, who responded with a guess or correct response to at least 102 items (out of 153), and who went beyond the training blocks in the segmental analysis test.

The results are shown in Table 1. Note that the correlations among the three reading tests, R, E, and N, are quite high. The magnitudes of these correlations are probably due to the careful matching of the stimuli and to the wide range of ability levels represented. As hypothesized, however, the correlation between E and N, r(E,N), is lower than the other two relevant correlations, r(R,E) and r(N,R) ($p < 0.01$, taking into account the dependence between measures). All tests are one-tailed unless otherwise noted. (Baron and Treiman, 1979, have discussed the advantages of comparing dependent correlations.) Thus, the three measures appear to tap somewhat different abilities. E is influenced more by use of word-specific associations, N by use of rules, and R by both. The lower correlation between N and E comes about because the ability to use word-specific associations and the ability to use rules are somewhat independent. Two extreme subjects illus-

Table 1. Means, standard deviations (in parentheses), and correlations for results bearing on use of rule and word-specific paths, 36 subjects

| Type of test | Mean score (SD) | Correlations | | | |
		Regular	Exception	Nonsense	Segmental
Regular	37.0 (12.3) out of 51				
Exception	32.4 (9.4) out of 51	0.943^b			
Nonsense	34.0 (12.8) out of 51	0.950^b	0.899^b		
Segmental	68.1 (9.7) out of 80	0.265	0.271	0.422^a	
Greek	52.4 (16.9) out of 72	-0.220	-0.339	-0.226	-0.065

$^a p < 0.01$, one-tailed
$^b p < 0.001$

trate the origin of these results. One (not included in the analysis of Table 1 because of failure to meet the criteria) read 11 regular words, 11 exceptions, and no nonsense words correctly. The other read 50 of 51 regular words, 49 nonsense words, and 34 exception words. The former child seemed to be relying entirely on word-specific paths, the latter largely on rules.

The other results of interest concern the segmental analysis test, S. As hypothesized, r(S,N) was higher than r(S,E) ($p < 0.02$), indicating that segmental analysis is more strongly related to use of rules than to use of word-specific paths in reading words. (However, r(S,R) was as low as r(S,E), a result the authors cannot explain.)

The Greek test, G, correlated negatively with all other tests, possibly because better readers used an inefficient strategy of trying to discover letter-sound correspondences in this test.

In this group of 36 readers, age correlated 0.382 with E and 0.195 with N ($p < 0.01$, two-tailed, for the difference between correlations). This result suggests that years of reading instruction exert their effect most heavily on word-specific knowledge. The California Achievement Test arithmetic raw score (whose relation to reading would most likely be through general abilities) correlated more highly with E (0.535) than with N (0.364)—not quite a significant difference. However, in second graders alone, the arithmetic score correlated 0.847 with N and 0.723 with E. This result suggests that general ability is unrelated to use of one path or the other.

To assess the importance of rules in learning to read, we selected pairs of subjects who were equal in R but one subject was older by 2 years. Within each pair, then, the two children have achieved more or less the same reading level, but one child has learned much faster than the other.

Table 2.   Means, standard deviations (in parentheses) and correlations for results bearing on whole-word and analytic instruction, 15 readers and 20 nonreaders combined

Type of test	Mean (SD)	Correlations			
		Regular	Segmental	Greek	Whole-word
Regular	12.8 (15.0)				
Segmental	58.1 (12.1)	0.354[a]			
Greek	52.8 (14.1)	0.096	0.016		
Whole-word	62.3 (34.9)	0.470[b]	0.699[c]	0.232	
Analytic	52.4 (35.4)	0.726[c]	0.666[c]	0.313[a]	0.767[c]

[a] $p < 0.05$, one-tailed
[b] $p < 0.005$
[c] $p < 0.001$

The younger subjects had higher N but lower E($p < 0.05$ for the interaction, two-tailed). As argued by Baron (in press), rules seem more important than word-specific knowledge in early reading.

Analytic and Whole-Word Instruction

A major aim of the present study was to find out whether children differ in the optimal method of instruction. One analysis relevant to this question was done on all 35 readers who were given instruction of both types, even if there were not enough unknown words to complete the instruction. Readers were classified as rule-users if N was higher than E, and as word-specific-path-users if the reverse was true. For 15 of 19 word-specific-path-users, the whole word score (number correct in 10 trials) was higher than the analytic score. For 9 of 16 rule users, the analytic score was higher than or equal to the whole-word score. This difference is significant ($p < 0.05$, one-tailed) by a chi-squared test. Thus, there appears to be a relation between the use of rules in reading and the ability to learn from analytic instruction.

A second analysis used data from 15 readers and 20 nonreaders for whom the training did not have to be stopped for lack of unknown words. We could thus use the W and A scores parametrically. The data for these 35 subjects are shown in Table 2. The only measure that predicted A better than it predicted W was R, the ability to read regular words; r(R,A) was greater than r(R,W) ($p < 0.01$, two-tailed). Two negative results are of interest. First, S was just as highly correlated with W as with A. Second, G was just as highly correlated with A as with W. If whole-word learning were based on the formation of rote associations, of the sort required in the Greek learning test, we might have expected r(G,W) to be higher than r(G,A). And if learning from analytic instruction was affected by segmental analysis ability, we might have expected r(S,A) to be higher than r(S,W). Neither of these results was found.

Table 3.   Means, standard deviations (in parentheses), and correlations (based on different numbers of subjects) of predictor variables with learning from whole-word (W) and analytic (A) instruction in nonreaders

Type of test	Number of subjects used in correlations	Mean	(SD)	Correlation with W	Correlation with A
	20	7.1	(1.1)	0.494^b	0.281
Segmental	15	50.0	(9.9)	0.537^b	0.690^c
Greek	20	48.5	(13.9)	0.533^c	0.523^c
Inference	12	0.318	(0.282)	0.281	0.593^b
C.A.T. math (raw)	16	266	(19)	0.474^a	0.478^a
Whole-word	19	31.4	(15.1)		
Analytic	19	21.5	(14.9)	0.650^c	

$^a p < 0.05$, one-tailed
$^b p < 0.025$
$^c p < 0.01$

The most appropriate analysis of the ability to benefit from different kinds of instruction is done in the nonreaders. Since these subjects probably had little knowledge of the words they were taught, and since prior reading instruction, if any, had been ineffective, the results are not likely to be affected by reading instruction or by what the children had so far learned from reading. Correlations of the various measures with W and A are shown in Table 3. Although a number of variables correlated significantly with ability to learn from one kind of instruction or the other, only one variable, I (letter-inference ability), correlated more highly with A than with W ($p < 0.05$, given $r(W,A) = 0.783$ for these subjects). No variable correlated with W significantly more than with A. Here, as before, S and G did not correlate with benefit from one kind of instruction more than with benefit from the other.

Discussion

The results replicate the major findings of Baron (in press) and of Treiman and Baron (in press). Children differed in their use of rules and word-specific associations in reading words aloud. Furthermore, the segmental analysis test correlated more highly with N than with E, indicating that the correlation between segmental analysis and reading ability holds particularly strongly for use of rules rather than for other, more general abilities.

It was also possible to predict how quickly a child would learn from whole-word and analytic instruction, and some measures predicted ability to learn from analytic instruction better than they predicted ability to benefit from whole-word instruction. In particular, analytic learning (A) was better predicted than was whole-word learning (W) by R, by whether N was higher than E (for readers) and by letter-inference ability (I) for nonreaders.

In order to benefit from the analytic instruction over the whole-word instruction, a child must presumably be able to use the parts of the word to help him learn the pronunciation of the whole word. The fact that ability to benefit from analytic instruction correlated with inference ability (essentially a measure of the same thing) tends to validate the analytic learning measure. Better readers, in particular, readers who were better at using rules, seemed to be more able to make the sorts of inferences that were required to benefit from the analytic instruction.

Two of our initial hypotheses, however, were not confirmed. We hypothesized that segmental analysis would correlate more highly with A than with W, and that Greek learning would correlate more highly with W than with A. Neither of these results was found. One possibility is that our measures were insensitive. However, both Greek learning and segmental analysis did correlate highly with some other variables. It is also possible that the analytic and whole-word instruction tests were not extensive enough to tap effects of subtle differences between them, although, again, it was possible to predict differentially with other measures.

If the negative results are taken seriously, two explanations are plausible. One is that segmental analysis plays a smaller role in learning to read than has been thought. Our results, and most results of others, are consistent with the view that segmental analysis ability (as measured) is an *effect* of learning spelling-sound rules rather than a *cause*. This view would explain why the use of rules in reading correlates with segmental analysis, even though segmental analysis does not correlate with ability to benefit from rule-based instruction, either in readers or nonreaders. The ability to do segmental analysis tasks may result in large part from having learned how to spell. Adults often think of spelling when they do segmental analysis tasks; even when they do not, the fact that they have learned to *label* sound segments with letters may help them perform the task.

Consistent with the view that segmental analysis ability results from learning spelling-sound rules, adults have great difficulty with segmental analysis tasks when the segments are not represented in the spellings of their language. For example, many adults will say that there are four or five segments in *rocks* but three in *box*. This has been tested more systematically (with the help of R. Elias) by asking adults to make the following sort of inferences: If *1234* spells *fuel* and *134* spells *fool* in a phonetic alphabet, what does *2ail* spell? Or, if *5678* spells *chip* and *678* spells *ship,* what does *5oo* spell? Adults make many errors in these problems, but they perform without errors on similar problems in which new symbols stand for segments already represented by letters (see also I. M. Liberman et al., chapter 10, this volume).

It is possible that phonological abilities (like visual abilities; see Vellutino, chapter 16) might be sufficient for learning to read in almost all children. If so, failure to learn spelling-sound rules might result simply from a failure to use strategies that would be helpful for rule learning, such as searching memory for analogies (Baron, 1977, in press) or testing hypotheses about possible rules. If this is true, these strategies should be taught to those children who do not use them already. There is, however, some evidence that seems to contradict the view that segmental analysis is learned *from* learning to read and has little influence *on* that learning. Fox and Routh (1976) found that preschool nonreaders who were good at segmental analysis were good at learning and using letter-sound correspondences in a small artificial alphabet. However, this study did not rule out more general ability differences as an influence on both tasks. Rosner (1971) found that training in segmental analysis (and other tasks) increased the rate of learning to read in first graders. However, Rosner did not show that the training effect was specific to the learning of spelling-sound rules, or even to reading. "Further research is needed."

A second interpretation of our results is that phonological abilities often *do* limit ability to learn to read, but that these abilities are not well measured by current segmental analysis tests. We could then explain the negative findings by saying that the segmental analysis test (along with most others in the literature) does not really measure the phonological abilities that are necessary to learn spelling-sound rules. If what is required to learn an alphabet is the ability to represent spoken words in terms of phonemes, this ability might be most clearly reflected in the ability to imitate nonsense words.

APPENDIX A. STIMULI USED IN TESTS

Word Reading Test

Exception (E)	Regular (R)	Nonsense (N)
was	has	mas
have	gave	tave
what	flat	plat
said	maid	haid
some	home	lome
been	seen	deen
water	later	bater
come	dome	gome
does	goes	moes
both	moth	poth
want	pant	bant
country	counter	countly
father	rather	dather
whole	while	whule

Word Reading Test—*continued*

Exception (E)	Regular (R)	Nonsense (N)
toward	towers	towark
done	bone	yone
front	blond	bront
among	along	anong
gone	lone	sone
says	days	cays
watch	catch	satch
hours	holes	houls
hurt	yearn	hearn
having	saving	taving
hour	hear	houl
copy	dopy	hopy
wasn't	hasn't	rasn't
blood	brood	slood
women	homer	somer
wear	fear	mear
knowledge	snowplows	snowledge
touch	pouch	rouch
results	insults	besults
lose	rose	wose
wash	cash	fash
soul	foul	coul
sword	swore	swort
curtain	contain	cortain
closet	closer	closen
scarce	sparse	scarse
wander	sander	mander
chords	chairs	chaids
created	treated	gleated
wanting	panting	santing
layer	sayer	hayer
prayer	player	drayer
chute	choke	chuke
chef	chat	chaf
corps	harps	horps
liquor	liquid	liquod
sew	new	rew

APPENDIX B. LETTER INFERENCE TEST

After learning the responses (in parentheses for stimuli with artificial letter) to the items to the left of the slash, the training words, children were asked to identify items to the right, the testwords.

an set / san et
aish thealm / thaish ealm
run lad / lun rad
chaung knoosh / knaung choosh
■ it (hit) ham / ■am ■at
•oush (foush) awnk / •awnk•awsh
r*g (rag) men / m*g ren
wrθnk (wroank) shouph / wrounk shθph
sa $\neq$ (sat) bun / ba $\neq$ sun
quaiϕ (quaith) whoong / whaiϕ quoong
$\theta \chi$ (us) van / v $\theta \chi$ run
au$\rightarrow$ (auth) pheash / phea$\rightarrow$ phaush
hπp (hop) tuα (tug) / huα tπp
sh★ng (sheeng) quoa◢ (quoath) / qu★ng shoa◢

Section IV
READING PROCESSES
Skilled Reading

Chapter 13
HOW DOES ORTHOGRAPHIC STRUCTURE FACILITATE READING?

Dominic Massaro

It is well-known that the psychological processing of letter strings is facilitated to the extent the strings approximate the natural orthography, the rules of spelling of the written language. This result implies that readers utilize in some form the structural constraints given by rules during one or more processing stages in reading. The letters in a string conforming to the orthography are partially predictable or redundant when the visual information is incomplete. The goal of this chapter is to evaluate how knowledge about orthographic structure is represented and how it supplements visual letter information. This assessment is carried out within a general model of the processing stages in reading.

PROCESSING STAGES IN READING

A schematic representation of processing stages in reading is shown in Figure 1. At each stage of processing, memory and process components are represented. The memory component corresponds to the information available to the system at a particular stage of processing. The process component corresponds to the procedural operations on the information held by the memory component. In addition to the temporary memory structures, long-term memory contributes an additional source of information at some of the processing stages. The model will be elaborated simultaneously with the evaluation of how orthographic structure facilitates reading processes.

FEATURE DETECTION

A printed pattern is first transduced by the visual receptor system and the feature detection process detects features which are then stored in preperceptual visual storage. One of the simplest views of the contribution of orthographic structure is that experience with written language modifies the

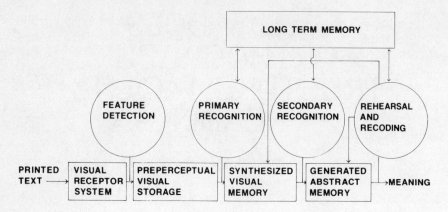

Figure 1.   Schematic representation of information processing model for reading.

feature detection process. Given this view, it is possible that orthographic structure enhances the visual feature analysis of the letters in a string. Familiar or frequent orthographic contexts might facilitate feature analysis of the component letters. Orthography may also be exploited to guide feature analysis; recognition of some letters may guide the feature analysis of other letters in the pattern. Accordingly, readers would resolve a greater number of letter features or would obtain better resolution of the features to the extent that the string contains common letter sequences. Another possibility is that experience with certain letter patterns allows the establishment of visual features that are defined across adjacent letters. These supra-letter features would make available additional visual information to the extent the letter string is redundant. The distinguishing characteristic of these mechanisms is that orthographic structure directly modifies the featural processing of visual information that the reader has available in reading.

Enhanced Feature Detection

Although it may seem reasonable, there is no evidence that orthographic redundancy enhances the detection of visual features of letters. The most direct test of the idea was carried out about a decade ago. Earhard (1968) asked subjects to indicate whether or not one of the letters in a string was thinner than the other letters. The letter strings were either words or random letter strings. The strings were presented at four different durations sufficient to cover the range from chance to perfect performance. There was absolutely no difference in tachistoscopic recognition of a thin letter between the word and random letter strings at any of the four exposure durations. These results argue that the visual system is *not* more finely tuned to visual features in common rather than in uncommon, letter patterns.

Earhard's results antedated two independent studies carried out by Krueger and Shapiro (1978) and Massaro (in press). In the Krueger and Shapiro study, subjects monitored lists of items presented one item at a time at varying rates of presentation. One-half of the lists of items were composed of six-letter words; the other one-half were lists of six-letter nonwords. In one experiment, subjects indicated whether a mutilated A or mutilated E appeared in a list. Performance was more accurate for word than for nonword lists. This result might be interpreted to mean that the word context enhanced the feature detection of the mutilated letter; however, enhanced performance with words may have resulted from the redundancy of the word context contributing to the interpretation of whether a mutilated letter was an A or an E. (The role of redundancy and interpretation is developed more fully in the section "Primary Recognition.")

To provide a more direct test of whether orthographic redundancy enhances feature detection, Krueger and Shapiro replicated their study but now eliminated any possible contribution of an interpretation advantage for words. In this experiment, subjects had to detect simply whether or not a mutilated A occurred. This task, therefore, directly taps how well the subject detects a mutilation and performance cannot be influenced by what the mutilated letter is interpreted to be. No performance differences were found as a function of word or nonword lists. This result indicates that detection of a mutilation was not modified by orthographic context, in agreement with the idea that orthographic context does not modify feature analysis.

Massaro's experiment involved the independent variation of the visual information about a letter and its orthographic context in a letter perception task. Consider the lowercase letters c and e. As can be seen by reading down a column of six items in Figure 2, it is possible to gradually transform the c into an e by extending the horizontal bar. To the extent the bar is long, the letter resembles e and not c. If the letter is now presented as the first letter in the context *-oin,* the context would support c but not e. Only c is orthographically legal in this context since three consecutive vowels would usually violate English orthography. This condition is defined as e illegal and c legal ($\bar{e}\Lambda c$). Only e is valid in the context *-dit* since the cluster cd is an invalid initial English pattern. In this case, the context *-dit* favors e ($e\Lambda\bar{c}$). The contexts *-tso* and *-ast* can be considered to favor neither e nor c. The first remains as illegal context whether e or c is present ($\bar{e}\Lambda\bar{c}$), and the second is orthographically legal for both e and c ($e\Lambda c$).

The experiment factorially combined six levels of bar length with these four levels of orthographic context, giving a total of 24 experimental conditions. The test letter was also presented at each of the four letter positions in each of the four contexts giving a total of 96 items. The test string was presented for a short duration followed after some short interval by a masking stimulus composed of random letter features. In all cases, the subject indicated whether an e or c was presented in the test display.

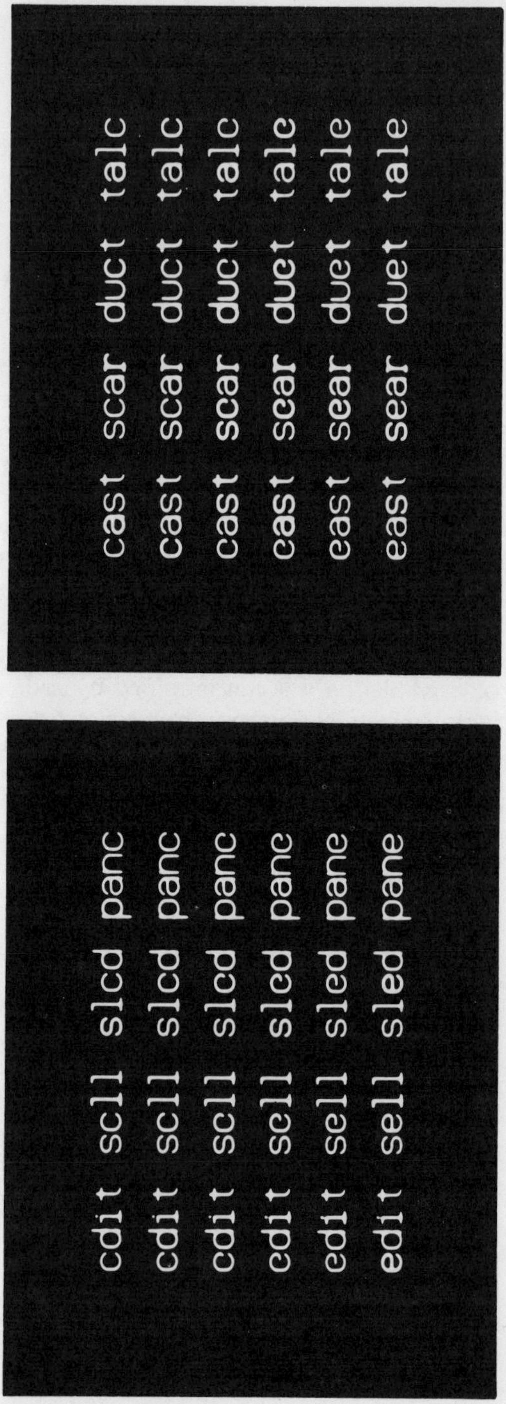

cast scar duct talc
cast scar duct talc
cast scar duct talc
cast scar duct tale
east sear duet tale
east sear duet tale

cdit scll slcd panc
cdit scll slcd panc
cdit scll slcd panc
cdit scll sled pane
edit sell sled pane
edit sell sled pane

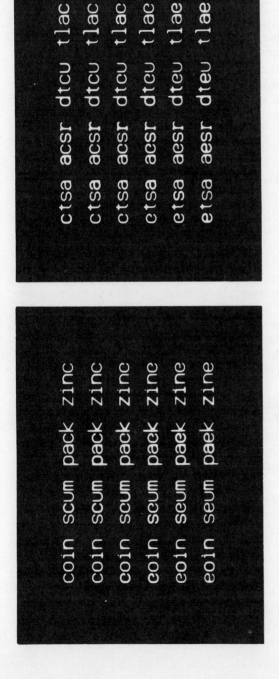

Figure 2. The 96 test items generated by the factorial combination of six bar lengths of the test letter, four serial positions of the test letter, and four orthographic contexts.

The experiment provides a direct test of whether orthographic context influences the feature detection process. One direct measure of feature resolution in the present experiment is the degree to which the reader can discriminate the bar length of the test letter. This discrimination can be indexed in the present experiment by the degree of differential responding to the successive levels of the bar length of the test letter. Better resolution of the test letter is assumed to occur to the extent the subject responds e to one length and c to another. In the ($e\Lambda c$) context, both letters spell words whereas neither letter spells a word in the ($\bar{e}\Lambda\bar{c}$) context. If the word context influences feature detection, then the discrimination of bar length should differ in the word and nonword contexts.

The visual resolution of the test letter should be critically dependent on the orthographic context if the latter modifies feature detection. An index of the discriminability of the bar length of the test letter is given by d' and can be derived from the identification responses (Braida & Durlach, 1972). The probabilities of responding e to each of the six levels of bar length are transformed to z-scores. The d' value between two adjacent levels of the bar length is simply the difference between the respective z-scores. Cumulating these successive d' distances across the levels of bar length gives a cumulative d' discrimination function. The subject shows good discrimination of bar length to the extent that cumulative d' values are large.

As can be seen in Figure 3 there is no consistent effect of orthographic context on the cumulative d' values. These results indicate that the discrimination of bar length of the test letter did not change with context. The observed equivalence between the both legal and both illegal contexts is direct evidence against the idea that context modifies feature detection. Subjects should have performed differently in the both legal than in the both illegal contexts since these models assume that the context modifies lower-level feature analyses, and therefore, the discriminability of bar length.

One might question whether the cumulative d' values are sensitive measures of the visual resolution of the target letter. Evidence on this question can be derived from the effect of some other variable on the cumulative d' values. It is well known that visual resolution improves with the processing time available for a test stimulus. Processing time was varied in this experiment by varying the blank interstimulus interval between the short test display presentation and the masking stimulus. The cumulative d' values in Figure 4 show a very consistent and large effect of processing time. Discriminability as measured by cumulative d' values increased with increases in the available processing time. The fact that processing time enhanced resolution of bar length shows that the failure to find an effect of orthographic context on discriminability cannot be due to an insensitive test. This conclusion is also supported by the good description of the data by a model based on the assumption that discriminability of the bar length is independent of orthographic context (see the section "Primary Recognition").

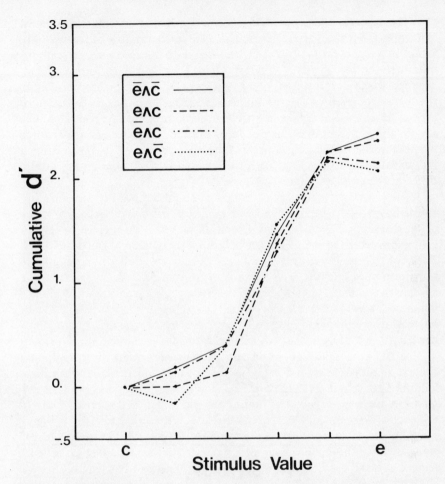

Figure 3.   Cumulative d' values as a function of the bar length (stimulus value) of the test letter and the orthographic content.

Supraletter Features

There appears to be sufficient empirical data to reject the idea that orthographic structure enhances feature analysis of letter features. Another more
popular alternative is that orthographic structure allows the establishment
of *supraletter* features that represent the overall shape and configuration of
common letter patterns or words. However, there is no evidence for this
idea (Anderson & Dearborn, 1952; Gibson & Levin, 1975; Huey, 1908/
1968). One of the strongest arguments against the idea of supraletter features is the small potential contribution of supraletter features to reading.
Overall word shape, for example, does not sufficiently differentiate among

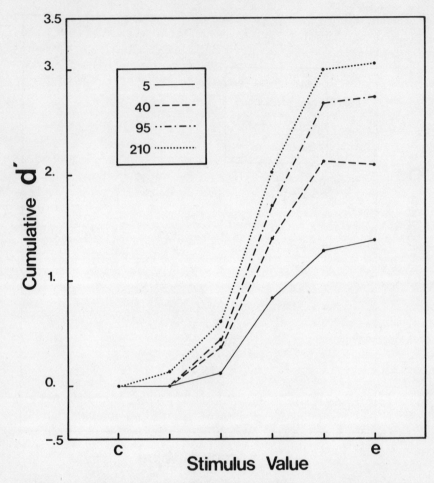

Figure 4.   Cumulative d′ values as a function of the bar length (stimulus value) of the test letter and the interstimulus in msec.

the words of a language. Groff (1975) examined the shapes of high-frequency words taken from school book sources. The shape was defined by drawing a contour around the letters so that elephant would be elephant. Only 20% of the 283 words were represented by a unique shape. Groff rightly concludes that the small number of words that can be represented by a unique shape precludes the utilization of this cue for accurate word recognition. It should be noted that although words may be recognized from just partial information about the letters, this does not necessarily imply that supraletter features were responsible. Nonvisual information about orthography might supplement the partial information from the letters.

There is also experimental evidence against the idea of word recognition based on supraletter features. Marchbanks and Levin (1965) and Williams, Blumberg, and Williams (1970) presented subjects a test pseudoword followed after a short delay by several other pseudowords. Subjects were required to choose the item that most resembled the test word. First-grade readers tended to choose the item that matched in first or final letter; they seldom matched on the basis of overall shape. Prereaders showed no consistent choices. These results show that beginning readers remember and recognize words on the basis of letter identity rather than overall word shape. Thompson and Massaro (1973) and Massaro (1973) found for adult readers that visual confusability between letters was equivalent in single letter and word presentations. Two letters likely to be confused for one another were just as confusing in single letter and word presentations. If recognition of words involved the utilization of different features than those contained in the component letters, different degrees of letter confusability in single letter and word presentations would have been expected.

The role of supraletter features has been evaluated in a number of studies by determining whether mixing the type fonts of letters eliminates the advantage of word over nonword letter strings. It should be pointed out, however, that attenuating the contribution of orthography by mixing type fonts does not necessarily implicate supraletter features as the cause of a word advantage. As will be discussed in the section "Primary Recognition," utilizing orthographic redundancy to narrow down the number of possible alternative interpretations of partial featural information may produce a word advantage. It is not unreasonable to assume that mixing type fonts may also disrupt the contribution of this process since the partial featural information is much more ambiguous when a variety of type fonts are represented in a letter string.

Although reducing the perceptual advantage of letter strings high in orthographic structure by mixing type fonts does not necessarily implicate supraletter features, an equivalent advantage with mixed type fonts would demonstrate that supraletter features were not responsible. Adams (1979) studied the tachistoscopic recognition of words, pseudowords very high in orthographic structure, and nonwords very low in structure. The items were presented in a single type font or the items were constructed from a variety of fonts. Figure 5 presents examples of the words, pseudowords, and nonwords in single and mixed type fonts. Performance was more accurate for words than pseudowords and poorest for nonwords. Most importantly, the size of the differences among the three types of items did not change when the letters of the items were presented in a variety of type fonts. If supraletter features or whole-word cues contribute to the perceptual advantage of well-structured strings, the advantage of the word and pseudoword strings should have been drastically attenuated in the mixed case presentation.

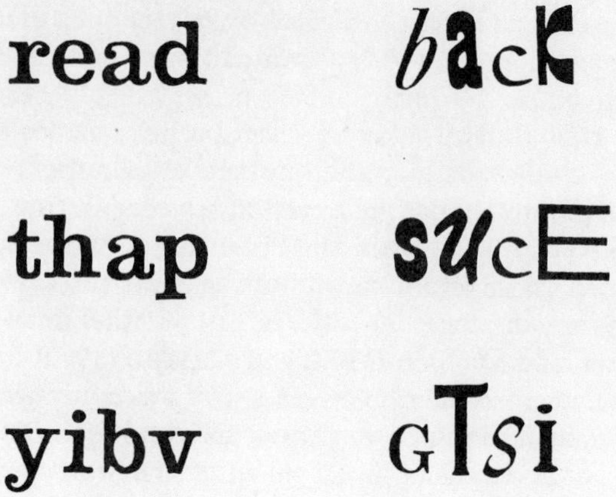

read   *back*

thap   *suc*E

yibv   G*Tsi*

Figure 5.   The word, pseudoword, and nonword items presented in a single type font or mixed type fonts (after Adams, 1979).

PRIMARY RECOGNITION

Faced with the set of features in preperceptual visual storage, the primary recognition process evaluates and integrates these features, producing a synthesized visual percept in synthesized visual memory. The primary recognition process operates on a number of letters simultaneously (in parallel). The visual features evaluated at each spatial location narrow down the set of possible letters for that position. The recognition process must choose from this candidate set the most likely letter alternative for each position. Knowledge in long-term memory can contribute to the primary recognition process. The accomplished reader knows not only what visual features define each letter but also something about the orthographic structure of the language. The primary recognition process, therefore, utilizes both the visual information in preperceptual storage and knowledge about the structure of legal letter strings. In the present model, it is assumed that the two sources of information make independent contributions to the recognition process (Massaro, 1973, 1975, in press; Thompson & Massaro, 1973).

This view of primary recognition was developed on the basis of experiments carried out using variants of the Reicher paradigm (Reicher, 1969; Wheeler, 1970). Subjects were presented with either a word or a single letter for a short duration followed immediately by a masking stimulus and two response alternatives. The response alternatives would both spell words in the word condition; for example, given the test word *word,* the response alternatives ---*d* and ---*k* would be presented. The corresponding letter condition would be the test letter *d* followed by the response alternatives *d* and *k*. Performance was about 10% better in the word than in the single-letter condition.

Given the two-alternative forced-choice control, it was argued that the reader was able to utilize orthographic context to eliminate possible alternatives during the perception of the test display before the onset of the masking stimulus (Thompson & Massaro, 1973). As an example, given recognition of the context *wor* and a curvilinear segment of the final letter, the reader could narrow down the alternatives for the final letter to d, o, and q. Given that o and q are orthographically illegal in the context *wor,* d represents an unambiguous choice. The reader will therefore perceive the word *word* given just partial information about the final letter. If the reader has recognized the same curvilinear segment in the corresponding letter condition, however, any of the three letters (*d, o,* and *q*) are still possible and the perceptual synthesis will result in *d* only one out of three times. What is critical in this analysis is that a word advantage is obtained even though the visual featural information available to the primary recognition process is equivalent in the word and letter conditions. The orthographic context of the word simply provides an additional but independent source of information. The featural information available to the recognition process does not change with changes in orthographic context. In this view, although orthographic context facilitates word perception, it does not modify the feature analysis of the printed pattern.

Quantitative Test

An experiment was carried out to test a quantification of this view of primary recognition (Massaro, in press). The logic of the experiment centered on the question of whether orthographic context and featural processing make independent contributions to letter perception. The experiment was described in the section "Feature Detection." Subjects viewed four-letter strings that differed in terms of the visual information about the critical letter and the orthographic context of surrounding letters. In the *e–c* identification task, the horizontal bar of the critical letter was presented at six different lengths covering the range of a good *c* to a good *e*. Each test letter was also presented at each of the four letter positions in each of four orthographic contexts (see Figure 2).

Figure 6 presents the probability of an *e* response at each of the experimental conditions. The results showed large effects of stimulus information and orthographic context on the identification of the test letter. The significant interaction of these two variables revealed that the magnitude of the context effect was large at the more ambiguous levels of visual information. Although the context effect decreased some with experience in the task, it was still highly significant on the fourth day of the experiment.

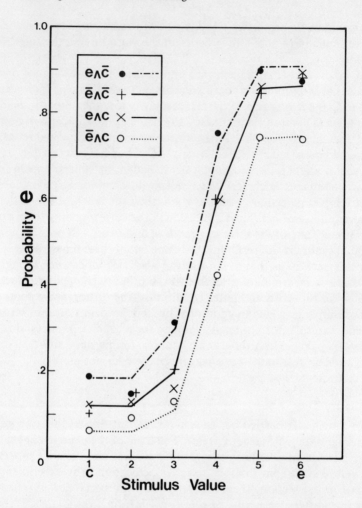

Figure 6.   Observed (points) and predicted (lines) probabilities of an *e* response as a function of the bar length (stimulus value) of the test letter and orthographic context.

The model provides a straightforward interpretation of the experimental situation. Two independent sources of information are available: the visual information from the critical letter and the orthographic context. The first source of information can be represented by V_i where the subscript i indicates that V_i changes only with bar length. For the *e–c* identification, V_i specifies how much *e*-ness is given by the critical letter. This value lies between zero and one and is expected to increase as the length of the bar is increased. With these two letter alternatives that differ only in bar length, it is reasonable to assume the visual information supporting c is simply one minus the amount of e-ness given by the same source. Therefore, if V_i specifies the amount of e-ness given by the test letter, then $(1 - V_i)$ specifies the amount of c-ness given by that same test letter.

The orthographic context provides independent evidence for e and c. The value C_j represents how much the context supports the letter e. The subscript j indicates that C_j changes only with changes in orthographic context. The value of C_j lies between zero and one and should be large when e is legal and small when e is illegal. The degree to which the orthographic context supports the letter c is indexed by D_j and is independent of the value of C_j. The value of D_j also lies between zero and one and should be large when c is legal and small when c is illegal.

Faced with two independent sources of information, the reader evaluates the amount of e-ness and c-ness from these two sources. In order to arrive at a combined value of e-ness and of c-ness, it is necessary to integrate the two sources. The amount of e-ness and c-ness for a given test display can therefore be represented by the conjunction of the two independent sources of information:

$$e\text{-ness} = (V_i \Lambda C_j) \tag{1}$$
$$c\text{-ness} = ((I - V_i)\Lambda(D_j)) \tag{2}$$

The e-ness and c-ness values given by both sources can be determined once conjunction is defined. Research in other domains has shown that a multiplicative combination provides a much better description than an additive combination (Massaro & Cohen, 1976; Oden, 1977; Oden & Massaro, 1978). Applying the multiplicative combination, Equations (1) and (2) are represented as:

$$e\text{-ness} = V_i \times C_j \tag{3}$$
$$c\text{-ness} = (1 - V_i) \times (D_j) \tag{4}$$

A response is based on the e-ness and c-ness values: a choice of e is assumed to be made by evaluating the degree of e-ness relative to the sum of the e-ness and the c-ness values. This choice rule is a direct application of Luce's (1959) choice axiom. The probability of an e response, P(e), is expressed as

$$P(e) = \frac{V_i C_j}{V_i C_j + (1 - V_i)(D_j)} \tag{5}$$

To derive P(e) for the four orthographic contexts, a simplifying assumption about context is that a given alternative is supported to the degree x by a legal context and to the degree y by an illegal context, where $1 \geq x \geq y \geq 0$. The values x and y do not have subscripts since they depend only on the legality of the context. Therefore, C_j is equal to x when e is legal in a particular context and equal to y when e is illegal. Analogously, D_j is equal to x when c is legal in a particular context and equal to y when c is illegal.

Given the context with e legal and c illegal

$$(e \wedge \bar{c}): P(e) = \frac{V_i x}{V_i x + (1 - V_i) y} \tag{6}$$

since the e-ness is given by $V_i x$ and the c-ness by $(1 - V_i) y$. Analogous expressions for the other three contexts are

$$(e \wedge c): P(e) = \frac{V_i x}{V_i x + (1 - V_i) x} = V_i \tag{7}$$

$$(\bar{e} \wedge \bar{c}): P(e) = \frac{V_i y}{V_i y + (1 - V_i) y} = V_i \tag{8}$$

$$(\bar{e} \wedge c): P(e) = \frac{V_i y}{V_i y + (1 - V_i) x} \tag{9}$$

Equations 6 and 9 predict an effect of context to the extent a legal context gives more evidence for a particular test letter than does an illegal context, i.e., to the extent $x > y$. A second feature of this model is that $P(e)$ is entirely determined by the visual information when the context supports either both or neither of the test alternatives; Equations 7 and 8 both predict $P(e) = V_i$.

This form of the independence model was tested against the observed response probabilities. Figure 6 gives the observed and predicted values. In order to fit the model to the data, it was necessary to estimate 6 values of V_i for each level of bar length of the critical letter and an x value for a legal context and a y value for an illegal context. The parameter values were estimated using the iterative routine STEPIT by minimizing the squared deviations between predicted and observed probability values (Chandler, 1969).

The model provided a good description of the results. In addition, the parameter estimates are psychologically meaningful. The value of V_i increased with increases in the length of the bar of the critical letter. The values were 0.11, 0.11, 0.19, 0.60, 0.85, and 0.86 for the six respective levels. The value of x was 0.76 for legal context and the value of y was 0.40 for the illegal context. The root mean squared deviation between the predicted and observed response probabilities was 0.02. It is clear that an additive combination of the two sources would fail since the curves would have to be parallel. Supporting this, the description was 2.5 times poorer for the same model based on the additive combination of the independent sources.

Johnston (1978) offers what he considers a critical test of a general form of this interpretation of the facilitating effects of orthographic redundancy. His goal was to provide a direct test of the assumption that a word context facilitates letter identification because its identity is constrained by the identity of the surrounding letters. Two classes of words were chosen and presented for tachistoscopic identification. Words were chosen to have either a high or low constraining context on a particular letter position. Consider the word pairs *date–gate* and *drip–grip* when the initial letter position is tested. Nine four-letter words end in ate whereas only three end in rip. If the primary recognition process utilizes information from the orthographic context to supplement featural information, Johnston reasoned that performance should be better when tested on the first letter of either of the first pair of words than the second, when the alternatives are limited to *d* and *g* in the Reicher-Wheeler task. Although the standard word advantage was found, Johnston found no performance difference between these two classes of words.

Johnston's experiment is limited in a number of ways and, therefore, cannot be taken as evidence against the idea that orthographic redundancy provides an additional source of information at primary recognition. With respect to his structure manipulation, Johnston varied lexical constraints at a given position, but there is no evidence that the psychological representation of orthography is limited to lexical constraints (Massaro, 1975). For example, although three times as many words are possible given the context *–ate* than given the context *–rip,* almost as many letters are legal in the second context as in the first. Our more recent studies have shown that the contribution of orthographic redundancy can be captured by descriptions that are independent of whether the letter string is lexically represented (Massaro, Taylor, Venezky, Jastrzembski, & Lucas, in preparation). Johnston equated the position-sensitive bigram frequency of the high and low constraint items and since we have shown that this variable captures nearly all of the contribution of orthographic redundancy, it is not surprising that there were no differences between the two classes of words.

SECONDARY RECOGNITION

The secondary recognition process transforms the synthesized visual percept into a higher-order code in generated abstract memory. Synthesized visual memory holds a sequence of letters that are analyzed by the secondary recognition process with the goal of closing off the letter string into a phonological, lexical, and/or meaning code. The secondary recognition process makes this transformation by finding the best match between the letter string and codes in long-term memory. Orthographic redundancy might facilitate the transformation from a visual to a higher-order code.

Mewhort (1974) presented first-order or fourth-order pseudowords one letter at a time horizontally across a visual display. Each letter was presented for 3 msec and the interletter interval was varied from 0 to 100 msec.

Although increasing the interletter interval from 0 to 50 msec did not change performance on the first-order strings, it decreased performance on the fourth-order strings. Because increasing the rate of presentation did not lower performance on the first-order strings, Mewhort argues that the disruption of performance on the fourth-order strings cannot be due to simple character identification. These results are taken by Mewhort to support the idea that orthographic structure aids transfer from a visual store to a verbal short-term memory.

Although feature analysis may not be influenced by increasing the interletter interval from 0 to 50 msec, the utilization of orthographic structure during perceptual recognition probably requires having featural information from adjacent letters simultaneously available. Therefore, the utilization of orthographic structure at primary recognition can also account for Mewhort's finding that increasing the interletter interval decreases performance on fourth-order but not first-order letter strings. Although Mewhort's results are ambiguous, it is still reasonable to expect that orthographic structure can facilitate the transfer of a visual percept into a higher-order code since a well-structured string will require fewer codes than a poorly-structured string.

REHEARSAL-RECODING

Recoding and rehearsal processes build and maintain semantic and syntactic structures at the level of generated abstract memory. Generated abstract memory corresponds to the short-term or working memory of most information processing models. In our model, this memory is common to both speech perception and reading. It is also possible to go from meaning to a visual or auditory percept in our model. The recoding operation can transform the meaning of a concept into its surface structure and auditory or visual form.

Baddeley (1964) questioned the perceptual contribution to the original psychological study of orthography carried out by Miller, Bruner, and Postman (1954). The authors had subjects reproduce letter sequences, eight letters in length, corresponding to different approximations to English based on Shannon's (1948) algorithms. The displays were exposed for durations of 10 to 500 msec and the number of letters reported increased with display duration. Also, performance was a systematic function of the order of approximation to English. By correcting for redundancy of the strings, the amount of information transmitted was shown to be equivalent for the four different approximations.

Baddeley (1964) observed that performance in the task was unlikely to be a direct index of how well the letter sequences were perceived. Observing that performance improved at a negatively accelerated function of log exposure duration, it was possible to extrapolate from the curves and observe that an exposure duration of one or two hours would be required for correct report of all eight letters. Baddeley argued that the results of Miller et al. (1954) may have reflected differences in memory for the sequences rather than visual perception. To test this idea, he presented the eight-letter sequences of Miller et al. at a duration that was sufficient for that subject to name each of the eight letters. Presentation times ranged between one and two seconds. The contribution of orthographic redundancy to performance was essentially identical to that reported by Miller et al. (1954). Baddeley concluded that both interletter redundancy and exposure time allow a more effective coding and, therefore, better memory and recall of the letter sequence.

Krueger (1971) evaluated the influence of orthographic redundancy on short-term recognition memory. In one study, a string of six letters was presented one letter at a time at a rate of four letters per second. The letters were presented either left to right or right to left across the display screen. Words produced only a 3% performance advantage over corresponding nonwords whereas the left-to-right presentation gave about a 7% advantage relative to the right-to-left presentation for both types of strings. Slowing the presentation rate to 2.5 letters/sec eliminated the left-to-right advantage but not the word advantage. These results replicate Baddeley's findings that orthographic structure can improve short-term memory and extend them to a recognition memory situation that eliminates output interference present in free recall studies.

SUMMARY

There is now good evidence that orthographic structure does not modify featural processing of the visual information in reading, although it contributes a significant source of information to perceptual recognition. Knowledge of the orthography allows the reader to constrain the set of admissable letters in a letter string when only partial featural information is available. Orthographic structure not only facilitates perceptual recognition, the phenomenal experience of a visual pattern, it enhances accessing higher-order codes for the pattern, and maintenance and elaboration of the codes in memory.

Chapter 14
READING IN A NONALPHABETIC WRITING SYSTEM
Some Experimental Studies

Ovid Tzeng and Daisy Hung

There is a growing concern among reading specialists (e.g., Gibson & Levin, 1975; Gleitman & Rozin, 1977) as well as cognitive psychologists (Biederman & Tsao, 1977; Park & Arbuckle, 1977; So, Potter, & Friedman, in preparation; Tzeng, Hung, & Wang, 1977) about the effects of orthographic differences on visual information processing. It is not an unreasonable conjecture that human information processing strategies may differ because information is presented in different formats. For example, it has been suggested that the meaning of words and of pictures are recovered via different processing routes (Paivio, 1971). Thus, depending upon how meanings are represented in print (i.e., what type of writing system is used), a reader may have to develop different strategies to achieve reading proficiency. Hence, by comparing experimental results of reading behaviors across languages as well as across different writing systems, we should be able to gain some insights into the various processes involved in reading. Our experimental work so far has been concerned mainly with adult, fluent readers. It is our belief that it is more important to identify the property of the target skill than to deal with problems associated with the acquisition of these skills. Two major questions were asked in a series of experiments to be reported below. First, we have been interested in whether or not visual lateralization effects, which have been observed in the study of reading alphabetic materials (Hardyck, Tzeng, & Wang, 1977, 1978), would also occur in

---

[1]There are phonograms in Chinese characters in which one part of the character functions as a phonetic clue. Examples of these can be found in Figure 1. However, one has to know how to pronounce the base character to be able to sound out the derived phonogram. Sometimes a character may contain a certain character as its component, but its pronunciation may have nothing to do with that particular character. In other words, the same character may carry a phonetic clue when embedded in a certain derived character but may also carry no clue at all when embedded in other characters. According to a recent analysis carried out in mainland China, the success rate of using a base character to sound out another character is only about 39%.

reading nonalphabetic symbols. Second, we would also like to find out the extent of phonetic recoding, if any, in the processes of reading nonalphabetic materials.

THE CHINESE CHARACTERS AND READING DISABILITY

Generally speaking, the Chinese characters represent a type of logography that utilizes written signs to express the words or morphemes of the spoken language (Gleitman & Rozin, 1977). It is important to realize that Chinese, like other logographic scripts, is meant to express a single particular word while ignoring many grammatical marking elements (e.g., *I want go* instead of *I wanted to go*). That is, the character remains the same regardless of the syntactical structure. Thus, for Chinese children the task of learning to read means simply to learn to associate each spoken word with a particular character. In general, the orientation and the number of strokes that form the basis of a character bear no relationship to the sound of the spoken word.[1] This lack of symbol-to-sound correspondence leaves the beginning readers a most straightforward way (and probably the only way) to master the thousands of distinctive characters, namely, the way of rote memorization. This situation is very different from that of learning the alphabetic writing system where one has to be able to extract the orthographic regularities embedded in written words in order to master the letter-sound correspondence rules. Therefore, the beginning readers of Chinese are facing a more concrete learning situation than those who are learning the alphabetic writing system.

Besides these linguistic considerations, several research reports have suggested that students of Chinese characters may be immune to the problems of dyslexia. Makita (1968) observed that reading disability is ostensibly uncommon in Japanese children. Since Japanese orthography has two types of writing symbols—kana (phonetic symbols for syllables) and kanji (nonphonetic logographic symbols borrowed from the Chinese characters), the rarity of dyslexia may be attributable either to the fact that kana characters map onto speech at the level of syllables rather than that of the more abstract phonemes, or to the fact that kanji is a sign script where each word has its own symbol, or both. Results of reports have indicated that Chinese orthography is more easily comprehended by a beginning reader than alphabetic material. Rozin, Ponitsky, and Sotsky (1971) showed that a group of second-grade school children with serious reading problems that had persisted even after extensive tutoring by conventional methods were able to make rapid progress in learning and reading sentences written in Chinese characters. Moreover, a recent large-scale survey in Taiwan has also shown that reading disability rarely exists in the primary schools, even in the most deprived rural school districts (Kuo, 1978). Therefore, the experimental studies of reading Chinese characters will undoubtedly help us in constructing a better theory of visual information processing in general and in designing a better reading instruction in particular (Rozin & Gleitman, 1977).

CEREBRAL LATERALIZATION
EFFECTS IN READING CHINESE CHARACTERS

The term *lateralization* refers to the specialization of the left or right hemisphere of the brain for different functions. In most right-handed persons, for example, speech is generally lateralized in the left cerebral hemisphere. Sperry, Gazzaniga, and Bogen's (1969) research on split-brain patients provides direct evidence of hemispheric specialization of function. In these patients, due to the cutting of the corpus callosum, the two cerebral hemispheres are able to function separately and independently. Sperry et al. (1969) found that written and spoken English were processed in the left hemisphere, while the right hemisphere was superior in performing various visual and spatial tasks. Evidence for asymmetrically represented functions has also been found in behavioral research with normal subjects (Hardyck, Tzeng, & Wang, 1977, 1978). Kimura (1973), in a dichotic listening experiment, found that subjects were quicker and more accurate in identifying speech sounds processed in the left hemisphere than in the right. Similarly, in visual hemifield experiments, in which English words were tachistoscopically presented to either the left or the right of a central fixation point, Mishkin and Forgays (1952) found a differential accuracy of recognition, favoring words presented to the right of the fixation point. This finding has been termed the right-visual-field, RVF, (left-hemisphere) superiority effect of language processing.

Since most experiments demonstrating the RVF superiority effect have used alphabetic materials, the results may not be generalized to other nonalphabetic materials. Of particular interest is the possibility that visual lateralization effects may not show up with nonalphabetic material such as the Chinese characters. Or, if the effect does occur, one question still remains to be answered: Which visual field will have the advantage? In accord with the experimental research cited above, many psychologists would agree that spoken and written English words enjoy an RVF advantage because it is believed that the phonetic blending required for processing alphabetic materials is carried out in the left hemisphere. However, the case for logographic symbols, exemplified by the Chinese characters, is not as clear. It has been suggested that these symbols map directly onto meaning, and thus by-pass the intermediate stage of speech recoding between symbol and meaning. Hence, reading Chinese characters is much more like a pattern recognition task, which is presumably carried out in the right hemisphere. Consequently, one would expect a left visual field, LVF, (right hemisphere) superiority, if there is indeed a visual lateralization effect.

Two main approaches have been used to examine the cerebral lateralization functions for processing Chinese characters. The first is to study the effects of brain lesions on reading behavior and thereby infer the psychological functions of the corresponding structures of the nervous system. This approach has been used by Sasanuma (1972, 1974a, 1974b, 1974c) in several studies of Japanese aphasics. It is well known that among the many writing systems in the world today, Japanese is unique in the sense that three different types of script are used simultaneously to represent text. Most words in Japanese are written in kanji (Chinese characters) while grammatical particles are usually written in hiragana, and loan words (i.e., foreign words such as television) in katakana. The latter two types of prints are called kana scripts and each symbol represents a syllable of the spoken language. So, a fluent reader of Japanese has to know all three types of scripts. Sasanuma (1974a, 1974b, 1974c) reported a series of studies that showed some evidence for the selective impairment of kana and kanji. She has carefully examined the characteristics of the aphasic's speech production and reception and has followed up any speech recovery that occurred. Rather than postulating a right and left hemisphere dichotomy, Sasanuma has argued for differential disruptions of language attributable to localized lesions in the left hemisphere. The primary difference between kana and kanji is the suggestion of phonological processor for kana, which is needed to mediate the graph-sound-meaning correspondence. A similar processor has been postulated for the reading of alphabetic materials (Rozin et al., 1971). Therefore, Sasanuma's argument has potential for explaining characteristics of language processing beyond Japanese. A detailed review and some criticisms of Sasanuma and her associates' work can be found in Tzeng, Hung, and Garro (1978).

The second approach is to study visual lateralization effects with respect to kanji and kana scripts. Hirata and Osaka (1967) and Hatta (1976) both found a superior performance of the left hemisphere in the perception of kana characters. Stimuli presented first to the left visual field and then to the right visual field produced more errors in a recognition matching task than the converse order of presentation. This indicates a left hemisphere superiority for kana. Recently, Hatta (1977) reported an experiment measuring recognition accuracy of kanji characters. Left visual field superiority was found for both high and low familiarity kanji characters, suggesting that kanji characters are processed in the right hemisphere. However, a similar experiment by Sasanuma, Itoh, Mori, and Kobayashi (1977) complicates the seemingly clear picture. Also using a recognition experiment, Sasanuma et al., presented kana and kanji words to normal subjects and found a significant RVF superiority for the recognition of kana words, but

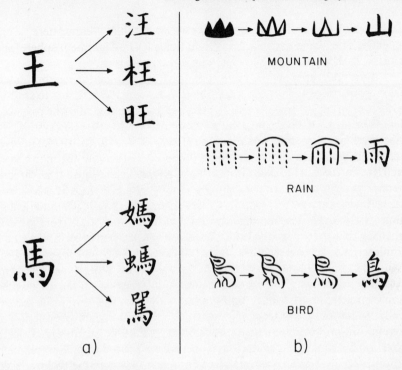

Figure 1. a) Examples of Chinese phonograms. b) Examples of the pictograms and their transformations through hundreds of years.

a nonsignificant trend toward LVF superiority for kanji. The discrepancy between these two studies could possibly be explained by methodological differences in the two experiments. The Hatta experiments used either kana or kanji characters for individual subjects, whereas Sasanuma et al. presented a mixed list of kana and kanji to all subjects. It is possible that in the Hatta study the hemisphere most appropriate for the task was primed to handle the stimuli. Furthermore, in the Sasanuma et al. study, subjects were asked to identify two characters at a time. Putting two characters together may involve some phonetic recoding, thus reducing the LVF advantage. In fact, the Sasanuma et al. data were much noisier than Hatta's.

Three experiments on visual lateralization effects were conducted in our laboratory to test the above arguments (Tzeng, Hung, & Cotton, 1978). In the first experiment, we followed Hatta's (1977) procedure very closely but with an additional manipulation. Eighty stimulus characters were selected from commonly used characters which can be broken into two different categories: (1) phonograms—those characters that contain a certain base character as a clue to their pronunciation (see Gleitman & Rozin, 1977, pp. 12–13); and (2) pictograms—those characters that are pictographic in origin. Examples of these types of characters are presented in Figure 1. In

Table 1.   Mean numbers of correct identifications as
a function of type of character and of visual field

Visual field	Pictograms	Phonograms
Right	5.20	5.60
Left	13.30	14.20

the upper panel of the figure, the character on the left hand side is the base character and is pronounced as /wáng/ (meaning *king*). The three characters on the right are derivatives that contain the base character as a clue to their pronunciation. In fact, they are pronounced as /wāng/, /wǎng/, and /wàng/ from top to bottom, meaning *the barking sound of dogs* (or alternatively, *deep and wide*), *not straight,* and *properity* for the three characters respectively. In the lower panel, the base character on the left is pronounced as /mǎ/. It means *horse* and it is a pictogram by itself (see Wang, 1973). Similarly, the three derivative characters on the right are pronounced as /mā/, /má/, and /mà/, meaning *mother, ant,* and *to acold,* respectively. Thus, if a reader knows how to pronounce the base character, he can guess the pronunciation of a derived phonogram which contains the base character as its partial component. However, one should be cautious in making generalizations because in many cases the base character only gives a clue to how a particular phonogram sounds (sometimes the clue refers only to the vowel ending) and the tonal patterns (-, ´, ∨ , `) are not included. The subjects in the experiments were 20 Chinese students enrolled in the graduate school of the University of California, Riverside. They were asked to identify orally a single character very briefly exposed via a tachistoscope. The exposure duration was readjusted for each individual subject according to his recognition threshold, determined before the experimental trials. The experiment employed a 2 (type of character)× 2(LVF versus RVF) design and the dependent measure was the number of correct identifications. The results are summarized in Table 1.

A 2×2 ANOVA was performed on the data. Only the main effect of the visual field was statistically significant, $F(1,19) = 49.56$, $p < 0.001$. A strong LVF superiority effect was obtained, but neither the type of character nor the interaction between visual field and type of character was significant. In general, the results replicated those reported by Hatta (1977). Furthermore, the results showed that regardless of whether or not the character contains any phonetic clue, it is processed mainly in the right hemisphere.

Although the result of a right hemisphere (RH) processing is clearcut, its implication for reading is less clear. It should be noted that modern Chinese tends to be multiple-syllabic in nature. Hence, the perceptual unit in reading may be much larger than the single characters. Thus, a major task in reading is to generate meaning by putting together several characters to form meaningful terms. The second experiment, therefore, was con-

Table 2. Mean reaction times (in msec) for correct decisions as a function of imagery value and visual field

| Visual field | Positive response | | Negative response |
	High imagery	Low imagery	
Right	827.82	863.18	1382.95
Left	906.34	993.52	1391.32

ducted to investigate whether the results obtained in the previous experiment would be generalized to the tachistoscopic recognition of multiple-character terms. The procedure was exactly the same as the first experiment except that the stimulus terms were always two characters (e.g., 學校 for school; 鉛筆 for pencil, etc.) arranged vertically in either LVF or RVF of the tachistoscope. The results showed that of the 80 stimulus terms presented (40 for each field) the numbers of correct identification were 36.5 and 22.5 for stimulus terms presented in the RVF and LVF, respectively. The difference is statistically significant, $t(19) = 7.49$, $p < 0.001$. This result suggested a left hemisphere (LH) dominance, a complete reversal from that of the previous experiment. Therefore, the locus of the cerebral lateralization cannot be the on the logographic symbols per se; rather, it must be on the type of task that the subject has to perform in order to meet the experimental requirement.

One may still object to the result of the second experiment on the basis that LVF-RH effect as observed in the first experiment might be overridden by the LH function (it is conceivable that more effort is required to pronounce two characters) of motor programming in the oral report. To circumvent this objection, a third experiment was run which investigated the visual lateralization effect with the subject making a semantic decision on multiple-character terms. Twenty Chinese graduate students were instructed to make a YES/NO response as quickly and as accurately as possible to stimuli briefly exposed in either the RVF or LVF of the tachistoscope. They were asked to press the YES key only if the characters formed a meaningful term; otherwise they were to press the NO key. The right- or left-hand responding to the YES or NO key was counterbalanced across the subjects. The imagery value was also manipulated by dividing the stimulus terms into 16 high and 16 low imagery terms. Thirty-two meaningless character strings were constructed to balance the positive and negative instances. The dependent measure was the reaction time (RT) required to make a correct decision. The results are summarized in Table 2.

First of all, subjects took much longer to make a negative response than a positive response and the data on negative responses were much noisier than those on the positive responses. Since our particular interest was in the positive response under various experimental conditions, an ANOVA for a 2 (RVF versus LVF) × 2 (high versus low imagery) factorial design with both factors as repeated measures was performed on RTs of the correct, positive responses. The main effect of imagery was significant with the high imagery terms having a 62 msec advantage over the low imagery terms, $F(1,19) = 5.69$, $p < 0.05$. This is consistent with previous findings (Paivio, 1971). The main effect of visual field was also highly significant, $F(1,19) = 14.52$, $p < 0.002$, with the RVF performance having a 104.1 msec advantage over the LVF performance. In other words, the results showed a RVF-LH superiority effect. On the surface, this result, together with that of the second experiment, seems to be in conflict with those of the first experiment. However, a moment's reflection reveals that these data are in fact compatible with the current view of cerebral organization which maintains that for most right-handed people, the left hemisphere is better at handling sequential and analytical tasks while the right hemisphere is better at handling holistic pattern recognition tasks. Since the experimental task in the first experiment emphasizes a holistic recognition of the single characters and since the experimental task in the second and third experiments emphasizes putting character strings together to get at the lexemes of the terms, the results of these three experiments not only do not conflict with each other but rather they support the differential function views of cerebral organization.

From the interpretation above, we are able to generate a further prediction: there should be a significant interaction effect between the visual field and the imagery values of the stimulus terms. That is to say, the difference in performance between the RVF and LVF should be greater for the low imagery terms than for the high imagery terms. This is because a low imagery, abstract term may require more complicated analyses to recover its semantic content, while it is possible that many high imagery, concrete nouns may only require a simple pattern recognition (i.e., visual reading). Thus, most low imagery terms can only be handled by the left hemisphere whereas most high imagery terms can easily be handled by both right and left hemispheres. A glance at Table 2 shows that the data are entirely consistent with this prediction: the difference between RVF and LVF under the low imagery condition is 129.67 msec whereas the difference between RVF and LVF under the high imagery condition is only 78.52 msec. Statistical analyses also substantiate this interaction, $F(1,19) = 4.44$, $p < 0.05$.

The results of these three experiments should be a lesson to most investigators: It is most important to evaluate experimental results from the viewpoint of what the subject's actual task is in an experiment and to make conclusions based upon data from more than one experiment. Otherwise, we would conclude that "the Chinese verbal ability is wired at the right hemisphere" from the results of the first experiment and "the Chinese verbal ability is wired at the left hemisphere" from the results of the second and third experiments. In fact, what has been demonstrated here is that reading involves various subtasks with different levels of complexity and a reader uses whatever strategies are available to him to accomplish these sub-tasks. Given the ingenuity of the investigator, one can always isolate one component of the task and conduct a certain experiment. Nevertheless, the conclusion generated from such an isolated experiment can never tell the whole story about reading. The interaction between visual hemifield and imagery points out a possible methodological strategy for future investigation. One may not be really interested in the problem of cerebral lateralization. Nevertheless, one still can utilize the more or less established functions of the left (sequential and analytical) and right (holistic, Gestalt-like pattern recognition) hemispheres to reveal various stages of information processing during reading. In fact, we adopted this strategy to conduct another experiment. The procedure is exactly the same as the first experiment reported above except that native English speakers were asked to name briefly presented, common, four-letter monosyllabic nouns. For one group of subjects, all stimulus items were presented in normal fashion, such as *FISH,* whereas for another group all stimulus terms were presented in alternating upper and lower cases, such as *fIsH.* The results showed a strong RVF superiority effect for the nouns presented in alternating cases, but a much reduced, although still significant, RVF superiority effect for the nouns presented in normal fashion. Presumably in the former case, the orthographic regularity has been destroyed so that direct lexical access (visual reading) is impossible.

We have mentioned that an increasing number of expressions in modern Chinese are multisyllabic in nature. However, the combinatory principle is not based upon phonetic consideration; rather, in most cases it is based upon semantic consideration. For example, 圖書館 (library) consists of three different characters. The first one means "pictures," the second means "books," and the third "a building." Together, they mean "a building for holding books and pictures"—library. Thus, the logographic principle differs from the alphabetic principle in that the former requires the extraction of meaning of each syllable (character) before the whole term can be comprehended, whereas the latter requires the identification of phonetic sound of each syllable before the whole word can be comprehended. Thus, the initial perception of Chinese characters and of English words may entail different processes. This is supported by the findings of an LVF superiority effect for single Chinese character identification but an RVF superiority effect for English word identification.

Biederman and Tsao (1977) reported a study in which they found that a greater Stroop interference effect (Stroop, 1935) was observed for Chinese subjects engaging in a Chinese version of the Stroop-color naming task than for American subjects in an English version. They attributed this difference to the possibility that there may be some fundamental differences in the perceptual demands of reading Chinese and English. We conducted two experi-

Table 3. Magnitude (in sec) of Stroop interference[a] as a function of stimulus language and of response language

Stimulus	Response	
	English	Chinese
English	33.38	23.42
Chinese	18.16	27.83

[a]Magnitude of Interference = RTs for Experimental condition -RTs for Control condition.

Table 4. Magnitude (in sec) of Stroop interference as a function of stimulus language and of response language

Stimulus	Response	
	English	Spanish
English	30.91	26.22
Spanish	20.26	24.71

ments on the Stroop effect but with a more complicated design. Preston and Lambert (1969) and Dyer (1971) both showed that for bilinguals, the condition where the interfering words were in one of the bilingual's languages and the color naming was to be done with the other language produced a great amount of interference, although significantly less than when color naming and interfering words were both in the same language. All the languages chosen in these two studies have alphabetic writing systems. No study has employed logographic symbols as experimental material and contrasted their effect with that produced by alphabetic materials. Our two experiments followed the procedure used by Preston and Lambert (1969). Subjects were asked to name the color of color patches (control condition) or of incongruent color names (experimental condition). The difference in reaction times (i.e., experimental condition minus control condition) was taken as the magnitude of the Stroop interference effect. The first experiment employed English-Chinese bilinguals and the second experiment employed English-Spanish bilinguals. In both experiments, subjects named the colors in the language consistent with the printed color names for one-half of the time; in the remaining time they named the colors in a language other than that of the printed color names. Note that the color patches were named twice, once in each language, to provide the appropriate baseline for gauging the Stroop effect in each respective responding language. The results are presented in Table 3 and Table 4, for English-Chinese bilinguals and English-Spanish bilinguals, respectively.

Clearly, a tremendous Stroop interference effect occurs in every experimental condition. Also consistent with the results reported by both Dyer (1971) and Preston and Lambert (1969), the interlanguage color naming produced much less interference than the intra-language color naming. The most important finding, however, is that the magnitude of reduction because of switching languages is greater in the case of English-Chinese bilinguals (Table 3) than in the case of English-Spanish bilinguals (Table 4). Since Spanish and English are both alphabetic systems, switching languages does not change the processing demands. However, since English and Chinese represent two different writing systems (i.e., alphabetic versus logographic), switching from one to another may prevent the subject from employing the same processing mechanism and consequently cause him to be released from the Stroop effect. The results of these two experiments seem to support Biederman's and Tsao's (1977) contention that reading English and Chinese entail two different perceptual demands, at least at the level of single character recognition.

PHONETIC RECODING IN READING CHINESE CHARACTERS

Ever since Conrad (1964) demonstrated that phonetic recoding occurs in processing verbal materials even if they are presented visually, a large number of experiments have investigated the role of phonetic recoding in reading. One of the major issues involved in these experiments is whether phonetic recoding is necessary in ordinary reading. An answer to this question is not easy since the experimental evidence is not consistent from one study to another. On the pro speech recoding side, Krueger (1970) demonstrated that acoustic confusability affected the speed of searching for a particular letter, and Corcoran and Weening (1968) also showed that omission of pronounced letters was easier to detect in proofreading than that of unpronounced letters. Furthermore, Rubenstein, Lewis, and Rubenstein (1971) presented evidence showing that pronounceable nonwords which sound like words are more difficult to classify than are pronounceable nonwords which do not sound like words. So it seems that phonetic recoding is necessarily involved in reading.

The seemingly clear picture becomes messy if we consider the experimental results obtained by Baron and his associates (Baron, 1973; Baron & McKillop, 1975). They found that the reaction time to determine if a short phrase makes sense is not affected by the phonetic factor. For example, Baron (1973) showed that homonyms that are not homographs (e.g., *knot–not; pane–pain; piece–peace*) do not confuse skillful or fluent readers. In his experiment, subjects were asked to read different types of phrases, some of which were meaningful both as written and as they would be pronounced (e.g., *My new car; He sees poorly*), some of which were meaningful as they would be pronounced but which were meaningless as written (e.g., *My knew car; He seas poorly*), and some of which were meaningless in either case (e.g., *pie pot; nut and bout*). Reaction times for judgments of *makes no sense* were the same for items like *My knew car* as for items like *pie pot*. Baron argued that if a subject uses phonetic recoding to mediate in converting the message to meaning, then he would hear in his head *My knew car* as meaningful and either make a wrong judgment or take extra time to notice the spelling and respond correctly. Since his results disconfirmed this hypothesis, Baron concluded that a phonetic stage is not necessary for reading.

A more detailed analysis of the phonetic factors at the lexical access stage was provided by Meyer and Ruddy (1973) in two experiments. Again, the findings are contradictory. It was found that reaction times for negative responses in a spelling task were slower for pseudo-members than for non-members. This suggests that speech recoding is occurring. They also found that responses to nonmembers were faster in the spelling than the pronunciation task, and the positive responses in the pronunciation task were faster for members than for pseudo-members. A phonetic recoding view would predict no difference in both these cases.

To account for all these inconsistencies, Meyer and Ruddy (1973) proposed a "parallel horse-race model," in which lexical memory is accessed through both visual and speech representation of a word. On a given trial, phonetic properties will affect reaction time only if the speech route locates the lexical entry first. Since it is obvious that lexical entries can be accessed via phonemic codes, the interesting claim is that they can also be accessed via visual code. Kleiman (1975) speculates that skilled readers may use the visual routes most of the time. It is also possible that perhaps the visual route is usually preferred by readers of logographic symbols. A skillful reader can go directly from orthographically coded information to meaning if the material is not difficult. When material is difficult, people tend to subvocalize the sentence. In this situation, phonetic recoding is used as a means of retaining orthographic material in the immediately activated working memory until the whole sentence is comprehended. However, we should notice that all the subjects in the experiments mentioned above were fluent readers. These results may not be applicable to beginning readers. I. Y. Liberman, Shankweiler, A. M. Liberman, Fowler, and Fischer (1977) demonstrated that phonetic recoding is almost a necessary stage toward reading comprehension for beginning readers. Most children learn to read English by learning to produce sounds in response to printed text, and to derive meaning from the text by listening to the sounds they produce. For some beginning readers, it may be a difficult job to break down the words they hear into separate phonemes, so that they cannot come up with the sound that corresponds to the printed text. There is indeed some evidence for such a type of dyslexia. Rozin et al. (1971) taught a group of second grade children with serious reading problems some ideographic characters. They hypothesized that since logographic writing systems such as Chinese have a one-to-one correspondence between sound to meaning, children do not need to break down words into phonemes in order to sound them out; consequently, they should be able to read Chinese with little trouble. Their results seem to support this hypothesis. Rozin et al. (1971) suggested that the success of their program can be attributed to the fact that Chinese characters map onto speech at the level of words rather than of phonemes. Therefore, Rozin et al. and many other reading researchers have come to the conclusion that since a logographic language has printed forms that do not contain information about pronunciation, people must be able to read without speech recoding. We think this is an overstatement and therefore do not totally agree with it.

Phonetic recoding is claimed to be an important factor in reading for two reasons. First, in blending the individual sounds of words, the phonetic recoding of the individual letter sounds can plausibly be argued as an important intervening stage, at least for children learning to read. Clearly this view is concerned with the problem of lexical recognition and is relevant to the claim that inadequate phonetic recoding can be avoided by logographic scripts such as Chinese characters. A second way in which phonetic coding may be involved in reading is concerned with the question of whether fluent adult readers need to recode phonetically printed material or are assisted by doing so. In this view the phonetic recoding is seen as a general strategy of human information processing, and thus the orthographic differences in the printed materials become less important.

So our view is that even if the thesis that lexical access can occur directly from visual input is valid in reading individual Chinese characters, it is possible that phonetic recoding may still be needed at a later stage (e.g., the working memory stage) of text comprehension. There are at least three reasons why phonetic recoding might be needed at the working memory stage. One is that maybe the storage component operates efficiently only if the representation of the lexical information is in a phonetic code (Atkinson & Shiffrin, 1968). Another reason is that the process involved in the parsing and abstraction of syntactic structures may be able to function only on phonetic codes (Kleiman, 1975). The third reason is that phonetic coding might transform the text into a motor program that would operate at a higher speed (see, for example, Hardyck & Petrinovich, 1970). From these viewpoints, the phonetic recoding can facilitate temporary storage, or comprehension processes, or both. Thus, it is plausible to expect that the phonetic recoding would occur even in the reading of Chinese characters and this is exactly what was found by Tzeng, Hung, and Wang (1977).

Recently in our laboratory two other experimental paradigms have been used to examine the role of phonetic recoding in reading Chinese characters embedded in unrelated character strings, in sentences, and in paragraphs. The first one involved asking Chinese subjects to make decisions about strings of characters with or without a concurrent shadowing task. Since the shadowing task (i.e., subjects had to repeat digits in Chinese delivered through a headphone) presumably disrupts phonetic recoding, a measure of the shadowing effect on a given decision should provide an estimate of how much recoding facilitates that decision. That is, a decision not requiring recoding should show a relatively small shadowing effect, which would be due only to general disruption, while a decision requiring recoding

Table 5.   Mean reaction times (in msec) for the three types of decisions with or without concurrent shadowing task

Type of decision	Examples		Without shadowing	With shadowing
	True	False		
Graphemic	汪沅 花芸	見好 元父	650	777
Phonetic	江香 冬公	春面 才里	974	1294
Semantic	哀悲 兵軍	工古 法豆	878	1011

should show a large effect resulting from both the general disruption and the specific disruption of recoding. Two experiments were conducted with this paradigm. In the first experiment, the subject, wearing a headphone, sat in front of a tachistoscope in which two characters were presented simultaneously. The subject's task was to make one of the following three decisions about these two characters: 1) share an identical radical (graphemic), 2) rhyme with each other (phonetic), or 3) are synonyms (semantic). The presentation of the characters, the recording of reaction time (RT), the manipulation of the tape recorder (for the shadowing task), and all necessary randomization procedures were monitored by a PDP 11/34 computer. Before the presentation of the characters, the subject was briefly instructed about what type of decision was to be made in the following trial. The results of this experiment are summarized in Table 5.

The last two columns of Table 5 list the mean RTs required for making the three types of decisions with or without the concurrent shadowing task. Apparently, only the phonetic decision has been affected tremendously by the shadowing task. Both the graphemic and semantic decisions seem to suffer only the general disruption caused by the shadowing task. Thus, it can be concluded that for single characters lexical access does not require the intermediate stage of phonetic decision.

In the second experiment, we modified the procedure to allow the presentation of sentences. The subject was asked to make one of three decisions: 1) graphemic decision, 2) phonetic decision, or 3) sentence judgment in which the subject was asked to determine whether a string of characters formed a meaningful and grammatically correct sentence. For both the graphemic and phonetic decision tasks, a target character was presented above a string of seven or eight different characters and the subject was asked to look at the target character and then scan the string of characters in order to make the appropriate decisions. Once again the important comparisons are between the RTs for various decisions with or without shadowing the concurrent task. The results are summarized in Table 6.

Table 6. Mean reaction times (in msec) for the three types of decisions with or without concurrent shadowing task

Type of decision	Example		Without shadowing	With shadowing
Graphemic	吃 用強張死女銀吵叔	(True)	977	1069
	打 包布名土治甲衣短	(False)		
Phonetic	皮 天間米水回耕人土	(True)	1063	1160
Sentence	昨天老張又去賭博了	(True)	997	1302
	文明在高進大很無趣	(False)		

The results are similar to those in the previous experiment in that the shadowing task has little effect on the graphemic decision but has a tremendous effect on the phonetic decision. Of particular interest in this experiment is the effect of shadowing on the sentence judgment. An inspection of Table 6 reveals that the sentence judgment is also affected greatly by the shadowing task, suggesting that a phonetic recoding process occurs during sentence processing. All these results are consistent with those reported by Tzeng et al. (1977).

Another experimental paradigm we used in evaluating the role of phonetic recoding in reading was a detection task in which Chinese subjects were asked to read a section of prose containing about 1,500 characters and concurrently circle all characters that contained certain grapheme components, such as 台 and 由. We found that subjects detected characters most often when the designated grapheme component carried a phonetic clue (i.e., phonograms). This result is similar to a corresponding case in English which showed that American subjects were better at detecting an embedded sounded e than an embedded silent e while reading prose (Corcoran & Weening, 1968).

The results of all these experiments enable us to conclude that phonetic recoding does play an important role even in reading a logographic writing system.

CONCLUSION

Whether differences in writing systems would result in different information processing strategies during reading has been a major concern of reading specialists for a long time (Gibson & Levin, 1975). However, most experimental investigations of this problem in the past have always focused on some gross measures such as the reading rate (i.e., number of words or characters read per minute) and eye-voice span (the distance, usually measured in number of words or characters, that the eyes are ahead of the voice when reading aloud). The results of such cross-language and cross-writing system comparisons yield nothing but very crude guesses as to reading behaviors in general. Little can be said about whether there are indeed different problems faced by beginning readers in different language environments.

In this chapter, two current major research approaches were reviewed which attempt to reveal the functional properties of reading Chinese characters from an information processing perspective. The first line of research shows that one can demonstrate the right- or left-hemisphere superiority in visual processing of Chinese characters depending upon what the subjects have to do to meet the experimental requirements. Therefore, the visual lateralization difference found previously on the various writing systems (e.g., kanji and kana) reflects a task-specific property of the two hemispheres rather than the orthographic-specific localization property hypothesized by previous researchers (Hatta, 1976, 1977; Sasanuma et al., 1977). The second line of research provides evidence that speech recoding does occur in processing Chinese characters beyond the working memory stage. This fact enables us to argue for the facilitative role of the speech code in reading difficult materials. Together, we begin to understand human reading behaviors as general linguistic activities. However, we are still only at the edge of understanding the total processes of reading. Much research work waits to be done, and experimental studies of reading Chinese characters definitely will provide some very fruitful results.

Chapter 15
SOME EXPERIMENTS ON THE ROMAN AND CYRILLIC ALPHABETS OF SERBO-CROATIAN

Georgije Lukatela and Michael T. Turvey

CROSS-LANGUAGE COMPARISONS: SERBO-CROATIAN ORTHOGRAPHIES AND THEIR SPECIAL PROPERTIES

Much if not most of current theorizing on the reading process and visual information processing is based on investigations with English language materials. Perhaps such processes vary but little across languages and orthographies and therefore a theory based on one language will suffice for all. However, what variations there are may prove to be revealing. We have been asking whether or not the reading of Serbo-Croatian may make use of different characteristics of the written word or different encoding routines than are used in the reading of English.

A distinction that is often made between logographic writing systems, such as Korean, Chinese, and Japanese kanji, and alphabetic systems, such as English and Serbo-Croatian, is that the former refer to the morphology, while the latter refer to the phonology. The logographic system is said to specify units of meaning, whereas the alphabetic system is said to specify the sounds of the spoken language, although the distinction is not as sharp. Indeed, this interpretation of the alphabet is less than ideal as far as English is concerned, for the correspondence between written and spoken English is opaque: graphemes can be made silent by context and, in general, graphemes take on different phonetic trappings in different graphemic contexts. Looking for regularity in the English orthography, Gibson, Pick, Osser, and Hammond (1962) advanced the idea of a spelling pattern, a cluster of letters that corresponds to a sound. While individual letters in English do not have invariant phonetic interpretations, certain arrangements of letters do, particularly when their locations within words are taken into consideration. Whether or not the notion of spelling pattern is valid, the point is obvious: the cipher relating script to utterance in English is complex. We argue that the cipher in Serbo-Croatian is considerably more transparent; and that for the Serbo-Croatian orthography the claim that it specifies the

227

sounds of speech is potentially closer to the mark. But let us pursue the English orthography a little further.

The opaqueness of the script to utterance relation in English is owing, by and large, to two reasons. First, the pronunciation of the language evolved along different lines from the spelling of the language. Consider the following example cited by Henderson (1977). The English digraph *gh* as in *bough* and *rough* specified a unique gutteral utterance until the seventeenth century. After the seventeenth century the pronunciation of *gh* took two directions, it either became silent as in *night* or took the phonetic interpretation /f/ as in *enough*. But the spelling had already become standardized largely owing to the efforts of the fifteenth century English printers, such as Caxton; and, in consequence, *gh* is handed down to the contemporary reader of English as an orthographic anomaly.

The second reason for the spelling-sound opaqueness is that the English orthography may be as close to the morphology as it is to the phonology. Indeed, in the evolution of the English language, Henderson (1977) has stated that the tendency has been for the orthography to reflect etymology, which is tantamount to saying that it reflects the basic units of meaning. In this vein Chomsky (1970b) has argued that the English orthography is near optimal for writing the English language. The orthography preserves the morphology, which would not be the case if the optimality principles were phonetic correspondences. Thus, the spelling preserves the following morphological similarities—tele-graphy, tele-graph-ic, tele-graphy-y—in the face of the obvious phonetic variability. Similarly *anxious* and *anxiety* by virtue of their visual likeness permit the reader, in principle, to go directly from the appearance of the letter sequence to its meaning. Therefore, the fundamental point made by Chomsky (1970) and also by Venezky (1970) (but for somewhat different reasons) should be noted, namely, that the English orthography is systematic in its own right. It is specific to linguistic structure at a deep level and is not to be understood just as a phonemic transcription. Indeed, on the Chomsky-Venezky view, the script-utterance relation is opaque precisely because the script and utterance are *alternative* specifications of the same underlying structure (cf. Francis, 1970). However, the tempering conclusion of Gleitman and Rozin's (1977) thorough analysis is that it is not so much that English orthography is optimal for this or that grain-size of linguistic analysis, but rather that English writing is a rich mixture of a number of grains of linguistic representation, together with more than a sprinkling of arbitrary features.

Let us now turn to Serbo-Croatian, Yugoslavia's major language. Serbo-Croatian, unlike English, is pronounced as it is written; that is, individual letters have phonetic interpretations that remain consistent throughout changes in the context in which they are imbedded. All written letters are pronounced; hence, in Serbo-Croatian there are no silent letters and no double letters.

This state of affairs—a straightforward regularity between script and utterance—is by virtue of a historical development that sharply contrasts the evolution of the Serbo-Croatian orthography with that of the English orthography. The modern Serbo-Croatian orthography was constructed at the beginning of the nineteenth century by Karadić on the basis of a simple rule: "Write as you speak and read as it is written!" In Serbo-Croatian, therefore, constraints on sound sequences are the sole sources of constraints on letter sequences. This contrasts with English in which restrictions on letter sequences derive not only from phonological constraints but also from a desire to preserve the etymology and graphemic convention. That is, from a "...1400-year accumulation of scribal practices, printing conventions, lexicographers' selections, and occasional accident which somehow became codified as part of the present orthographic system" (Venezky & Massaro, 1976, p. 25). In English, illegal phonological sequences (such as /wh/) can be orthographically regular spellings (such as wh) but no such peculiarity is permitted in Serbo-Croatian.

Karadić (1814) selected the speech spoken in mid-Yugoslavia as the ideal and to each phonemic segment of the speech he assigned a letter character or, in a few cases, a combination of letters. Karadić took the majority of letters from the alphabet existing at the time but since the number of letters available was less than the number of phonemes needed, he borrowed or modified several letters from other alphabets. In fact, two alphabets were constructed: a Roman alphabet and a Cyrillic alphabet. In modern Yugoslavia, Eastern Serbo-Croatian uses primarily the Cyrillic script whereas Western Serbo-Croatian uses primarily the Roman. In some regions (e.g., Bosnia, Herzegovinia), however, both scripts are used about equally.

The Serbo-Croatian language has 30 phonemes. In the Cyrillic alphabet there is one letter for each phoneme; in the Roman, 27 phonemes are represented by single letters and three phonemes by pairs of letters: LJ, NJ, DZ. Figure 1 compares the Roman and Cyrillic alphabets in uppercase and in Table 1 the letters (both uppercase and cursive) of the alphabets are given their corresponding letter-names in the International Phonetic Alphabet (IPA) transcription.

An important fact about the Roman and Cyrillic alphabets is that they map onto the same set of phones but still comprise two sets of letters that are, with certain exceptions, mutually exclusive. Of the total set of letters comprising the two alphabets the majority are unique to one or the other alphabet (see Figure 1). A number of letters, however, are shared by the two alphabets. Of these shared letters, some receive the same phonetic interpretation whether read as Roman or Cyrillic (referred to as common letters) and some receive two phonetic interpretations, one in the Roman reading and one in the Cyrillic reading (referred to as ambiguous letters). Therefore, one may recognize instances in which letters are different in shape but pronounced the same way, e.g., the Cyrillic И and the Roman I are both pro-

Serbo-Croatian Alphabet
—Uppercase—

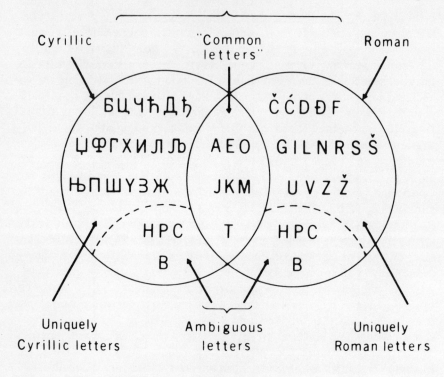

Figure 1.   The two alphabets of the Serbo-Croatian language.

nounced like the *ea* in *seat;* instances in which letters are the same in shape and pronunciation; and instances in which the letters are of the same shape but pronounced differently, e.g., the Cyrillic *H* is pronounced like the *n* in *wine,* the Roman *H* like the *ch* in the Scottish rendering of *loch.*

Three examples underscore the unusualness of Serbo-Croatian bi-alphabetism. The sentence, *This is my mother,* translated into Serbo-Croatian is spelled: *TO JE MOJA MAJKA.* In IPA it is rendered as: [to je moja majka]. There is no way to tell whether this particular sentence is written in Roman or Cyrillic, since only the common letters have been used. The sentence, *The deer climbs,* translated into Serbo-Croatian is spelled in Cyrillic as: *CPHA CE BEPE.* In IPA it is rendered as: [srna se vere]. However, if *CPHA CE BEPE* were read as Roman, it would be uttered as: [tspxa tse bepe], which is a meaningless utterance. Finally, one may note the sentence, *The pupil studies reading,* which is written in Cyrillic, ЂАК УЧИ ДА ЧИТА but in Roman as, *ĐAK UČI DA ČITA.* Regardless of which alphabet has

Serbo-Croatian				
Roman		Cyrillic		
Printed Upper Case	Cursive Lower Case	Printed Upper Case	Cursive Lower Case	Letter Name in I.P.A.
A	*a*	А	*a*	a
B	*b*	Б	*ð*	bə
C	*c*	Ц	*ц*	tsə
Č	*č*	Ч	*ч*	tʃə
Ć	*ć*	ħ	*ħ*	tʃjə
D	*d*	Д	*g*	də
Đ	*đ*	ħ	*ħ*	dʒjə
DŽ	*dž*	Џ	*џ*	dʒə
E	*e*	Е	*e*	ɛ
F	*f*	Ф	*φ*	fə
G	*g*	Г	*ʒ*	gə
H	*h*	Х	*x*	xə
I	*i*	И	*и*	i
J	*j*	Ј	*j*	jə
K	*k*	К	*k*	kə
L	*l*	Л	*л*	lə
LJ	*lj*	Љ	*љ*	ljə
M	*m*	М	*м*	mə
N	*n*	Н	*н*	ne
NJ	*nj*	Њ	*њ*	njə
O	*o*	О	*c*	ɔ
P	*p*	П	*ū*	pə
R	*r*	Р	*р*	rə
S	*s*	С	*c*	sə
Š	*š*	Ш	*ш*	ʃə
T	*t*	Т	*ū*	tə
U	*u*	У	*у*	u
V	*v*	В	*b*	və
Z	*z*	З	*з*	zə
Ž	*ž*	Ж	*ж*	ʒə

Table 1.   Letters of the Serbo-Croatian alphabet

been used, the phonetic transcription is the same in both cases: [dzjak uči da čita], as is the meaning.

A most central feature is that both alphabets are taught in the schools and by most accounts the letter forms and the letter-to-sound correspondences of both alphabets are learned by the end of the second grade. The children are taught one alphabet in the first year and a half and then master the other by the end of the second year. In the western part of the nation the Roman alphabet is learned first and in the eastern part of the nation it is the Cyrillic alphabet that the children master initially. This geographically based ordering of acquisition of the two alphabets provides a model for examining the relation of two separate symbol systems, learned at different times—a bi-alphabetism if you wish—of which bilingualism is the fashionable example. It deserves reemphasizing that the two alphabets map onto the same phonetic and semantic structure.

At this juncture let us collect the preceding discussions of the phonetic regularity and the bi-alphabetism of Serbo-Croatian in order to highlight several important contrasts with English orthography. First, where it can be claimed that the English orthography more directly represents the morphology, it can be claimed that the Serbo-Croatian orthographies more directly represent the phonology. Common to the views of Chomsky and Venezky, a reader of English often needs to know more about a word than its surface orthographic structure in order to pronounce it. One would say of Serbo-Croatian that knowledge about any word's surface orthographic structure is generally all that is needed in order to pronounce it. Second, English spelling more than occasionally reveals the etymology of words but the radical reworking of the Serbo-Croatian writing system according to Karadić's injunction ensured that the contemporary orthography would be essentially ahistorical. Third, because of the virtually invariant relation between letter and sound there are no true homophones in Serbo-Croatian. (Situations such as *tale/tail, crews/cruise, wait/weight* could never arise.) We emphasize *true* because the bi-alphabetic nature of Serbo-Croatian permits homophones of a very special kind, precisely, letter sequences that are visually quite distinct—for one is composed mainly of uniquely Cyrillic and the other of uniquely Roman letters—but which are identical in pronunciation and meaning.

It is the case, however, that Serbo-Croatian, like English, allows true homographs. It is for this reason that a reader can *generally,* rather than *always,* pronounce a word correctly on the basis of knowing only its surface orthography. Two words may be written the same way, but, owing to different assignments of vowel length and accent type, can be pronounced differently and mean different things. In Serbo-Croatian a vowel can be short or long and its accent can or can not extend into the following syllable.

Sometimes these contrasts are noted by diacritical marks. More commonly, however, the ambiguity must be resolved, as in English, by sentential context. The language gives rise additionally to a special kind of homography, again made manifest over the two alphabets. Thus a given letter sequence such as *POTOP* can be read one way in Roman and another way in Cyrillic (see Table 1), and mean two entirely different things (respectively, *inundation* and *rotor*).

There is a further feature of the Serbo-Croatian language on which we now pass remark by way of concluding our delineation of the language's special properties. It is that inflection is the principal grammatical device in the language in contrast with English which uses inflection for grammatical purposes only sparingly. Thus for nouns, all grammatical cases in Serbo-Croatian are formed by adding to the root form an inflectional element, namely, a suffix consisting of one syllable of the vowel or vowel-consonant type. The Serbo-Croatian nouns, pronouns, and adjectives are declined in seven cases of singular and seven cases of plural whereas verbs are conjugated by person and number in six forms.

ERROR PATTERN IN BEGINNING READING

Where other languages with a close match between sound and writing have been examined, the evidence is that children learned very rapidly to read aloud letter sequences congruent with the orthographic rules of the language (Elkonin, 1963; Venezky, 1973b). Nevertheless, it can be noted that indifferent to the script-to-utterance correspondence reading differences emerge early (Gibson & Levin, 1975) and that some children will continue to have problems even where the spelling of the words on which they are instructed is phonetically regular and maps to sound directly (Savin, 1972). Reading skill, in the long run, appears to be largely indifferent to the language being read (Gray, 1956). A not overly venturesome claim is that different writing systems induce differences in acquisition of reading and differences in the reading process without necessarily affecting the ultimate proficiency of reading. The point to be emphasized, perhaps, is that of Carroll (1972): "A perfectly regular alphabetic system may facilitate word-recognition processes but its use does not alter the fact that the learning of reading entails the acquisition of skills in composing word units from their separate graphic components and practice, large amounts of it, in recognizing particular word units."

Given the orthographic distinction between English and Serbo-Croatian one can ask: In what ways does the beginning reader in Serbo-Croatian differ from his counterpart in English and in what ways are they the same? One can ask, in short, with respect to the acquisition of reading, what changes across orthographies and what remains invariant? We are examining this question in relation to research already conducted and currently underway at the Haskins Laboratories.

A point of departure for the reading research of the Haskins Laboratories' group is that reading is somehow parasitic on speech. One recent focus has been the notion of "linguistic awareness" (Mattingly, 1972). A child might try to read words by the mediary of shape. But this nonanalytic strategy, while useful to a point, is far from optimal; the child cannot benefit from the fact that the alphabet permits its users to generate a letter string's pronunciation from the spelling. But what is required of the child to know how the alphabet works? I. Y. Liberman and Shankweiler (in press) argue that the child must realize that speech can be segmented into phonemes and he must know how many phonemes any given word in his vocabulary contains and their order. He must know that the letters of the alphabet represent phonemes, not syllables or some other unit of speech (see also Gleitman & Rozin, 1977; Rozin & Gleitman, 1977).

The difficulty and significance of phonemic segmentation has been frequently noted (e.g., Elkonin, 1973; Gibson & Levin, 1975; Rosner & Simon, 1971); the inability to analyze syllables into phonemes marks the child who has failed to learn how to read or, at least, who reads poorly (I. Y. Liberman, Shankweiler, A. M. Liberman, Fowler, & Fischer, 1976, Savin, 1972).

Exemplary of the difficulty with phonemic segmentation is the pattern of errors a child makes in reading syllables. For simple English consonant-vowel-consonant structures the error rate on the final consonant is larger than that on the initial consonant while the error rate on the vowel is largest of all (Shankweiler & I. Y. Liberman, 1972). Moreover, the form of the vowel and consonant errors differ in nontrivial ways (I. Y. Liberman & Shankweiler, in press). To what extent, one might ask, are these patternings of errors orthographically based? Are they indigenous to the writing system of English or would they be as likely in the orthographies of Serbo-Croatian? For example, the greater error rate on vowels might be owing to the fact that in English vowel pronunciation is extremely context conditioned. On the other hand, it might be owing to the differential status of vowels and consonants in the perception and production of speech; in which case one might treat the different error rates of vowels and consonants and the direction of the difference as indexing a universal property of phonographic writing systems.

We have begun an examination of these questions through an experiment that is closely comparable to one previously conceived and conducted by the Haskins Laboratories group.

The 65 subjects in the experiment all tested within the normal range of intelligence. They were selected from the first grade population of an elementary school system located in Belgrade. Their ages ranged from 6.5 to

7.5 years. They had completed their first semester and had an active knowl-edge of the Cyrillic alphabet.

We devised two lists of the CVC-type monosyllables written in Cyrillic. One hundred CVCs were words and 100 CVCs were nonwords. The words were familiar to first graders. In the word and nonword lists the 25 Serbo-Croatian consonant phonemes that can occur in both the initial and in the final positions of a word appeared twice in each position. In the majority of the trigrams the medial letter was one of the five Serbo-Croatian vowels (/i/, /e/, /a/, /o/, /u/) as in ДИБ 'giant,' ЦЕВ 'pipe,' ДАР 'gift,' СОН 'juice,' and ВУН 'wolf.' In some trigrams, however, the medial letter was the semi-vowel /r/. In Serbo-Croatian monosyllabic words of the type con-sonant–semivowel /r/–consonant, as in ВРХ 'top,' ТРН 'thorn,' ГРБ 'emblem,' are not infrequent. And finally, it should be noted that of the 100 words, 25 could be reversed to produce other words: For example the word БОР 'pine' if read from right to left reads РОБ 'slave.'

A string of three uppercase Cyrillic letters arranged horizontally at the center of a separate $3'' \times 5''$ white card defined a stimulus. The cards were placed face down in front of the subject and were turned over one by one by the examiner. The subject was asked to read each letter string aloud as it was presented. Responses were written down by the examiner and were re-corded simultaneously on magnetic tape. A complete list was presented in a single session with each child participating in two separate sessions. If in the first session the child read the word list, then in the second session he read the nonword list and vice versa. The order of presentation was balanced across children.

The responses to the stimuli revealed several types of errors: 1) substi-tution, 2) addition, 3) omission, and 4) reversal of sequence when a letter string or a part of it was read from left to right. Single letter orientation er-rors did not occur because the Cyrillic uppercase letters did not provide op-portunity for reversing letter orientation.

The analysis of errors showed that sequence reversals accounted for only a small proportion of the total of misread letters, although the lists were constructed to provide ample opportunity for the complete reversal of sequences. (As noted, 25% of the words were "reversible"; and 13% of the nonwords were words if read from right to left, for example, the nonword НИС would become СИН 'son').

The complete sequence reversals are distinguished from the partial and the total reversal scores for words and nonwords are given in Table 2. Pro-portions of opportunity for error (in percentages) are presented within parentheses. We note that sequence reversals were rare.

Single letter omission errors were also quite rare. Their distribution on initial and final consonants and on the medial vowel/semivowel is presented in Table 3. Omissions of the final consonant in words seem to be more fre-

Table 2.   Sequence reversals

	Complete sequence reversal	Partial sequence reversal	Total
Words	17 (1.1%)	6 (0.0%)	23
Nonwords	21 (2.5%)	13 (0.0%)	34

quent than in nonwords, but the respective proportions of opportunity are too small to allow any reliable conclusion on their distribution.

Additional errors were distributed in a nonrandom manner (See Table 4). Additions of a single phoneme in front of the final consnant (FC_1) were more frequent than after the final consonant (FC_2), other types of additions being relatively infrequent.

In words and nonwords of the consonant–semivowel /r/–consonant type, additions of a single phoneme in front of the final consonant were relatively the most frequent. For example, the word ГРБ was often misread as /grab/, /grub/, /greb/, or /grob/. In four words (ГРБ, ВРХ, ТРГ , ТРН) there were 45 single vowel additions, and in four nonwords (БРС, ДРН, КРП, ПРК) there were 47 single vowel additions of the FC_1 type. Viewed in terms of opportunities for this particular error in the four words, the percentage amounts to 17% and in the four nonwords up to 18%. This is a notable result. Apparently, to facilitate the phonetic representation of the letter string, the child inserted a vowel between the medial semivowel and the final consonant.

Substitutions of single phonemes were the major source of errors in the experiment. Distribution of substitution errors on initial and final consonant and on the medial vowel/semivowel is presented in Table 5. Raw error scores and the respective percentages (within parentheses) indicate that final consonant (FC) errors exceed initial consonant (IC) errors. A Wilcoxon signed-rank test on proportions of correct responses revealed that this difference was significant ($T_{52} = 252$, $p < 0.001$), a result that agrees with the findings for beginning readers of English. The occurrence of phoneme sub-

Table 3.   Omission errors

	Initial consonant	Medial vowel	Final consonant	Total
Words	1	4	11 (0.2%)	16
Nonwords	4	3	3	10

Table 4. Additions of a single phoneme

	Initial consonant	Medial vowel	Before final consonant FC_1	After final consonant FC_2	Total
Words	6	10	52	12	80
Nonwords	1	9	52	25	87

stitutions on medial vowel segments was, however, less frequent than on initial ($T_{53} = 273$, $p < 0.001$) or final ($T_{57} = 202$, $p < 0.001$) consonant segments. Serbo-Croatian differs from English: consonants cause more difficulty for beginning readers than vowels. In an attempt to understand this finding one is reminded that the vowel set in Serbo-Croatian comprises only five vowels and that the Serbo-Croatian vowels are neatly distinctive in the F_1–F_2 plane. On the contrary, within some groups of the Serbo-Croatian consonants the distinctiveness is poor. For example, within the group of four affricates /tʃ/, /tʃj/, /dʒ/, /dʒj/ the phoneme boundaries are extremely fragile. Moreover, in some regions of Yugoslavia the native population replaces the voiced affricates /tʃ/ and /dʒ/ by their respective voiceless mates /tʃj/ and /dʒj/.

In our opinion the result of this experiment indicates that the substitution errors (both the initial consonant and final consonant) were phonetically biased. By far the more frequent errors were the substitutions within the group of the Serbo-Croatian affricates. All proportions of opportunity for substitution in Table 5 are small in comparison with the corresponding figures in the report of Shankweiler and I. Y. Liberman (1972).

A last but not the least interesting finding of this experiment is the fact that the final consonant substitution errors (see Table 5) were more frequent for nonwords than for words. This suggests that even at an early stage of learning to read the process of decoding is sensitive to lexical content and that the child may possess both nonlexical (orthographic) and lexical routes to the phonology (Baron & Strawson, 1976; Forster & Chambers, 1973; Patterson & Marcel, 1977).

Table 5. Single phoneme substitution errors

	Initial consonant	Medial vowel	Final consonant	Total
Words	172 (2.6%)	93 (1.4%)	264 (4.1%)	529
Nonwords	213 (3.3%)	113 (1.7%)	368 (5.7%)	693

LEXICAL DECISION AND PHONOLOGICAL ANALYSIS

It is commonplace to underscore the fact that English spelling is a less than perfect transcription of the phonology. Nevertheless, English is an alphabet in spite of its apparent phonological capriciousness—for each spelled English word provides strong hints as to its pronunciation. Some students of reading (e.g., Smith, 1971), however, have felt that the hints are so obscure, the relation between script and phonology so opaque, that the fluent reading of English by-passes what must be the complex and arduous process of converting the letter patterns into their related phonological forms. The idea that the fluent reading of English may proceed without reference to the phonology is buttressed by the claim that the English spelling optimally transcribes the morphology, that is, the meaning structure (Chomsky, 1970b). Given this claim, it is a simple step to supposing that the fluent reading of English proceeds as one might suppose that the fluent reading of logographic writing proceeds, that is, without a phonological intermediary between the printed word and its meaning (e.g., Goodman, 1973).

But forceful arguments can be made and have been made by Rozin and Gleitman (1977) to counter these denials of a phonologic strategy. Indeed, as Rozin and Gleitman (1977) take pains to point out, the observations questioning a phonological mediary cut two ways and when looked at carefully add strength to, rather than weaken, the notion of phonological involvement in the reading of English.

It is evident from what has been said about Serbo-Croatian writing, that neither of the two foregoing arguments against a phonological encoding is especially compelling from the perspective of that orthography. Indeed, if an opaque relation between script and phonology and an optimal transcription of the morphology are advanced as reasons *against* phonological involvement in the reading of English, then a transparent relation between script and phonology and an optimal transcription of the phonology should be received as reasons *for* phonological involvement in the reading of Serbo-Croatian.

At all events, this general issue of the contribution of phonological encoding to reading is given particular expression in various laboratory tasks. An extremely popular task is that of lexical decision, a task in which the subject must decide as rapidly as possible whether a visually presented letter string is a word. A finding often presented as evidence for phonological involvement in accessing English lexical items is that rejection latencies for nonhomophonic nonwords are shorter than for homophonic nonwords (Rubenstein, Lewis, & Rubenstein, 1971). That is, it takes longer to initiate response (say, pressing a telegraph key) to indicate "no" (it is not a word) to a nonword that sounds exactly like a real word than to a nonword that does not sound like any word (also Coltheart, Davelaar, Jonasson, & Besner, 1977). While, in general, lexical decision experiments support the idea of a phonologically mediated access to English lexical items (e.g., Meyer, Schvaneveldt, & Ruddy, 1974), other experiments that use other tasks imply no phonological analysis or, at best, a phonological analysis that occurs subsequent to lexical evaluation (e.g., Green & Shallice, 1976; Kleiman, 1975).

All things considered, however, the emerging orthodoxy appears to be that there is both a phonologically mediated route to the lexicon and a more direct, nonphonological route with the two modes of access relatively independent and possibly parallel in operation. As Gleitman and Rozin (1977) express it, reading probably proceeds at a number of grains of linguistic analysis simultaneously.

We wish to support the claim of phonological involvement in lexical decision. Evidence is presented that suggests that in lexical decision on Serbo-Croatian letter strings the phonological representation cannot be bypassed and that the phonological interpretation of a letter string is obligatory and automatic. Additionally, evidence is presented to show a complicity between the phonological evaluation and the lexical evaluation of letter strings that is of significance to the construction of a theory of word recognition.

Given the nature of and the relation between the two Serbo-Croatian alphabets it is possible to create a variety of types of letter strings. Thus, a letter string composed of uniquely Roman letters or of uniquely Cyrillic letters (in Figure 1) would receive single phonological interpretation and could be either a word or not a word. In contrast, a letter string composed of the common and ambiguous letters (see Figure 1) would receive two distinct phonological interpretations and could be either a word or not a word; more precisely, it could be a word in one alphabet and a nonword in the other or it could represent two different words, one in one alphabet and one in the other.

In a series of three experiments (Lukatela, Savić, Gligorijević, Ognjenović, & Turvey, 1978a) bi-alphabetic subjects were invited—by experimental design and by instruction—to relate to letter strings (block capitals) in the Roman alphabet mode. None of the letter strings seen by a subject were comprised of uniquely Cyrillic letters and relatively few of the letter strings were composed of common and ambiguous letters, that is to say, could even be read as Cyrillic. The conclusion on which all three experiments converged was that lexical decision to a letter string was slower when that string could be given two phonological readings (that is, could be read in either the assigned Roman alphabet mode or the nonassigned Cyrillic alphabet mode) but *if and only if* the letter string was a word in at least one of the alphabets. Nonwords that could be read in both alphabets were rejected no slower than nonwords constructed from the set of letters unique to the Roman alphabet.

Type of letter string (LS)	Lexical entry (L)		Phonological representation (P)		Symbolic representation	Is it a word? (in Roman or in Cyrillic)
	In Roman (L_R)?	In Cyrillic (L_C)?	In Roman (P_R)?	In Cyrillic (P_C)?		
LS1	Yes	No	Yes	No	LS1 ⟨ ○ L_R / ○ P_R	Yes
LS1a	No	Yes	No	Yes	LS1a ⟨ ● L_C / ● P_C	Yes
LS3	Yes	Yes	Yes	Yes	LS3 ⟨ ◑ L_R, L_C / ◑ P_R, P_C	Yes
LS4	Yes	No	Yes	Yes	LS4 ⟨ ○ L_R / ◑ P_R, P_C	Yes
LS5	Yes	Yes	Yes	Yes	LS5 ⟨ ○ $L_R = L_C$ / ○ $P_R = P_C$	Yes
LS6	No	Yes	Yes	Yes	LS6 ⟨ ● L_C / ◑ P_R, P_C	Yes
LS7	No	No	Yes	Yes	LS7 ⟨ ◑ P_R, P_C	No
LS8	No	No	Yes	No	LS8 ⟨ ○ P_R	No
LS8a	No	No	No	Yes	LS8a ⟨ ● P_C	No
LS9	No	No	Yes	Yes	LS9 ⟨ ○ $P_R = P_C$	No

Table 6.   Types of letter strings in the Roman and Cyrillic alphabets

This result is nicely illustrated by a recent experiment in which there was no imposed alphabet bias: The adult bi-alphabetic subject (there were 48 subjects in the experiment) decides whether a string of (capital) letters is a word in the Serbo-Croatian language. In this experiment, unlike the previous ones, letter strings containing uniquely Roman letters *and* letter

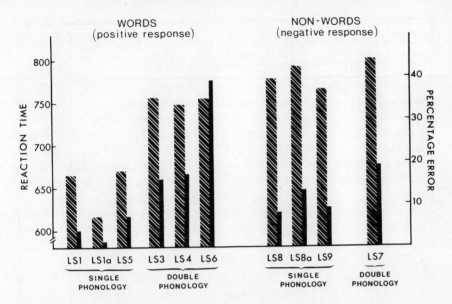

Figure 2.   Lexical decision latencies and errors for Serbo-Croatian letter strings that are readable in only one alphabet or readable in both alphabets.

strings containing uniquely Cyrillic letters were presented. The types of letter strings (LS) examined are shown in Table 6 together with the correct lexical decision for each type. (The odd labeling of letter strings is to maintain consistency with the table of letter strings given previously in Lukatela et al., 1978a; the present table is more inclusive). Table 6 is self-explanatory although it needs remarking that LS5 and LS9 are composed solely from the common letters (see Figure 1) and are therefore read the same way and mean the same thing (in the case of LS5) in Roman and Cyrillic. The results of the experiment are shown in Figure 2. It is apparent from inspection of Figure 2 that lexical decision was impaired for those letter strings that could be given both Cyrillic and Roman interpretations but only if the letter string was a word. To give two of the relevant comparisons, decision times to LS4 were significantly slower than decision times to LS1 ($F' = 11.72$; df = 1,26; $p < 0.01$); decision times to LS3 were significantly slower than decision times to LS1a ($F' = 33.4$; df = 1,27; $p < 0.001$). The latter contrast is especially interesting since letter strings of type LS3 are words in both alphabets and since a general observation in the literature on English words is that letter strings with multiple meanings are accepted as words faster than letter strings with a single meaning (e.g., Jastrzembski & Stanners, 1975). Clearly, the present observation is counter to this general finding. It should also be noted that the slower decision time to LS3 was witnessed in our previous research (Lukatela et al., 1978a). Returning to the data represented by Figure

2, where the letter string was not a word, the lexical decision was not retarded by phonological bivalence: decision times to LS7 did not differ, for example, from those to LS8 (F' = 2.44, df = 1,50).

As anticipated, these data on bi-alphabetic lexical decision permit two conclusions of some significance to an understanding of the reading of Serbo-Croatian. (We are assuming like others—for example, Coltheart et al., 1977—that lexical decision is a laboratory task well suited to investigating the nature of the information extracted from a printed word for use of lexical access.) First, the data suggest strongly that phonological encoding of Serbo-Croatian words is an automatic and extremely rapid process; as we have seen, phonological bivalence interferes with lexical decision. Second, the data suggest that it is not phonological bivalence per se that retards lexical decision, rather the necessary contingency is that the phonologically bivalent letter string being evaluated must be a word in the Serbo-Croatian language.

There are a number of theories that could be pursued by way of explaining this curious result of bi-alphabetic lexical decision. They are not pursued here for there is little to be gained at this stage by adjusting the details of this or that account of lexical decision (e.g., Coltheart et al., 1977; Meyer & Ruddy, 1973) so as to force a fit with the present data. It suffices, perhaps, to note the Coltheart et al. (1977) concluding lament that for English there is no compelling evidence for the view that the mapping from printed word to lexical entry references the phonology. They propose that:

> Unequivocal evidence for this view would be obtained by demonstrating that the phonological code for a word is sometimes used in making the "yes" response to that word in a lexical decision or categorization task; such a demonstration remains to be achieved (Coltheart et al., 1977, p. 551).

Do the present data constitute such a demonstration for Serbo-Croatian?

THE PROCESSING RELATION BETWEEN THE TWO SERBO-CROATIAN ALPHABETS

A question that has been pursued at some length is how the Roman and Cyrillic alphabets relate psychologically. For the reader of Serbo-Croatian the alphabets must be kept distinct at some level (or in some manner) of processing in order to circumvent the ambiguous characters as a potential source of phonetic confusion. Might we therefore speak of an alphabet mode implying perhaps that the reader can be in one mode or the other but not in both concurrently? The experiments just described bear on this question.

And how are the two alphabets memorially represented? If there are two alphabet spaces are all the letters of the Roman alphabet stored in one space and all the letters of the Cyrillic alphabet stored in the other? Or is there a region of overlap, say, the representations of the common letters? Given that the meaning of one alphabet precedes the other, how is priority in learning manifest in either the processing or the representation of the two alphabets? These questions and others guided our attempts to understand the psychological fit between the two Serbo-Croatian writing systems (Lukatela, Savić, Ognjenović, & Turvey, 1978); a part of that research is reported here.

A very simple experiment proved exceptionally instructive. Native Eastern Yugoslavians (those who learn Cyrillic first) were presented individual Roman and Cyrillic letters in random order and pressed a key as quickly as possible in answer to the question "Is this letter Cyrillic?" or to the question "Is this letter Roman?" The results are given in Figure 3. It took considerably longer to verify that the common letters (see Figure 1) were Roman in the "Is this letter Roman?" condition than to verify that the common letters were Cyrillic in the "Is this letter Cyrillic?" condition. The suggestion is that the subjects of the experiment viewed the common letters as essentially members of the Cyrillic alphabet and only indirectly as members of the Roman alphabet. Arguing in like style, the ambiguous characters would appear to inhabit both alphabet spaces. The most telling observation however was this: rejecting Cyrillic letters in the Roman alphabet mode took appreciably longer than rejecting Roman letters in the Cyrillic alphabet mode.

We have come to look at these data in the following way. We reasoned that the average latency for rejecting a Cyrillic character as Roman is an index of the degree to which a description of a Cyrillic character is, on the average, similar to a description of a Roman character. In the notation of Tversky (1977) this similarity may be written as $s(c,r)$ where the perceptual representation of the target Cyrillic letter (c) is the *subject* of the relation and where the memorial representation of an individual Roman letter (r) is the *referent*. Similarly, the average latency for rejecting a Roman character as Cyrillic indexes $s(r,c)$. It follows, therefore, that $s(c,r) > s(r,c)$. In other words, for speakers of Serbo-Croatian who have learned the Cyrillic alphabet first, the perceptual descriptions of Cyrillic characters are, on the average, more similar to the memorial descriptions of Roman characters than the perceptual descriptions of Roman characters are, on the average, similar to the memorial descriptions of Cyrillic characters.

What is the basis for this asymmetry? By Tversky's (1977) argument asymmetric similarities such as X is more similar to Y than vice versa hold if and only if Y, the referent term, is more salient on some nontrivial dimension from X, the subject term. The putative salience of (processing) the Roman alphabet may arise because the dimensions of description of the Roman alphabet include those of the Cyrillic; or that the descriptors of the

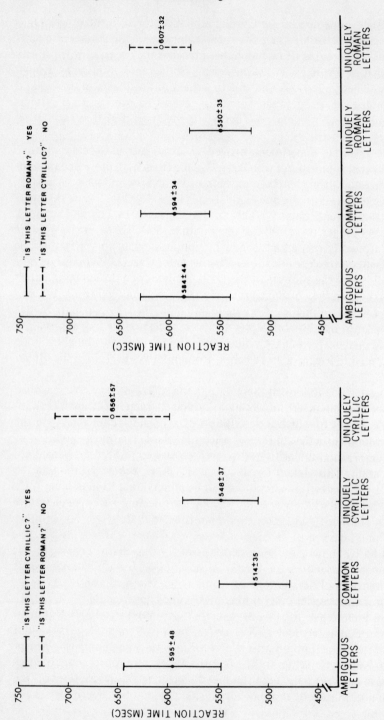

Figure 3.   Mean latencies and their range of variation for the alphabet decision task performed by subjects who learned the Cyrillic alphabet first.

Roman alphabet distinguish the Roman characters more efficiently than the descriptors of the Cyrillic alphabet distinguish Cyrillic characters. In short, the basis for the asymmetry may lie in some absolute property distinguishing the structure of the two alphabets. If true, the direction of the asymmetry should be indifferent to the order in which the alphabets are acquired. On the other hand, the basis for the asymmetry may just be the order of acquisition. To this purpose, the alphabet-decision task described above was replicated with subjects who had acquired the Roman alphabet first and the Cyrillic alphabet second. The results are shown in Figure 4. They reveal that under the two question regimes ("Is this letter Roman?"; "Is this letter Cyrillic?") these subjects behaved differently, as did the subjects in the first experiment. But most importantly the behavior of the subjects indigenous to Western Yugoslavia was diametrically opposite to that of the subjects indigenous of Eastern Yugoslavia (compare Figure 4 with Figure 3). By the same reasoning as outlined above we conclude, for subjects who learned the Roman alphabet first, that $s(r,c) > s(c,r)$. That is, for Roman-first subjects, processing Roman letters is more similar to processing Cyrillic letters than vice versa. More generally we conclude that the alphabet-processing asymmetry is owing not to a fixed structural property of the alphabets but to their order of acquisition. One tentative conclusion to be drawn is that the procedure developed by the child to decode the letters of the first acquired alphabet is modified for the second acquired alphabet so that decoding the second acquired alphabet necessarily entails the procedure for decoding the first acquired alphabet but not vice versa.

But perhaps the more outstanding, although equally tentative, conclusion to be drawn is that the order in which the alphabets are acquired, and the concomitant early bias in reading toward one of the alphabets, leaves a profound impression on the letter decoding processes of adult readers of Serbo-Croatian. This conclusion is not unrelated to some results recently published by Jackson and McClelland (in press). In the view of some students of reading (e.g. Kolers, 1969; Smith, 1971) individual differences in the reading ability of experienced readers are solely differences in comprehension ability. The research of Jackson and McClelland brings this view into question by showing individual differences in the ability of American college student readers to access letter codes, an ability that accounts for a significant portion of the variance in effective reading speed. What has been noted with mature Serbo-Croatian readers is that in the alphabet decision task there is an interaction between the alphabet first learned and the alphabet being decided upon. The pattern of decision times for Roman-first subjects is, on the significant contrasts, a mirror image of the pattern for the Cyrillic-first subjects. What is surprising about this interaction is that the subjects have been reading in the two alphabets for between 12 and 16 years and yet on a simple decision task the alphabet learned first makes its mark. The point on which our data and those of Jackson and McClelland would

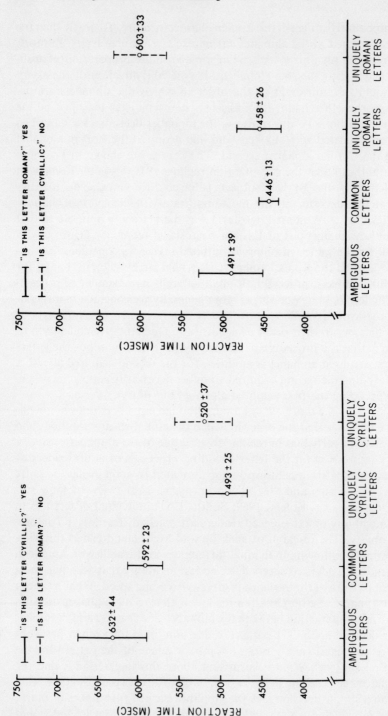

Figure 4.   Mean latencies and their range of variation for the alphabet decision task performed by subjects who learned the Roman alphabet first.

appear to converge is that the basic encoding processes by which letters of the alphabet are distinguished and named are not necessarily asymptotic in mature readers; nor is mature reading indifferent, perhaps, to the manner of their acquisition.

Section V
DYSLEXIA AND RELATED LINGUISTIC DISORDERS

Chapter 16
DYSLEXIA
Perceptual Deficiency
or Perceptual Inefficiency

Frank Vellutino

Dyslexia or specific reading disability[1] as it is called, has most often been attributed to dysfunction in the visual system, in particular to disturbances in spatial orientation and form perception. Orton (1925, 1937) proposed that reading difficulties may be caused by delayed lateral dominance for language resulting in spatial confusion manifested only in the perception of written symbols: e.g., "seeing" *b* as *d* or *was* as *saw*. Hermann (1959) advanced a similar theory, while others have ascribed reading disability to aberrant form perception associated with such diverse factors as dysfunction in visual-motor integration (Bender, 1956; Drew, 1956), the failure to develop visual hierarchical dominance (Birch, 1962), optical deficiencies (Anapolle, 1967; Getman, 1962), and abnormally persistant after-images (Stanley & Hall, 1973). Implied in each of these conceptualizations is the notion that dyslexia is ultimately caused by basic disorders in the central nervous system, resulting in significant impairment in visual perception and visual memory.

However, deficiency in visual perception, in the sense in which this difficulty is typically conceptualized, seems an unlikely source of reading disability. I suggest instead that many of the discrimination errors often observed in the poor reader's efforts at word decoding result from selective attention problems, which are themselves secondary manifestations of a more basic malfunction in visual-verbal learning, rather than the result of primary *deficiency* in visual perception. Thus, while poor readers can rea-

---

[1]The terms *dyslexia* and *specific reading disability* are intended to refer to children who sustain severe impairment in word decoding and consequent impairment in all aspects of reading. Such children are apparently normal in all other respects, and their reading difficulties occur in spite of average or above average intelligence, adequate exposure to the material to be learned, and the absence of sensory acuity problems, severe neurological disorder, gross physical disabilities, serious emotional or social disorder, and socioeconomic or cultural bias (Benton, 1975; Eisenberg, 1966; Rabinovitch, 1957). While it is often assumed that dyslexia is caused by basic disorder(s) in the central nervous system, the author is somewhat guarded as to this possibility, and is more inclined toward Applebee's (1971) suggestion that reading disability in otherwise normal children is best viewed as associated with variance in reading ability that is yet unaccounted for.

sonably be described as characteristically *inefficient* in the processing of orthographic information, such inefficiency is not caused by an organic disorder resulting in literal distortion of the distal stimulus, as is commonly inferred.

This chapter attempts to document the above distinction. It will be argued that efficient and economical analysis of the graphic and orthographic features of printed letters and words, while obviously an interactive process that necessitates reciprocity between the visual and verbal systems, is structured largely by the acquisition of, and ready access to the verbal components of these stimuli, as well as by knowledge of and facility with the various components of language. Evidence will be presented to support this view, highlighting the contention that inefficiency in the visual processing of written material results primarily from specific language impairment, or dysfunction in cross-referencing and integrating the visual and linguistic counterparts of letters and words.

PERCEPTUAL INEFFICIENCY AS A SECONDARY PROBLEM

Aside from the logical inconsistency inherent in the claim that dyslexics are subject to anomalous perception (e.g., optical reversibility, and spatial confusion) only in the processing of printed words, the most basic argument that may be advanced in support of the position taken here is that reading is primarily a linguistic function (Kavanagh & Mattingly, 1972), contrary to the more traditional conceptualizations that suggest that vision is the dominant system in acquiring skill in reading (Young & Lindsley, 1970). Indeed, in learning to read, children are required to "code" or symbolize their natural language and they must "decode" to that language. This means that the way in which they deploy their attention to the graphic and orthographic information contained in written words and their discrimination of those words are not random or arbitrary processes; in fact, they are largely determined by one's knowledge of a word's verbal constituents, as well as by verbal context in general.

Furthermore, a careful analysis of the reading process reveals that this enterprise makes unequal demands upon the visual and linguistic systems. This is not only because reading necessitates a functional knowledge and, perhaps, explicit awareness (Gleitman & Rozin, 1977; I. Y. Liberman & Shankweiler, in press) of *three* different categories of linguistic information (semantic, syntactic, and phonological) and only *two* different categories of visual information (graphic and orthographic), but also because the learner has to remember a good deal more about a word's verbal attributes than about its visual attributes. In reading, the (printed) symbols employed are stationary, requiring only discrimination and recognition of visual features and not reproduction or recall of those features. Since recall involves the recollection of much more detailed information than does discrimination and recognition (Underwood, 1972), it can reasonably be suggested that the reading process taxes verbal memory much more than it does visual memory.

This point may be reinforced by underscoring the fact that the redundancy which characterizes English orthography actually allows for considerable economy in visual processing. Such redundancy is reflected in the iterative use of alphabetic characters and the high frequency with which those characters occur in predictable spatial locations and combinations (e.g., *tion, qu, ing*). Unlike the poor reader who does not as readily become conversant with orthographic structure, the normal reader soon learns to capitalize upon this characteristic of the orthography (cf. Rosinski & Wheeler, 1972), theoretically because of the basic difficulty in associating the visual and linguistic counterparts of printed words. This, in effect, creates an implicit disposition toward inefficiency in processing orthographic information and consequent problems in discrimination.

Yet the foregoing remarks should *not* be taken as an indication that I underestimate either the complexity of English orthography or the amount of visual information that must be integrated before one becomes a fluent reader. Indeed as with any written language based on an alphabet, those attributes that ultimately distinguish letters and words are not immediately apparent, given the degree of visual similarity evident among words that have several characters in common.

Therefore, in order to make the decoding process a manageable enterprise, the fledgling reader has little choice but to find ways of reducing the amount of visual information with which he is initially confronted. Yet, herein lies a built-in hazard in that most learners will initially pick up too little (visual) information in word recognition and thereby occasionally fail to make the critical discriminations necessary for accurate decoding (Biemiller, 1970; Gibson, 1971; Weber, 1970).

How then does the beginning reader come to approximate an effective balance between processing too little and too much visual information in acquiring skill in reading? Or stating the question more generally, how does he effect reliable and accurate perception of the letters in a word so as to maximize the probability of identifying that word? It seems that he optimizes his efficiency in processing graphic and orthographic stimuli, in direct proportion to his ability to abstract and integrate spelling-to-sound correspondences for functional use, and to isolate visual representations of semantic and syntactic units that exist in the spoken language. Here I refer to the child's growing ability to attend selectively to distinguishing features of letters and words by virtue of his expanding knowledge of their phonological, semantic, and syntactic attributes. Thus, the individual who has become sensitized to the commonalities in the sounds of both spoken and printed words (I. Y. Liberman & Shankweiler, in press; Mattingly, 1972; Savin, 1972) will synthesize increasingly large amounts of auditory and visual information, which, in turn, will facilitate efficiency in discrimination and decoding.

Reciprocally, the child who can readily recall the names of words has a potentially useful means by which to detect similarities and differences in their orthographic structures provided that he becomes attuned to the similarities and differences in their phonetic structures.

And the child who comprehends most of the words and sentences he hears and reads by virtue of an age appropriate vocabulary and a knowledge of syntax has the potential use of a large amount of contextual information to assist in decoding, not only in the case of words appearing in running text, but also with words presented in isolation.

To illustrate, children who acquire a functional acquaintance with the initial consonant sounds in visually similar word pairs, such as *was/saw, not/ton,* will no doubt be able to employ these sounds as convenient mnemonics to assist in retrieving the names of those words and in stabilizing the serial order of their letters in both reading and writing. Similarly, explicit knowledge of the phonemic counterparts of redundant letter clusters such as *cl, sn, ng* and *oi* quite likely implies unit perception of these clusters, which would in turn facilitate discrimination between respective word pairs, such as *clam/calm; snug/sung; loin/lion,* that are identical, save for the order of the letters in the medial position.

At the same time, familiarity with the meanings of each pair of words, and experience with these words in spoken and written discourse would also aid one in visually discriminating between them, given the likelihood that their structural differences would eventually be detected by virtue of their differential use in particular linguistic contexts. The child who becomes conversant with both the structural and meaning attributes of these and like word pairs is much better equipped to detect the critical differences between them, than the child who lacks either or both types of information, and attempts to discriminate on the basis of global or idiosyncratic stimulus characteristics. Such children tend to identify visually similar words on a chance basis, thereby prompting the suspicion that they suffer basic perceptual deficiency.

To employ a slightly different type of example, consider the initial difficulty encountered by the child who must devise appropriate strategies for discriminating between, and identifying words like *fathead* and *father* that contain common letter sequences characterized by different sound values. The inherent problem confronting the inexperienced reader in decoding such words is the organization of their constituent letters into perceptual units that can facilitate detection of subtle disparities in their makeup. This process necessitates focal attention upon distinguishing combinations of letters in each word, such attention itself being a function of the reader's knowledge of phonemic and morphophonemic associates that define critical differences in their graphic and orthographic structures. Thus the ability to identify the component morphemes *fat* and *head,* would readily facilitate decoding of the compound word *fathead,* but this strategy would not be useful with the word *father,* since this word's morpheme boundaries and its phonetic characteristics define spelling-to-sound correspondences that are quite different from those in the word *fathead:* i.e., *f at h ea d* versus *fa th er.* Familiarity with these correspondences would no doubt aid in discriminating between *fathead* and *father* as would knowledge of the semantic and syntactic characteristics of these words.

The point being made is that the fine-grained discrimination of graphic and orthographic featural differences in words with similar visual characteristics, and the unit perception of these words, is initially dependent upon an increasingly functional acquaintance with their linguistic counterparts. Thus word identification in the developing or less than fluent reader is conceptualized as the end product of an elaborate series of cross-referencing maneuvers, whereby specific characteristics or subunits of given words are related to their meaning-bearing or sound counterparts heuristically, in systematic attempts to abstract those letter groupings that will both stabilize word perception and mediate to the correct response in spoken language.

However, if, for any reason, the learner has difficulty in the "cross-referencing" process, or in establishing visual-verbal relationships in general, it can be anticipated that his discovery of the redundancies embedded in the text, and the necessary synthesis of increasingly large amounts of visual material into functional units, will be inefficient at best. In other words, because of symbol-sound association difficulties, the child does not become sufficiently aware of the internal structure of the orthography and is thereby subject to a significant degree of *perceptual inefficiency* in letter and word discrimination. And, owing to his inability to systematically unitize letter sequences, particularly those of a redundant nature, he is often confronted with the burden of processing too much visual information, and he may frequently process too little in his natural attempts to economize.

Perceptual inefficiency is not, however, the same as *perceptual deficiency,* as defined in visual deficit theories of reading disability. Such theories typically suggest that poor readers are characterized by deficient form perception, optical reversibility, spatial disorientation, and related anomalies as a result of central nervous system disorder. Perceptual inefficiency, in contrast, simply refers to pervasive and chronic difficulties in selectively attending to and "automatizing" (Doehring, 1976; LaBerge & Samuels, 1974) critical discriminating cues, as a result of more basic difficulties in establishing visual-verbal relationships. In short, children who call *b d* or *was saw* do not literally misperceive these stimuli, but, instead have not yet encoded the differences that characterize their spatial attributes, because their attention to these differences is not sufficiently monitored by knowledge of their verbal components.

RESEARCH EVIDENCE

Evidence in support of the ideas is both direct and indirect, and emanates from *three* different sources. One source of support inheres in the results of studies conducted by Vellutino and his colleagues demonstrating that perceptual deficiency is not a significant correlate of reading disability.

Supporting evidence for this position is also derived from a number of investigations that indicate that poor readers are not as efficient as normal readers in the visual processing of letters and words, and are less sensitive than the normal readers to orthographic structure. The third source of support is more indirect as well as theoretical and comes from the results of seminal studies suggesting that contextual information possessed by the reader, greatly influences selective attention in letter and word processing. A number of investigations concerned with each of these areas of inquiry is discussed.

STUDIES EVALUATING PERCEPTUAL DEFICIT THEORIES OF DYSLEXIA

The literature is replete with accounts of empirical research evaluating perceptual deficit theories of dyslexia and the data are conflicting. I have reviewed critically the most influential of these studies in some detail and have concluded that there is no compelling support for the contention that specific reading disability is caused by basic dysfunction in visual perception and visual memory (Vellutino, in press). I shall therefore defer from making any further comment about this work and focus upon studies issuing from our laboratory, addressing the visual deficit explanation of reading disability.

Our major research objective in designing these studies was to evaluate the possibility that the so-called perceptual deficiencies, observed in the word identification errors of poor readers, are actually secondary manifestations of more basic dysfunction in visual-verbal association learning, resulting in a paucity of verbal mediators to assist in word decoding. Two specific hypotheses were evaluated. First, poor readers would not differ significantly on measures of form perception and visual memory when the confounding effects of *verbal mediation* were controlled.[2] Second, poor

---

[2]The term *verbal mediation* refers, in the present context, to the implicit use of various types of verbal information (semantic, syntactic, and phonological) as an aid to word decoding. Such information may either be embedded within a word, or within a phrase or sentence in which the word appears. The examples given in this paper illustrate the process.

readers would be comparable to normal readers on various measures of visual-*non*verbal learning, but would perform less proficiently than normal readers on learning tasks involving both a verbal and visual component.

Two separate studies compared reader groups on immediate recall of letters and words, when directions to subjects were varied so as to facilitate selective attention to either the visual or verbal features of these stimuli (Vellutino, Smith, Steger, & Kaman, 1975; Vellutino, Steger, & Kandel, 1972). Our samples were carefully selected so as to include only intellectually capable children whose reading problems were not ostensibly caused by environmental and other extrinsic factors (see Footnote 1). Poor readers were generally between 2 and 4 years below their grade placement on an individually administered oral reading test, while normal readers were at or above grade level. The groups were also matched for sex and school location. The age range for children in both studies was between 7 and 14.

Subjects in each study were given brief (600 to 1000 msec) tachistoscopic presentations of English words, randomly arrayed letters, and numerals, varying in number of items per set (e.g., 3, 4, or 5). They were also presented with geometric designs, all stimuli being randomly administered (see Figure 1). There were two stimulus presentations. On the first presentation, subjects were asked simply to copy each design from memory. On the second, only the verbal stimuli (words, random letters, and numerals) were shown (again tachistoscopically), but on this presentation, subjects were asked to pronounce the words when they appeared, and then to "spell out" their letters in correct order. They were also required to spell out the random letters and numerals in order when these stimuli appeared. The results in both of these studies were clear-cut. First, there were no differences between reader groups on immediate recall of geometric designs. Second, in all instances, poor readers performed significantly better on the graphic reproduction of the verbal stimuli than they did on the naming of those stimuli. Moreover, the performance of poor readers was comparable to that of the normal readers on the graphic reproduction of the verbal stimuli, but this was not the case when identification of these same stimuli was indexed with a naming response. Of additional interest is the observation (Vellutino, Smith, Steger, & Kaman, 1975) that poor readers in the second grade did not copy the five letter sets as well as their normal reading peers, quite possibly because these stimuli began to tax the upper limits of short-term memory (Miller, 1956; Simon, 1972). Yet poor readers at the sixth grade level reproduced all stimulus sets as well as normal readers at this level and better than the children at the lower grade level, including those in the normal reader group. Especially impressive in the case of the word stimuli was the fact that the poor readers in sixth grade could spell out the letters in given words more accurately than the normal readers in second grade, even though their pronunciations of those words was not substantially better than the normal readers at the lower grade level, and was, in some in-

REAL WORDS

Three Letter	Four Letter	Five Letter
fly	loin	blunt
bed	form	drawn
was	calm	chair

SCRAMBLED LETTERS

Three Letter	Four Letter	Five Letter
dnv	jpyc	ztbrc
hbd	gzfs	yfpqg
mcw	qvlt	qldnr

NUMBERS

Three Digit	Four Digit	Five Digit
382	4328	96842
974	3724	31579
296	9156	86314

GEOMETRIC DESIGNS

Two Items   Three Items

Figure 1.   Examples of verbal and nonverbal stimuli employed in the studies by Vellutino, Smith, Steger, & Kaman (1975). Reprinted by permission.

stances, worse. This finding suggests that poor readers eventually acquire some degree of familiarity with orthographic structure, while their difficulty in naming and pronouncing printed words persists.

The results of these studies constitute strong evidence that the difficulties poor readers encounter in the identification of printed words is in the storage or retrieval of the verbal counterparts of those words and *not* in the discrimination and visual encoding of their graphic features. This conclusion is reinforced by the results of a subsequent series of studies comparing poor and normal readers on visual recall of Hebrew letters and words (see Figure 2). The subjects were poor and normal readers (ages 7 to 12) who had no prior exposure to Hebrew and normal readers at the same age and grade levels who were learning to speak, read, and write the Hebrew language.

In two of these studies (Vellutino, Pruzek, Steger, & Meshoulam, 1973; Vellutino, Steger, Kaman, & DeSetto, 1975), subjects in respective reader groups were presented with three-, four- and five-letter Hebrew words (exposed for 3, 4 and 5 seconds, respectively) and were required to reproduce the letters in a word in correct order, immediately after the stimulus was terminated. In accord with the expectations, no significant differences were found between the dyslexics and the normal readers who were unfamiliar with Hebrew on the reproduction of the letters in these words in proper sequence. However, with the exception of the three-letter words (on which all groups were comparable), neither group performed as well as the children who were learning both the spoken and written forms of this language.

These data support our contention that poor readers are not perceptually impaired and compliment the results of the first two studies discussed above, employing Roman letters and English words. This idea is afforded additional confirmation by two other findings which we had not anticipated. First, poor and normal readers, unacquainted with Hebrew, were inclined to make more orientation errors in the recall of Hebrew letters that could be reasonably construed as disoriented versions of Roman letters (e.g., items 1B, 2A, 3C, Figure 2), than on those that either approximated Roman letters in *correct* orientation (e.g., 1C, 5B, Figure 2) or had no resemblance to these symbols. Particularly impressive was the fact that normal readers were observed to make *more* errors than the poor readers on the disoriented Roman letter facsimilies. A reasonable interpretation of these findings is that both groups were subject to verbal mediation errors, as a result of previous experience with Roman letters. However, the effect was more pronounced in normal readers, quite possibly because of their more stable experience in the phonetic encoding of these stimuli. Indeed, the data accord with the central theme of this chapter, that the orientation errors commonly observed in the oral reading and written productions of poor readers are, in fact, instances of linguistic intrusion rather than spatial confusion. This interpretation is consonant with the results of the first two studies discussed earlier, and is also consistent with the conclusions drawn from work done elsewhere (I. Y. Liberman, Shankweiler, Orlando, Harris, & Berti, 1971).

More direct confirmation that dyslexia is not attributable to spatial confusion comes from the second finding alluded to above. Briefly, it was observed that the poor and normal readers unacquainted with Hebrew manifested virtually identical tendencies to scan the letters in the Hebrew words from left to right as evident in a higher frequency of omission errors at the

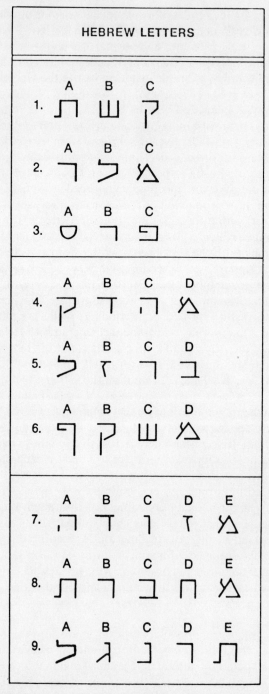

Figure 2.   Hebrew words presented to poor and normal readers for immediate visual recall in studies by Vellutino et al. (1973). Reprinted by permission.

right terminal positions of the words that at any other location. This pattern was diametrically opposed to the scanning tendencies manifested by the children learning Hebrew, whose omission errors were at the left terminal position of the words, consistent with the right-left direction in which Hebrew letters are ordered. These data are obviously at variance with the common belief that dyslexics are unable to establish a firm directional set as a result of spatial confusion.[3]

The results of the foregoing studies provide direct evidence that reading disability is not caused by *basic* dysfunction in visual perception. They indirectly support the suggestion that the visual discrimination errors that may be observed in poor readers, are, in fact, secondary manifestations of deficiencies in integrating visual and verbal information. More direct support for this point of view issues from several studies systematically comparing poor and normal readers on *visual-verbal* and *visual-nonverbal* learning tasks (Steger, Vellutino, & Meshoulam, 1972; Vellutino, Bentley, & Phillips, 1978; Vellutino, Steger, Harding, & Phillips, 1975; Vellutino, Steger, & Pruzek, 1973). In the visual-verbal learning conditions employed in these studies, subjects were asked to associate a variety of visual materials (e.g., designs, cartoon figures) with both meaningful words and pseudowords. The poor readers consistently performed below the level of normal readers on these measures. At the same time, the groups were found to be comparable in visual-nonverbal association learning, that is, in the pairing of stimuli devoid of phonetic structure or any uniform verbal meaning. Since given contrasts required that subjects learn to associate a visual stimulus with various sensory stimuli (visual, auditory, and kinesthetic) presented within and across given modalities, it seems a justifiable conclusion that the differential performance of reader groups on measures of verbal and nonverbal learning was attributable to the apparent difficulties encountered by poor readers on tasks involving a verbal rather than a visual component.

The results of these studies provide rather strong evidence that specific reading disability is not caused by basic disorders in visual perception and visual memory. They also provide both direct and indirect support for the contention that reading problems result either from deficiencies in one or more aspects of linguistic functioning, or from a specific disorder in visual-verbal integration. Vellutino (1977, in press) has discussed these latter alternatives in greater detail and space does not permit a more elaborate review of the evidence supporting his position. It will suffice to indicate, for present purposes, that research evaluating the linguistic correlates of reading disorder, while yet at the seminal stage, has, to date, yielded highly suggestive evidence that poor readers may be characterized by significant impair-

---

[3]While the Hebrew letter studies discussed above evaluated short-term visual memory in poor and normal readers, one other study (Vellutino, Steger, DeSetto, & Phillips, 1975) employed a Hebrew letter paradigm to assess long-term (visual) memory in these groups, and found no differences between the two.

ments in *semantic* (Denckla & Rudel, 1976a, 1976b; Perfetti & Goldman, 1976; Perfetti & Lesgold, 1978; Waller, 1976), *syntactic* (Cromer & Wiener, 1966; Fry, Johnson, & Muehl, 1970. Goldman, 1976; Oakan, Wiener, & Cromer, 1971; Vogel, 1974; Wiig, Semel, & Crouse, 1973) and *phonological* processes (I. Y. Liberman & Shankweiler, in press; I. Y. Liberman, Shankweiler, Fischer, & Carter, 1974; I. Y. Liberman, Shankweiler, A. M. Liberman, Fowler, & Fischer, 1977), as evidenced in respective deficiencies in related functions such as discourse memory, word encoding and retrieval, verbal concept formation, comprehension of specific syntactic constructions, phonetic encoding, phonemic segmentation, knowledge of words, verbal fluency, and expressive language.

In any event, the further elaboration of the linguistic correlates of dyslexia and the relationship of verbal processing deficiencies to this disorder would seem to be a promising avenue for additional study.

PERCEPTUAL INEFFICIENCY AND ORTHOGRAPHY

The central thesis of this chapter is that dyslexics, while not perceptually impaired in the strict sense, process orthographic information inefficiently because of significant difficulty in acquiring relevant verbal information that facilitates selective attention to critical discriminators. This generates the prediction that poor and normal readers would manifest qualitative differences in their ability to abstract and generalize spelling-to-sound correspondences, as well as in their overall sensitivity to orthographic invariance and redundancy. Inefficiency in abstracting orthographic patterns would, in turn, lead one to infer that poor readers are characterized by pedantic and idiosyncratic modes of processing letters in printed words. Evidence for these conjectures is somewhat limited, but the results of relevant studies are suggestive.

That proficient readers apprehend and generalize predictable spelling patterns more readily than less proficient readers is demonstrated in a series of studies conducted by Venezky, Calfee, and their associates. To illustrate, Calfee, Venezky, and Chapman (1969) evaluated good and poor readers (grades 3, 6, 11, 12 and college) on their knowledge of spelling-to-sound correspondence rules (e.g., final *e* pattern, initial *c* pattern) employing synthetic words (e.g., *cipe, cabe*) which incorporated both regular and irregular patterns. Subjects were simply asked to pronounce each of these words. It was found that correct pronunciation increased from third grade to high school, and that the better readers in the third and sixth grades gave more accurate responses to predictable patterns than did the poor readers in those grades. Also of interest is the fact that correlations between pronunciation of the synthetic words and reading ability was greater for third graders than for sixth graders. This finding suggests that success in mastering the code is a more important determinant of reading achievement in the lower grades than it is in the upper grades. Consistent with this interpretation is the fact that the good readers also gave many more "plausible" responses than did poor readers who often guessed "wildly" in response to given words.

The above findings are in accord with the results of two later studies conducted in this series. Venezky and Johnson (1972) tested children in first, second and third grades on their knowledge of the /k/ and /s/ sounds of c, along with knowledge of the long and short pronunciations of a (/e/ and /ae/). Poor readers did not perform as well on these patterns as the normal readers, although both groups had difficulty with c→/s/ in initial position. Similarly, Venezky, Chapman, and Calfee (1972) tested second, fourth, and sixth graders with synthetic words to determine development of invariant consonants (e.g., b, m, n), long and short vowels, and the variable sounds of c and g. Poor and normal readers did not differ in their rate of acquisition of the vowel sounds. There were, however, significant differences between these groups on acquisition of invariant consonants in the medial and final positions, but not in initial positions. Venezky et al. inferred a qualitative difference between good and poor readers on word attack strategies, with poor readers using only the first few letters and perhaps word length for making identifications. Reader groups also differed on their knowledge of the sounds associated with c and g, although all subjects acquired the less common patterns (i.e., c→/s/ and g→/ǰ/) later.[4]

These findings support the suggestion that poor readers encounter more difficulty than normal readers in acquiring spelling-to-sound correspondences and are less sensitive than the normal readers to orthographic redundancies. Additional confirmation for this suggestion is derived from the results of a study by Mason (1975). Mason hypothesized that poor readers do not "directly perceive" the redundancy characteristic of the spatial locations of letters and have little awareness of the fact that not all letters of the alphabet occur in the same spatial locations with equal frequency (Mayzner & Tresselt, 1965). Mason (1975) distinguishes between direct perception of spatial redundancy and inferential knowledge of such redundancy as a result of experience with the orthography. Thus, the insensitivity to letter locations attributed to poor readers is apparently conceived as a basic process disorder stemming from central nervous system dysfunction.

In an initial test of her hypothesis, Mason (1975) conducted a series of four related studies comparing poor and normal readers on visual search tasks. Target stimuli were individual letters embedded in letter strings which

---

[4]The results obtained in the studies by Venezky and his associates are in accord with the results of a later study by Rayner and Habelberg (1975) finding that poor readers in first grade were more variable than normal readers in this grade in using initial letters in printed words as a discriminating cue.

varied with respect to spatial redundancy. The subjects in each study were sixth graders selected only on the basis of reading achievement.

The first experiment simply compared these groups on the speed with which they searched for a target letter embedded either in real English words, or pseudowords. Since the normal readers were faster only on the word stimuli, it was inferred that these subjects differed from poor readers only in their ability to employ letter redundancies to assist in word identification, and not in their ability to perceive the distinctive features of the letters.

Similar results were obtained in the second study in this series, employing English words, as well as pseudowords that were anagrams of these words, and which varied as to degree of redundancy (e.g., *seldom, somled, sdelmd*). Normal readers were again observed to be faster than poor readers in locating target letters embedded in the spatially redundant letter sets.

The third study employed materials and a procedure similar to those used in experiment two; but because Mason was interested in evaluating letter processing strategies in the reader groups, the target letters in the three types of display were counterbalanced to evaluate serial position effects. Thus, all target letters appeared equally often in each serial position.

Contrary to expectations, normal readers were faster than poor readers in locating letter targets under all three redundancy conditions, except when target letters appeared in improbable spatial locations. Under these circumstances, normal readers were faster than poor readers only when nontarget letters were in spatially redundant locations.

Especially relevant to the present discussion is the disparity in the shapes of the error curves (collapsed over display types) yielded by analyses of serial position effects for each word set. The distribution for the normal readers was bow shaped, suggesting faster search times for letters located at the end points of letter sets. In contrast, the distribution for poor readers was roughly linear, indicating a distinct tendency toward an increase in search times as target letters moved toward the right terminal position of given letter sets. These trends suggest that the skilled readers were inclined to process the constituent letters in a set simultaneously or in parallel, while the less skilled readers adopted a serial or left-right processing strategy. The data support the suggestion that poor and normal readers may be characterized by qualitatively different strategies in processing the letters in words. Insofar as serial processing can be considered an inefficient means by which to detect and apprehend orthographic redundancies,[5] it may reasonably be concluded that poor readers process the letters in words less efficiently than normal readers.

---

[5] A quote from Venezky (1970) will be instructive on this point: "...a person who attempts to scan left to right, letter by letter, pronouncing as he goes could not correctly read most English words. Many of the English spelling-to-sound patterns require, at a minimum a knowledge of succeeding graphemic units. How, for example, is initial *e* to be pronounced if the following units are not known (cf. *erb, ear, ewer, eight*)? This is just the beginning of the

The fourth and final study in this group evaluated the effects of spatial frequency of the target letters themselves. The stimuli were pseudoword sets, one type comprised of letters occurring in positions in which they frequently occur, and another comprised of letters occurring in unlikely spatial positions. Consistent with the results obtained in the other studies conducted, normal readers had faster search times than poor readers, but only under the high redundancy condition.

Mason (1975) concluded from the findings that normal readers are more attuned to and make more effective use of redundancy information than poor readers. This conclusion seems reasonable and is basically consonant with the position being taken here. However, I disagree with Mason's (1975) suggestion that the poor reader's lack of sensitivity to spatial redundancy is due to qualitative differences between reader groups in the neurological functions involved in perceiving spatial location.[6] Indeed, the "plodding" and less efficient serial processing strategy manifested by these subjects would be a more parsimonious explanation of the poor readers' failure to detect spatial redundancy than the one offered by Mason (1975).

Additional confirmation that less skilled readers tend toward component letter rather than parallel processing comes from some recent work done by Samuels and his associates. Briefly, Samuels, LaBerge, and Bremer (1977) presented subjects (grades 2, 4, 6 and college) with words varying in length (3 to 6 letters) and asked them simply to press a response button if the word presented was from an animal category. The dependent measure was latency of response. It was found that response times for children in the lower grades increased sharply with an increase in letter length, implying component letter or serial processing in these subjects. However, in the older more experienced readers, response times did not vary as a function of letter length, thereby suggesting that the subjects were inclined toward parallel or holistic processing of the letters in the words. More importantly,

---

problem. In some patterns the entire word must be seen—and this is true of almost all polysyllabic words since stress patterns are significant for vowel quality. The implication here is that single pass left-to-right scanning is unproductive except for some monosyllabic words." (Venezky, 1970, p. 129).

[6]Mason attempted to provide more direct confirmation of this conjecture in a later study (Mason & Katz, 1976) in which good and poor readers were compared in the processing of spatially redundant and nonredundant arrays comprised of IBM characters. The results in this study were similar to those obtained in the study described above (Mason, 1975). That is, good readers were observed to be faster in locating characters embedded in redundant as compared with nonredundant arrays. However, the groups did not differ with respect to accuracy in locating these characters. Since the stimuli employed in this study were non-alphabetic, the authors concluded that the reader group differences observed in the previous study by Mason (1975) were not due to negative experience with English orthography, but to basic dysfunction in "spatial order perception." However, this interpretation of the results may not be the most parsimonious one. It is sufficient to point out that inefficient search strategies (e.g., serial vs. parallel processing) acquired over a protracted period of negative learning involving alphabetic stimuli, may well be transferred to non-alphabetic stimuli, particularly those that are letter-like in their appearance, as with the IBM characters employed in the Mason and Katz (1976) study. Thus, the authors' conclusion is debatable.

it was found that the unskilled readers at different grade levels were more apt to process letters serially than in parallel. Similar results were obtained in a recently completed study by McCormick and Samuels (1978). Also noteworthy are the results of a study by Terry, Samuels, and LaBerge (1976) who found that college students employed component letter processing with words presented as mirror image transforms. Thus, it would seem that serial processing is the natural course with material that is not well integrated. It may therefore be suggested that the poor reader persists in his tendency to process letters serially, because he does not have an integral knowledge of orthographic relationships and often relies upon idiosyncratic cues for word identification.

CONTEXTUAL EFFECTS IN LETTER AND WORD PERCEPTION

It has been suggested throughout this chapter that impaired readers are inefficient in dissecting the orthography because of basic difficulty in integrating visual and linguistic information. The assumption is made that such difficulty limits the poor reader's ability to acquaint himself with the internal structure of English words, and that this, in turn, impairs efficiency in letter and word discrimination. However, it must be acknowledged that the suggested relationship between verbal context and the processing of letters and words in print is largely inferential, since there is very little in the way of empirical study evaluating this relationship, in particular with dyslexics. However, LaBerge (1977) provides a useful approximation to the type of conceptualization I have in mind, and has generated research results that lend credence to the point of view expressed here.

In expanding the model of the reading process articulated by LaBerge and Samuels (1974), LaBerge (1977) again underscores the notion that *automaticity* and *unitization* in word perception take place gradually in stages, beginning with 1) detection of distinctive features necessary for discrimination, 2) progression through the integration of such features into a unit, and 3) selective and minimal attention to word features, conforming to automatic recognition. This model also incorporates the notion of "multiple pathways," by which the visual system makes contact with the semantic system (e.g., visual → phonological → semantic or visual → semantic), in addition to the idea that this system contains multilevel codes, representing the visual constituents embedded in a written word. Thus there are postulated codes for features, letters, spelling patterns, and words. It is assumed that such codes are gradually linked to the phonological, semantic, and syntactic systems during the course of perceptual learning, as well as to each other. Indeed, the interconnections established among these word components no doubt become a rather elaborate network that ultimately permits a variety of means by which a word might be identified or information embedded in the word may be conveyed, depending upon the type of decoding enterprise in which the reader happens to be engaged at any given moment: i.e., identification of letters, spelling clusters or words; comprehension of sentences, etc. The problem is then to determine the means by which one selectively attends to the perceptual unit that most effectively satisfies task demands.

The solution to this problem, as posited by LaBerge (1977), inheres in the existence of contextual structures, termed *contextual nodes* (Estes, 1975). These appear to be stored bits of information of given types (visual, phonological, semantic, or syntactic) that are selectively activated by cognitive and perceptual sets determined by the nature of the task and that combine with activation from the sensory stimulus to "produce a higher activation for the particular code at the desired level." It is in this way that an appropriate level of visual processing is selected so as to maximize the probability of identification and comprehension.

Three prototypical experiments were designed to test the conceptualization described above. An initial test of the hypothesis was carried out in a study by Petersen and LaBerge (1977) which evaluated the effect of "priming" the visual system with contextual information relevant to the unit processing of either letter pairs (spelling clusters) or individual letters. The subjects were college students and the basic experimental paradigm was referred to as the "list induction technique." This procedure was essentially a visual matching task, wherein subjects were presented either with a list consisting primarily of familiar spelling patterns (e.g., *cl, sh, tr,* and *ph*) interspersed with a few unfamiliar pairs (e.g., *lc,* and *hs*), or a list consisting primarily of unfamiliar letter pairs ·vith a smaller number of familiar patterns. The list containing predominantly familiar clusters was designed to induce subjects to "read out" visual codes at the level of spelling patterns, while the list comprised predominantly of unfamiliar clusters was designed to induce visual processing at the level of the component letter.

Subjects were presented with two pairs of letter clusters from a given list, and asked to press a button if they matched, but to withhold a response if they did not match. The dependent measure, in each instance, was latency of response. The major contrasts involved comparisons of latencies in matching pairs of familiar and unfamiliar letter pairs in lists representing each condition.

The general finding was that response times varied as a function of word list. In the list containing mostly unfamiliar letter pairs, the latencies for matching familiar clusters and unfamiliar letter pairs were *not* significantly different, suggesting that familiar and unfamiliar pairs were processed in a similar manner, presumably at the level of component letters. However, in the case of the list consisting primarily of familiar clusters, it was found that the unfamiliar letter pairs took 100 msec longer to process than familiar letter pairs. This suggested that the expectation to perceive familiar clusters had biased subjects so that processing time was slower when presented with an unfamiliar cluster. The data supported the hypothesis that the context provided by the different lists could selectively activate different levels of letter processing.

Two other experiments employing the list induction technique were reported by LaBerge (1977). One evaluated the possibility that syntactic information can influence visual processing, and a second evaluated the question of whether or not semantic information can do likewise.

In the study evaluating the influence of syntax on visual processing, it was found that in lists comprised mainly of adjective–noun pairs and a few noun–verb pairs, processing time was greater when the noun–verb items appeared. However, in lists containing mostly noun–verb pairs, there were no significant differences in processing time between adjective–noun and noun–verb probes. These results are, of course, analogous to the results obtained with letter clusters. They suggest that the effects were induced primarily by the context provided by a syntactic rule, that is, that *adjective-noun* elements are typically grouped into noun phrases, whereas *noun-verb* elements are separated into subjects and predicates.

Similar results were reported for the study evaluating semantic information and visual processing. Lists consisting of words from various taxonomic categories were presented, and probe words from either same or different categories were interspersed with each list. It was found that probe words from different categories occasioned longer latencies than probe words from the same category. The data therefore suggest that the semantic system can significantly influence visual processing.

These results are, of course, consistent with the position taken in this chapter, and are therefore promising. Unfortunately, they provide no *direct* evidence for the argument that visual processing is impaired in poor readers, because of their inability to employ contextual information as well as normal readers. However, the results of two studies involving contrasts between poor and normal readers provide suggestive support to this idea.

Oakan, Wiener, and Cromer (1971) evaluated the effect of training in organization of discourse material on word identification in poor and normal readers in fifth grade. Each subject read aloud four different passages under four experimental conditions: stories presented either one word at a time, or in paragraphs, with or without comprehension training. Comprehension training consisted of providing each subject with an aural summary of a specific passage before having him read it.

The provision of contextual information did *not* significantly reduce word identification errors in poor readers, either under the word or paragraph reading conditions. This suggested that these subjects tended to treat words as unrelated items, and were not inclined to utilize syntactic information and other context cues to organize word strings into larger units. Interestingly enough, the comprehension training actually caused in normal readers a *higher* proportion of word identification errors than did reading a selection to which they had no prior exposure, presumably because the information provided beforehand induced more "economical" visual processing. These data are, of course, consistent with the notion that syntactic information can significantly influence word identification.

Similarly, Samuels, Begy, and Chen (1975) compared the effects of context words and partial letter cues on latency of word recognition in fourth grade readers. The words were presented tachistoscopically for variable durations and responses were oral. It was found that poor readers generally had longer response latencies than did normal readers, and furthermore, that context words (e.g., *black*) presented for longer durations, just prior to the brief presentations of target words (e.g., *cat*), did not facilitate recognition for poor readers as well as for normal readers. The poor readers were also found to be less proficient than normal readers in generating target words from partial letter cues (e.g., black c __). Samuels et al. concluded that poor readers are less efficient than normal readers in utilizing contextual information for word decoding.

SUMMARY AND CONCLUSION

This chapter addressed the hypothetical distinction between *perceptual deficiency* and *perceptual inefficiency,* as alternative explanations for the apparent visual discrimination errors (e.g., *b–d, was–saw, clam–calm*) observed in the reading and written language of children who sustain specific reading disability. Perceptual deficiency has been traditionally conceptualized as a central nervous system disorder, presumably leading to inferred disruptions in the visual system, for example, optical reversibility, spatial confusion, and figure-ground dysfunction. Perceptual inefficiency, on the other hand, is conceived as a secondary attentional problem that would theoretically occur when *both* the information network and the psychological dispositions necessary for optimal efficiency in letter and word perception have not been acquired. Perceptual inefficiency is not, however, viewed as originating from organic dysfunction causing literal distortion of the distal stimulus. Rather, it appears to be a by-product of basic deficits in various aspects of language or specific disorder in visual-verbal association learning. Such disturbances presumably impede the acquisition of spelling-to-sound correspondences, which, in turn, curtails the development of more sophisticated and efficient strategies for processing orthographic information.

Research data were reviewed that strongly contradicted perceptual deficit explanations, while providing both direct and indirect evidence for verbal processing deficiencies as a central problem in learning to read. At the same time, considerable evidence was presented to show that poor readers dissect the orthography inefficiently, and that their acquaintance with orthographic structure does not develop at a rate commensurate with normal readers. Of particular interest are recent studies with adults lending credence to the hypothesized relationship between verbal context and qualitative differences in visual processing. However, there are very few studies currently available which have directly explored these relationships with the population of interest here and such study would seem to be imperative.

It may be suggested that the characterization of perceptual inefficiency advanced herein constitutes a more viable explanation of the types of visual discrimination errors commonly observed in the oral reading and written productions of poor readers than the notion of perceptual deficit as it has been traditionally conceptualized.

Chapter 17
DEFICIENCIES IN RESEARCH ON READING DEFICIENCIES

Renate Valtin

Despite over 30 years of research on specific reading and writing disabilities in children with normal intelligence, experimental results continue to be discrepant or contradictory not only with regard to the causal factors of reading problems, but also with regard to remedial programs. The catalog of the causal factors of dyslexia includes almost 20 separate cognitive, emotional, motivational, environmental, constitutional, and physiological factors. Since German studies did not yield any evidence for the existence of dyslexia as a specific reading disability with typical reading errors (e.g., letter reversals) or characteristic deficiencies (e.g., directional confusion) the term *dyslexia* is used by German researchers (Angermaier, 1974; Niemeyer, 1974; Valtin, 1973b) only in a descriptive way as a synonym for disabilities in reading or spelling of various origins, although current usage assumes a causality ("This child reads poorly because he is dyslexic.") While it is generally agreed upon that dyslexia is due to multiple causation, there is considerable disagreement as to which factors are more relevant and which remedial procedures are more promising.

There seem to be at least two reasons for these discrepancies: the concept of dyslexia and the variety of approaches that try to assess dyslexia.

A CRITICISM OF THE CONCEPT OF DYSLEXIA

The concept of specific reading disability is a purely formal one and each researcher can more or less arbitrarily choose the operational definition and the criteria concerning the degree of reading retardation and the measure of intelligence. In Germany this issue becomes even more complicated by the fact that most of the researchers use spelling tests, or in some instances a combination of reading and spelling tests, as a diagnostic tool for dyslexia.

Schlee (1976, p. 291) has pointed out that the often cited discrepancy between relatively high IQ and poor reading and spelling achievement (frequently considered as a criterion for dyslexia) is of no special importance since there is nothing remarkable about discrepancies in performance on variables that are only moderately correlated. The purely conventional character of the concept of dyslexia has been expressed most clearly by Angermaier (1974, p. 148):

> Thus the concept of reading disability points to the multiple causal factors of a relatively (!) limited learning disturbance: the higher one sets the percentage of dyslexics, the less limited the learning disability will be. And this percentage must be *set:* the limits of dyslexia have to be *determined, established,* not *recognized* or *discovered.* There is no unmistakable collection of symptoms or argument for a specific reading disability...the concept does not refer to an "illness" but at most to divergences toward the lower end of a continuum of performance that displays heterogenous composition and whose extent must be determined.

Thus every researcher is free to choose an operational definition and select the criteria that will be used for the severity of the reading/spelling/writing disability and for the level of IQ. In this purely conventional concept of specific reading disability (dyslexia), research encounters a vicious circle. Working from an arbitrary and unclear diagnostic construct, the researcher attempts to discover the particularities of that construct or, expressed differently, an arbitrary diagnosis produces a necessarily arbitrary cluster of research results that vary according to criteria for reading or spelling disability, choice of diagnostic instruments, and selection of the investigative sample.

Most often the samples of dyslexic children are very heterogeneous with regard to the reading disabilities, a fact that is partly a consequence of the tests used for diagnosis. The diagnosis of dyslexia, at least in Germany, is based on standardized reading and spelling tests that refer to the relative position of an individual compared with the norm group, but these tests do not provide reliable knowledge of the specific strengths and weaknesses in the reading or spelling process since they lack adequate criterion measures. Moreover, this diagnostic approach based on the normal distribution will always produce failures.

AN ANALYSIS OF DIFFERENT APPROACHES TO DYSLEXIA

At least five approaches try to assess reading or spelling difficulties:

1. The etiological approach
2. The cognitive deficit approach
3. The symptom approach
4. The process-oriented approach
5. The task-analysis or subskill approach

Each of these approaches is discussed in terms of their implicit assumptions and inherent difficulties and their usefulness to diagnosis and remedial and therapeutic teaching.

The Etiological Approach

The *etiological approach* tries to identify physical, environmental, or educational factors that impede the reading process. There seem to be at least three inherent difficulties in this approach. First, there is a lack of criteria for differential diagnosis and the problem of overlap. Rabinovitch (1962) categorized reading problems into three major groups:

Secondary reading retardation   The capacity to learn to read is intact but utilized insufficiently because of emotional blocking, limited schooling opportunity, or other external factors.
Brain injury with reading retardation   The capacity to learn to read is impaired by brain damage manifested by clear-cut neurological deficits.
Primary reading retardation   The capacity to read is impaired in such factors as visual memory, association, and auditory discrimination. The causes are considered biological or endogenous.

But Rabinovitch admits frankly that the criteria for differential diagnosis are still uncertain and "Despite the neatness of all our attempted theoretical formulations, I must confess that in practice our group not infrequently arrives at a diagnosis such as 'a secondary retardation with a touch of primary disability' " (Rabinovitch, 1962, p. 76).

The second difficulty of the etiological approach lies in the uncertainty of the direct causal relationship. The interdisciplinary study of Robinson (1946) revealed that there was a lack of agreement among her group of specialists as to which factor caused the reading problems. There is no theoretical agreement whether these factors are causative, contributory, or merely coincidental to the reading retardation. Practical evidence for a direct causal relationship is also lacking. As Merritt (1971, p. 186) points out: "In the case of every factor that is supposed to contribute to reading disability we can find a child who should be at risk who can read perfectly well."

Another problem arrives because of the multiplicity of the causal factors. Robinson reports that those children most retarded in reading exhibited the greatest number of anomalities. The open question is, as Kasdon (1970, p. 5) puts it: "How many etiological factors do we have operative? How much are they interacting to produce different effects than any one would have by itself?" We must look for the missing link, the mechanisms through which these causative or contributory factors may affect certain reading subskills, and we need a fruitful theory of the reading process as a precondition for this.

Third, another problem of the etiological approach is its low and indirect therapeutical value. Having diagnosed etiological factors as brain damage or poor home conditions, the teacher is unable to remove or correct these factors. Furthermore, this approach does not give any direct evidence for specific remedial instruction since the mechanisms operating and the points in the reading process where these factors lead to a disturbance are unknown. "If a child's difficulty with orientation does owe something to a neurological deficit of some kind we certainly cannot operate on his brain. Whatever may have predisposed the child to experience difficulty, the remedial problem consists of developing the appropriate learning sets. This is where more attention is really needed both for practical and theoretical reasons" (Merritt, 1971).

The Cognitive Deficit Approach

The cognitive deficit approach tries to isolate various types of reading problems. Some researchers are looking for deficits of reading disabled children in various cognitive functions, such as visual and auditory discrimination, memory, and language. Again, there are many shortcomings of this attempt, the most important of which are listed below.

From a pragmatic point of view, the attempts to classify poor readers for visual-spatial, auditory-linguistic, or symbol-learning difficulties were not very successful because of the considerable overlap between these categories (for a review of studies see Vernon, 1977).

The assumptions about the process of reading underlying the deficit approach are inadequate. It is significant that in studies of this type one scarcely ever finds a definition of the reading process that goes beyond banal paraphrases (reading is making sense out of signs, or some such), let alone a discussion or proposal of a theory of reading. Authors seem to be content to list the skills that are used during reading and writing. Behind these studies lies the unexpressed assumption that reading is some sort of a product of a variety of cognitive functions (such as visual and auditory discrimination, language skills, memory and comprehension of symbols) whose undisturbed functioning guarantees reading achievement and that reading will be impaired if one of these functions is deficient. That reading is a result of a specific learning and instructional process seems to be ignored in this model. Consequently, specific reading disability implies a specific causal attribution: the causes are primarily attributed to the child and his lack of capacities and not so much to the instruction process itself. Most of the research on dyslexia is based on this *function model* or *reading-readiness model*. Groups of poor and normal readers are compared in these functions and low achievement of backward readers is interpreted as a *deficit* that impedes normal progress in reading (compare Angermaier's interpretation, 1974, p. 19). The fallacy of this conclusion is obvious: correlations are interpreted as causal factors, although the design of the studies doesn't permit this.

The third fallacy of the deficit approach is the implicit assumption that the cognitive functions are a unitary process operating relatively independently of the stimulus material and the task so that a transfer effect from one task to another will take place (see also Scheerer-Neumann, 1977a). The underlying assumption seems to be that visual perception, for example, is a unitary psychic entity that the child possesses to certain degrees and that operates uniformly on all visual materials like pictures, geometric or abstract designs, numbers, letters, and words. Or that auditory discrimination operates uniformly on noises, musical notes, letter sounds, or words. Or that there is one directional ability equally effective in discriminating one's own body parts, body parts of other persons, objects in a two- and three-dimensional space or the sequence of letters in a word.

As various investigations have shown (Malmquist, 1958; Neisser, 1967), the visual processes are not unitary, but highly specific, and must be trained on different materials. A good discrimination ability in the pictorial domain does not guarantee the discrimination of letters and words. To learn to discriminate letters, the child must learn the specific distinctive features of the letters. Similar conclusions were reached about auditory discrimination ability by Dykstra (1966). Dykstra used seven independent tests of auditory discrimination with over 600 first grade pupils and reported that the intercorrelations among these measures were consistently low, almost always below 0.40. The implication of these results is that auditory discrimination is highly test specific.

Based on the assumption of the uniformity of the cognitive functions, the function model also serves as a theoretical basis for remedial treatment. The deficient visual, auditory, and motor functions are trained by specific programs and the improvement of these functions, so it is hoped, will result in an improvement of reading (see for instance the Frostig program [Frostig and Maslow, 1973]). There is neither theoretical nor empirical evidence for the validity of such a transfer. The numerous American experiments with visual training programs have not proven themselves helpful in increasing reading achievement (Valtin, 1972). Eggert, Schuck, and Wieland (1973) have stated that motor and cognitive-verbal training (that is, training in writing and functional exercises) resulted in very unspecific effects: both treatment groups showed improvement in both the trained and the untrained areas. Thus, the assumption of a transfer of such training programs is highly questionable.

Moreover, when one looks at the low correlations that have been obtained between the functions that have been tested and the reading achievement scores, the impression arises that factors have been measured that are rather irrelevant to the reading process. A further verification for this is that in a longitudinal study (Valtin, 1972) scarcely any relationships worth mentioning were observed between reading and writing achievement in the first, second, and third school years and some variables measured at the beginning of school (visual perception, directional confusion, articulation, auditory discrimination, vocabulary, school readiness, IQ).

Another objection against this approach is that the observed deficits of the poor readers might be an artifact of the research method used. If representative samples of good and poor readers are compared, they will differ in background variables, such as intelligence and socioeconomic status, and consequently they will differ also in correlated psychological tests of visual, auditory, memory, or language abilities. Thus, the poor readers will show many cognitive deficits; but, if we take into consideration the IQ of the poor readers and investigate only children with specific reading disabilities, that is, individuals whose reading progress is unsatisfactory in terms of their potential, then the deficits will vary with the measure of potential ability that is used (Verbal IQ, Performance IQ, or Full scale IQ). Reed (1970), in a most interesting study, investigated the effects of different IQ measures of the Wechsler Intelligence Scale for Children in studies of specific reading disabilities and showed that the nature of the IQ test not only determines the number of poor readers in a sample, but also determines the results on other psychological tests. He concluded that "the pattern of deficits found among retarded readers will depend upon the index used to estimate reading potential" (Reed, 1970, p. 348).

Since Reed's criterion for reading retardation (poor readers were defined as those children whose reading scores were among the lowest one-third of the group and whose IQs were 90 or above) differed from the usual definition, his investigation was replicated by the author of this paper. Third graders of 13 classes in West Berlin were tested with a reading test, a spelling test, the Primary Mental Abilities Test (German version), and other visual, auditory, and language tests. Poor readers and poor spellers (below one standard deviation in the applied tests) were defined as retarded if one of their IQ measures was 90 or above. If Full Scale IQ or Performance IQ was chosen as the IQ criterion, the number of poor readers/spellers was about 30% higher than with the Verbal IQ since fewer children with low reading and spelling abilities reached a Verbal IQ above 90. Thus the IQ measure determines the number of children with specific reading or writing problems and the results in the other tests.

The groups of disabled children with reading or spelling difficulties as a whole showed a significantly lower Verbal IQ (about 95) and a comparatively higher Performance IQ (about 105), whereas among the good readers/spellers the relationship of the Verbal IQ and the Performance IQ was nearly balanced (about 110 each). From this typical IQ pattern of poor and good readers/spellers, we might deduce the results that would be obtained if we compared matched groups of poor and good readers/spellers with different IQ measures as matching variables (see Figure 1).

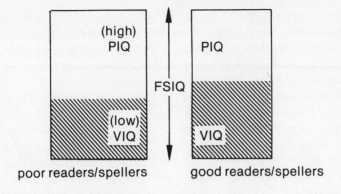

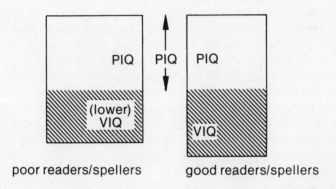

Figure 1.   Consequence of the comparison of good and poor readers matched on Full Scale IQ or Performance IQ. *Top:* Matching on the Full Scale IQ will result in a higher Performance IQ of the poor readers (and in better results in tests correlating with PIQ) and in a lower Verbal IQ (and in poorer results in tests correlating with VIQ). *Bottom:* Matching on the PIQ will result in a lower FSIQ and a lower VIQ of the poor readers.

The actual outcome of our study confirmed these reflections. The IQ measure used to define the reading or spelling disability not only influenced the pattern of the relationship between Verbal IQ and Performance IQ, but also the results in tests correlated with these IQ measures. If groups were matched on Performance IQ, the poor readers/spellers showed "deficits," especially in the language tests. If the Verbal IQ was chosen for the matching variable, the differences tended to disappear. When the Full scale IQ was used as the matching variable, the poor readers/spellers showed better results in the visual tests.

Other studies using the matched pair design also showed a superiority of the poor spellers in the visual domain (Kemmler 1967, Oehrle 1975, Valtin, 1973).

In the Berlin study (Valtin, 1979) the results varied even in those variables such as poor vocabulary, field dependence, poor auditory discrimination ability, difficulties in coding and symbol learning, and poor memory for digits which are frequently quoted as reliable deficits of reading disabled children.

To explain these results, Reed (1970) turned to the principle of the correlation between two or more variables. When matching is done on the basis of Verbal IQ, good and poor readers will show similar scores in those variables that correlate higher with Verbal IQ than with reading achievement. They are more likely to be different in characteristics that are more closely related to reading achievement than to Verbal IQ. When, on the other hand, the Performance IQ of both groups is comparable, good and poor readers will achieve similar scores in tests that are highly correlated to Performance IQ. Thus, conclusions about lower achievement or deficits among children with specific reading or spelling difficulties on cognitive, speech, or visual tests can only be drawn with extreme care.

In summary, it can be stated that the acceptance of the etiological approach and the functional model of reading has had an unfortunate consequence: it has led researchers (the author of this paper included) in a circle round about the reading process (in areas such as sociocultural milieu, dominance factors, early childhood development, personality characteristics), while scarcely anything is known about specific deficits in the reading process itself. What is needed is a theory about the specific visual, auditory, memory, and language functions which operate in the reading process.

The Symptom Approach

The third approach to discover varieties of reading and spelling difficulties is called the *symptom approach*. Some researchers believe that an analysis of the reading and writing errors of an individual may give hints about the specific difficulty in the reading and writing process. Three approaches can be differentiated:

1. The descriptive approach
2. The function-oriented approach
3. The process-oriented approach

Oral reading tests in Germany are based on the principle that each error of the child is scored. The teacher has to compare the standard word with the word the child has read and then count letter for letter how many omissions, additions, reversals, or substitutions of letters the individual has produced. By comparing the input letters and the output sounds, this black-box-error-counting-model arrives at highly formal quantitative measures which do not account for the inner cognitive processes and strategies the reader uses in interacting with a given text.

Since reading errors are made rather unreliably and in no systematic way and since the classification of the errors is more or less subjective this approach does not seem fruitful.

The function-oriented approach tries to identify the cognitive deficits which underly certain errors. Müller (1974) has developed a functional-etiological classification scheme for spelling errors. He believes that each spelling error can be linked directly to a cognitive deficit. For instance, substitutions of acoustically dissimilar sounds were caused by an auditory discrimination disability, or reversals of letters were caused by directional confusion. This approach ignores the possibility that errors are multifactorial, caused by dialect, lack of concentration, unfamiliariarity with the word, or poor memory for word structures, to name only a few potential causes. Due to a lack of an adequate theory of the spelling process, Müller's approach does not take into consideration the operations that the speller uses during the writing act.

The process-oriented symptom approach tries to identify the cognitive operations of the reader. Goodman (1970) views reading as a psycholinguistic guessing game in which language and thought interact. His miscue analysis gives evidence about the strategies readers use and the kind of information (graphemic, phonetic, syntactic, semantic) they process in interacting with a given text. This approach seems very promising. A pilot study by Hofer (1977) has identified individual differences in the reading strategies of poor readers:

Difficulties in word identification (The child is so busy in recoding letter by letter that he does not get the meaning.)
Difficulties in the segmentation of the words in economical and meaningful units
Difficulties in using syntactic and semantic restrictions of the text

Further studies of this kind are needed to identify the individual difficulties and their interactions.

THE PROCESS-ORIENTED APPROACH

A fourth attempt to identify variables in reading difficulties is the process-oriented approach. This attempt is an alternative to the function model of reading. Researchers of this type try to identify partial processes of reading in which children with reading problems are deficient.

Vernon (1977) suggests a classification scheme of poor readers according to four types of failures in reading (although she admits that there may be much overlap from one type to another):

In the initial learning phases there may be deficiencies in the capacity to analyze complex, sequential visual and/or auditory-linguistic structures. These deficiencies prevent the coding of the linguistic structures and their organization in short- and long-term memory...

The second point at which reading difficulty is likely to occur is in the linking of visual and auditory-linguistic structures...

A third type of failure, the inability to establish regularities in variable grapheme-phoneme correspondences, may be the most frequent cause of poor reading...

A fourth type of poor readers may recognize words but cannot group them into meaningful phrases (Vernon, 1977, pp. 406–407).

Lastly, however, Vernon is dedicated to a function-oriented approach to reading. She assumes that the development of reading skills is "dependent on the normal functioning of a number of different psychological processes, including visual and auditory perception, memory, linguistic ability, and reasoning...and deficiencies in any of the psychological processes on which reading is based can lead to disturbances" (Vernon 1977, p. 396).

Thus, she seems to have adopted the implicit assumption of unitary psychological functions, which is questionable.

In this same article Vernon does not mention a major finding of her prior publication on reading retardation (Vernon, 1960), which is highly relevant for the initial stages of reading. In her review of the literature on backwardness in reading, Vernon had concluded: "Thus the fundamental and basic characteristic of reading disability appears to be cognitive confusion." She stated that poor readers are "hopelessly uncertain and confused as to why certain successions of printed letters should correspond to certain phonetic sounds in words." In his cognitive clarity theory of reading Downing (1973b) also stresses the point that one source of difficulty in the early stages of reading is the child's lack of understanding of the purpose of written communication and its lack of basic concepts of language such as words, phonemes, letters, or sentences. This linguistic awareness seems to be an important factor in reading and learning to read. A finding of the Berlin study (Valtin, 1979) might be interpreted in light of this cognitive clarity theory. An interesting result of this study was the fact that poor readers/spellers showed poor performance in a German auditory discrimination test (requiring comparison of two spoken words and judgment concerning likeness and differences) but normal results in the similarly constructed Wepman Test with English words.[1] This result is in contradiction to the widespread assumption that specific reading disability is connected with poor auditory discrimination ability.

---

[1]We bypass the problem of validity of tests of the Wepman type which assess much more than the auditory discrimination ability (Blank, 1968; Skelfjord, 1975). Many children react to semantic features. Vellutino, DeSetto, and Steger (1972) have shown that response bias spuriously influences categorical judgments on discrimination tasks with unequal response alternatives.

Similarly, Katz (1967) observed that English-speaking poor readers had greater difficulties in the auditory discrimination of English words than with Hebrew words and supposed the familarity with the words to be the critical factor. Another explanation also seems plausible: that good readers use a different strategy when presented with words of their native language. They might not rely only on the auditory stimuli but figure out the written form of the orally presented words, thus possessing more critical cues for the differentiation. With this strategy they have an advantage over the poor readers and spellers whose knowledge of the written forms of the word often is deficient. This hypothesis should be further investigated, however. According to this interpretation, the apparent discrimination disability of the dyslexics is not so much a perceptual difficulty in discriminating speech sounds but a cognitive confusion about the nature of phonemes which do not have the same acoustic quality in all linguistic contexts (see Vellutino, chapter 16). Since phonemes are not always identical with the acoustical units of a spoken word, the phonemes that are relevant for a particular alphabetic writing system must be learned by the pupils and cannot be identified only by hearing (auditory discrimination) or a good pronunciation of the words. This learning process may not be fully accomplished by the reading disabled.

Let me cite another example for my hypothesis that poor readers/spellers have adequate phonetic discrimination abilities. The German linguist Jung (1977) carried out a tricky experiment to show that phonemic discrimination is influenced by the orthographic knowledge of an individual. In the German language, long and short vowel sounds are represented by different orthographic rules. Jung constructed pairs of sentences, each which contained a verb with a short and a long vowel sound:

Die Schwalbe ist ein Zugvogel, weil sie nach Suden fliegt.

Der Schuster ist ein Handwerker, der kaputte Schuhe flickt.

These sentences were videotaped and some of the verbs were interchanged. Children with poor and normal spelling abilities heard the sentences and were asked whether the verb contained a long or a short vowel sound. Most of the good spellers did not notice the manipulation of the verbs and gave the right answer in respect to the orthographic representation of the sound, while more of the poor spellers noticed the manipulation. Obviously, the poor spellers relied on the acoustic signal while the good spellers referred to the written form of the word. Thus the orthographic knowledge influenced their phonetic judgment.

To summarize, the findings reported in this chapter indicate that children with poor reading and spelling abilities possess adequate perceptual discrimination abilities, but lack phonemic awareness, especially the ability to segment words phonemically. The poor ability of dyslexics to segment

282　　Dyslexia and Related Disorders

spoken words into phonemes has been demonstrated by Valtin (1972). In this study the poor readers/spellers showed normal results in segmenting words into syllables, but had difficulties in segmenting at a phoneme level. This result is in agreement with other findings that the syllabic segmentation is easier than the phonemic segmentation (Goldstein, 1976; I. Y. Liberman, Shankweiler, Fischer, & Carter, 1974). This inability to segment words into phonemes is an explanation for certain errors in spelling: errors that are not phonemically accurate. Since children with reading and spelling difficulties in general are able to write letters after dictation (Valtin, 1974), these phonetic errors in spelling cannot be attributed to poor sound-letter conversion skills alone but they seem to indicate a failure in the accurate phonemic segmentation of the word.

In the Berlin study (Valtin, 1979) the spelling errors of the sample were classed into two broad categories: phonemic errors, which distorted the sound pattern of the word, and orthographic errors, which were phonemically accurate but violated specific orthographic rules. In the factor analysis of all administered tests, six factors were extracted.

F_1　Inability to segment words phonemically (with loadings in all phonemic misspelling categories as letter omission, letter insertion, vowel and consonant substitution, and reversal and translocations of letters)
F_2　Orthographic rule knowledge
F_3　With the only loadings in the two auditory discrimination tests
F_4　Verbal knowledge (with a loading in the silent reading test)
F_5　A numerical factor
F_6　A visual-spatial factor

This factor analytic study has indicated that auditory discrimination is, in fact, independent of phonemic segmentation ability. Another finding of this study supports this argument: children with poor auditory discrimination skills did not show more phonemic errors in their spellings. This casts doubt on the widely accepted hypothesis in Germany that phonemic errors are an indicator of deficiencies in auditory perception.

Another proponent for the process-oriented approach is the German psychologist Scheerer-Neumann. She also questions the value of the traditional research studies on specific reading disabilities and argues "that most studies in the medical-neurological and the psychological tradition (i.e., the etiological and deficit approach) are of limited usefulness due to their aim to discover *causes* of dyslexia thereby neglecting the actual disturbed *cognitive processes*" (Scheerer-Neumann 1977a, p. 125). In her attempt to identify partial processes of reading in which poor readers are deficient, she outlines a model of reading, limited to the reading of single words, which has been influenced also by American researchers. According to this model three operations take place sequentially during the process of word identification:

1. The *visual operation* consisting of a distinctive feature analysis and a segmentation of the linguistic material into manageable chunks
2. The *phonetic recoding* of chunks into a phonetic pattern
3. The *semantic decoding* which can take place parallel or prior to the phonetic coding

Scheerer-Neumann's studies show that poor readers have difficulties with the segmentation of words into economical units because they either try to read words as a whole or try to code letter by letter. In a tachistoscopic experiment (Scheerer-Neumann, 1977b) the performance of good and poor readers in identifying eight-letter pseudowords of either first- or fourth-order approximation to German were compared (*aejnarte* and *pulmerat*).

Both groups showed better results with the more redundant pseudowords, but the difference between these two experimental conditions was much greater for the poor readers who could apparently not profit from the better segmentation possibility of the fourth-order pseudowords. Another study showed that the identification of pseudowords by poor readers could be improved when the stimulus material was segmented into syllables.

Still another study (Scheerer-Neumann, 1978) throws an interesting light on the reversal errors of poor readers, which within the deficit approach are linked to a directional confusion. Using letter sequences ordered by chance, the poor readers were even better than the good readers in reporting the left-right sequence, but the good readers showed better results when letter sequences that could be segmented into chunks were used. Thus, it is apparent that the poor readers have internalized the left-right scanning process, but fail because of their uneconomical segmentation strategy. If the phonetic coding process operates on syllables *(pul-me-rat)*, the order of the letters within the syllable is already fixed; but if one recodes single letters *(p-u-l-m-e-r-a-t),* it is far more difficult to keep the right order (Scheerer-Neumann 1978).

As Scheerer-Neumann (1977a, p. 134) points out, her reading model has to be refined by investigating mastery of the partial processes under three aspects: accuracy, speed, and automaticity. Interfacilitation among these processes is another aspect worth studying. Furthermore, this model must be elaborated for reading passages (words in context) where other languages and cognitive skills are involved. In this respect a differentiation of skills suggested by Merritt (1975) seems useful. He distinguishes between intermediate reading skills, or the ability to profit from contextual cues, and higher order comprehension skills. The intermediate skills, or "the ability to anticipate or predict that certain letters, word classes, word forms, meanings, or actual words are more or less likely in a given context" facilitate the recognition of unfamiliar words, understanding of word and sentence reading, and fluent reading (Merritt, 1975).

Linguistic awareness and knowledge about the redundancy of language seem to be prerequisites of these skills. Scheerer-Neumann (1978) showed that poor readers showed poorer results in guessing a missing letter (vowel or consonant) in a pseudoword, thus demonstrating a lack of sensitivity for allowable letter combinations. Deficiencies in verbal processing will also affect the intermediate skills. (For an extensive discussion of this point see Vellutino, 1977.)

Another skill involved at this intermediate level is text-organization or the ability to make use of units larger than a word in reading. Golinkoff (1976), in a review of studies on good and poor comprehenders, cites evidence for a lack of text organization of poor comprehenders. Studies with the eye-voice-span (EVS) show that the EVS for good readers usually is 14 letter spaces (or about 2 words), while the EVS for poor comprehenders is about 9 letter spaces or a little more than a word. Golinkoff concludes "the preceding studies characterize the poor comprehender as concerned with decoding each word and failing to utilize the interword relationships that could speed up the decoding process and permit more efficient text sampling" (p. 646).

A further differentiation by Cromer (1970) of the poor comprehenders into deficit and difference types seems most plausible. Due to a lack of some ability, for instance poor vocabulary skills, the deficit type of poor comprehender displays poor comprehension abilities. The difference type of poor reader has not yet achieved the right strategy: he reads the text word-by-word and does not organize the text into meaningful units. The difficulty of the deficit type seems to be a generally inadequate language comprehension skill, while the problem of the difference type is one of text organization. This assumption is confirmed by Cromer (1970) who demonstrated that the difference type of poor comprehenders could improve their comprehension ability when the presented text was organized into meaningful units.

The higher order comprehension skills refer to the ability to deal with larger units of meaning whereby the material can be differently used according to the purpose of the reader:

Literal comprehension (ability to select relevant details, perception of main ideas and understanding of their structure)
Inferential comprehension (ability to make inferences about implicit meaning)
Evaluation and critical appraisal of the reading material (cf. Merritt, 1975)

It is obvious that the comprehension skills are directly related to the differentiation and complexity of the concepts, the cognitive organization, the general level of cognitive development, and the cognitive style of an individual.

THE TASK-ANALYSIS OR SUBSKILL APPROACH

A fifth promising approach to assess reading disabilities can be labeled the "subskill" or task-oriented approach. Guthrie (1973) and Guthrie and Seifert (1977) identified subskills or direct components of the reading process with respect to the development of phoneme-grapheme association skills. Guthrie (1973) found that the strength of subskills in a group of poor readers was similar to the comparable subskills in normal readers with a similar reading level but was inferior to normal readers of the same age who completely mastered these skills. Although the intercorrelations among the subskills were high positive for the normal readers, they were largely insignificant for the poor readers. Guthrie (1973) suggests that "interfacilitation among subskills is necessary for normal reading. One source of disability for poor readers is lack of integration and interfacilitation among subskills."

Guthrie and Seifert (1977), in a longitudinal study, demonstrated that the acquisition of letter-sound correspondence rules was similar for good and poor readers and depended on the complexity of the rules. The specific task (including consonant-vowel combinations, short vowel words, long vowel words, special rule words, and nonsense words), which includes a hierarchy of difficulty, could be used to reveal specific strengths and weaknesses of poor readers in word identification.

RECOMMENDATIONS FOR FUTURE RESEARCH

In future research, the following points should be taken into consideration.

1. Because dyslexia or specific reading deficit is a collective term for various disturbances in the ability to read and spell, the oft-used method of group comparisons for research is not appropriate for uncovering evidence about the different types of reading and spelling failures. Data on mean scores do not reveal whether or not weaknesses of a particular type are being offset by relative strengths of another type. In order to develop initial hypotheses about different sorts of disturbances in reading and writing, an exploratory approach based on individual case studies is recommended. Also, the prevailing practice of testing for the range of certain psycho-physical functions, which are assumed to re-

strict reading performance, should in the future be supplemented with or replaced by an approach that aims at isolating the partial processes of reading and writing themselves.

2. or this it will be necessary that research be based on an explicit, theoretical model of the reading process, one in which the individual subskills are identified and their interactive connections laid open to view. Also, only those research studies that clarify individual components of the reading process itself can provide the practitioner with concrete guidance in the structuring of (remedial) classwork.

3. Studies with an ex post facto design should be replaced by longitudinal studies.

Chapter 18
RELATIONSHIPS BETWEEN READING AND SPELLING

Uta Frith and Christopher Frith

It seems obvious that reading a word correctly is merely the inverse of spelling it. It is the same written word that is the stimulus in one case and the response in the other. Letter-to-sound and sound-to-letter relationships should logically be identical, just working in opposite directions. However, there are several facts that are incompatible with this apparently obvious and logical relationship.

First, there are patients who after cerebral accidents have lost their ability to write but not to read, and those who have lost their ability to read, but not to write. This means that they are unable to read what they themselves have written (Benson & Geschwind, 1964; Weigl & Fradis, 1977). If reading and writing were just the same process in reverse, such a specific disability would be hard to explain.

Second, it has often been observed that reading skill exceeds spelling skill. This might not necessarily mean more than the well-known fact that in language skills comprehension exceeds production. Rather less trivial is the observation that spelling sometimes exceeds reading. This has been described by Read (1971) and C. Chomsky (1971) who noticed this phenomenon in very young children who could write before they could read and who spelled in a phonologically plausible way without concern for potential readers, including themselves. Bryant and Bradley (1979) demonstrated experimentally that 7-year-olds often spelled words correctly that they were unable to read. Interestingly enough, if they were induced to use a phonological reading strategy they were able to read these words. Bryant and Bradley concluded that children often read words on the basis of visual chunks and often spell words on the basis of phonological segments.

Third, there can be very marked dissociation between reading and spelling skills. We have studied 12-year-old children with and without such a dissociation and shall summarize some of the experiments of this study.

Table 1 shows the relevant data for the three groups that were compared: one dissociated group, which consisted of children who were good readers and at the same time atrocious spellers; one group good at both reading and spelling; and one group poor at both reading and spelling. All children had about average verbal IQs, which presumably guarantees that

Table 1.   Comparison of three groups of children: good readers/good spellers, good readers/poor spellers, and poor readers/poor spellers.

	Good	Dissociated	Poor
n	10	10	9
PPVT IQ	117(15)	100(14)	100(13)
Reading Quotient	106(6)	101(9)	81(10)
Spelling Quotient	109(6)	90(10)	83(9)

Age 12:12 (range 11–13)

there were no gross differences in intelligence/language skill that might (un-interestingly) account for differences in educational attainments. Despite the similarities in terms of these variables and in terms of educational and social background, there were differences in reading and spelling as assessed by Schonell graded word lists (Schonell, 1942). The dissociated group was as good in reading as a generally good group and was as poor in spelling as a generally poor group. Of course the same level of achievement may never-theless have been gained by qualitatively different strategies. Consequently, we tried to look at the quality of both reading and spelling. Reading and spelling nonsense words can reveal some of the strategies being used (see Baron & Treiman, chapter 12, this volume). With nonsense words, the reader cannot use rote memory for specific words, but must use rules of some kind. Grapheme-to-phoneme correspondence rules are the most ob-vious ones, but analogies to real words also can be used.

Nonsense words were developed, each of which was based on a real word of the Schonell list and exemplified a particular grapheme-to-pho-neme rule. Examples are: c before e → /s/ (laucer–saucer) and ph → /f/ (crephew–nephew). If the critical graphemes were pronounced incorrectly, an error was scored, regardless of the rest of the word. Conversely, if the critical grapheme was pronounced correctly, no error was scored, even if the rest of the word was incorrect.

The good group made 11% reading errors, the dissociated group 24%, and the poor group 44%, all significantly different from each other. The large difference between good and poor readers on this test is, of course, ex-pected. However, the difference between good readers who were good spellers and good readers who were poor spellers is surprising since both groups had achieved the same attainment level on word recognition. Most of the words on which the nonsense words were based had been read cor-rectly by these children. Yet, the dissociated group made letter-to-sound translation errors in about one-quarter of the nonsense words. This must mean that they read the corresponding real words not by such translation rules, but by look-and-say strategy. If they recognized the underlying real word in the nonsense word then they could bypass the grapheme-to-phoneme conversion even in this task, so that their ability to use conver-

Table 2.   Spelling nonsense words

Type of response	% responses			Example
	Good	Dissociated	Poor	
Phonetic-Conventional	90	75	60	usterand
Phonetic-Unconventional	3	10	7	asterand
Non-phonetic	7	15	33	austeran

sions may well be overestimated. The three groups also had to spell non-sense words. These words were dictated, i.e., clearly pronounced three times, and the written spellings were scored according to how well the original sound could be reconstructed from them. Two judges decided to-gether what could count as a phonetic or a nonphonetic rendering. A rela-tively lenient criterion was set so that nonphonetic renderings were indisput-ably wrong spellings.

Such wrong spellings were significantly more frequent in the poor group than in the dissociated group (t = 2.20; df = 17; $p < 0.01$). It can there-fore be concluded that they had poorer phoneme-to-grapheme conversion skills. The dissociated group, on the other hand, did not differ in this re-spect from good spellers and must therefore be supposed to be reasonably good at phoneme-to-grapheme conversion. At first sight it seems surprising that these poor spellers were no worse at spelling nonsense words than the good spellers. However, close examination of the correct renderings showed that there was a subtle difference in their spelling responses.

The class of phonetic renderings was subdivided into those spellings that exactly reproduced the original (which was never seen, only heard) and into others. Since we had tried hard to use only regular spellings and un-equivocal sound-letter relationships, all phonetic spellings should have been like the original spelling. Table 2 shows that conventional phonetic spellings made up the majority of phonetic responses in all three groups. However, the good spellers had significantly more of these conventional spellings ($t = 2.46$, df = 18, $p < 0.01$) than the dissociated spellers, who did not differ from the other poor spellers in this respect. Interestingly enough, the disso-ciated group produced a relatively large proportion of unconventional spell-ings which nevertheless were phonetically acceptable significantly more than good spellers. One problem with these unconventional renderings is that they are more difficult to read since the graphemes used are often more ambiguous, i.e., they can be pronounced in many different ways. This can also explain the paradoxical result that poor spellers can't read their own misspelled words very well (Frith, 1978).

Similar results have been obtained (Frith, 1978) that support the hy-pothesis that good readers/poor spellers know and use phoneme-to-grapheme rules but rely less on grapheme-to-phoneme rules. Poor readers/poor spellers on the other hand, are poorly skilled at both processes.

Thus, our initial contention that reading and spelling are not one and the same process in opposite directions has received support. There can be a remarkable lack of reciprocity between phoneme and grapheme translation rules. If the dissociated group can produce an acceptable phoneme-to-grapheme translation, but has difficulty in choosing the best of the many grapheme alternatives, then they should have particular difficulty in spelling homophones. However, since these are real words, additional cues are available, such as a rote memory for the appearance of the word from reading it and morphological information. If the dissociated group did use such cues, they should find the homophone problem easier than the nonsense word problem.

Therefore we selected about 20 homophone pairs, such as *beach-beech,* all in the reading vocabulary of the children, and dictated them in meaningful sentence frames. The error of interest was the production of the wrong homophone. Good spellers showed only 6% of such errors, but both groups of poor spellers showed 14%, which is significantly more. Since the dissociated group was no better than the other poor spellers, it seems likely that their better reading ability does not help them to make use of rote memory for these words, nor of morphological cues.

The children were also asked to recognize which of the alternatives of the homophones was correct in a particular sentence. All of them could do the task very well, with an error rate of only 6%–8%, and there was no group difference. This suggests dissociation between reading and spelling for both groups of poor spellers, since they can distinguish between some homophones when reading them, but not when spelling them.

DIFFERENCES IN RECOGNITION AND RECALL

It would be trivial to rephrase differences between reading and spelling in terms of recognition and recall processes, if the difference was simply in the mode of testing; however, there are more than merely methodological differences. It is often held (e.g., Kintsch, 1970) that recall involves two phases, first generating, then recognizing the product. Written spelling is also often subjectively experienced as involving a subsequent recognition test. Simon (1976) proposes this in an explicit model for spelling. The difficulty with this two-phase model is that just as it cannot account for superiority of recall over recognition, it cannot account for superiority of spelling over reading.

Very relevant to our discussion is the distinction of recall and recognition tasks in terms of different modality codes. The discovery of acoustic confusions in recall of visually presented letters (Conrad, 1964) has given

Table 3.   Recall of nonsense words simultaneously seen and heard

Conditions	Examples		Phonetic errors (max = 6)
	Seen	Heard	
Same letter/different sound	plear hearf	/plɪr hɛrf/	0.70
Different letter/different sound	pleer herf	/plɪr hɛrf/	1.10
Same letter/same sound	steane dease	/stɪn dɪs/	1.30
Different letter/same sound	stene deese	/stɪn dɪs/	2.40

rise to the theory that items in short term memory are auditorily encoded. Cohen and Granström (1970) and Vingilis, Blake, and Theodor (1977) have suggested that auditory coding plays a role mainly in recall, whereas visual coding plays a role in recognition. O'Connor and Hamelin (1978) have suggested that different modality codes go together with different encoding strategies. Specifically, they hypothesize that items related sequentially favor auditory coding, whereas items related spatially favor visual coding. Thus, a visual code may be in terms of whole words, without letter by letter detail. This code would be sufficient for recognition purposes, and moreover especially suited to "noisy" conditions. Exact details of the stimulus are bound to vary and an exact code would therefore not be helpful. In contrast, an auditory code may be in terms of an exact letter by letter sequence. An exact and detailed code is necessary to produce correct spellings.

The hypothesis that a sound code is preferred for spelling recall derives support from spelling error analysis. It is well known that the majority of spelling errors are based on correct sound. When words are written to dictation, as in conventional spelling tests, by definition, only the sound of the word is provided. Therefore it need not be surprising to find that sound dominates spelling. In order to investigate more rigorously the role of sound in spelling we carried out an experiment where both the sound and the written form of the word were presented simultaneously, so that subjects could use either or both types of cues. The test stimuli were pairs of short nonsense words. To minimize reliance on auditory cues there was a 10 sec interval between presentation and writing down the words during which subjects had to count. All stimuli were one syllable words of four to six letters with a central vowel sound. In each pair the sound of the central vowel could be the same or different, and its graphic representation could also be the same or different. All the usual experimental controls were applied in a balanced two-factor repeated measures design. Thus, sometimes the same vowel sound in both members of the stimulus pair was represented by the same letter (*steane–dease*), sometimes by different letters (*stene–dease*). For each condition there were 6 different word pairs (see Table 3).

Subjects were ten adults, all skilled spellers, as we wanted to see whether the role of sound was predominant beyond the initial learning stages. We looked only at the letters the subjects had used to represent the central vowel sound in each pair of stimuli. Misspellings that were phonemically incorrect were very rare. In other words, the sound was almost always preserved. This alone suggests that a sound-based code must have been used. The errors shown in Table 3 refer strictly to the phonemically correct, but graphemically incorrect, renderings of the given vowel sounds. These errors were most frequent when one and the same phoneme mapped onto two different graphemes. The phoneme gives no clue as to which grapheme is to be used in either pair. There were significantly more confusions of the critical graphemes in this (homophone) condition than in the obverse (homograph) condition. This might simply be because in the homograph condition only one grapheme has to be remembered. However, the condition in which different letters were associated with different sounds was also easier than the homophone condition, even though two graphemes had to be remembered.

Phonetic misspellings could have been avoided simply by ignoring the sound and by remembering only the visual representation. This would effectively remove the homophone effect obtained. Since people did not ignore sound, even when this led to confusion, one may well talk about a dominance of sound in this task. Since this effect was shown by experienced adult spellers, it is probably not restricted to the early stages of reading, but reflects a dominance of sound in sequential processes in general of which spelling is an example.

A similar experiment has been reported by Crowder (1978). He asked subjects to recall (write down) lists of homophonic words (or nonsense words), e.g., *write–right–rite–right–write–rite–write*. This strictly tested the ability of subjects to use a graphemic memory code, since a phonemic code would clearly not help at all. Recall was very much poorer in this condition than one would get under "normal" conditions of different sounding words. Interestingly enough, when using nonwords the performance was decreased even further, essentially to chance level. This suggests that a purely graphemic code is not viable unless it is also a lexical code. That is, the different spellings of homophones can be recalled by virtue of their being familiar words, carrying meaning.

A second experiment, using the same subjects and similar stimuli, was carried out in order to contrast the previous recall task with a recognition task. Here it was predicted that visual cues rather than sound would dominate, as stimuli are spatially rather than sequentially processed.

The subjects had to read silently through lists of 96 lines with three one-syllable words and nonsense words per line. The subjects were asked to scan the list as fast as possible and to cancel all nonsense words. For example, one line might read *tool–rule–nool* (same sound, different letters for the central vowel in both words), another, *love–move–sove* (different sound,

Table 4. Recognition of words and nonsense words

Conditions	Word	Word	Nonword	Errors (max = 12)
Same letter/different sound	weight	height	seight	2.33
Different letter/different sound	blue	hear	plon	1.86
Same letter/same sound	coarse	hoarse	loarse	2.00
Different letter/same sound	tool	rule	nool	1.80

same letters). Table 4 shows examples and error rates. Each condition was represented by 12 triads of 2 words and 1 nonsense word, all randomly presented and mixed with as many dummy triads that had none, two, or three nonsense words.

Errors were mainly due to not recognizing nonsense words, but also to judging a real word to be nonsense. Although there was no significant difference between the error rates for the four conditions, there was a tendency for performance to be worse when the critical letters were the same in the triad. This is opposite to the homophone effect obtained previously. If anything, it is a homograph effect. There was no effect whatever attributable to different or same sounds. The effect of different or same letters was greater, although still not significant. However, the important point is that sound cannot be said to dominate performance in this task. This gives weak support for the hypothesis that recognition, as in silent reading, is associated with a visual rather than auditory code. Once again, this seems a general phenomenon that is not restricted to the early stages of reading.

DIFFERENT DEMANDS OF INPUT AND OUTPUT SKILLS

If we accept the notion that spelling as a recall process relies heavily on phonological coding, and reading as a recognition process, if anything, on visual coding, then there is nothing abnormal with the unexpectedly poor speller precisely following this pattern. What may be abnormal is a lack of connection between the two codes. The good speller can presumably easily go from grapheme to phoneme and from phoneme to grapheme. Ideally, sound, spelling, meaning, and other linguistic attributes of a word should be accessible simultaneously and with equal facility (see Ehri, chapter 11, this volume).

An important difference between good and unexpectedly poor spellers can be seen in the ability to go beyond phoneme to grapheme rules: good spellers can spell words where sound is an insufficient or misleading cue. In order to spell these words, there are at least two options, either using an immensely complex set of deeper level linguistic rules, or using thousands of specific spelling programs for individual words. Among the various rules, it would be useful to know the roots of words, their provenance from other languages, and their syntactic function. This is in addition to a number of spelling rules that specify which graphemes can occur in particular positions in a word, and when to change letters with particular suffixes and prefixes. However, rather than trying to learn the rationale for each spelling by a host of rules and relationships, one can just remember the spelling of individual words by rote. One wonders whether the rules mentioned are often known by hindsight only. If one knows how to spell *hyperbole* one can guess that it is a Greek word with the prefix *hyper* as in *hyperactive* and not as in *highway*.

Therefore, it seems plausible that good spellers use specific programs learned by rote, rather than rules. Unexpectedly poor spellers, on the other hand, may try to use rules rather than rote. Rules undoubtedly permit flexibility. Only by using rules can we spell entirely novel words. However, we would like to put forward the hypothesis that flexibility is not desirable in spelling. While flexibility is desirable in reading, rigidity is desirable in spelling. A similar argument has previously been applied to the forms taken by single letters (Frith, 1974).

The reader finds the written word in many different and novel forms. It may be the product of many different writers. The variety makes the appearance of written words unpredictable, and hence input analyzing strategies cannot be entirely preprogrammed. Since input conditions normally vary tremendously with context, purpose, and background noise, we must presume that reading, like all other perceptual processes, requires strategies that adapt themselves to these different conditions. Flexibility would entail that reading can be guided by sound, sight, orthographic pattern, etc., depending on the task conditions.

Quite the opposite applies to output processes. The writer produces the written word for many different readers to look at. Hence, it should be reliable, predictable, i.e., rigidly controlled. This can be done by preprogramming. Such preprogramming is evident in handwriting movements (it is essentially the same characteristic pattern that is produced), but spelling programs need not be tied to writing movements. Evidence for spelling programs has been collected by Henderson, Chard, and Clark (1977), who showed that oral spelling is subject to a word superiority effect.

Beginners and poor spellers who have no spelling programs have to spend much effort in order to spell a word and often produce different spelling variants for the same word. Good spellers rarely spend any conscious effort in spelling. They typically say that they "just know" how to spell a word. But once programs are established they will always lead to the same (correct) response. This rigidity in output processing, in turn, benefits input processing. Rigidly consistent spelling makes for easy reading, inconsistent spelling demands attention from the reader. Presumably this is one of the reasons why spelling has become standardized.

CONCLUSION

This chapter shows that the relationship between reading and spelling, which seems such an obvious and close one, is in fact quite complex and interesting. Some results have been presented from children who are good readers, but unexpectedly poor spellers, as an example of possible dissociations between these two processes.

Whenever phoneme-to-grapheme rules are insufficient to produce the correct spelling (which is the case for about every other English word), specific spelling programs probably have to be used. This is where poor spellers fail, possibly because they have failed to acquire such programs by rote. Instead of rote learning, an immensely complex set of rules can be used and this would undoubtedly allow for flexibility in spelling unfamiliar words. However, while such flexibility is characteristic of input processes, rigidity is characteristic of output processes. Skilled reading, as a typical input process, is flexible. A visually based code seems well suited for this as it allows for "whole" word encoding without letter by letter detail. Skilled spelling, as a typical output process, is rigid and based on preprogrammed letter sequences. A phonologically based code is appropriate for detail sequential information.

We have suggested that the dominant coding strategy for sequential processes, such as spelling and writing, is essentially auditory. This leads to difficulties particularly with English orthography since a sound-based strategy can only be partially successful. Spelling reform aimed at a straightforward phonetic orthography would necessarily be detrimental to reading. A sound-based strategy for reading seems at least unnatural, and the dissociation between the strategies for reading and spelling, found in children who are good readers and poor spellers, is still present to some extent in adults, who are highly skilled in both tasks. It has been frequently mentioned by other contributors to this volume that English has a deep orthography, which precisely because of its relative lack of phonetic correspondence, is able to carry linguistic and semantic information. Presumably, this deep orthography is particularly helpful for reading, as it allows immediate access to meaning (See Baron & Treiman, chapter 12, this volume).

Thus we must conclude that the ideal orthography for spelling is incompatible with the ideal orthography for reading. Any useful orthography must be a compromise between these two requirements. A similar incompatibility has been suggested by Wang (1976) for speech and listening.

Although our arguments are speculative, they would provide a deeper reason for dissociations between reading and spelling skills and would make this dissociation a specific instance of a general psychological principle.

References

Adams, J. J. Models of word recognition. *Cognitive Psychology,* 1979, *11,* 133–176.

Adar, L. [A study of scholastic difficulties of immigrant children.] *Megamot,* 1956, *7,* 139–180. (In Hebrew)

Adiel, S. [Reading ability of culturally deprived first graders.] *Megamot,* 1968, *15,* 345–356. (In Hebrew)

Adiel, S. (Ed.). [*Ten years of compensatory education.*] Jerusalem: Ministry of Education, 1970. (In Hebrew)

Adler, C., & Peleg, R. [*Evaluating the results of studies and experiments in compensatory education.*] Jerusalem: Hebrew University, School of Education, 1976. (In Hebrew)

Ahvenainen, O., Karppi, S., & Aström, M-L. [*Children's reading and writing difficulties.*] Helsinki, 1977. (In Finnish)

Alahuhta, E. On the defects of perception, reasoning and spatial orientation ability in linguistically handicapped children. *Annales Academiae Scientiarum Fennicae,* Ser.B. Tom 6. Helsinki, 1976.

Amano, K. [Formation of the act of analyzing phonemic structure of words and its relation to learning Japanese syllabic characters (kanamoji).] *The Japanese Journal of Educational Psychology,* 1970, *18,* 76–89. (In Japanese with a 1½ page English summary.)

Anapolle, L. Visual training and reading performance. *Journal of Reading,* 1967, *10,* 372–383.

Anderson, I. H., & Dearborn, W. F. *The psychology of teaching reading.* New York: Ronald Press, 1952.

Angermaier, M. *Multikausale Erklarung der Legasthenie. Fernstudienlehrgang Legasthenie.* Vol. 2. Weinheim: Beltz, 1974.

Applebee, A. N. Research in reading retardation: Two critical problems. *Journal of Child Psychology and Psychiatry,* 1971, *12,* 91–113.

Arab Regional Literacy Organization (ARLO). *Facilitating the Arabic writing: Report of ARLO's experiment for facilitating the Arabic writing.* Cairo: ARLO, 1977.

Arajarvi, T., Louhivuori, K., Hagman, H., Syvälahti, R., & Hietanen, A. The role of specific reading and writing difficulties in various school problems. *Annales Paediatrica Fennicae,* 1965, *11,* 138–147.

Aspinall, A. *Politics of the press.* London: Home and Van Thal Ltd., 1949.

Atkinson, R. C., & Shiffrin, R. M. Human memory: A proposed system and its control processes. In K. W. Spence & J. T. Spence (Eds.), *The psychology of learning and motivation* (Vol. II). New York: Academic Press, 1968.

Baddeley, A. D. Immediate memory and the "perception" of letter sequences. *Quarterly Journal of Experimental Psychology,* 1964, *16,* 364–367.

Baddeley, A. D. Short-term memory for word sequences as a function of acoustic, semantic, and formal similarity. *Quarterly Journal of Experimental Psychology,* 1966, *18,* 362–365.

Baddeley, A. D. How does acoustic similarity influence short-term memory? *Quarterly Journal of Experimental Psychology,* 1968, *20,* 249–264.

Baddeley, A. D. *The psychology of memory.* New York: Basic Books, 1976.

Baddeley, A. D. Working memory and reading. In P. A. Kolers, M. E. Wrolstad, & H. Bouma (Eds.), *Processing of visible language,* (Vol. 1). New York: Plenum Publishing Corporation, 1979.

Baron, J. Phonemic stage not necessary for reading. *Quarterly Journal of Experimental Psychology,* 1973, *25,* 241–246.

Baron, J. Successive stages in word recognition. In S. Doric & P. Rabbitt (Eds.), *Attention and Performance V.* New York: Academic Press, 1975.

Baron, J. Mechanisms for pronouncing printed words: Use and acquisition. In D. LaBerge & S. J. Samuels (Eds.), *Basic processes in reading: Perception and comprehension.* Hillsdale, N.J.: Lawrence Erlbaum Associates, 1977.

Baron, J. Orthographic and word-specific mechanisms in children's reading of words. *Child Development,* in press.

Baron, J., & Hodge, J. Using spelling-sound correspondences without trying to learn them. *Visible Language,* 1978, *12,* 55–70.

Baron, J., & McKillop, B. J. Individual differences in speed of phonemic analysis, visual analysis and reading. *Acta Psychologica,* 1975, *39,* 91–96.

Baron, J., & Strawson, C. Use of orthographic and word-specific knowledge in reading words aloud. *Journal of Experimental Psychology: Human Perception and Performance,* 1976, *2,* 386–393.

Baron, J., & Treiman, R. *Some problems in the study of differences in cognitive processes.* Unpublished manuscript, 1979.

Baron, J., Treiman, R., Wilf, J., & Kellman, P. Spelling and reading by rule. In U. Frith (Ed.), *Cognitive processes in spelling.* London: Academic Press, 1980.

Barron, R. W. Access to the meanings of printed words: Some implications for reading and for learning to read. In F. B. Murray (Ed.), *The development of the reading process* (International Reading Association Monograph No. 3). Newark, Del.: International Reading Association, 1978.

Barron, R. W., & Baron, J. How children get meaning from printed words. *Child Development,* 1977, *48,* 487–594.

Bataille, L. (Ed.). *A turning point for literacy.* Paris: Pergammon Press, 1976.

Baucom, K. L. *The ABCs of literacy: Lessons from linguistics.* Amersham, U.K.: Hulton Educational Publications Ltd., 1978.

Bauer, E. Bilingual Education in BIA Schools. *TESOL Quarterly,* 1970, *4,* 223–229.

Bautista y Piño, P. *Exposicion Succinta y Sencilla del Nuevo Mexico.* Cadiz, 1812.

Bazany, M. Evaluating an experimental functional literacy project: the Esfahan experience. In J. Ryan (Ed.), *Planning out-of-school education for development.* Paris: UNESCO (IIEP), 1972.

Bender, L. A. *Psychopathology of children with organic brain disorders.* Springfield, Ill.: Charles C Thomas, 1956.

Benson, F., & Geschwind, N. The alexias. In P. Vinken & G. DeBruyn (Eds.), *Handbook of clinical neurology.* Amsterdam: Elsevier, 1964.

Benton, A. L. Developmental dyslexia: Neurological aspects. In W. J. Friedlander (Ed.), *Advances in neurology* (Vol. 7). New York: Raven Press, 1975.

Berkel, J. A. Th. M. van, Brandt Corstius, H., Mooken, R. J., & Wijngaarden, A. van. *Formal properties of newspaper Dutch* (Mathematical Centre Tracts, 12). Amsterdam: Mathematisch Centrum, 1965.

Berko, J. The child's learning of English morphology. *Word,* 1958, *14,* 150–177.

Berry, J. The making of alphabets revisited. In T. P. Gorman (Ed.), *Language and literacy: Current issues and research.* Tehran: International Institute for Adult Literacy Methods, 1977.

Betts, E. A. Reading: Phonemic basis of word perception. *Spelling Progress Bulletin,* 1973, *XIII*(4), 10–15.

Betts, E. A. Phonics: Methods and orthography. *Spelling Progress Bulletin,* 1974, *XIV*(2), 7–12.

Biederman, I., & Tsao, Y. C. *Chinese readers show more Stroop-type interference than readers of English.* Paper presented at the Annual Meeting of the Psychonomic Society, Washington, D.C., 1977.

Biemiller, A. The development of the use of graphic and contextual information as children learn to read. *Reading Research Quarterly,* 1970, *6,* 75–96.

Birch, H. Dyslexia and maturation of visual function. In J. Money (Ed.), *Reading disability: Progress and research needs in dyslexia.* Baltimore: Johns Hopkins Press, 1962.

Bishop, C. H. Transfer effects of word and letter training in reading. *Journal of Verbal Learning and Behavior,* 1964, *3,* 215–221.

Bläfield, L., & Kuusinen, J. *[The psychometric characteristics of the Finnish language.]* KTL 241, Jyvaskyla, 1974. (In Finnish)

Blank, M. Cognitive processes in auditory discrimination in normal and retarded readers. *Child Development,* 1968, *39,* 1091–1101.

Bloom, S. Israeli reading methods for their culturally disadvantaged. *Elementary School Journal,* 1966, *66,* 304–310.

Bloomfield, L. Tagalog texts. *University of Illinois studies in language and literature,* 1917, *3,* 2–4.

Bloomfield, L. *Language.* New York: Holt, 1933.

Blumberg, P., & Block, K. K. *The effects of attempting spelling before feedback on spelling acquisition and retention.* Paper presented at the meeting of the American Educational Research Association, Washington, D.C., 1975.

Boas, F. *Handbook of American Indian languages.* (Bulletin 40). Washington, D.C.: Smithsonian Institute, Bureau of American Ethnography, 1911.

Boder, E. Developmental dyslexia: A diagnostic approach based on three atypical reading-spelling patterns. *Developmental Medicine and Child Neurology,* 1973, *15,* 663–687.

Bond, G., & Dykstra, R. The cooperative research program in first-grade reading instruction. *Reading Research Quarterly,* 1976, *3,* 5–142.

Boogaart, P. C. uit den. *[Word frequency in written and spoken Dutch.]* Utrecht: Oosthoek, Scheltema en Holkema, 1975. (In Dutch).

Boring, E. G. *A history of experimental psychology* (2nd ed.). New York: Appleton-Century-Crofts, 1950.

Bormuth, J. On the theory of achievement test items. Chicago: University of Chicago Press, 1970.

Bouma, H., & Voogd, A. H. de. On the control of eye-saccades in reading. *Vision Research,* 1974, *14,* 273–284.

Braida, L. D., & Durlach, N. I. Intensity perception, II: Resolution in one-interval paradigms. *Journal of the Acoustical Society of America,* 1972, *51,* 483–502.

Brandt Corstius, H. *Exercises in computational linguistics.* Amsterdam: Mathematisch Centrum, 1970.

Brink, D. T. *Problems in phonological theory: A generative phonology of Dutch.* Unpublished doctoral dissertation, University of Wisconsin, 1970.

Brooks, L. Visual pattern in fluent word identification. In A. S. Reber & D. L. Scarborough (Eds.), *Toward a psychology of reading: The proceedings of the CUNY conference.* Hillsdale, N.J.: Lawrence Erlbaum Associates, 1977.

Bryan, W. L., & Harter, N. Studies on the telegraphic language. *Psychological Review,* 1899, *6,* 345–375.

Bryant, P., & Bradley, L. Why children sometimes write words which they do not read. In U. Frith (Ed.), *Cognitive process in spelling.* London: Academic Press, 1980.

Buck, C. D. *A grammer of Oscan and Umbrian.* Boston: Ginn and Co., 1929.

Caeser, F. B. [*Teaching reading/evaluating reading: a brief overview of the services of the teaching academy.*] Tilburg: Zwijsen, 1971. (In Dutch)

Calfee, R. C., Chapman, R. S., & Venezky, R. L. How a child needs to think to learn to read. In L. W. Gregg (Ed.), *Cognition in learning and memory.* New York: Wiley, 1972.

Calfee, R. C., Venezky, R. L., & Chapman, R. S. *Pronunciation of synthetic words with predictable and unpredictable letter-sound correspondences.* (Technical Report No. 71). Wisconsin Research and Development Center for Cognitive Learning, 1969.

Carroll, J. B. Defining language comprehension: Some speculations. In J. B. Carroll & R. O. Freedle (Eds.), *Language comprehension and the acquisition of knowledge.* Washington, D.C.: V. H. Winston, 1972.

Central Bureau of Statistics. *Statistical Abstracts of Israel.* Jerusalem: Government Printing Press, 1977.

Chall, J. *Learning to read: The great debate.* New York: McGraw-Hill, 1967.

Chall, J. Reading 1967-1977: A decade of change and promise. Bloomington, Ill.: Phi Delta Kappa Educational Foundation, 1977.

Chandler, J. P. Subroutine STEPIT—finds local minima of a smooth function of several parameters. *Behavioral Science,* 1969, *14,* 81-82.

Chomsky, C. Write first, read later. *Childhood Education,* 1971, *47,* 296-299.

Chomsky, N. Comments for Project Literacy meeting. Project Literacy Report No. 2. Reprinted in M. Lester (Ed.), *Readings in applied transformational grammar.* New York: Holt, 1970. (a)

Chomsky, N. Phonology and reading. In H. Levin & J. P. Williams (Eds.), *Basic studies on reading.* New York: Basic Books, 1970. (b)

Chomsky, N., & Halle, M. *The sound patterns of English.* New York: Harper & Row, 1968.

Cohen, A., Stilitz, I., & Feitelson, D. *Reading ability and reading mistakes of Israeli first and second graders,* in preparation.

Cohen, R. L., & Grandstrom, K. Reproduction and recognition in short-term visual memory. *Quarterly Journal of Experimental Psychology,* 1970, *22,* 450-457.

Coltheart, M., Davelaar, E., Jonasson, J., & Besner, D. Access to the internal lexicon. In S. Dornic (Ed.), *Attention and Performance VI.* London: Academic Press, 1977.

Conrad, R. Acoustic confusions in immediate memory. *British Journal of Psychology,* 1964, *55,* 75-84.

Conrad, R. Speech and reading. In J. F. Kavanagh & I. G. Mattingly (Eds.), *Language by ear and by eye: The relationships between speech and reading.* Cambridge: The MIT Press, 1972.

Corcoran, D. W., & Weening, D. L. Acoustic factors in visual speech. *Quarterly Journal of Experimental Psychology,* 1968, *20,* 83-85.

Cromer, W. The difference model: A new explanation for some reading difficulties. *Journal of Educational Psychology,* 1970, *61,* 471-483.

Cromer, W., & Wiener, M. Idiosyncratic response patterns among good and poor readers. *Journal of Consulting Psychology,* 1966, *30,* 1-10.

Crowder, R. G. Memory for phonologically uniform lists. *Journal of Verbal Learning and Verbal Behavior,* 1978, *17,* 73-89.

Damsteegt, B. C. Spelling and spelling reform in the Netherlands. In P. Brachin, J. Goossens, P. K. King, & J. de Rooy (Eds.), *Dutch studies: Annual review of the language, literature and life of the Low Countries* (Vol. II). Den Haag: Hijhoff, 1976.

DeFrancis, J. The alphabetization of Chinese. *Journal of the American Oriental Society*, 1943, *63*, 225-240.

DeFrancis, J. *Nationalism and language reform in China*. Princeton: Princeton University Press, 1950.

Delacato, C. H. *Neurological organization and reading*. Springfield, Ill.: Charles C Thomas, 1967.

Denckla, M. B., & Rudel, R. Naming of pictured objects by dyslexic and other learning disabled children. *Brain and Language*, 1976, *39*, 1-15. (a)

Denckla, M. B., & Rudel, R. Rapid 'automatized' naming (R.A.N.): Dyslexia differentiated from other learning disabilities. *Neuropsychologia*, 1976, *14*, 471-479. (b)

Dighe, A. Case study of curriculum development for an experimental non-formal education project for rural women. New Dehli: Council for Social Development, 1977.

Diringer, D. *The alphabet: A key to the history of mankind*. New York: Hutchinsons, 1948.

Doehring, D. G. Acquisition of rapid reading responses. *Monographs of the Society for Research in Child Development*, 1976, *41*, 1-54.

Doggett, D., & Richards, L. G. A re-examination of the effect of word length on recognition thresholds. *American Journal of Psychology*, 1975, *88*, 583-594.

Doman, G. *Teach your baby to read*. London: Jonathan Cape, 1964.

Downing, J. *Comparative reading*. New York: Macmillan, 1973. (a)

Downing, J. Causes of reading disability in different languages. *Dyslexia Review*, 1973, *10*, 4-7. (b)

Downing, J. *The child's understanding of the functions and processes of communication*. Paper presented at the World Congress on Reading, Hamburg, 1977.

Drew, A. L. A neurological appraisal of familial congenital word-blindness. *Brain*, 1956, *79*, 440-460.

Dror, R. Educational research in Israel. In A. M. Dushkin & C. Frankenstein (Eds.), *Studies in education—Scripta hierasolymitana*. Jerusalem: Magnes, 1963.

Dyer, F. N. Color naming interference in monolinguals and bilinguals. *Journal of Verbal Learning and Verbal Behavior*, 1971, *10*, 297-302.

Dykstra, R. Auditory discrimination abilities and beginning reading achievement. *Reading Research Quarterly*, 1966, *1*, 5-34.

Earhard, B. Perception and retention of familiar and unfamiliar material. *Journal of Experimental Psychology*, 1968, *76*, 584-595.

Edfeldt, A. W. *Silent speech and silent reading*. Chicago: University of Chicago Press, 1960.

Eggert, D., Schuck, K. D., & Wieland, A. J. Ergebnisse eines Untersuchungsprogramms zur kontrollierten Behandlung leserechtsch-tschreibschwacher Schuler. In R. Valtin (Ed.), *Einfuhrung in die Legasthenieforschung*. Weinheim: Beltz, 1973.

Ehri, L. C. Word consciousness in readers and prereaders. *Journal of Educational Psychology*, 1975, *67*, 204-212.

Ehri, L. C. Word learning in beginning readers and prereaders: Effects of form class and defining contexts. *Journal of Educational Psychology*, 1976, *68*, 832-842.

Ehri, L. C. Beginning reading from a psycholinguistic perspective: Amalgamation of word identities. In F. B. Murray (Ed.), *The development of the reading process* (International Reading Association Monograph No. 3). Newark, Del.: International Reading Association, 1978.

Ehri, L. C. Reading and spelling in beginners: The development of orthographic images as world symbols in lexical memory. In U. Frith (Ed.), *Cognitive processes in spelling*. London: Academic Press, 1980.

Ehri, L. C. Linguistic insight: Threshold of reading acquisition. In T. G. Waller & G. E. MacKinnon (Eds.), *Reading research: Advances in theory and practice*. New York: Academic Press, in press.

Ehri, L. C., & Roberts, K. T. *Do beginners learn printed words better in contexts or in isolation?* Unpublished manuscript, 1978.

Ehri, L. C., & Wilce, L. S. The mnemonic value of orthography among beginning readers. *Journal of Educational Psychology*, 1979, *71*, 26–40.

Eisenberg, L. The epidemiology of reading retardation and a program for preventive intervention. In J. Money (Ed.), *The disabled reader*. Baltimore: Johns Hopkins Press, 1966.

Elkonin, D. B. The psychology of mastering the elements of reading. In B. Simon & J. Simon (Eds.), *Educational psychology in the U.S.S.R.* London: Routledge & Kegan Paul, 1963.

Elkonin, D. B. U.S.S.R. In J. Downing (Ed.), *Comparative reading*. New York: Macmillan, 1973.

Enoch, C. [Early school leavers in the municipal schools of Tel Aviv.] *Megamot*, 1950, *2*, 34–51. (In Hebrew)

Erickson, D., Mattingly, I. G., & Turvey, M. T. *Phonetic activity in reading: An experiment with kanji* (Haskins Laboratories Status Report on Speech Research, SR-33). New Haven, Conn.: Haskins Laboratories, 1973.

Estes, W. K. Memory, perception, and decision in letter identification. In R. L. Solso (Ed.), *Information processing and cognition: The Loyola symposium*. Hillsdale, N.J.: Lawrence Erlbaum Associates, 1975.

Experimental world literacy programme: A critical assessment. Paris: The UNESCO Press, 1976.

Feitelson, D. *Causes of scholastic failure among first graders*. Jerusalem: Henrietta Szold Foundation, 1953. (In Hebrew) (Summarized in: *International Child Welfare Review*, 1954, *8*, 64–71.)

Feitelson, D. On the teaching of reading in non-European languages. *English Language Teaching*, 1961, *16*, 39–43.

Feitelson, D. The alphabetical principle in Hebrew and German contrasted with the alphabetic principle in English. In P. Tyler (Ed.), *Linguistics and reading*. Newark, Del.: International Reading Association, 1966.

Feitelson, D. Choice of basal readers in two school districts. In *Compensatory programs*. Jerusalem: Ministry of Education, 1967, 81–94. (In Hebrew)

Feitelson, D. The relationship between systems of writing and the teaching of reading. In M. D. Jenkinson (Ed.), *Reading instruction: An international forum*. Newark, Del.: International Reading Association, 1967.

Feitelson, D. Teaching reading to culturally disadvantaged children. *The Reading Teacher*, 1968, *22*, 55–61.

Feitelson, D. Israel. In J. Downing (Ed.), *Comparative reading*. New York: Macmillan, 1973.

Feitelson, D. *Transferring insights gained in developing teaching strategies in one writing system to other writing systems with similar problems: The case of Hebrew and Arabic*. Paper presented at The Seventh World Congress on Reading. Hamburg, August, 1978. (a)

Feitelson, D. (Ed.), Cross-cultural perspectives on reading and reading research. Newark, Del.: International Reading Association, 1978. (b)

Fellman, J. The teacher did it: A case history of the revival of the mother language. In D. Feitelson (Ed.), *Mother tongue or second language: On the teaching of reading in multi-lingual societies*. Newark, Del.: International Reading Association, 1979.

Ferguson, C. A. Contrasting patterns of literacy acquisition in a multilingual nation. In W. H. Whiteley (Ed.), *Language use and social change.* London: Oxford University Press, 1971.

Ferguson, C. A. Aspects of literacy teaching in the People's Republic of China. In T. P. Gorman (Ed.), *Language and literacy: Current issues and research.* Tehran: International Institute for Adult Literacy Methods, 1977.

Ferguson, C. A. Contrasting patterns of literacy acquisition in a multilingual nation. In W. H. Whiteley (Ed.), *Language reading and reading research.* Newark, Del.: International Reading Association, 1978.

Firth, I. *Components of reading disability.* Unpublished doctoral dissertation, University of New South Wales, 1972.

Forster, K. K., & Chambers, S. M. Lexical access and naming time. *Journal of Verbal Learning and Verbal Behavior,* 1973, *12,* 627–635.

Foster, P. J. Problems of literacy in Sub-Saharan Africa. In T. P. Gorman (Ed.), *Language and literacy: Current issues and research.* Tehran: International Institute for Adult Literacy Methods, 1977.

Fowler, C. A., Liberman, I. Y., & Shankweiler, D. On interpreting the error pattern of the beginning reader. *Language and Speech,* 1977, *20,* 162–173.

Fowler, C. A., Shankweiler, D., & Liberman, I. Y. *Apprehending spelling patterns for vowels: A developmental study* (Haskins Laboratories Status Report on Speech Research, SR-57), in press.

Fox, B., & Routh, D. K. Phonemic analysis and synthesis as word-attack skills. *Journal of Educational Psychology,* 1976, *68,* 70–74.

Francis, W. N. Linguistics and reading. In H. Levin & J. P. Williams (Eds.), *Basic studies on reading.* New York: Basic Books, 1970.

Franciscan Fathers. *An ethnologic dictionary of the Navajo Language.* St. Michaels, Ariz.: St. Michaels Press, 1910.

Fries, C. C. *Linguistics and reading.* New York: Holt, 1963.

Frith, U. Internal schemata for letters in good and bad readers. *British Journal of Psychology,* 1974, *54,* 233–244.

Frith, U. From print to meaning and from print to sound, or how to read without knowing how to spell. *Visible Language,* 1978, *12,* 43–54.

Frith, U. Reading by eye and writing by ear. In P. A. Kolers, M. Wrolstad, & H. Bouma (Eds.), *Processing visible language.* New York: Plenum Publishing Corporation, 1979.

Frostig, M., & Maslow, P. *Learning problems in the classroom.* New York: Grune & Stratton, 1973.

Fry, M. A., Johnson, C. S., & Muehl, S. Oral language production in relation to reading achievement among select second graders. In D. J. Bakker & P. Satz (Eds.), *Specific reading disability: Advances in theory and method.* Rotterdam: Rotterdam University Press, 1970.

Gagg, J. C., & Gagg, M. E. *Teaching children to read.* London: Newnes, 1955.

Gelb, I. J. *A study of writing* (Rev. Ed.). Chicago: University of Chicago Press, 1963.

Getman, G. N. *How to develop your child's intelligence.* Luverne, Minn.: Announcer Press, 1962.

Gibson, E. J. Perceptual learning and the theory of word perception. *Cognitive Psychology,* 1971, *2,* 351–368.

Gibson, E. J. Perception. In N. S. Sutherland (Ed.), *Tutorial essays in experimental psychology.* Hillsdale, N.J.: Lawrence Erlbaum Associates, 1977.

Gibson, E. J., & Levin, H. *The psychology of reading.* Cambridge: The MIT Press, 1975.

Gibson, E. J., Pick, A., Osser, H., & Hammond, M. The role of grapheme-phoneme correspondence in the perception of words. *American Journal of Psychology,* 1962, *75,* 554–570.

Gleitman, L. R., & Rozin, P. The structure and acquisition of reading I: Relations between orthographies and the structure of language. In A. S. Reber & D. L. Scarborough (Eds.), *Toward a psychology of reading: The proceedings of the CUNY conference.* Hillsdale, N.J.: Lawrence Erlbaum Associates, 1977.

Goldman, S. R. Reading skill and the minimum distance principle: A comparison of listening and reading comprehension. *Journal of Experimental Child Psychology,* 1976, *22,* 123–142.

Goldstein, D. M. Cognitive-linguistic functioning and learning to read in preschoolers. *Journal of Educational Psychology,* 1976, *68,* 680–688.

Golinkoff, R. M. A comparison of reading comprehension processes in good and poor comprehenders. *Reading Research Quarterly,* 1976, *4,* 623–659.

Goodman, K. S. Reading: A psycholinguistic guessing game. In H. Singer & R. R. Ruddell (Eds.), *Theoretical models and processes of reading.* Newark, Del.: International Reading Association, 1970.

Goodman, K. S. Orthography in a theory of reading instruction. *Elementary English,* 1972, *49,* 1254–1261.

Goodman, K. S. The 13th easy way to make learning to read difficult: A reaction to Gleitman and Rozin. *Reading Research Quarterly,* 1973, *8,* 484–493.

Gorman, T. P. Literacy in the mother tongue: A reappraisal of research and practice. In T. P. Gorman (Ed.), *Language and literacy: Current issues and research.* Tehran: International Institute for Adult Literacy Methods, 1977.

Gray, W. S. *The teaching of reading and writing, an international survey.* Paris: UNESCO, 1956.

Green, D. W., & Shallice, T. Direct visual access in reading for meaning. *Memory & Cognition,* 1976, *4,* 753–758.

Grimes, B. F. (Ed.), *Ethnologue.* Huntington Beach, Cal.: Wycliffe Bible Translators, 1978.

Groff, P. Research in brief: Shapes as cues to word recognition. *Visible Language,* 1975, *9,* 67–71.

Gudschinsky, S. *A manual for literacy for preliterate pupils.* Papua, New Guinea, Summer Institute of Linguistics, 1973.

Gudschinsky, S. Linguistics and literacy. In T. P. Gorman (Ed.), *Language and literacy: Current issues and research.* Tehran: International Institute for Adult Literacy Methods, 1977.

Guthrie, J. T. Models of reading and reading disability. *Journal of Educational Psychology,* 1973, *65,* 9–18.

Guthrie, J. T., & Seifert, M. Letter-sound complexity in learning to identify words. *Journal of Educational Psychology,* 1977, *69,* 686–696.

Hakulinen, L. *The structure and development of the Finnish language.* Bloomington: Indiana University Publications, 1961.

Halvorson, M. An adult literacy program: Central Tanzania 1955–1968. *Notes on Literacy,* 1970, *7.*

Hansen D., & Rodgers, T. S. An exploration of psycholinguistic units in initial reading. In K. S. Goodman (Ed.), *The psycholinguistic nature of the reading process.* Detroit: Wayne State University Press, 1968.

Hardyck, C., & Petrinovich, L. Subvocal speech and comprehensive level as a function of the difficulty level of reading material. *Journal of Verbal Learning and Verbal Behavior,* 1970, *9,* 647–652.

Hardyck, C., Tzeng, O. J. L., & Wang, W. S.-Y. Cerebral lateralization effects in visual half-field experiments. *Nature,* 1977, *269,* 705-707.

Hardyck, C., Tzeng, O. J. L., & Wang, W. S.-Y. Cerebral lateralization of function and bilingual decision processes: Is thinking lateralized? *Brain and Language,* 1978, *5,* 56-71.

Harman, D. A different approach to the teaching of reading to illiterate adults: an example from Thailand. In T. P. Gorman (Ed.), *Language and literacy: Current issues and research.* Tehran: International Institute of Adult Literacy Methods, 1977.

Harris, J. W. *Spanish phonology.* Cambridge: The MIT Press, 1969.

Hart, J. [*The phonetic structure.*] *De Nieuwe Taalgids,* 1969, *62,* 168-174. (In Dutch)

Hatta, T. Asynchrony of lateral onset as a factor in difference in visual field. *Perception and Motor Skill,* 1976, *42,* 163-166.

Hatta, T. Recognition of Japanese *kanji* in the right and left visual field. *Neuropsychologia,* 1977, *15,* 585-588.

Helfgott, J. Phoneme segmentation and blending skills of kindergarten children: Implications for beginning reading acquisitions. *Contemporary Educational Psychology,* 1976, *1,* 157-169.

Henderson, L. Word recognition. In N. S. Sutherland (Ed.), *Tutorial essays in experimental psychology.* Hillsdale, N.J.: Lawrence Erlbaum Associates, 1977.

Henderson, L., Chard, J., & Clark, A. *Spelling as a transcription process.* Paper presented at the BPS Conference, London, December, 1977.

Hendrickson, G. L. Ancient reading. *Classical Journal,* 1929-30, *XXV,* 182-196.

Henry, G., & Grisay, A. *Methodological aspects of evaluation in primary reading.* Liege: IEA, 1972.

Hermann, K. *Reading disability.* Copenhagen: Munksgaard, 1959.

Heuven, V. J. J. P. van. Effects of person marking suffixes in the present singular in Dutch, obtained from oral and silent reading tasks. *Progress Report of the Institute of Phonetics Utrecht,* 1976, *1,* 26-35.

Heuven, V. J. J. P. van. Effects of tense marking suffixes in plural finites in Dutch, obtained from oral and silent reading tasks. *Progress Report of the Institute of Phonetics Utrecht,* 1977, *2,* 10-31. (a)

Heuven, V. J. J. P. van. Silent reading with aspect marking verb suffixes in dependent clauses in Dutch. *Progress Report of the Institute of Phonetics Utrecht,* 1977, *2,* 24-37. (b)

Heuven, V. J. J. P. van. [*Spelling and reading, the problem of the meaning of words.*] Assen: Van Gorcum, 1978. (In Dutch)

Heuven, V. J. J. P. van, & Broecke, M. P. R. van den. Perceptual discrimination of Dutch velar fricatives. *Progress Report of the Institute of Phonetics Utrecht,* 1977, *2,* 38-48.

Hintzman, D. L., & Summers, J. J. Long-term visual traces of visually presented words. *Bulletin of the Psychonomic Society,* 1973, *1,* 325-327.

Hirata, K., & Osaka, R. Tachistoscopic recognition of Japanese letter materials in left and right visual fields. *Psychologia,* 1967, *10,* 17-18.

Hirvonen, P. Finnish and English communicative intonation. Turku: University of Turku, Department of Phonetics, August, 1970.

Hockett, C. Review of *Nationalism and language reform in China* by J. DeFrancis. *Language,* 1951, *27,* 439-445.

Hofer, A. Lesediagnosen in der Grundschule mit Hilfe des Verlesungskonzepts. In Gudrun Spitta (Ed.), Legasthenie gibt es nicht...Was nun? Kronberg: Scriptor, 1977.

Holm, W. *Some aspects of Navajo orthography*. Unpublished doctoral dissertation, University of New Mexico, 1972.

Hotopf, N. Slips of the pen. In U. Frith (Ed.), *Cognitive processes in spelling*. London: Academic Press, 1980.

Huey, E. B. *The psychology and pedagogy of reading*. Cambridge: The MIT Press, 1968. (Originally published, 1908, Macmillan.)

Husén, T. *International impact of evaluation*. N.S.S.E. Yearbook, No. 68: II, 1969.

International African Institute. Practical orthography of African languages (Memorandum No. 1). London: Oxford University Press, 1930.

International Institute for Adult Literacy Methods (IIALM). *Literacy projects: Report on the replies received to the Institute's questionnaire*. Tehran: IIALM, 1971.

International Institute for Adult Literacy Methods (IIALM). *Literacy teachers: Interpretative bibliography*. Prepared by K. D. Sharam. Tehran: IIALM, 1978.

Ishikawa, S. [*A follow-up study of letter reading ability of infants.*] The 1969 Annals of the Early Childhood Education Association of Japan. Tokyo: Froebel-kan, 1970. (In Japanese)

Israeli Ministry of Education. [Reading steering committee protocols.] 1977-78. (In Hebrew, mimeographed)

Izumoji, T., Takenoya, M., & Mitsui, K. [Mothers' concerns about picture books.] *The Science of Reading,* 1975, *19,* 1-12. (In Japanese with a 1½ page English summary.)

Jackson, M. D., & McClelland, J. L. Processing determinants of reading speed. *Journal of Experimental Psychology: General,* in press.

Jastrzembski, J. E., & Stanners, R. Multiple-word meanings and lexical search speed. *Journal of Verbal Learning and Verbal Behavior,* 1975, *14,* 534-537.

Jeffrey, W. E., & Samuels, S. J. Effects of method of reading training on initial learning and transfer. *Journal of Verbal Learning and Verbal Behavior,* 1967, *6,* 354-358.

Johnston, J. C. A test of the sophisticated guessing theory of word perception. *Cognitive Psychology,* 1978, *10,* 123-153.

Jones, D. *The phoneme*. Cambridge: W. Heffer & Sons, Ltd., 1950.

Jung, U. O. H. Zur auditiven Diskrimination legasthener und normaler Schuler. *Linguistik und Didaktik,* 1977, *31,* 210-218.

Kahneman, D. *Attention and effort.* Englewood Cliffs, N.J.: Prentice-Hall, 1973.

Karadić, V. S. Pismenica serbskoga jezika po govoru prostoga naroda. Wien: J. Schnirer Press, 1814.

Karam, F. X. Literacy and language development. In T. P. Gorman (Ed.), *Language and literacy: Current issues and research*. Tehran: International Institute for Adult Literacy Methods, 1977.

Karlsson, F. [Morphotactic structure and word cohesion.] *Contrastive Studies,* 1977, *4,* 59-74. (In Finnish)

Kasdon, L. M. Causes of reading difficulties: Facts and fiction. In W. K. Durr (Ed.), *Reading difficulties: Diagnosis, correction, and remediation*. Newark, Del.: International Reading Association, 1970.

Katz, P. A. Verbal discrimination performance of disadvantaged children: Stimulus and subject variables. *Child Development,* 1967, *38,* 234-242.

Kavanagh, J. F., & Mattingly, I. G. *Language by ear and by eye: The relationships between speech and reading*. Cambridge: The MIT Press, 1972.

Kemmler, L. *Erfolg und Versagen in der Grundschule*. Gottingen: Hogrefe, 1967.

Kerek, A. The phonological relevance of spelling pronunciation. *Visible Language,* 1976, *10,* 323-338.

Kimura, D. The asymmetry of the human brain. *Scientific American,* 1973, *228,* 70–78.

Kintsch, N. Models for free recall and recognition. In D. A. Norman (Ed.), *Models of human memory.* New York: Academic Press, 1970.

Kipling, R. *Just so stories.* London: Macmillan, 1902.

Kirsner, K. An analysis of the visual component in recognition memory for verbal stimuli. *Memory & Cognition,* 1973, *1,* 449–453.

Kleiman, G. M. Speech recoding in reading. *Journal of Verbal Learning and Verbal Behavior,* 1975, *14,* 323–339.

Kok, G. H. A. [The automatic translation of written Dutch to phonetic notation. Report MR 130/72.] Amsterdam: Mathematisch Centrum, 1972. (a) (In Dutch)

Kok, G. H. A. *The automatic conversion of written Dutch to a phonetic notation* (Papers in Computational Linguistics). Budapest: Publishing House of the Hungarian Academy of Sciences, 1972. (b)

Kolers, P. A. Reading is only incidentally visual. In K. S. Goodman & J. Fleming (Eds.), *Psycholinguistics and the teaching of reading.* Newark, Del.: International Reading Association, 1969.

Kooreman, H. J. [Construction and results of a test package for the evaluation of reading comprehension.] *Pedagogische Studien,* 1974, *51,* 398–412. (In Dutch)

Kooreman, H. J. Leren lezen: letterkennis en klankpositie. *Pedagogische Studien,* 1975, *52,* 218–230.

Kozma, T. *Hungarian studies on primary reading.* Stockholm, IEA, 1972.

Krueger, L. E. Search time in a redundant visual display. *Journal of Experimental Psychology,* 1970, *83,* 391–399.

Krueger, L. E. Effect of direction and sequential presentation and redundancy on short-term recognition memory. *Perception and Psychophysics,* 1971, *9,* 121–124.

Krueger, L. E., & Shapiro, R. C. *Visual search for intact and mutilated letters through rapid sequences of words and nonwords.* Unpublished manuscript, 1978.

Kuo, W. F. *A preliminary study of reading disabilities in the Republic of China.* Collection of papers by National Taiwan Normal University, Graduate School of Education, Vol. 20, 1978, 57–78.

Kuusinen, J. [*The psycholinguistic abilities of children suffering and not suffering from reading and writing disorders*] KTL 129, Jyvaskyla, 1972. (In Finnish)

Kyöstiö, O. K. Finland. In J. Downing (Ed.), *Comparative reading.* New York: Macmillan, 1973.

Kyöstiö, O. K. [*The child and his environment*] 32, Oulu, 1977. (In Finnish)

Kyöstiö, O. K., & Vaherva, T. Reading and forgetting among young children. *Scandinavian Journal of Educational Research,* 1969, *3,* 129–146.

LaBerge, D., & Samuels, S. J. Toward a theory of automatic information processing in reading. *Cognitive Psychology,* 1974, *6,* 293–323.

LaBerge, D. *Unitizing and automaticity in reading.* Address to the American Psychological Association Convention, San Francisco, August, 1977.

Lastra, Y. Literacy in Ibero-America and the Caribbean. In T. P. Gorman (Ed.), *Language and literacy: Current issues and research.* Tehran: International Institute for Adult Literacy Methods, 1977.

Lefevre, C. A. *Linguistics and the teaching of reading.* New York: McGraw-Hill, 1964.

Lehtonen, J., Sajavaara, K., & May, A. *Spoken English.* Gummerus: Jyvaskyla, 1977.

Lepisto, M. [*Comparative analysis of textbooks used in mother tongue teaching in the first grade.*] KTL 267, Jyvaskyla, 1976. (In Finnish)

Lepsius, C. R. *Standard orthography for reducing unwritten languages and foreign graphic systems to a uniform orthography in European letters* (2nd ed.). London, 1863.

Levin, H. Reading research: What, why, and for whom? *Elementary English,* 1966, *44,* 138–147.

Levy, B. A. Vocalization and suppression effects in sentence memory. *Journal of Verbal Learning and Verbal Behavior,* 1975, *14,* 304–316.

Levy, J. Teaching reading and writing in first grade. In J. Levy & U. Blum (Eds.), *Handbook for the first grade.* Tel Aviv: Urim, 1952. (In Hebrew).

Lewis, E. G. The development of literacy in the Soviet Union. In T. P. Gorman (Ed.), *Language and literacy: Current issues and research.* Tehran: International Institute for Adult Literacy Methods, 1977.

Liberman, A. M., Cooper, F. S., Shankweiler, D., & Studdert-Kennedy, M. Perception of the speech code. *Psychological Review,* 1967, *74,* 431–461.

Liberman, I. Y. Basic research in speech and lateralization of language: Some implications for reading disability. *Bulletin of the Orton Society,* 1971, *21,* 71–87.

Liberman, I. Y. Segmentation of the spoken word and reading acquisition. *Bulletin of the Orton Society,* 1973, *23,* 65–77.

Liberman, I. Y., Mark, L. S., & Shankweiler, D. Reading disability: Methodological problems in information processing analysis (Letter to the editor). *Science,* 1978, *200,* 801–802.

Liberman, I. Y., & Shankweiler, D. Speech, the alphabet and teaching to read. In L. B. Resnick & P. A. Weaver (Eds.), *Theory and practice of early reading.* Hillsdale, N.J.: Lawrence Erlbaum Associates, in press.

Liberman, I. Y., Shankweiler, D., Camp, L., Heifetz, B., & Werfelman, M. *Steps toward literacy. A report prepared for the Working Group on Learning Failure and Unused Learning Potential.* President's Commission on Mental Health, Washington, D.C., 1977.

Liberman, I. Y., Shankweiler, D., Fischer, F. W., & Carter, B. Explicit syllable and phoneme segmentation in the young child. *Journal of Experimental Child Psychology,* 1974, *18,* 201–212.

Liberman, I. Y., Shankweiler, D., Liberman, A. M., Fowler, C., & Fischer, F. W. Phonetic segmentation and recoding in the beginning reader. In A. S. Reber & D. Scarborough (Eds.), *Toward a psychology of reading: The proceedings of the CUNY conference.* Hillsdale, N.J.: Lawrence Erlbaum Associates, 1977.

Liberman, I. Y., Shankweiler, D., Orlando, C., Harris, K. S., & Berti, F. B. Letter confusion and reversals of sequence in the beginning reader: Implications for Orton's theory of developmental dyslexia. *Cortex,* 1971, *7,* 127–142.

Longacre, R. E. Discourse analysis and literacy. In T. P. Gorman (Ed.), *Language and literacy: Current issues and research.* Tehran: International Institute for Adult Literacy Methods, 1977.

Luce, R. D. *Individual choice behavior.* New York: Wiley, 1959.

Lukatela, G., Savić, M., Gligorijević, B., Ognjenović, P., & Turvey, M. T. Bi-alphabetical lexical decision. *Language and Speech,* 1978, *21,* 142–165.

Lukatela, G., Savić, M., Ognjenovic, P., & Turvey, M. T. On the relation between processing the Roman and Cyrillic alphabets: A preliminary analysis with bi-alphabetical readers. *Language and Speech,* 1978, *21,* 113–141.

Lyytinen, P. The acquisition of Finnish morphology in early childhood. *Jyvaskyla Studies in Education,* 1977, *37.*

Maamoori, M. Illiteracy in Tunisia: An evaluation. In T. P. Gorman (Ed.), *Language and literacy: Current issues and research.* Tehran: International Institute for Adult Literacy Methods, 1977.

Makita, K. The rarity of reading disability in Japanese children. *American Journal of Orthopsychiatry,* 1968, *38,* 599–614.

Malmquist, E. *Factors related to reading disabilities in the first grade of the elementary school.* Unpublished doctoral dissertation, Stockholm, Uppsala, 1958.

Marchbanks, G., & Levin, H. Cues by which children recognize words. *Journal of Educational Psychology,* 1965, *56,* 57–61.

Mark, L. S., Shankweiler, D., Liberman, I. Y., & Fowler, C. A. Phonetic recoding and reading difficulty in beginning readers. *Memory & Cognition,* 1977, *5,* 623–629.

Marshall, J. C., & Newcombe, F. Patterns of paralexia: A psycholinguistic approach. *Journal of Psycholinguistic Research,* 1973, *2,* 175–199.

Martin, S. E. Nonalphabetic writing systems. In J. F. Kavanagh & I. G. Mattingly (Eds.), *Language by ear and by eye: The relationships between speech and reading.* Cambridge, Mass.: The MIT Press, 1972.

Mason, M. Reading ability and letter search time: Effects of orthographic structure defined by single-letter positional frequency. *Journal of Experimental Psychology: General,* 1975, *104,* 146–166.

Mason, M., & Katz, L. Visual processing of non-linguistic strings: Redundancy effects and reading ability. *Journal of Experimental Psychology: General,* 1976, *105,* 338–348.

Massaro, D. W. Perception of letters, words, and nonwords. *Journal of Experimental Psychology,* 1973, *100,* 349–353.

Massaro, D. W. Primary and secondary recognition in reading. In D. W. Massaro (Ed.), *Understanding language: An information-processing analysis of speech perception, reading, and psycholinguistics.* New York: Academic Press, 1975.

Massaro, D. W. Letter information and orthographic context in word perception. *Journal of Experimental Psychology: Human Perception and Performance,* in press.

Massaro, D. W., & Cohen, M. M. The contribution of fundamental frequency and voice onset time to the /zi/–/si/ distinction. *Journal of the Acoustical Society of America,* 1976, *60,* 704–717.

Massaro, D. W., Taylor, G. A., & Venezky, R. L., Jastrzembski, J. E., & Lucas, P. A. *Letter and word perception: The role of visual information and orthographic structure in reading,* in preparation.

Matthews, W. *Memoirs of the American folklore society.* New York: G. E. Stechert, 1897.

Mattingly, I. G. Reading, the linguistic process, and linguistic awareness. In J. F. Kavanagh & I. G. Mattingly (Eds.), *Language by ear and by eye: The relationships between speech and reading.* Cambridge: The MIT Press, 1972.

Mayakovsky, V. Translated by M. Hayward & G. Reavy in P. Blake (Ed.), *The bed bug and selected poetry.* New York: Meridan Books, 1960.

Mayzner, M. S., & Tresselt, M. E. Tables of single-letter and diagram frequency counts for various word-length and letter-position combinations. *Psychonomic Monograph Supplements,* 1965, *1,* 1.

McClelland, J. L. Letter and configuration information in word identification. *Journal of Verbal Learning and Verbal Behavior,* 1977, *16,* 137–150.

McCormick, C., & Samuels, S. J. *Word recognition by second graders: The unit of perception and interrelationships among accuracy, latency, and comprehension.* Unpublished manuscript, University of Minnesota, 1978.

McGrady, H. J. Language pathology and learning disabilities. In H. R. Myklebust (Ed.), *Progress in learning disorders* (Vol. I). New York: Grune & Stratton, 1968.

McIntosh, J. B. y Jose Grimes. Niuqui 'lquisicayari: vocabulario huichol-castellano, castellano-huichol. Mexico, D. F.: Instituto Linguistico de Verano, 1954.

Merritt, J. E. Reading: Seven to eleven. *Education,* 1975, *2.*

Merritt, M. E. Reading failure: A reexamination. In J. F. Reid (Ed.), *Reading: Problems and practices.* London: Ward Lock, 1971.

Mewhort, D. J. K. Accuracy and order of report in tachistoscopic identification. *Canadian Journal of Psychology,* 1974, *28,* 383-398.

Meyer, D. E., & Ruddy, M. G. *Lexical-memory retrieval based on graphemic and phonemic representations of printed words.* Paper presented at the meetings of the Psychonomic Society, St. Louis, 1973.

Meyer, D. E., Schvaneveldt, R. W., & Ruddy, M. G. Loci of contextual effects on visual word recognition. In S. Dornic & P. M. A. Rabbitt (Eds.), *Attention and Performance V.* London: Academic Press, 1974. (a)

Meyer, D. E., Schvaneveldt, R. W., & Ruddy, M. G. Functions of graphemic and phonemic codes in visual word-recognition. *Memory & Cognition,* 1974, *2,* 309-321. (b)

Miller, G. A. The magical number seven, plus or minus two: Some limits on our capacity for processing information. *Psychological Review,* 1956, *63,* 81-97.

Miller, G. A., Bruner, J. S., & Postman, L. Familiarity of letter sequences and tachistoscopic identification. *Journal of General Psychology,* 1954, *50,* 129-139.

Miller, G. A., & Friedman, E. A. The recognition of mutilated English texts. *Information and Control,* 1957, *1,* 38-55.

Mishkin, M., & Forgays, D. G. Word recognition as a function of the retinal locus. *Journal of Experimental Psychology,* 1952, *43,* 43-48.

Morais, J., Cary, L., Alegria, J., & Bertelson, P. Does awareness of speech as a sequence of phones arise spontaneously? Mimeo draft, Free University of Brussels, 1978.

Morris, J. M. *Standards and progress in reading.* London: National Foundation for Educational Research in England and Wales, 1966.

Moskowitz, B. A. On the status of vowel shift in English. In T. E. Moore (Ed.), *Cognitive development and the acquisition of language.* New York: Academic Press, 1973.

Müller, R. *Leseschwache-Leseversagen-Legasthenie.* Weinheim: Beltz, 1974.

Murata, K. [*Reading and writing of young children.*] Tokyo: Baifukan, 1974. (In Japanese)

Myklebust, H. R. (Ed.), *Progress in learning disorders* (Vol. I). New York: Grune & Stratton, 1968.

National Language Research Institute. [*Reading and writing ability in pre-school children.*] Tokyo: Tokyo Shoseki Publishers, 1973. (In Japanese)

Neisser, U. *Cognitive psychology.* New York: Appleton-Century-Crofts, 1967.

Nickjoo, M. *A century of struggles for the reform of the Persian script: A historical study and proposal for a resolution of the problem,* undated.

Nida, E. Practical limitations to a phonetic alphabet. *The Bible Translator,* 1954, *15,* 35-39, 58-62.

Niemeyer, W. *Legasthenie und Milieu.* Schroedel-Verlag, Hannover, 1974.

Nooteboom, S. D., & Cohen, A. [*To speak and understand: An introduction to experimental phonetics.*] Assen: Van Gorcum, 1976. (In Dutch)

Norman, D. A., & Bobrow, D. G. On data-limited and resource-limited processes. *Cognitive Psychology,* 1975, *7,* 44-64.

Oakan, R., Wiener, M., & Cromer, W. Identification, organization, and reading comprehension for good and poor readers. *Journal of Educational Psychology,* 1971, *62,* 71-78.

O'Connor, N., & Harmelin, B. *Seeing and hearing and space and time*. London: Academic Press, 1978.

Oden, G. C. Integration of fuzzy logical information. *Journal of Experimental Psychology: Human Perception and Performance*, 1977, *3*, 565–575.

Oden, G. C., & Massaro, D. W. Integration of featural information in speech perception. *Psychological Review*, 1978, *85*, 172–191.

Oehrle, B. D. *Visuelle Wahrnehmung und Legasthenie*. Weinheim: Beltz, 1975.

Ormian, H. (Ed.). *Education in Israel*. Jerusalem: Ministry of Education, 1973.

Orton, S. T. "Word blindness" in school children. *Archives of Neurophysiology and Psychiatry*, 1925, *14*, 581–615.

Orton, S. T. *Reading, writing and speech problems in children*. London: Chapman and Hall, 1937.

Paivio, A. *Imagery and verbal processes*. New York: Holt, Rinehart, and Winston, 1971.

Park, S., & Arbuckle, T. Y. Ideograms versus alphabets: Effects of script on memory in "Biscriptual" Korean subjects. *Journal of Experimental Psychology: Human Learning and Memory*, 1977, *3*, 631–642.

Patterson, K. E., & Marcel, A. J. Aphasia, dyslexia and the phonological coding of written words. *Quarterly Journal of Experimental Psychology*, 1977, *29*, 307–318.

Perfetti, C. A., & Goldman, S. R. Discourse memory and reading comprehension skills. *Journal of Verbal Learning and Verbal Behavior*, 1976, *14*, 33–42.

Perfetti, C. A., & Hogaboam, T. The relationship between single word decoding and reading comprehension skill. *Journal of Educational Psychology*, 1975, *67*, 461–469.

Perfetti, C. A., & Lesgold, A. M. Discourse comprehension and sources of individual differences. In M. J. Just & P. A. Carpenter (Eds.), *Cognitive processes in comprehension*. Hillsdale, N.J.: Lawrence Erlbaum Associates, 1978.

Perfetti, C. A., & Lesgold, A. M. Coding and comprehension in skilled reading and implications for reading instruction. In L. B. Resnick & P. A. Weaver (Eds.), *Theory and practice of early reading* (Vol. I). Hillsdale, N.J.: Lawrence Erlbaum Associates, 1979.

Petersen, R. J., & LaBerge, D. Contextual control of letter perception. *Memory & Cognition*, 1977, *5*, 205–213.

Pike, K. L. *Phonemics: A technique for reducing language to writing*. Ann Arbor: University of Michigan Press, 1947.

Preston, M. S., & Lambert, W. E. Interlingual interference in a bilingual version of the Stroop color-word task. *Journal of Verbal Learning and Verbal Behavior*, 1969, *8*, 295–301.

Pritchard, J. B. *Archaeology and the Old Testament*. Princeton: Princeton University Press, 1958.

Rabinovitch, R. D. Reading and learning disabilities. In S. Arieti (Ed.), *American handbook of psychiatry*. New York: Basic Books, 1959.

Rabinovitch, R. D. Dyslexia: Psychiatric considerations. In J. Money (Ed.), *Reading disability: Progress and research needs in dyslexia*. Baltimore: Johns Hopkins Press, 1962.

Rayner, K., & Habelberg, E. M. Word recognition cues for beginning and skilled readers. *Journal of Experimental Child Psychology*, 1975, *20*, 444–455.

Rayner, K., & Posnansky, C. Stages of processing in word identification. *Journal of Experimental Psychology: General*, 1978, *107*, 64–80.

Read, C. Pre-school children's knowledge of English phonology. *Harvard Educational Review*, 1971, *41*, 1–34.

Read, C. *Children's categorizations of speech sounds in English* (NCTE Research Report 17) ERIC, 1975.

Reed, J. C. The deficits of retarded readers: Fact or artifact? *The Reading Teacher,* 1970, *23,* 347–352 and 393.

Reicher, G. M. Perceptual recognition as a function of meaningfulness of stimulus material. *Journal of Experimental Psychology,* 1969, *81,* 275–280.

Rijnsoever, R. van. [*Psychological introduction to the processes of learning to read and write: an introductory report.*] Nijmegan, 1977. (In Dutch)

Rispens, J. [*Auditory aspects of reading comprehension: A study of the relative factors of auditory discrimination, quality analysis and auditory synthesis in reading comprehension.*] Utrecht: Elinkwijk, 1974. (In Dutch)

Robinson, H. M. *Why pupils fail in reading. A study of causes and remedial treatment.* Chicago: University of Chicago Press, 1946.

Rosier, P., & Farella, M. Bilingual education at Rock Point—Some early results. *TESOL Quarterly,* 1976, *10,* 379–388.

Rosier, P., & Holm, W. *Saad Naaki: Bee Na'nitin: Bilingual education in a Navajo school.* In preparation.

Rosinski, R. R., & Wheeler, K. E. Children's use of orthographic structure in word discrimination. *Psychonomic Science,* 1972, *26,* 97–98.

Rosner, J. *Phonic analysis training and beginning reading skills* (Publication No. 1971/19). Pittsburgh: University of Pittsburgh, Learning Research and Development Center, 1971.

Rosner, J., & Simon, D. P. The auditory analysis test: An initial report. *Journal of Learning Disorders,* 1971, *4,* 40–48.

Rowe, H. D. Materials in English for study of the Finnish. Studia Fennica, Tome XIV, Suomalaisen kirjallisuuden seura, Helsinki 1969 (taken from a bibliography in progress: Materials in English for the Study of the Finnish Language, Western Michigan University).

Roy, P., & Kapoor, J. M. *The retention of literacy.* Delhi: Macmillan, 1975.

Rozin, P., & Gleitman, L. R. The structure and acquisition of reading II: The reading process and the acquisition of the alphabetic principle. In A. S. Reber & D. L. Scarborough (Eds.), *Toward a psychology of reading: The proceedings of the CUNY conference.* Hillsdale, N.J.: Lawrence Erlbaum Associates, 1977.

Rozin, P., Ponitsky, S., & Sotsky, R. American children with reading problems can easily learn to read English represented by Chinese characters. *Science,* 1971, *171,* 1264–1267.

Rubenstein, H., Lewis, S. S., & Rubenstein, M. A. Evidence for phonetic recoding in visual word recognition. *Journal of Verbal Learning and Verbal Behavior,* 1971, *10,* 647–657.

Ruoppila, I., Västi, M. [*The structure of mistakes made by pupils suffering from reading and writing disorders and the relation of these to some variables on the cognitive development level.*] KTL 81, Jyvaskyla, 1971. (In Finnish)

Ryan, J. W. (Ed.). *Planning Out-of-School Education for Development.* Paris: I.I.E.P., 1972.

Sakamoto, T. Preschool reading in Japan. *The Reading Teacher,* 1975, *29,* 240–244.

Sakamoto, T. Writing systems in Japan. In J. E. Merritt (Ed.), *New horizons in reading.* Newark, Del.: International Reading Association, 1976.

Sakamoto, T., & Makita, K. Japan. In J. Downing (Ed.), *Comparative reading.* New York: Macmillan, 1973.

Sales, B. D., Haber, R. N., & Cole, R. A. Mechanisms of aural encoding IV: Hear, see, say-write, interactions for vowels. *Perception and Psychophysics,* 1969, *6,* 385–390.

Samuels, S. J., & Anderson, R. H. Visual recognition memory, paired-associate learning, and reading achievement. *Journal of Educational Psychology,* 1973, *65,* 160–167.

Samuels, S. J., Begy, G., & Chen, C. C. Comparison of word recognition speed and strategies of less skilled and more highly skilled readers. *Reading Research Quarterly,* 1975, *1,* 73–86.

Samuels, S. J., LaBerge, D., & Bremer, C. *A developmental study of the unit of perceptual processing in word recognition.* Unpublished manuscript, University of Minnesota, 1977.

Sapir, E. Athapaskan tone. *American Anthropologist,* 1922, *24,* 390–391.

Sarton, G. *A history of science.* Cambridge, Mass.: Harvard University Press, 1952.

Sasanuma, S. An analysis of writing errors in Japanese aphasic patients: Kanji versus Kana words. *Cortex,* 1972, *8,* 256–282.

Sasanuma, S. Kanji vs. Kana processing in alexia with transient agraphia: A case report. *Cortex,* 1974, *10,* 89–97. (a)

Sasanuma, S. Impairment of written language in Japanese aphasics: Kana vs. kanji processing. *Journal of Chinese Linguistics,* 1974, *2,* 141–157. (b)

Sasanuma, S. Kana and Kanji processing in Japanese aphasics. *Brain and Language,* 1974, *2,* 369–383. (c)

Sasanuma, S., Itoh, M., Mori, K., & Kobayashi, Y. Tachistoscopic recognition of Kana and Kanji words. *Neuropsychologia,* 1977, *15,* 547–553.

Saville-Troike, M. *Variation and change in Navajo: Some preliminary notes* (Languages and Linguistic Working Papers, No. 7). Washington, D.C.: Georgetown University Press, 1973.

Savin, H. B. What the child knows about speech when he starts to learn to read. In J. F. Kavanagh & I. G. Mattingly (Eds.), *Language by ear and by eye: The relationship between speech and reading.* Cambridge, Mass.: The MIT Press, 1972.

Scheerer-Neumann, G. Funktionanalyse des Lesens. *Psychologie in Erziehung und Unterricht,* 1977, *24,* 125–135. (a)

Scheerer-Neumann, G. Prozessanalyse von Lesestorungen. In Volker Ebel (Ed.), *Legasthenie.* Koblenz: Bundesverband Legasthenie, 1977. (b)

Scheerer-Neumann, G. Die Ausnutzung der sprachlichen Redundanz bei leseschwachen Kindern: I Nachweis des spezifischen Defizits. Zeitschrift für Entwicklungspsychologie und Padagogische. *Psychologie,* 1978, *1,* 35–48.

Schlee, J. *Legasthenieforschung am Ende?* Munich: Urban & Schwarzenberg, 1976.

Schonell, F. G. *Backwardness in the basic subjects.* London: Oliver and Boyd, 1942.

Schonell, F. G. *The psychology and teaching of reading.* London: Oliver and Boyd, 1946.

Shankweiler, D., & Liberman, I. Y. Misreading: A search for causes. In J. F. Kavanagh & I. G. Mattingly (Eds.), *Language by ear and by eye: The relationship between speech and reading.* Cambridge, Mass.: The MIT Press, 1972, 293–317.

Shankweiler, D., & Liberman, I. Y. Exploring the relations between reading and speech. In R. M. Knights & D. J. Bakker (Eds.), *Neuropsychology of learning disorders: Theoretical approaches.* Baltimore: University Park Press, 1976.

Shannon, C. E. A mathematical theory of communication. *Bell System Technical Journal,* 1948, *27,* 379–423, 622–656.

Sharma, K. D. *Interpretative bibliography: A review of Drop-Out.* Tehran: International Institute for Adult Literacy Methods, in press.

Shiffrin, R. M., & Schneider, W. Controlled and automatic human information processing: II. Perceptual learning, automatic attending, and a general theory. *Psychological Review,* 1977, *84,* 127–190.

Siirala, S. [*Delayed speech development.*] HYKS, Helsinki, 1969. (In Finnish)

314   References

Silva, M. W. Sugathapala de. Problems of literacy in diglossic communities. In T. P. Gorman (Ed.), *Language and literacy: Current issues and research*. Tehran: International Institute for Adult Literacy Methods, 1977.

Simon, A. [On the scholastic achievements of immigrant children in the lower grades.] *Megamot,* 1958, *8,* 343–368. (In Hebrew)

Simon, D. P. Spelling—A task analysis. *Instructional Science,* 1976, *5,* 277–302.

Simon, H. On the development of the processor. In S. Farnham-Diggory (Ed.), *Information processing in children*. New York: Academic Press, 1972.

Singh, S. *Learning to read and reading to learn: An approach to a system of literacy instruction*. Amersham, U.K.: Hulton Educational Publications Ltd., 1976.

Skjelfjord, V. J. Problems of validity in connection with the concept of auditory discrimination between speech sounds. *Scandinavian Journal of Educational Research,* 1975, *19,* 153–173.

Smith, F. *Understanding reading: A psycholinguistic analysis of reading and learning to read*. New York: Holt, 1971.

Smith, F. Alphabetic writing—A language compromise? In F. Smith (Ed.), *Psycholinguistics and reading*. New York: Holt, 1973.

Smith, L. B., & Kemler, D. G. Developmental trends in free classification: Evidence for a new conceptualization of perceptual development. *Journal of Experimental Child Psychology,* in press.

So, K. F., Potter, M. C., & Friedman, R. B. *Reading in Chinese and English: Naming versus understanding,* in preparation.

Sperry, R. W., Gazzaniga, M. S., & Bogen, J. E. Interhemispheric relationships: The neocortical commissures; syndromes of hemispheric disconnection. In P. H. Vinken & G. W. Bruyn (Eds.), *Handbook of clinical neurology* (Vol. 4). Amsterdam: North-Holland Publisher, 1969.

Spolsky, B. *Navajo language maintenance: Six-year-olds in 1969* (Navajo Reading Study Progress Report No. 5). Albuquerque: University of New Mexico, 1969.

Spolsky, B. *Navajo language maintenance II: Six-year-olds in 1970* (Navajo Reading Study Progress Report No. 13). Albuquerque: University of New Mexico, 1970.

Stanley, G., & Hall, R. Short-term visual information processing in dyslexics. *Child Development,* 1973, *44,* 841–844.

Steger, J. A., Vellutino, F. R., & Meshoulam, U. Visual-tactile and tactile-tactile paired associate learning in normal and poor readers. *Perceptual and Motor Skills,* 1972, *35,* 263–266.

Stroop, J. R. Studies of interference in serial verbal reactions. *Journal of Experimental Psychology,* 1935, *18,* 643–662.

Sugiyam, Y., & Saito, T. [Variables of parent reading in relation to the social traits of kindergarten pupils.] *The Science of Reading,* 1973, *15,* 121–130. (In Japanese with a brief English summary.)

Terry, P., Samuels, S. J., & LaBerge, D. The effects of letter degradation and letter spacing on word recognition. *Journal of Verbal Learning and Verbal Behavior,* 1976, *15,* 577–585.

Thompson, M. C., & Massaro, D. W. The role of visual information and redunduncy in reading. *Journal of Experimental Psychology,* 1973, *98,* 49–54.

Treiman, R. *Children's ability to segment speech into syllables and phonemes as related to their reading ability*. Unpublished manuscript, Yale University, Department of Psychology, 1976.

Treiman, R., and Baron, J. Segmental analysis ability: Development and relation to reading ability. In T. G. Waller & G. E. MacKinnon (Eds.), *Reading research: Advances in theory and practice* (Vol. 2). In press.

Treiman, R., Baron, J., & Luk, K. *Type of orthography affects use of sound in silent reading.* Paper presented to Eastern Psychological Association, Philadelphia, April 18-21, 1979.

Tuunainen, K. *[Diagnosing school beginner's language learning difficulties.]* Sarja A9, 1977. (In Finnish)

Tversky, A. Features of similarity. *Psychological Review,* 1977, *84,* 327-352.

Tzeng, O. J. L., Hung, D. L., & Cotton, B. *Visualization effect in reading Chinese characters.* Paper presented at the annual meeting of the Psychonomic Society, San Antonio, Texas, November, 1978.

Tzeng, O. J. L., Hung, D. L., & Garro, L. Reading the Chinese characters: An information processing view. *Journal of Chinese Linguistics,* 1978, *6,* 285-305.

Tzeng, O. J. L., Hung, D. L., & Wang, S.-Y. Speech recoding in reading Chinese characters. *Journal of Experimental Psychology: Human Learning and Memory,* 1977, *3,* 621-630.

Underwood, B. J. Are we overleading memory: In A. W. Melton & E. Martin (Eds.), *Coding processes in human memory.* Washington, D.C.: V. H. Winston and Sons, 1972.

Vachek, J. Some remarks on writing and phonetic transcription. *Acta Linguistica,* 1945-1949, *5,* 86-93.

Vähäpassi, A. *[On the structure and variability of reading skill in grade 3 of the comprehensive school in the school year 1973-1974.]* KTL/283, Jyvaskyla, 1977. (In Finnish)

Vähäpassi, A. [The level of reading and writing in grade 6 of the comprehensive school year.] Jyväskylä, Institute for Educational Research Series 88/1977. (In Finnish)

Valtin, R. *Legasthenie—Theorien und Untersuchungen.* Weinheim: Beltz, 1970.

Valtin, R. *Empirische Untersuchungen zur Legasthenie.* Schroedel-Verlag, Hannover, 1972.

Valtin, R. *Einfuhrung in die Legasthenieforschung.* Weinheim: Beltz, 1973. (a)

Valtin, R. Report of research on dyslexia in children. Paper presented at the International Reading Association Meeting, Denver, Colorado, 1973. (ERIC Document Reproduction Service No. ED 079 713.) (b)

Valtin, R. *Legasthenie—Theorien und Untersuchungen* (3rd ed.). Weinheim: Beltz-Verlag, 1974.

Valtin, R. Dyslexia: Deficit in reading or deficit in research? *Reading Research Quarterly,* 1979, *14,* 201-221.

Vanderslice, R., & Ladefoged, P. Binary suprasegmental features and transformational word-accentuation rules. *Language,* 1977, *48,* 819-838.

Velde, I. Van der. *[The problem of vocabulary development: An historical and didactic study.]* Groningen: Wolters, 1956. (In Dutch)

Vellutino, F. Alternative conceptualizations of dyslexia: Evidence in support of a verbal-deficit hypothesis. *Harvard Educational Review,* 1977, *47,* 334-354.

Vellutino, F. R. *Dyslexia: Theory and research.* Cambridge: The MIT Press, in press.

Vellutino, F. R., Bentley, W., & Phillips, F. Inter- vs. intrahemispheric learning in dyslexic and normal readers. *Developmental Medicine and Child Neurology,* 1978, *20,* 71-80.

Vellutino, F. R., DeSetto, L., & Steger, J. A. Categorial judgment and the Wepman test of auditory discrimination. *Journal of Speech and Hearing Disorders,* 1972, *37,* 252-257.

Vellutino, F. R., Pruzek, R. M., Steger, J. A., & Meshoulam, U. Immediate visual recall in poor and normal readers as a function of orthographic-linguistic familiarity. *Cortex,* 1973, *9,* 368–384.

Vellutino, F. R., Smith, H., Steger, J. A., & Kaman, M. Reading disability: Age differences and the perceptual deficit hypothesis. *Child Development,* 1975, *46,* 487–493.

Vellutino, F. R., Steger, J. A., DeSetto, L., & Phillips, F. Immediate and delayed recognition of visual stimuli in poor and normal readers. *Journal of Experimental Child Psychology,* 1975, *19,* 223–232.

Vellutino, F. R., Steger, J. A., Harding, C. J., & Phillips, F. Verbal vs. non-verbal paired-associates learning in poor and normal readers. *Neuropsychologia,* 1975, *13,* 75–82.

Vellutino, F. R., Steger, J. A., Kaman, M., & DeSetto, L. Visual form perception in deficient and normal readers as a function of age and orthographic-linguistic familiarity. *Cortex,* 1975, *11,* 22–30.

Vellutino, F. R., Steger, J. A., & Kandel, G. Reading disability: An investigation of the perceptual deficit hypothesis. *Cortex,* 1972, *8,* 106–118.

Vellutino, F. R., Steger, J. A., & Pruzek, R. M. Inter- vs. intra-sensory deficit in paired associate learning in poor and normal readers. *Canadian Journal of Behavioral Science,* 1973, *5,* 111–123.

Venezky, R. L. *The structure of English orthography.* The Hague: Mouton, 1970.

Venezky, R. L. The notion of regularity in reading and spelling. *Spelling Progress Bulletin,* winter 1973. (a)

Venezky, R. L. The letter-sound generalizations of first, second, and third grade Finnish children. *Journal of Educational Psychology,* 1973, *64,* 288–292. (b)

Venezky, R. L. Research on reading processes: An historical perspective. *American Psychologist,* 1977, *32,* 339–345.

Venezky, R. L. From Webster to Rice to Roosevelt. In U. Frith (Ed.), *Cognitive processes in spelling.* London: Academic Press, 1980.

Venezky, R. L., Chapman, R. S., & Calfee, R. C. The development of letter-sound generalizations from second through sixth grade (Technical Report No. 231). Wisconsin Research and Development Center for Cognitive Learning, 1972.

Venezky, R. L., & Johnson, D. The development of two letter-sound patterns in grades 1–3. *Journal of Educational Psychology,* 1973, *64,* 109–115.

Venezky, R. L., and Massaro, D. W. The role of orthographic regularity in word recognition. In L. B. Resnick & P. A. Weaver (Eds.), *Theory and practice of early reading* (Vol. I). Hillsdale, N.J.: Lawrence Erlbaum Associates, 1979.

Vernon, M. D. *Backwardness in reading.* Cambridge, Mass.: Harvard University Press, 1960.

Vernon, M. D. Varieties of deficiency in the reading process. *Harvard Educational Review,* 1977, *47.*

Vingilis, E., Blake, J., & Theodor, L. Recognition vs. recall of visually vs. acoustically confusable letter matrices. *Memory & Cognition,* 1977, *5,* 146–150.

Viitaniemi, E. [*The efficiency of oral and silent reading instruction.*] Helsinki: Otava, 1971. (In Finnish)

Vogel, S. A. Syntactic abilities in normal and dyslexic children. *Journal of Learning Disabilities,* 1974, *7,* 103–109.

Vorih, L., & Rosier, P. Rock Point Community School: An example of a Navajo-English bilingual elementary school program. *TESOL Quarterly,* 1978, *12,* 263–269.

Walker, W. Notes on native writing systems and the design of native literacy programs. *Anthropological Linguistics,* 1969, *11,* 148–166.

Waller, T. G. Children's recognition memory for written sentences: A comparison of good and poor readers. *Child Development,* 1976, *47,* 90–95.

Wallis, E. E. The word and the phonological hierarchy of Mezquital Otomi. *Language,* 1968, *44,* 76–90.

Wang, W. S-Y. The Chinese language. *Scientific American,* 1973, *228,* 50–60.

Wang, W. S-Y. Language change. *Annals of the New York Academy of Science,* 1976, *280,* 61–72.

Weber, R-M. First graders' use of grammatical context in reading. In H. Levin & J. P. Williams (Eds.), *Basic studies in reading.* New York: Basic Books, 1970.

Weigl, E., & Fradis, A. The transcoding processes in patients with agraphia to dictation. *Brain and Language,* 1977, *4,* 11–22.

Weir, R., & Venezky, R. L. Spelling to sound correspondences. In K. S. Goodman (Ed.), *The psycholinguistic nature of the reading process,* 1973.

West, E. G. *Education and the state.* London: Institute of Economic Affairs, 1970.

Wheeler, D. D. Processes in word recognition. *Cognitive Psychology,* 1970, *1,* 59–85.

Wickens, D. D. Encoding categories of words: An empirical approach to meaning. *Psychological Review,* 1970, *77,* 1–15.

Wiig, E. H., Semel, M. S., & Crouse, M. B. The use of English morphology by high-risk and learning disabled children. *Journal of Learning Disabilities,* 1973, *6,* 457–465.

Wiik, K. *Finnish and English vowels.* Turku: University of Turku, Series B, Tome 94, 1965.

Willett, T. The Southeastern Tepehuan verb. *Anthropological Linguistics,* in press.

Williams, J. P. Successive versus concurrent presentation of multiple grapheme-phoneme correspondences. *Journal of Educational Psychology,* 1968, *59,* 309–314.

Williams, J. P., Blumberg, E. L., & Williams, D. V. Cues used in visual word recognition. *Journal of Educational Psychology,* 1970, *61,* 310–315.

Ylinentalo, O. [*Reading ability and the differences in it in the middle and upper primary school.*] KTL 62, Jyvaskyla, 1970. (In Finnish)

Young, F. A., & Lindsley, D. B. (Eds.), *Early experience and visual information processing in perceptual and reading disorders.* Washington, D.C.: National Academy of Sciences, 1970.

Young, R. W. *Written Navajo: A brief history.* (Navajo Reading Study Progress Report No. 19). Albuquerque: University of New Mexico, 1972.

Young, R. W., & Morgan, W. *The Navaho language.* Window Rock, Ariz.: United States Indian Service, 1943.

Zhurova, L. E. [The development of analysis of words into sounds by preschool children.] *Soviet Psychology and Psychiatry,* 1963, *2,* 17–27. (In Russian)

Zifcak, M. *Phonological awareness and reading acquisition in first grade children.* Unpublished doctoral dissertation, University of Connecticut, 1977.

Index

Adult literacy, *see* Literacy
African languages, 95, 97, 112
  number of, 110
  unified orthographic system, 112
Alphabetic orthography, teaching
  beginning readers, 142
Alphabetic writing, 122–123, 129, 139,
  149
  logographic systems compared with,
  227, 228
American spelling, 7
Amharic, 95
Aphasia, 150
  Japanese studies of, 214
Arab Regional Literary and Adult
  Educational Organization, 116
Arabic
  Modern Standardized and Tunisian,
  113
  teaching, 34
  writing, 95
Arabic Language Academy, Cairo, 116
Arabic script
  diacritics missing in, 116–117
  Persian language in, 115–118
  phonemes and graphemes, 117–118
Athapaskcan languages, Cree-type
  syllabaries, 87

Beginning readers, 137–153
  linguistic awareness, *see* Linguistic
  awareness
  linguistic sophistication, 137–138,
  140–149
  paths and codes in learning, 171–189
  perceptual inefficiency and perceptual deficiency in, *see* Dyslexia
  phonological maturity, 138–140,
  146–149
  phonological recoding, 149–153
  test methods and results, 178–189

Cerebral lateralization
  and Chinese characters, 211, 213–221
  and dyslexia, 251
  and English words, 213, 219
Cheremiss, 35

Cherokee syllabary, 4
Children's reading, *see* Beginning
  readers; Cross-national primary
  reading studies
Chinese, 211–226
  Cantonese, 97
  cerebral lateralization effects and
  reading, 211, 213–221
  characters in tests, 179
  color names, Stroop interference,
  219–220
  ideographs and phonetic values, 96
  logographies, 146, 148, 227
  morphemic transcription, 148
  nonalphabetic writing system,
  211–226
  occurrence of reading disability,
  212–213
  phonetic recoding, 221–226, 283
  phonograms, 211, 215–216
  pictograms, 215–216
  reading, 151, 211–216
  sentences, 224–225
  Yao in Chinese characters, 97–98
Chō-on, 18, 19, 22
Color names, Stroop interference,
  219–220
Consonant-vowel dichotomy, 3–5
Cree-type syllabaries, 87
Cross-National Conference on Orthography, Reading, and Dyslexia, 1
Cross-national primary reading studies,
  125–133
  alphabetic system used, 129
  collection of printed materials, 133
  equivalent tests in different languages, 131
  hypotheses, 127–128
  implications of outcomes, 126–127
  literacy level of countries, 130
  objectives, 126
  questionnaires, 132
  research design, 128–129
  sampling of children, 130–131
  selection of countries for participation, 129–130
  test types and testing procedures,
  131–133
Cyrillic alphabet, 112
  of Serbo-Croatian, 227–247

319